Uisneach
or the Center of Ireland

The hill of Uisneach lies almost exactly at the geographical center of Ireland. Remarkably, a fraction at least of the ancient Irish population was aware of that fact. There is no doubt that the place of Uisneach in Irish mythology, and more broadly speaking the Celtic world, was of utmost importance: Uisneach was – and probably still is – best defined as a sacred hill at the center of Ireland, possibly the sacred hill of the center of Ireland.

Uisneach or the Center of Ireland explores the medieval documents connected with the hill and compares them with both archaeological data and modern Irish folklore. In the early 21st century, a *Fire Festival* started being held on Uisneach in connection with the festival of Bealtaine, in early May, arguably in an attempt to echo more ancient traditions: the celebration was attended by Michael D. Higgins, the current president of Ireland, who lit the fire of Uisneach on 6 May 2017.

This book argues that the symbolic significance of the hill has echoed the evolution of Irish society through time, be it in political, spiritual and religious terms or, perhaps more accurately, in terms of identity and Irishness. It is relevant for scholars and advanced students in the fields of cultural history, Irish history and cultural studies.

Frédéric Armao is currently an Associate Professor at the University of Toulon (France). His primary research focuses on the link between Irish folklore (both modern and contemporary) and Celtic mythology. His work has examined the evolution of Irish calendar festivals from their pre-Christian beginnings through their syncretic contemporary celebration.

Studies for the International Society for Cultural History

Series Editors: Patryk Babiracki and Filippo Carlà-Uhink

In both research and teaching, the study of cultural history is burgeoning, with a variety of interpretations of culture cross-fertilizing between disciplines – history, critical theory, literature and media, anthropology and ethnology, and many more. This series focuses on the study of conceptual, affective and imaginative worlds of the past, and sees culture as encompassing both textual production and social practice. It seeks to highlight historical and cultural processes of meaning-making and explore the ways in which people of the past made sense of their world.

Cultural History in France
Local Debates, Global Perspectives
Edited by Evelyne Cohen, Anaïs Fléchet, Pascale Gœtschel, Laurent Martin, and Pascal Ory

New Perspectives on Jewish Cultural History
Boundaries, Experiences, and Sensemaking
Edited by Maja Gildin Zuckerman and Jakob Egholm Feldt

Reconstructing Minds and Landscapes
Silent Post-War Memory in the Margins of History
Edited by Marja Tuominen, T. G. Ashplant, and Tiina Harjumaa

Cultural Translation and Knowledge Transfer on Alternative Routes of Escape from Nazi Terror
Mediations Through Migrations
Edited by Susanne Korbel and Philipp Strobl

Uisneach or the Center of Ireland
Frédéric Armao

For more information about this series, please visit: https://www.routledge.com/Studies-for-the-International-Society-for-Cultural-History/book-series/SISCH

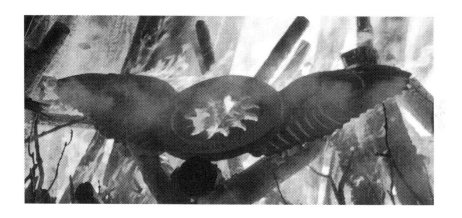

Uisneach
or the Center of Ireland

Frédéric Armao

NEW YORK AND LONDON

First published 2023
by Routledge
605 Third Avenue, New York, NY 10158

and by Routledge
4 Park Square, Milton Park, Abingdon, Oxon, OX14 4RN

Routledge is an imprint of the Taylor & Francis Group, an informa business

Library of Congress Cataloguing-in-Publication Data
Names: Armao, Frédéric, 1978- author.
Title: Uisneach or the center of Ireland / Frédéric Armao.
Description: New York : Routledge, 2023. |
Series: Studies for the international society for cultural history |
Includes bibliographical references and index.
Identifiers: LCCN 2022035118 | ISBN 9780367697709 (paperback) |
ISBN 9780367697693 (hardback) | ISBN 9781003143161 (ebook)
Subjects: LCSH: Westmeath (Ireland)--Antiquities. |
Hill of Uisneach (Ireland) | Civilization, Celtic. | Mythology, Celtic. |
Ireland--Social life and customs. | Ireland--Civilization. |
Ireland--Religious life and customs. | Ireland--Politics and
government. |
National characteristics, Irish. | Ireland--In literature.
Classification: LCC DA990.W4 A76 2023 | DDC 941.8/15--dc23/
eng/20221013
LC record available at https://lccn.loc.gov/2022035118

ISBN: 978-0-367-69769-3 (hbk)
ISBN: 978-0-367-69770-9 (pbk)
ISBN: 978-1-003-14316-1 (ebk)

DOI: 10.4324/9781003143161

Typeset in Sabon
by MPS Limited, Dehradun

Contents

Acknowledgment

I wish to express my gratitude to Ruairí McKiernan, whose help has been most valuable; to David Clarke: I am greatly indebted to your help, cooperation and support; to Justin Moffatt and everybody at the Visitor Center of the hill of Uisneach for their time and patience; to Patsy Preston, Treasa Kerrigan and all those who were kind enough to answer my questions; to Pr. Christophe Gillissen for his help and advice; to Pr. Gilles Leydier, Pr. Catherine Maignant, Pr. John Mullen, Pr. Clíona Ní Riordáin, Dr. Jenny Butler for their guidance and interest; to Pr. Filippo Carlà-Uhink and the International Society for Cultural History for believing in this project; to everyone at the *National Folklore Collection*, University College Dublin, whose expertise and effectiveness were very much appreciated.

I am extremely grateful to Dr. Roseanne Schot whose constructive comments proved crucial in final revisions and whose research was invaluable in the making of this book.

A very special thanks to Gregory Gipson for his time, patience and thoughtful remarks; to the whole Gipson family for their inspiring kindness and constant support; to Mickaël Garde for his help; to friends and family anywhere near Toulon, Boston, Tampa or *the center of Ireland*.

Ba mhaith liom buíochas ó chroí a ghabháil le hUachtarán na hÉireann Michael D. Higgins agus a fhoireann.

A Elizabeth et Cassandre

Foreword

"It was a pleasure and a privilege for me, to become the first President of Ireland to light the Bealtaine fire at the Hill of Uisneach, at a ceremony in May 2017.

The Uisneach festival is a tribute to our rich cultural heritage and a celebration not only of Ireland's history and rituals, but also its mythical past.

Marking the beginning of Bealtaine, the summer season, Uisneach celebrates the power of the sun's warmth, and its associated wonders of birth and fertility.

Throughout history, the people of Ireland have used the power of fire, to set flames blazing to herald a new beginning, and a new light. It is a wonderful experience to see this tradition being enjoyed to bring our communities together, to emphasise our togetherness, and to re-awaken our sense of belonging as people on a shared planet."

Michael D. Higgins
11 February 2020

Introduction

The hill of Uisneach lies about 15 kilometers west-south-west of the village of Mullingar, County Westmeath, Éire,[1] at the approximate geographical center of Ireland. Pinpointing the precise center of an island like Ireland, with its irregular and fluctuating coastline, remains difficult even for contemporary scientific geographers. These geographers have wrestled with the question, and now place the precise, geometrical center of Ireland by convention at 53°30'00"N/ 8°00'00"W,[2] less than 30 kilometers west of Uisneach. A fraction at least of the ancient Irish population was aware of this approximate correspondence: Uisneach was – and probably still is – best defined as a sacred hill at the center of Ireland, possibly *the* sacred hill *of* the center of Ireland.

The literally central nature of Uisneach and its symbolic corollary were undoubtedly known to the successive waves of population that settled on or around the hill throughout centuries. Some elements suggest that its sanctity could even be multi-millennial, which may seem surprising given the modest dimensions and unimpressive overall appearance of the place.

Uisneach (modern pronunciation: /ˈɪʃnə/)[3] rises to only 182 meters above sea level, which is far from imposing, even for Ireland and its usually gentle and uniform terrain. Even if the general appearance of what could be described as a mere mound is by no means remarkable,[4] a short walk to the summit gives a first idea of its strategic and symbolic importance. From the top of Uisneach, the view over the surrounding area, although arguably neither breathtaking nor unique, is intriguing: it extends for many kilometers[5] and one can see or be seen from 360 degrees around.[6]

A fairly large number of monuments, either natural or artificial, compete for the attention of the visitor. To name but a few for now, *Ail na Mireann*, also called the *Catstone*, is an imposing rock – or rather, a conglomerate of glacial origin – that can be found a few hundred meters from the top of Uisneach. Reaching nearly five meters in height and almost as much in width, the rock has played a major role in the symbolism of the place. According to several sources,[7] it corresponded to the point where the provinces of ancient Ireland met, further reinforcing the emblematic centrality of Uisneach. The small oval pond of *Lough Lugh* is another natural

DOI: 10.4324/9781003143161-1

attraction of the hill: the god Lugh, the main deity of the Irish pantheon, is said to have drowned there.

It is, however, the dozens of monuments[8] erected by men on Uisneach throughout centuries – the oldest of which apparently dating back to the prehistoric[9] period – that catch the attention of the scholars and confirm the importance of the hill in the context of Irish history. This importance, once again as strategic as it was symbolic, is attested as early as the Middle Ages: a "convention", *Mórdháil Uisnigh* in ancient Irish, was supposedly held on Uisneach by the "men of Ireland" since "time immemorial". As will be shown, the historical veracity of such a gathering is debatable: the convention is mainly mentioned in mythological and late pseudo-historical accounts. *Mórdháil Uisnigh*, the great periodic assembly of Uisneach, is almost always cited in relation to the Irish festival of *Bealtaine*, in early May of our modern calendar. The fact remains that a great deal of ancient sources tend to associate Uisneach with that festival of *Bealtaine*, of which much will be said hereafter.

Irish mythology laid special emphasis on the hill. A famous episode shows the druid called Mídhe, a renowned member of the mythological tribe of the Nemedians, light a "mystic fire" on top of Uisneach; it was said to be the first fire ever lit in Ireland, a prototypical flame from which all other fires following originated. More recently, the local folklore marginally took hold of the place and included it in a number of rituals and traditions. Some of those traditions reached us, notably thanks to the investigative works of the *Irish Folklore Commission* in the 20th century. It is once again during the month of May, at the time of the festival of *Bealtaine*, that the veneration and celebration of Uisneach found their most vivid fruitions. Today, a new – and in many re-spects very contemporary – way of celebrating the hill seems to have taken over. Uisneach is now privately owned. Its *Fire Festival*, which is organized by the owner and his team every year, gathers thousands of visitors who take part in various merriments and attractions, not the least of which being the bonfire lit on top of the hill. These first examples shed some light on the importance of Uisneach and its remarkable place in Irish history and Irish imagination for centuries onward. Its strong symbolism inspired the *creators* and later *mediators* of myths, the members of the ruling classes – either royal or religious – and also the people, the "common crowd", as the folklore connected to the place seems to confirm.

Still, in spite of its apparent impact on Irish society throughout time, the hill now remains confidential, often unknown and overlooked by the general public, not only outside of Ireland but for most Irish people themselves. Even if thousands of visitors have gathered on Uisneach to celebrate *Bealtaine* in early May for about a decade, the popularity of the place does not compare to other touristic or spiritual attractions such as the hill of Tara – although it is closely connected to Uisneach – the tumulus of Newgrange or even Croagh Patrick and its world-renowned pilgrimage.

The reason(s) that led to the relative lack of popularity of Uisneach as a destination for contemporary tourists and "Celtic enthusiasts" ought to be investigated. But it will be even more useful to try and understand the underlying substance and significance of the hill of Uisneach throughout centuries in Ireland, its mythical and historical reach, the origin of this importance, its precise nature and its evolution. As far back as can be traced, Uisneach appears to have been a seat of power, a power that was fundamentally connected to the notion of centrality.

The question of whether this central power was mainly and initially sacerdotal and religious, royal and warlike, or linked to fecundity and agrarian production is obviously essential. Answering it would potentially clarify the original symbolic nature of the hill. Was Uisneach originally significant because it correlated to religion and the spiritual world, to politics and the ruling class or because of more secular and down-to-earth reasons, potentially connected with the common men and women? The answer to this crucial question will not be as clear-cut as hoped for and it will be argued that the centrality of Uisneach should above all be related to the idea of *juste milieu*, a "just middle-ground" or "midpoint", theorized by Celtic expert Donatien Laurent.[10] As will be demonstrated, this *juste milieu*, this symbolic midpoint ought to be understood and apprehended both in spatial and temporal terms and will hold implications for all members of the ancient Irish society.

***

A study of Uisneach, from its origins (or at least what can be discerned of those origins) to this day, poses a number of methodological problems. It notably implicates the analysis of disparate and controversial documents. Let us proceed in order.

The terms "*ancient* Ireland" refer to "pre-Christian Ireland" – sometimes called "prehistoric Ireland" – although most of the documents shedding light on this era were written down between the 7th and 17th centuries. Those primary (or pseudo-primary) sources are of variable nature and reliability: mythological narratives, lives of saints, compilation of laws and rights, genealogies, poems and songs, alleged collections of old traditions, onomastics studies, glossaries, annals etc. The myths relating to the hill and, broadly speaking, the written medieval sources mentioning Uisneach were therefore transcribed and compiled over the course of a millennium at least. Although they are extremely heterogeneous in nature, they share at least one common trait: an overwhelming majority was transcribed by Irish monks. Since the dawn of Christianity in Ireland – that is, by convention, the 5th century or perhaps more accurately the 6th and 7th centuries[11] – Irish monks have attempted to transcribe traditions anterior to the arrival of the New Religion.[12] It should be remembered that the erudites that preceded the introduction of Christianity in Ireland, i.e. druids and poets, did not put their knowledge into writing. As Julius Caesar explains: "They are said there to learn by heart a great number of verses; accordingly some remain in the course of training twenty years. Nor do they regard it lawful to commit these to writing".[13] Of course, Caesar's point of view on the Celtic world is often doubtful. For instance, his attempt to draw a comparison between the Celtic and Roman pantheons is famously debatable. Here, it does not seem necessary to question his words, all the more so as his statement is confirmed by other commentators – and arguably by the fact that no pre-Christian Irish written document exists. The members of the Celtic sacerdotal class seem to have believed all knowledge ought to be passed down orally and not through perishable media: confiding science to the material world amounted to tarnishing it; bringing knowledge within reach of the layman and attempting to pin it to the material world was not considered a viable option.[14]

As a consequence, the oldest written references to the hill of Uisneach are medieval Christian transcriptions. No matter how precious and irreplaceable the work of the Irish monks was – and still is – those transcriptions cannot be considered as absolutely dependable, trustworthy primary sources that actually account for and describe ancient Celtic knowledge. It will be necessary to understand and interpret them, to discriminate between the Christian gloss and the original text – or rather "concept", provided that it is still accessible. Then and only then will it be possible to rely on those mythological texts – that is, those texts aiming at transcribing the pre-Christian myths of Ireland.

Other sources, with the same sorts of caveats, can prove useful. For example, some hagiographies (including those of Saint Patrick) or medieval texts claiming and discussing laws and rights do mention, sometimes very laconically, the hill of Uisneach. Their study will not always lead to spectacular finds: the primary sources of that period, which stretches over one millennium at least, are abundant but the direct allusions to Uisneach are marginal and often very concise. Fortunately, cross-references between those different sources are eloquent enough to establish new evidence and disclose original data.

Some later sources will complete this investigation: the Irish Annals are chronicles of medieval history that also belong to the Irish monastic context. Most do mention the hill several times and will confirm some of the hypotheses put forward. Finally, Geoffrey Keating and his famous *History of Ireland* (*Foras Feasa ar Éirinn*) written down in the 17th century will potentially substantiate a number of claims. It must, however, be analyzed with a critical, if not circumspect eye; in the words of Celticists Françoise Le Roux and Christian Guyonvarc'h, the methodology of Keating is closer to Gregory of Tours' than to Jules Michelet's.[15] The knowledge transmitted by the author, perhaps more a *mediator of myths* than a historian in the modern sense of the term, remains pertinent and useful to this study, as long as the precise nature of this "knowledge" and "transmission" is truly understood. Keating's *History of Ireland* arguably provides interesting insights regarding some of the customs in ancient Ireland and must therefore be considered as a late medieval addition to the set of documents mentioned above. Precisely for this reason, the term *medieval* will hereafter be used as a reference to a period starting with the introduction and early development of Christianity in Ireland and ending, by convention, in the 17th century, i.e. the "long" Middle Ages.

The analysis of those diverse sources will aim at clarifying the symbolic and historical import of Uisneach and explaining its origin or even identifying its causes, provided that such a complex phenomenon can be contemplated in sheer rational terms. Similarly, Chapters III and IV of this study will examine the two major features associated with the sacredness of the place: on the one hand, its connection with the insular festival of the month of May, *Bealtaine* (a celebration that will be inscribed in the wider context of disputably "Celtic" festivals); on the other, *Mórdháil Uisnigh*, this ancient assembly that was apparently held on the date of *Bealtaine*.

Once those medieval writings are reviewed and perused, it will be fitting to describe precisely, that is in archaeological terms, the site known under the name of "Uisneach": this study will highlight congruence or, on the opposite, potential disparities and incoherence with the elements brought forward by the medieval sources. Fortunately, a number of archaeologists looked into the case of Uisneach. The first mentions of monuments were quite elusive. They can be found in the *Ordnance Survey Letters* (a topographical compilation and administrative inventory initiated by the British Parliament) in the first half of the 19th century. The studies of Macalister and Praeger date back to the 1920s–30s and are also moderately controversial. However, more recent – and excellent – investigations were carried out by experienced archaeologists about a decade ago. The historiography of the archaeological studies of Uisneach is now solid enough to allow for a thorough and relevant description and a better historical comprehension of the site.

The last part of this study will be dedicated to modern and contemporary traditions. Whereas early written sources and archaeological studies will confirm the considerable importance of Uisneach in Ireland in past centuries, the modern and contemporary periods contribute in their own specific ways to the aura and overall status of the hill. For several centuries following the Middle Ages, the prestige and reputation of Uisneach admittedly remained more confidential: its political and religious importance eroded and faded to almost nothing – albeit temporarily. Only but a handful of people living in the parishes nearby seem to have sustained the symbolic position of the hill in Irish tradition. It is quite fortunate that, in the beginning of the 20th century, the *Irish Folklore Commission* (hereafter *IFC*) engaged in a double task of collecting traditions.

First, the *Schools' Collection*[16] regroups the manuscripts issued from a pioneering and nation-wide effort initiated by this same commission. During the 1937–9 school years, the *IFC* asked the schoolteachers of the Irish Free State, recently turned into a full Republic, to systematically collect folkloric data among their pupils aged 11 to 14. A phenomenal production ensued: around 750,000 pages were written down by 50,000 children and their teachers, originating from some 5,000 Irish schools. The data that were collected tackle almost all domains of so-called folkloric customs, beliefs and traditions in Ireland.[17] Each manuscript, or fraction of manuscript, deals with local traditions, which were specific to the vicinity of the said school. In the present case, the manuscripts 742 to 744, which corresponds to the hill of Uisneach and its surroundings,[18] will be studied so as to understand the survival or popular (re-)inventions mentioned by the pupils from the 12 schools nearby. The 1,131 pages pertaining to the barony of Rathconrath will reveal precious, often previously unpublished information.

The second folkloric tool will be provided by another nation-wide investigation carried out by the *IFC*: as already mentioned, Uisneach seems to have been intimately, if not fundamentally, connected to the festival of *Bealtaine*, celebrated in the beginning of the month of May in Ireland. In the 1940s, the *IFC* undertook a collection of data relative to the four main Irish seasonal festivals, including *Bealtaine*. The apposite manuscripts date from 1947[19] and will complete this folkloric investigation of Uisneach. For this reason, the word *modern* will hereafter refer to traditions from the 18th century to 1947 (i.e. the *Late* Modern Period) and the term *contemporary* to traditions or observations post-1947 and, even more so, from the past 30 years.

If used cautiously and with scientific rigor, the combined study of folklore and mythology is a most potent tool. Folklore must be understood as the popular epiphenomenon of myth. In other words, the popular traditions and customs, which were passed down from generation to generation, usually from word of mouth, were *a priori* inspired by myths,[20] at least for the most part. Folkloric traditions must therefore be considered as a form of ritualized mythology, a peculiar collection of ritualized myths that were appropriated by the people year after year, century after century, and that became part of their lives. The knowledge and understanding of myths enables the careful analyst to better understand modern folkloric customs and potentially trace back their origin. On the other hand, a reverse approach is a serious methodological pitfall and would be unsustainable: assembling a patchwork of modern traditions in order to find or recreate *a posteriori* supposedly ancient myths is out of the question.

The analysis of *contemporary* folklore[21] will conclude this investigative work: onsite original fieldwork was conducted between 2017 and 2019 for this study and it will constitute an important primary source of information. A new *Fire Festival* is now held on the hill in early May, in relation to the festival of *Bealtaine*. A number of interviews were conducted, including that of the owner of the hill and his team. They will enable a better understanding of the motivations of the organizers of the contemporary festival as well as a fraction of its participants. As a consequence, the chapter dedicated to folklore will also stand as a witness of the contemporary customs of Uisneach, including limited speculation as to what extent those customs are the creature of their time rather that the continuation, re-enactment or revival of a supposedly millennial tradition.

***

From archeological investigations and the processing of popular and folkloric data to the examination of old sources of various vintage and origin, this study aims at a "total" understanding of the hill of Uisneach. Obviously, "total" should not be interpreted as exhaustive, let alone definitive. The cross-use of several fields of research – the study of myths and medieval texts, archeology, linguistics, folklore and traditions – suggests a potentially fruitful form of comparative study. This methodology will aim at shedding new light on the symbolism, the importance, perhaps the origin and very substance of this geographical place, at the "center" of Ireland in many respects. The following pages are purposely placed at the intersection of different sciences and methodological perspectives. They will hopefully bring new, or at least newly refined, answers to the questions raised and will confirm that Uisneach was and remains a sacred hill, at the center of Irish and Celtic history and identity, a hill of symbol and a hill of power: that of the "just middle-ground".

Notes

1 ~53°29'25"N/7°33'30"W. See Annex II.1.
2 "Where the 8° Meridian West meets the 53°-30' North Latitude in the townland of Carnagh East Co. Roscommon. On the western shore of Lough Ree, opposite the Cribby Islands and 5.5 miles N.N.W of Athlone Town." https://web.archive.org/web/20120228155031/http://www.osi.ie/en/faq/faq3.aspx; all websites mentioned hereafter were last consulted in May 2020 unless specified otherwise
3 Among other variants, /ˈʃnə/, /ˈʃnəχ/ or /ˈɒʃnəχ/ are common modern pronunciations.
4 See Annex I.1.
5 See Annex II.1-6 and chapter V for a more thorough description.
6 It should be noted however that other hills tend to moderately block the horizon on its north and east sides as discussed in Chap. V.1.
7 The precise nature of those sources will be detailed *infra*.
8 See Annex II.3.
9 See Annex IV.
10 Laurent, Donatien. 1990. "Le Juste milieu. Réflexion sur un rituel de circumambulation millénaire: la troménie de Locronan" in Tenèze, Marie Louise (ed.). 1990. *Tradition et Histoire dans la culture populaire. Rencontres autour de l'œuvre de Jean-Michel Guilcher*. Grenoble: Centre Alpin et Rhodanien d'Ethnologie.
11 Although tradition kept 432 as the official date of the landing of Saint Patrick in Ireland, "evangelization [was] an extremely slow process that actually spanned three centuries. The turning point of this process arguably took place in the first half of the 7th century, although when precisely the scale tipped in favor of Christianity remains difficult to assess". Maignant, Catherine. 1996. *Histoire et Civilisation de l'Irlande*. Paris: Nathan, 18. All translations from French by F.A. unless otherwise noted.

12 However, the most important documents – from either a historical or mythological perspective – were only transcribed or redacted centuries later: "Everything truly ancient in Irish literature is Christian, liturgical or hagiographical. It is only later, it the 12th century, that oral narratives were finally transcribed". Le Roux, Françoise & Guyonvarc'h, Christian-Joseph. 1986. *Les Druides*. Rennes: Ed. Ouest-France, 29.

13 McDevitte, W. A. & Bohn, W. S. (ed.). 2012 (1869). *The Gallic Wars. Julius Caesar*. Merchants Books, VI, §14.

14 See Dumézil, Georges. 1940. "La Tradition druidique et l'écriture: le vivant et le mort" in *Revue de l'Histoire des Religions*, CXXII, 125-33.

15 Le Roux, Françoise & Guyonvarc'h, Christian-Joseph. 2015 (1995). *Les Fêtes celtiques*. Fouesnant: Ed. Yoran, 28.

16 https://www.duchas.ie/en/cbes.

17 For a historiographical perspective and global methodology, see Briody, Mícheál. 2016. *The Irish Folklore Commission 1935-1970, History, Ideology, Methodology*. Helsinki: Studia Fennica Folkloristica, 260-70.

18 More specifically, the hill lies in the parish on Conry and the townland of "Ushnagh Hill" but also covers the townlands of Clonownmore, Kellybrok, Lockardstow, Mweelra, Rathnew and Togherstown. For precise locations and detailed maps, see https://www.townlands.ie/westmeath/conry/ See also Annex II.1-2.

19 Manuscripts noted *NFC* (for *National Folklore Collection*) *1095* to *1097* and, for Uisneach, more specifically *NFC 1097*, pages 57 to 106.

20 "Myths" are probably best defined as ancient stories, which are intrinsic to the society and culture that produced them.

21 Or arguably, contemporary *popular culture* inspired by folkloric traditions.

1 Centrality of Uisneach

Understanding the importance of Uisneach in Ireland requires understanding the most prominent characteristic of the hill: its centrality. Whenever the hill is mentioned in Irish literature – either medieval, modern or contemporary – the fact that Uisneach is supposed to stand at the center of the island is inevitably implied. This recurrence cannot be coincidental and constitutes the starting point of the present study.

The idea comes in a variety of forms and from the pen of many authors and transcribers throughout history. This chapter will survey the most ancient sources at our disposal, from the dawn of Christianity in Ireland – the hagiography of Saint Patrick by Tírechán is for instance dated to the 7th century. By convention, this set of sources stops at the *History of Ireland* written by Geoffrey Keating in the 1630s. Keating represents a sort of lynchpin in the making of Irish history: the historian – or rather pseudo-historian – is supposed to take his knowledge from the Irish oral tradition and to have been inspired by ancient documents, now missing. The author consequently inscribes himself in the continuity of "mediators of Irish myths" and is ostensibly the last major representative of the allegedly ancient Irish tradition: this point will be discussed later in more detail.

Uisneach was, then, supposed to be the center of Ireland. The assertion is nonetheless debatable and the reasons for such an emphasis – along with its potential repercussions on Irish society – must also be clarified. Most medieval documents – that is, once again, comprised between the 7th and the 17th centuries – refer to Uisneach under the full name of "Uisneach Mide" or "Uisneach Midi", i.e. "Uisneach in the Province of Mide". This denomination is interesting in many respects, including its meaning and possible origin.

1.1 The Five Provinces

Background

Contemporary Ireland is now politically divided into four provinces (Leinster in the east, Munster in the south-west, Connacht in the west and Ulster[1] in the north). Early Irish literature tends to add a fifth, mythical

DOI: 10.4324/9781003143161-2

province, Meath, the historical reality of which has never been conclusively demonstrated. This ancient province of Meath must not be confused with the current counties of Meath or Westmeath: the *counties* (not *provinces*) of Meath and Westmeath belong to the province of Leinster and are quite real. In order to avoid any confusion, the mythical province of Meath will be referred to as Mide, its ancient Irish name. The term "Co. Meath" will be used whenever a mention of the (historical and contemporary) County of Meath will prove necessary.

Each of the five provinces of Ireland – Connacht, Ulster, Leinster, Munster and Mide – is associated with distinct functions in the manuscript called *The Settling of the Manor of Tara* (*Do Shuidigiud Tellaich Themra*), transcribed in the 14th–15th centuries:[2] "knowledge in the west, battle in the north, prosperity in the east, music in the south, kingship in the centre".[3] In other words, Connacht, the province of the west, is associated by the redactor with knowledge; Ulster, in the north, with battle; Leinster, in the east, prosperity; Munster, in the south, music or perhaps the arts generally; finally, Mide, placed at the center, with sovereignty. The latter assertion is indeed congruent with what is known of the symbolic importance of the province "in the middle".

Uisneach, in Mide

From a purely technical and administrative perspective, Uisneach can now be found in the contemporary province of Leinster. However, in the course of all of its "mythical history", the hill is associated with Mide, the mythical province of the center.[4] Though not systematic, the pairing Uisneach/Mide is a recurring one.

It is not essential to be exhaustive at this point and a couple of relevant examples will suffice to substantiate that claim. When the protagonists of *The Cause of the Exile of Fergus Mac Roig* (*Fochonn loingse Fergusa maic Roig*) – a manuscript possibly transcribed in the 9th century – decide to stop for the night after a long looting session, they indeed choose "Uisneach in Mide":

> [Fergus and his followers] proceeded in that wise to smooth Uisneach in [Mide][5]. And they stayed there that night. And they rose early on the morrow, and deliberated as to which of the provinces of Ireland they should go.[6]

Fergus and his disciples debate shortly and their choice finally settles on Connacht, the "best province", host of the "best king" (Ailill) and the "greatest of warriors" (Medb). Ailill and Medb are actually the masters of Cruachan, the stronghold of Connacht and one of the gates to the Otherworld – the *sídh* – in Irish tradition.[7] They are two of the central characters of *The Cattle Raid of Cooley* (*Táin Bó Cúailnge*), the major epic of Irish literature.

In this warlike context, the fact that Fergus chose to settle for the night on "smooth, beautiful"[8] Uisneach in Mide is probably not insignificant: the debate over the qualities of the different Irish provinces takes place on the central point of the island, Uisneach, which is associated with the province of kingship and stands as the epitome of the center.[9]

The Irish Annals

A lot of attention is paid by Irish Annals to the association between Uisneach and Mide. For instance, the *Annals of the Four Masters*, dated to the beginning of the 17th century, use this "Uisneach, in Mide" as a geographical reference point.[10] A looting that was said to happen in 1414 is mentioned as follows:

> John Stanley, the Deputy of the King of England, arrived in Ireland, a man who gave neither mercy nor protection to clergy, laity, or men of science, but subjected as many of them as he came upon to cold, hardship, and famine. It was he who plundered Niall, the son of Hugh O'Higgin, at Uisneach, in [Mide].[11]

John Stanley will eventually be killed by the harsh verbal abuse and taunting of the O'Higgins, which should not come as a surprise. History and its rewriting, exaggerations and reinventions are distinctive features of a large portion of early Irish literature. In the wording of Marie-Louise Sjoestedt, the ancient Irish "thought their history in mythical terms".[12] Perhaps what must be remembered from the peculiar episode is that a confrontation between different parties (in that case, English and Irish, which is always significant) happened on Uisneach, in Mide. This is not an isolated case as antagonisms are commonplace on the hill.

In the same *Annals of the Four Masters*, Uisneach is presented as the limit of a territory claimed by *Cenél Fiachach*, the clan of Fiachu mac Néill.[13] This territory was supposedly gained following a battle at Druim Dergaighe, of which nothing is known except that it caused "the plain of [Mide to be] detached"[14], i.e. created.

The *Annals of Tigernach*, dating back to the 12th century, confirm the statement:

> The battle of Druim Deargaige over Foilge Berraide by Fiacha son of Niall, and it is in that battle their portion of [Mide] as far as Uisneach was taken from the Leinstermen. As Cennfaeladh sang:
>
> 1. Vengeance that day seven years,
> That was the consolation of their hearts:
> The battle on Drommann Dergaige, Thence fell the plain of [Mide].[15]

Thus, Fiachu and his men invaded the province of Mide – which comprised Uisneach. Fiachu's conquest of and the domination by his clan, *Cenél Fiachach*, over a territory that included Uisneach seems to be a historical fact.[16] As will be seen later, a number of documents even honor Fiachu with the title of "Second King of Uisneach", which is rather telling.

Uisneach: Etymologies

The study of the etymology of Uisneach may shed light on the link uniting Uisneach to the province of Mide: a clear meaning of the term "Uisneach" might indicate an original significance and symbolic import of the place.

A first theory is put forward by the *Dindshenchas* (literally the *History* or the *Lore of Places*),[17] an onomastic treatise, which is deeply inspired and influenced by myths. Uisneach is said to stem from *ós neoch*, which means "above" or "over things" in ancient Irish and usually translated as "over somewhat".[18] Other pseudo-etymological interpretations associate Uisneach to *uais nech* or "person of excellence".[19] According to most scholars, both hypotheses are fanciful. If anything, they reveal the perception of Uisneach held by the different authors and transcribers: Uisneach, the hill of the center, is "above" things, both in a factual way – as it hangs over a vast plain –[20] and symbolically speaking.

There is actually no consensus over the etymology of Uisneach. The same can be said about its spelling. MacKillop reminds us that it varies widely, which is common in Irish, both ancient and modern. Thus, mentions of Uisneach, "Uisneagh, Uishnach, Ushnagh, Ushney, Usna, Usnagh, Usnech, Usney, Uisnig (gén.), Uisnigh (gén.)"[21] are all acknowledged.

O'Rahilly believed the toponym was a reference to **ostināko-* or the "angular place" from the root **ost-*, the bone. Eric Hamp derived it from **us-tin-āko*, the "place of the hearth", from a root connected to the idea of burning:[22] it is an appealing idea, especially when bearing in mind the importance of fire in the myths connected to the hill.[23] However, this plausible symbolic compatibility does not suffice to corroborate an etymological claim.

According to another hypothesis, Uisneach could stem from *uss* ("up/high/above") and *enech* ("the front") and stand for a reference to a high plateau.[24] Finally, other researchers suggested a derivation from *uss* (in the sense of "above") followed by *inne* ("the center/middle") and the suffix **-ako*.[25] Uisneach would therefore be the place "of the middle that is above". Even if this latter hypothesis seems attractive, it remains once again unprovable. Furthermore, reconstructed etymologies – i.e. etymologies fashioned *a posteriori* so as to conform to the idea one holds of the original word – are always a risk. It is sufficient then to remark on the lack of consensus regarding the etymology of Uisneach among scholars, and to note similarities – or discrepancies – between those different theories and some of the traditions connected to the hill.

Uisneach, in Mide: Etymologies

"Uisneach, in Mide" is "Uisnech Midi" in ancient Irish. The words are often translated into "Uisneach, in the center", from ancient Irish *an mhí*,[26] or even "the hearth/temple of the center".[27] Occasionally, "Mide" is translated as "neck": this led Michael Dames to assert that the Fifth Province played the role of "joining head to body, idea to thing, and body to soul"[28].

This interpretation, like other interpretations made by Dames, is rather perplexing. It seems at least partially inspired by an excerpt from the *Book of the Taking of Ireland* also called the *Book of Invasions* (*Lebor Gabála Érenn*) a collection of narratives and poems compiled from the 11th century onward, which details the different mythical waves of invasions of Ireland. The original text, however, is much more factual than what Dames implies:

> It was in the reign of Hadrian that Tuathal took the kingship of Ireland. (...) By Tuathal was each province in Ireland lopped of its head, and so "Mide" was the name given to them, that is "the neck" of every province.[29]

Tuathal Techtmar is said to be a High King – *Ard Rí Érenn* or *Ard-Rí na hÉireann*, that is a king claiming the whole of the Irish territory – from the 2nd century CE. Tuathal literally means "ruler of all people".[30] The historicity of the character is still debated and most scholars believe that he was probably a mythical king. In any case, Tuathal is here simply presented as the creator of the province of Mide, which was fashioned by taking the "head", i.e. a large portion of the land and wealth, either factual or symbolic, from each province. The idea is taken up in the 17th century by Geoffrey Keating: "it is why it is called [Mide], because that it is from the neck of each province Tuathal Teachtmhar cut [the mensal land]".[31] The etymology here proposed (Mide/neck) remains hypothetical, so much so that the word "Mide" did not originally refer to a province but rather a precise district – the one that surrounded the hill of Uisneach.[32]

In any case, it seems that the authors – or, more appropriately, the transcribers-glossators – usually specify that the hill is situated in the mythical province of Mide whenever they deal with claims of dominance and power, be it royal[33] or mystical and symbolic.

To put it more clearly, if "Uisneach" is a merely a hill, "Uisneach, in Mide" is presented as a place of power: the association of the hill with the province of the center must be regarded as an emphasis on its central nature and, as a consequence, on its symbolic and political relevance.

Royal Power

For instance, according to the *Annals of Inisfallen* – the compilation of which started in the 11th century – the very famous Brian Boru, whose legend asserts that he unified Ireland, gathered an impressive fleet in 988 on *Lough Ree*, a large lake situated about 30 kilometers west of Uisneach. Boru is said to have attacked Uisneach. The date seems to be an important turning point in the history of the hill.

> A fleet, viz. 300 boats, [was put] on Loch Rí by Brian, and they harried Mide and went to Uisnech. And twenty five boats of these went into [Connacht], and a great slaughter of their crews was inflicted there.[34]

At that time, Brian Boru was not yet High King of Ireland: he therefore proceeded to Uisneach – whose connection with the province of Mide is here clearly underlined – and invaded it. From here, it is just a short step to concluding than taking Uisneach amounted to claiming sovereignty on all or part (Mide?) of the Irish territory. Other examples are needed however to completely back up this claim.

The Vision of Ferchertne (*Brinna Ferchertne*), dated to the 10th century by Kuno Meyer, begins as follows:

1   I see two Hounds manfully fighting a glorious combat: Cuchulinn is boasting of the death of Curoi, Dare's son.
2   The Eraind seized Erin, numerous were their families,
    They seized a province without mishap as far as Uisneach in [Mide].
3   Many battles they fought, hardy were the troops,
    They slept a night in Tara on their march to Emain Macha.[35]

In this warlike episode, the dyad Uisneach/Mide is immediately followed by a mention of the hill of Tara, the royal site *par excellence*, and Emain Macha, the Fort of Navan, one of the other great royal sites of Ireland, situated today in the country of Armagh in Northern Ireland. Here, the emphasis is laid on the power and strategic efficiency of the fighters.

The Wooing of Emer (*Tochmarc Emire*), also dated to the 10th century by Meyer, explains:

> Three kings were reigning together over Érinn. They were from Ulster, viz. Dithorba, son of Diman, from Uisneach of [Mide], the Red, son of Badurn, son of Aircet the Bald, in the land of Aed, Cimbaeth, son of Findairget, from Finnabair of Mag Inis.[36]

One of the sovereign kings of Ireland therefore came from Uisneach: asserting that the hill stood in the mythical province of Mide was a way of justifying this title. Seven centuries later, Keating alludes to the same episode while using a similar process:

> Three kings out of Ulster held the sovereignty of Ireland, namely, Aodh Ruadh son of Badharn, from whom is named Eas Ruaidh, and Diothorba

son of Deaman of Uisneach in [Mide], and Ciombaoth son of Fionntan from Fionnabhair.[37]

Similarly, when the legendary High King Conaire Mór embarks upon a journey to the hill of Tara in the episode entitled *The Destruction of Da Derga's Hostel* (*Togail Bruidne Dá Derga*, compiled in the 14th century), the route chosen is quite informative:

> After settling the two quarrels, he was travelling to Tara. This is the way they took to Tara, past Uisneach of [Mide]; and they saw the raiding from east and west, and from south and north, and they saw the warbands and the hosts, and the men stark-naked; and the land of the southern [Uí] Néills was a cloud of fire around him.[38]

Roseanne Schot suggests an interpretation of this desire to associate Uisneach to the province of Mide, notably when Tara and the clans of the Uí Néill are implicitly alluded to:

> Uisneach is portrayed as the meeting place of the five ancient provinces, consisting of Ulster, Leinster, Connacht and Munster, the latter divided into two halves, either east–west or north–south. These and other alternative schema that purport to describe a proto-historic, five-fold division of the island become increasingly elaborate from about the tenth century, and have been shown to reflect a specific ideological agenda associated with the Uí Néill kings of Tara.[39]

The dynasty of the Uí Néill and its connection to Uisneach will be detailed *infra*. The main element to be remembered at this stage is that the association of the hill of Uisneach with the province of Mide recurs whenever a question of claiming power, particularly royal power, is at stake.

First Conclusion

The association of the hill of the center with this idea of sovereignty is obviously crucial. There is little point, however, in trying to make an exhaustive list of mentions of this "Uisneach, in Mide" in early Irish literature. Symbolically speaking, possessing Uisneach, being crowned at Uisneach, winning a battle at Uisneach amounted to asserting one's power over a much larger territory, possibly the whole of Ireland. It is at least the idea conveyed by a large number of medieval transcribers and authors. The hill is not only at the center of Ireland; it was, almost to the same extent as the hill of Tara,[40] at the heart of Irish sovereignty, which is itself embodied by the mythical province of Mide. Precisely because it is a hill, Uisneach is not only presented as being "at the center" but also as standing "above" the world: the superior, vertical aspect, which is inherent to any kind of sovereignty and dominance, is here exacerbated. Some etymological hypotheses seem to confirm this idea. A large portion of those hypotheses could, however, prove obsolete as they may simply be *a posteriori* constructions, mere attempts to apply to the hill one's own understanding of its function in Irish history. Such etymological fabrications could therefore shed light on the very idea and conception some transcribers – for example those of the *Dindshenchas* – may have had of the hill, which is no less interesting.

One last instance of this notion of "sovereignty gained on Uisneach, in Mide" must be mentioned. The example is remarkable as it clearly associates the Christian religion to the hill and therefore unmistakably connects religious and political matters.

Saint Patrick and Power

In this episode of *The Colloquy with* (/of) *the Ancients* (*Acallam na Senórach*, sometimes translated as *The Tales of the Elders of Ireland*), Saint Patrick gathers the great kings of Ireland on top of the hill of Uisneach:

> When they came up where should Patrick be but on Usnach's summit, with Dermot son of Cerbhall on his right hand, and on his left Ossian son of Finn, beside whom sat Muiredach mac Finnachta, king of Connacht; by him again was Eochaid *leithderg* king of Leinster, and next to him Eoghan *derg* mac Angus, king of Munster's both provinces.[41]

The presence of Mide is here implicit: the provinces of Ireland, together with their kings, meet at the center of Ireland, on the hill of Uisneach. Conall mac Néill, a distinguished member of the dynasty of the Uí Néill and future first King of Uisneach,[42] arrives and pledges allegiance to Patrick by resting his head on his chest while kneeling. Patrick is quick to respond:

> Patrick made answer: "regal power I convey to thee, and that of thy seed thirty kings shall reign; my metropolitan city and mine abbacy moreover I make over to thee, and that thou enjoy all whatsoever I shall have out of Ireland's five great provinces".[43]

Once again, supreme sovereignty is conferred for generations from Uisneach to the whole of Ireland and its *five* provinces. This time, it is by the hand of the most renowned Irish saint, Patrick, a most notable representative of the New Religion, or rather new religious power. More than ever, Uisneach is implicitly "at the center" and "above". Transcribers or redactors tend to focus on the province of Mide when the protagonists of their narratives, either kings or saints, need to transcend the hill of Uisneach and to take it out of the purely factual domain. Whenever Mide is mentioned, either implicitly or explicitly, Uisneach becomes "at the center" and "above" of this world.

In this excerpt, the Christian saint becomes a part of the story and overarching myth. It is by no means an isolated case. Tírechán, hagiographer of Patrick, places a famous episode on Uisneach, "in Mide" where he asserts his power – as well as that of the Kings of Uisneach he has chosen – over Ireland.[44] The saint is said to settle precisely at the "Stone of Coithrige," Coithrige being an alternate name of Patrick. The stone here mentioned most likely refers to *Ail na Mireann*, the imposing rock that lies near the top of Uisneach.

1.2 Ail na Mireann

Background and Etymologies

Ail na Mireann is an essential element of the symbolism of Uisneach. Of course, the geographical position of the hill already granted it a significant import. It must be noted, however, that Uisneach is certainly not the only hill that stands at just about the center of Ireland. The presence of this impressive-looking rock on its side undoubtedly reinforced its sacredness: without *Ail na Mireann*, Uisneach may have been merely one of many hills at the approximate center of Ireland.

What is referred to as *Ail na Mireann* is in fact a conglomerate stone, approximately five meters in length on each edge[45]. Today, it still stands at about 300 meters from the top of the hill. It is a natural monument, a remainder of the last Ice Age. Its structure and appearance has apparently not been modified – at least in any great degree – by the human hand. The rock, now commonly referred to as the *Catstone*, is still held in high regard by a fringe of the population.[46]

The conglomerate is mentioned on multiple occasions in medieval texts. It bears the name of *Ail na Mireann* in Irish and is sometimes referred to as *Lapis divisiorum* (the "Stone of Division") or *Umbilicus Hiberniae* ("the umbilicus" or "navel of Ireland") in Latin or even *Carraig Choithrigi* or *Petra Coithrigi* (the "Stone of Patrick"). The fact that those terms actually refer to the same stone will be debated on a case-by-case basis.

There is no consensus about the meaning of the term *Ail na Mireann*. It is usually translated to the "Stone of Divisions", which seems in keeping with what is known of the stone: its central and "divisional" aspect is indeed the focus of most medieval texts. However, some recent studies consider it a faulty translation that could be owed to Geoffrey Keating. The 17th-century historian may have been inspired by William Camden and have derived his translation from the term "Elnamirand", used in 1586 by the English scholar to allude to Mide in his *Britannia*. In his article published in *Eigse - Journal of Irish Studies* called "A Review of Some Placename Material from Foras Feasa Ar Éirinn" (2005), Diarmaid O'Murchadha suggests that *Ail na Mireann* might be derived from "Ail na Midhreadh" or "the Rock of Judgments"[47], which is an intriguing hypothesis.

Ail na Mireann and the "Catstone"

Ail na Mireann is now commonly referred to as the *Catstone* (sometimes spelled *Cat Stone*). The origin of this current denomination is equally obscure. Some see an allusion to the shape of the rock, which could look like a huge sitting cat or even a cat chasing a mouse.[48] Some other theories are even more peculiar: the *Catstone* could be the "Stone of the Cat" because the animal was allegedly a psychopomp in ancient mythologies; in other cases, a connection with the Irish *Cath*, that is "battle", is put forward, which is clearly unsustainable.[49]

Be it as it may, the modern denomination (or its potential Irish or Latin translation or equivalent) is never used as such in medieval texts. When and how *Ail na Mireann* became the famous *Catstone* is hard to establish. We only know that John O'Donovan referred to the conglomerate as the *Cat's Rock* in 1837 and the name *Catstone* was already known at the beginning of the 20th century at least.[50] Generally speaking, it seems more prudent and probably more accurate to refer to the rock as "*Ail na Mireann*", which will be the name used hereafter, along with other neutral denominations such as the "conglomerate" or the "stone of Uisneach".

According to Keating

In the 17th century, Geoffrey Keating confirms that, according to tradition, the five provinces were supposed to meet at a precise point:

> And it is where the common centre of these five provinces was, at a pillar-stone which is in Uisneach, until that Tuathal Teachtmhar came, into the sovereignty, and that he took away a portion of each province as mensal land for every high-king who should be in Ireland: so that it is of these [Mide] was formed, as we shall show in the reign of Tuathal.[51]

In this excerpt, Tuathal Techtmar, once again a – most likely mythical – High King of the 2nd century CE, is presented as the creator of the province of Mide. As noted before, Keating is not, however, a perfectly reliable source – even though one could ponder over the reasons that may have led the historian to invent such a connection out of thin air. Thankfully, the writings of Giraldus Cambrensis, which are four centuries older, confirm this ancient association.

According to Giraldus Cambrensis

In his *Topography of Ireland*, the author provides a very detailed and most precious pseudo-historical description:

These events having occurred in the order related, at length five chiefs, all brothers, who were the sons of Dela, and among the descendants of Nemedus, who had taken refuge in Greece, arrived in Ireland, and, finding it uninhabited, divided the country into five equal parts, of which each took one. Their bounds meet at a stone standing near the castle of Kyllari, in [Mide], which stone is called the navel of Ireland [*Umbilicus Hiberniae*], because it stands in the middle of the country. Hence that part of Ireland is called [Mide] (Media), because it lies in the middle of the island; but it formed neither of the five famous provinces whose names I have before mentioned. For when the aforesaid [five brothers], had divided the island into five parts, each of those parts had a small portion of [Mide], abutting on the stone just mentioned; inasmuch as that territory had from the earliest times been the richest part of the country, having a level plain, and being very fertile and productive of corn.[52]

In order to fully grasp the implications of this passage, it must be remembered that, according to the *Book of Invasions of Ireland*, the island had witnessed several mythical waves of settlement: Ireland was successively invaded by the tribes of Cessair, Partholón, Nemed, the Fir Bolg (here called "sons of Dela", after their leader) and the Tuatha Dé Danann, then followed by the Milesians, that is Men, whose arrival stands for the ultimate wave of invasion.

The fundamental idea behind this excerpt is that five leaders, descendants of the Fir Bolg and the tribe of Nemed, divided the country in five "equal parts" around *a stone situated at the center of the island, in Mide*. The etymology here submitted, that is "the middle", from ancient Irish *an mhí*, seems more convincing than the usual references to the "neck". The rock quite plausibly corresponds to the very real *Ail na Mireann* of Uisneach, which is here presented as the "navel" of Ireland, source – or at least focus – of wealth and fertility.

Interestingly enough, it is here specified that, although the stone is at the center of the five provinces, it is not an integral part of any of them: "Each of those parts had a small portion of [Mide], abutting on the stone just mentioned". *Ail na Mireann* – and probably the whole of the hill of Uisneach – appears to be outside of Ireland, perhaps, symbolically speaking, "outside" of the world.

In the Book of Invasions

The idea according to which a rock used to divide Ireland can also be found in the First Redaction of the *Book of Invasions*, compiled between the 12th and 14th centuries:

> The five parts of Ireland
> Between sea and land,
> I entreat the fair candles
> Of every province among them. (...)
>
> The points of those provinces
> To Uisne[a]ch did they lead,
> Each of them out of its ...
> [To the stone?] till it was five.[53] (...)
>
> About the stone in cold Uisneach
> in the plain of Mide of the horseman-bands
> on its top—it is a fair co-division--
> is the co-division of every province.[54]

There is little doubt that the stone here mentioned is indeed the Stone of Division: even if the name *Ail na Mireann* is not specified, it is literally a "stone" that "divides" and is situated on Uisneach.

Pillar or Navel?

Whereas the *Book of Invasions* merely mentions a stone, Giraldus goes further and associates it to a navel when Keating, on the other hand, writes about a pillar. The problem is that the peculiar shape of the rock of Uisneach is closest to that of an eroded cube or, at best, a broken sphere than a pillar or a column.[55] It may therefore be necessary at this point to digress a little: the symbolic and historical differentiation between a "pillar" and a "navel" is critical to the present study. The following discussion, although rather technical, will nonetheless prove quite useful.

The "stone pillar" described by Keating is somewhat reminiscent of the concept of a "cosmic pole" or *Axis mundi*, i.e. the symbolic axis around which the universe is supposed to revolve in many ancient traditions. The concept has been studied in detail by Mircea Eliade among others. Although Eliade is a controversial scholar,[56] his well-known propensity to over-generalize must not deprive us from his work as a collector of myths and traditions as well as a number of valuable – or at least intriguing – analyses. Eliade found references, either direct or indirect, to this "cosmic pole" in a great deal of traditions across the globe. He sums up the symbolism behind this axis as follows:

> This communication is sometimes expressed through the image of a universal pillar, *Axis mundi*, which at once connects and supports heaven and earth and whose base is fixed in the world below (the infernal regions). Such a cosmic pillar can be only at the very center of the universe, for the whole of the habitable world extends around it.[57]

Throughout the world – and depending on the various traditions studied – the *Axis mundi* takes the form of a pillar, a column, a stake, a pole or even a ladder, a tree, if not a mountain as a whole.[58] As Eliade remarks:

> Since the sacred mountain is an *Axis mundi* connecting earth with heaven, it in a sense touches heaven and hence marks the highest point in the world; consequently the territory that surrounds it, and that constitutes "our world", is held to be the highest among countries.[59]

If this view is accepted, Uisneach in its entirety could have originally played the role of an *Axis mundi*. Other sources suggest another possible analogy.

The Tree of Uisneach?

The *Dindshenchas* mentions the existence of an ash tree on Uisneach which collapsed at the time of Aed Slane, in the 7th century.[60] *The Settling of the Manor of Tara* (*Do Shuidigiud Tellaich Themra*) even tells about five legendary trees, including the "tree of Uisneach" or *Bile/Craeb Uisnig*. The five trees were said to have stemmed from fruits grown on one single branch:

> And these are the trees which grew up from those berries: the Ancient Tree of Tortu and the tree of Ross, the tree of Mugna and the Branching Tree of Dathe, and the Ancient Tree of Usne[a]ch.[61]

Nothing else is known about this tree of Uisneach[62] which is not mentioned in other early manuscripts.[63] In such an obscure context, it is difficult to picture it as an exact representation of an *Axis mundi*. The tree could as readily be a metaphor, for example, of power and sacredness in general, possibly dwelling on the symbolism of the five provinces of Ireland: the fact that the tree of Uisneach is mentioned last in this excerpt is probably not trivial. Alwyn and Brinley Rees, who had already identified this episode and noted its significance, gave the following interpretation:

> Though the location of most of these five places in uncertain, there can be no doubt that the underlying idea is that the trees symbolize the four quarters around the centre.[64]

For lack of better explanation or further points of comparison, it is tempting to accept this mention of a tree on Uisneach as a metaphor of the partition of Ireland into five provinces, Uisneach Midi at its center.

Axis Mundi and Omphalos

In any case and to return to Keating, the historian does mention a "pillar-stone", that is an actual pillar made of stone – not a tree. As for Giraldus Cambrensis, he believes that the stone of Uisneach was the "navel of Ireland" (*Umbilicus Hiberniae*), which does not make the interpretation simpler.

The umbilicus described by Giraldus rather recalls an *omphalos*, comparable to that of Delphi, than a pillar. In Greek, *omphalos* actually translates to "umbilicus". The importance of *omphaloi* – central objects reminding of a navel – has been confirmed in a great deal of peoples across the globe since the investigations of W.-H. Roscher at least.[65] Joseph Loth was the first to confirm its existence for the Celts.[66] Not so much an "axis" as a "navel of the world" – i.e. a potential source of creation – the term primarily referred to the ideas of birth and centrality.

Although not universal, the two concepts – *Axis mundi* and *omphalos* – are fairly common in many traditions around the world.[67] Jean-Loïc Le Quellec and Bernard Sergent remind us that the *omphalos* is usually a sacred stone of ovoid or conical shape whereas the *Axis mundi* is typically a central axis or pole, sometimes embodied by a natural object.[68] In Ireland, it is in general associated with the Stone of Fal, *Lia Fál*, next to the hill of Tara.

On Uisneach, however, the two symbolisms seem to conflate. On the one hand, the umbilicus – the *omphalos*, the navel of the world – and on the other hand the cosmic pillar – the *Axis mundi*, the central pole around which the world revolves, an in-between, a hyphen between the sky and the earth – are both mentioned. In this context, is it possible to contemplate that the "pillar" of Keating and the "navel" of Giraldus Cambrensis actually refer to one single object.

Two theories seem plausible and must be contemplated: first, it is possible to envisage two distinct objects on Uisneach, one standing for the navel of Ireland (as mentioned by Giraldus), the other the cosmic pillar (as referenced by Keating). According to a second conceivable theory, the center of Ireland could be embodied by one single object, which, by extension, would bear the double symbolism of navel and pillar – which is not, in essence, antinomic.

Of course, those theories hold water only if one accepts that the mentions of a stone on Uisneach by transcribers and authors from the Middle Ages actually refer to a real, historical object: this idea is in itself a preconception. If this postulate is accepted though, *Ail na Mireann* could stand as a plausible candidate to an Irish umbilicus, not least because of its sheer size and its subspherical, almost ovoid shape.[69] Moreover, it could be cautiously argued that the grooved, serrated, perhaps gnarled appearance of the rock may evoke the shape and overall appearance of a navel. On the other hand, even with a lot of imagination, it is hard to find even a remote resemblance between the boulder rock of Uisneach, almost five meters deep and across, and any sort of "pillar".

Pillar or Navel: Reality of Uisneach

Today, a number of objects stand on Uisneach and share some degrees of similarities with the shape of a pillar. For example, a short grey post is planted on the factual top of the hill, at a place called *Saint Patrick's Bed*. It is, however, a modern concrete triangulation pillar[70] that the current owner of the hill occasionally chooses to adorn with a gilded pyramidal structure, especially when festivals are held on the hill[71] – a fairly doubtful candidate for an ancient cosmic pole to say the least. Perhaps more interestingly, when describing the hill of Uisneach in archaeological terms, Roseanne Schot made the following account:

> on the south-western shoulder of the hill, is a small but interesting group of enclosures and a natural spring known as *Tobernaslath* (*Finnleascach*)—the "white rimmed well" of Uisneach. The spring issues near the base of a natural, rounded hillock on whose summit lies a large, prostrate pillar-stone. At some stage in the past the crown of this hillock was enclosed by a low, circular earthen bank (35m in diameter), thereby transforming this natural feature into a monument in its own right—a phenomenon which is paralleled, in an even more striking way, by the earthen enclosure (18m in diameter) erected around the "Catstone", some 400m to the north-west.[72]

The existence of a pillar-stone surrounded by an enclosure is intriguing, all the more so that it recalls the enclosure circling *Ail na Mireann*.[73] The prostrate pillar-stone near *Tobernaslath* could potentially be the "pillar" mentioned by Keating; this would imply the existence of a pillar (that of *Tobernaslath*) *and* a navel (*Ail na Mireann*), both circled by a similar-looking enclosure. Unfortunately, no one has made a thorough archaeological investigation of this enclosure and of the prostrate pillar-stone in such a way as to shed light on this possibility. The issue will be addressed in the apposite chapter, which nonetheless reaches the same conclusion: further archaeological investigations are needed for this theory to be conclusive.[74]

Most of all, one must bear in mind that a "cosmic pole" does not have to actually be a column. In terms of symbolism, the fact that *Ail na Mireann* is located close enough to the summit of a hill arguably conferred it a "vertical" dimension similar to that of a pillar pointed to the sky. Another interpretation would suggest that *Ail na Mireann* may have played the role of a navel that was situated on Uisneach, a hill which, because of its very nature, could itself represent the *Axis mundi*.

The concepts of *omphalos* and that of *Axis mundi* do not conflict with each other: on the contrary, in the case of Uisneach the two notions seem to coalesce. Similarly, the references to a "pillar" rather than a "rock" in the medieval texts describing the hill must not constitute an obstacle: this pillar could still be a reference to *Ail na Mireann*, possibly to the "prostrate pillar-stone" of *Tobernaslath* or even to the hill of Uisneach as a whole.

Eliade also believed the two concepts of *omphalos* and *Axis mundi* to be highly compatible. He considered that the *Axis Mundi* – the pole around which the world of Men expands – was supposed to be placed "in the middle", in the "navel of the Earth": most traditions held that it was supposed to stand at the Center of the World.[75] In that regard, Uisneach could have been considered both as the axis around which the world revolved and the navel, the symbolic center of this world.

The Settling of the Manor of Tara

One last example must be mentioned, as it is quite enlightening. *The Settling of the Manor of Tara* has already been briefly cited. It revealed the mythical existence of a "tree of Uisneach" and the episode was interpreted as a will to insist on the division of Ireland into five provinces. The manuscript, which is usually dated to the 14th-15th centuries, dwells on the dynasty of the Uí Néill, here simply referred to as the "nobles of Ireland":

> Then the nobles of Ireland came as we have related to accompany Fintan to [Uisneach], and they took leave of one another on the top of [Uisneach]. And he set up in their presence a pillar-stone of five ridges on the summit of [Uisneach]. And he assigned a ridge of it to every province in Ireland, for thus are Tara and [Uisneach] in Ireland, as its two kidneys are in a beast. And he marked out a *forrach* there, that is, the portion of each province in [Uisneach], and Fintan made this lay after arranging the pillar-stone:

> 33. The five divisions of Ireland, both sea and land, their confines will be related, of every division of them. (…) Wise the division which the roads have attained [?], perfect the arrangement dividing it into five. The points of the great provinces run towards [Uisneach], they have divided yonder stone through it into five (…). So Fintan then testified that it was right to take the five provinces of Ireland from Tara and [Uisneach] and that it was right for them also to be taken from each province in Ireland.[76]

In this passage, the stone is described as a pillar. However, three strophes prior, we find mention of a "navel of Uisneach": "It is long since I drank [?] a drink/of the Deluge over the navel of Uisneach".[77] In other words, the redactor seems to combine the two aspects (*omphalos/Axis mundi*) in the same tale. This tends to support the idea according to which Uisneach can be considered as both the umbilicus and the cosmic pole of Ireland, either because the hill in itself holds this dual identity or because *Ail na Mireann* (and/or possibly the broken pillar of *Tobernaslath*) express these aspects.

The term *forrach* mentioned in the extract refers to a zone of "protection or a sanctuary, similar in that respect to the Latin word *templum* or the Greek *temenos*, a 'sacred' enclosure".[78] Similarly to Giraldus Cambrensis' account, the stone is at the center of the five provinces but is not a part of any. In the words of Alwyn and Brinley Rees, it seems that Uisneach is "in all the four provinces, and in none of them".[79] The *forrach*, the sacred area, therefore, created on Uisneach is in fact excluded from the tangible world: it lies beyond it.

The erection of the pillar of Uisneach is supposedly owed to a certain Fintan, son of Bóchra, who is presented as the sole Irishman to have survived the Flood.[80] This five-sided stone[81] therefore divided Ireland in five parts and established the sovereignty of some members of the Uí Néill dynasty over the whole or part of Ireland.[82]

Ail na Mireann and the Uí Néill Dynasty

The Uí Néill dynasty – or at least some of its members – here finds its legitimacy on Uisneach reinforced. The hill lies at the center of the Irish provinces; each of these provinces is associated with a specific function ("knowledge in the west, battle in the north, prosperity in the east, music in the south, kingship in the centre");[83] being crowned or finding one's legitimacy as a King on Uisneach amounted to establishing one's power. Arguably, a correspondence with other, more ancient traditions, could also be put forward: we know many examples of other supposedly "Indo-European" kings who were crowned at the Center[84] of their territories, each territory being associated with a cardinal point and corresponding to one specific function.[85]

The Uí Néill dynasty is regularly associated with Uisneach, in particular in Christianized transcriptions and a number of hagiographies. Perhaps the place of the dynasty in the wider context of Irish history must now be scrutinized so as to better comprehend the stakes of such an association.

1.3 The Uí Néill and the "Kings of Uisneach"

The study of the Uí Néill dynasty and their connection with the hill of Uisneach is not an easy task. It will lead us to temporarily part from the analysis of the symbolic significance of the center in order to discuss historical issues. Unfortunately, most sources are not reliable: the main problem stems from the fact that history and myth are closely intertwined in the Ireland of the Early and High Middle Ages.

On top of these general remarks, it must be noted that the history of Ireland in the Early and High Middle Ages is particularly complex: from our contemporary perspective, the Irish genealogies are often obscure, their style convoluted, the narratives perhaps confusing. The analysis of this historic background must therefore be undertaken with a somehow didactic approach which, hopefully, will lead to intelligible and convincing conclusions while avoiding over-simplification.

Uí Néill Dynasty: General Statements

The Uí Néill were a powerful dynasty that ruled between the 5th and 12th centuries CE over a large portion of the Irish territory: it apparently dominated the northern half and the east of the island as early as the second half of the 6th century. It took its name from *Niall* or *Néill Nóigiallach* (Niall "the holder of the Nine Hostages" or simply "Niall of the Nine Hostages") who is said to have reigned in the late 4th or early 5th century. According to some traditions, he was a High King of Ireland – perhaps the first ever. Just like in the case of Tuathal Techtmar who, according to other transcribers, could have held the title of "first" High King of Ireland in the 2nd century, nothing seems to substantiate that claim.

It is not necessary here to go into much detail and enter scholarly debates on a highly complex issue.[86] What must be remembered is that the character of Niall of the Nine Hostages is the founding ancestor of a dynasty that will later be divided into rival branches: four of his sons were said to establish the northern Uí Néill lineage and settle in Ulster; four others, with the help of Diarmait mac Cerbaill, the southern Uí Néill at the *center* of Ireland, in a territory comprising Mide (and therefore Uisneach as well as the fortress of Tara) and roughly corresponding to the contemporary counties of Meath, Westmeath, Offaly and Longford.[87]

Tara, Uisneach and the Southern Uí Néill

The connection between the southern Uí Néill – also called *Cland Cholmáin* – and both the fortress of Tara and the hill of Uisneach seems to have been close. Many redactors insisted on the importance of that bond: this should not surprise us. As noted by Thomas Charles-Edwards in his phenomenal *Early Christian Ireland*, "Royal sites [were] entwined in the politics of the Uí Néill". The author continues:

> Early kings were not crowned and, in spite of some interest in royal unction in the *Hibernensis*,[88] they seem not to have been anointed either. The royal site was thus the throne of the early Irish kings, the pre-eminent sign of regality.[89]

Thus, establishing one's power on a specific place amounted to defining one's own symbolic power. This is by no means a revolutionary idea: the more sacred and well-known a place, the more legitimate the power. This clarifies why Tara and Uisneach, respectively royal fortress and center of Ireland, later described as the "two kidneys in a beast",[90] were at the core of the claims of the Uí Néill and their chroniclers.

The Southern Uí Néill, Kings of Uisneach

One of the most precious sources comes from the *Book of Leinster*. A whole section[91] is dedicated to some members of the Uí Néill lineage, there identified as the "Kings of Uisneach": about 50 kings of the royal dynasty succeeded each other between the 5th and 12th centuries and were said to hold the title of *ríg Uisnig*.

The list below is an attempt at reconstructing the history – or what is presented as history by the redactors – of the lineage of the Kings of Uisneach throughout centuries, from Conall mac Néill (also called Conall Cremthaind), the first to bear the title. It is based on the genealogical mentions that can be found in the *Book of Leinster* and is completed by data supplied by miscellaneous Irish Annals (*Annals of Ulster*: AU; *Annals of Tigernach*: AT; *Annals of the Four Masters*: AFM).[92]

Some inconsistencies remain: the work of the redactors of the Irish Annals was not infallible. However, those inconsistences do not completely prevent a global comprehension of the unfolding of history – or rather pseudo-history as exploited by the transcribers of Irish myth and history.

The asterisks indicate characters that were already explicitly mentioned or that will be detailed hereafter.

Kings of Uisneach		
Name	*Son of*	*Death (source)*
*Conall Cremthaind	*Niall of the Nine Hostages	480 (AU)
*Fiachu	*Niall of the Nine Hostages	514 (AU)
Ardgal	Conall	520 (AU)
Ma[i]ne	Cerbaill	537 (AT)
*Diarmait	Cerbaill	565 (AU)
Colman Mór	Diarmata	555/558 (AU)
Colman Bec	Diarmata	587 (AU)
Suibne	Colman	600 (AU)
Fergus	Colman	618 (AU)
Oengus	Colman	621 (AU)
Conall Guthbind	Subni	635 (AU)
Mael Doid	Suibni	653 (AT)
Diarmait	Airmedaig	689 (AT)
Murchad	Diarmata	715 (AT)
Aed & Colgu	Diarmata	? & 714 (AU)
Domnall	Murchada	758 (AFM)
Niall	Diarmata Airmedaig	826 (AU)
Muridach	Domnaill	802 (AU)
Dondchad	Domnaill f. Murchada	797 (AU)
Conchobor	Dondchada	833 (AU)
Mael Ruanaid	Dondchada	843 (AU)
*Mael Sechnaill[93]	Mael Ruanaid	862 (AU)
Lorcan	Cathail	864? (AU)
Dondchad	Eochocain	877 (AU)
Fland	Mael Sechnaill	916 (AU)
Conchobor	Mael Sechnaill	919 (AU)
Domnall	Flaind	921 (AU)
Dondchad Dond	Flaind	944 (AU)
Oengus	Dondchada	943 (AFM)
Dondchad	Domnaill	948 (AFM)
Fergal	Oengusa	?

(*Continued*)

Kings of Uisneach

Name	Son of	Death (source)
Aed	Mael Ruanaid	951 (AU)
Domnall	Dondchada	952 (AU)
Carlus	Duind Dondchada	960 (AU)
Murchertach	–	964 (AU)
Mael Sechnaill	[Domnail]	1022 (AU)
Mael Sechnaill Got	–	1025 (AU)
Roen	–	1127 (AFM)
Domnall Got	–	1130 (AFM)
Conchobor	Flaind	1073 (AFM)
Murchad	Flaind	1076 (AFM)
Mael Sechnaill Bán	Conchobuir	1087 (AFM)
Domnall	Flaind	1094 (AFM)
Conchobor	Mael Sechnaill	1105 (AFM)
Dondchad	Murchaid	1106 (AFM)
Mael Sechnaill & Murchad	Dondchada	1115 (AU) &?[94]

Elements of Genealogical Analysis of the Uí Néill

The main elements that must be kept in mind are as follows:

1   according to the different sources at our disposal, *Niall of the Nine Hostage* (Niall Noígíallach) was the founder of the Uí Néill dynasty.
2   his son, *Conall Cremthaind* (or Conall mac Néill) was the first to be considered a "King of Uisneach" and is believed to be an ancestor of the southern Uí Néill.[95]
3   Conall's brother, *Fiachu mac Néill* was the second King of Uisneach but he was, together with his lineage, ousted and disempowered. As a consequence, the successors to the title of King of Uisneach came from the lineage of his brother Conall.
4   among the descendants of Conall, *Diarmait mac Cerbaill* (anglicized Dermot) was famous for his founding of the dynasty of the southern Uí Néill.[96] Diarmait was said to hold in great respect the ancient Irish festivals and the great ritual Irish assemblies (fair of Tailtiu, convention of Uisneach and feast of Tara, the last of which was supposedly held by Diarmait in 558 or 560).[97] To that extent, he is often presented as the last great Pagan king of Ireland – or the first great Christian one.[98]

Importance of Fiachu Mac Néill

Fiachu mac Néill, second king of Uisneach (3/ above), is a character of cardinal importance. First, he is the founder of the clan called *Cenél*

Fiachach. *Cenél Fiachach* once ruled over the territory surrounding Uisneach[99] but was pushed toward the south by the other southern Uí Néill, the dynasty initiated by Diarmait, and was excluded for the kingship of Tara.[100] In other words, Fiachu is a founder of a clan that was ostracized by the other Uí Néill, i.e. the powerful southern Uí Néill of Diarmait. A second facet to bear in mind: some sources present Fiachu mac Néill as the ancestor – more specifically the great-great-grand-father – of Aed mac Bricc, the saint of *Cenél Fiachach*.[101] Aed eventually became one of the two main saints of the whole Uí Néill dynasty, in spite of the fact that he came from an outlawed dynasty.[102]

Aed Mac Bricc, Saint of the Uí Néill

An episode taken from the Latin life of Aed mac Bricc[103] is particularly interesting in the sense that it connects the Uí Néill dynasty not only to Uisneach but also to a gigantic stone which is not unknown to us.

The author of the hagiography first reveals that the main churches of the saint had been built in Killare (Cell Aír),[104] at the foot of the hill of Uisneach. While digging a ditch next to their quarters, the men of Aed discovered an immense buried rock "which no force of men was able to shift".[105] The saint had witnessed the discovery and:

> he ordered the rock to go to another place where it would harm no one. The rock withdrew at once to a different place, where it remains to this day and gives cures to the afflictions of all believers.[106]

Here, the central idea is to claim that the saint of the Uí Néill discovered *Ail na Mireann,* moved it to its current location[107] and blessed it with healing powers. The benefit for the hagiographer was twofold. First, by bestowing miraculous powers to the Stone, the latter is received into the bosom of the Christian tradition. The alleged prophylactic virtues of *Ail na Mireann* may find their origin in Pagan traditions, here Christianized – as was the case for hundreds of sacred places in Ireland and elsewhere. No credible source, however, confirms that the Stone was venerated by local Pagan communities before the arrival of Christianity or even at the time of the writing of this excerpt. Additionally, the interest of the episode is all the more compelling in the Irish historical and symbolic context, where "power" went together with "places of power" that could be claimed. This passage was as much about Christianizing *Ail na Mireann* as it was about establishing the power of the saint of the Uí Néill – and therefore of the Uí Néill as a whole – over the place. The saint and his men supposedly discovered the stone, which is the kernel of the symbolism of Uisneach, and Aed was the one to grant the rock its power and importance. This process is far from unique in Irish literature.

Conall and Patrick: The Colloquy with the Ancients

Another precious text dated to the 12th century,[108] *The Colloquy with the Ancients* (*Acallam na Senórach*), mentions Conall mac Néill, i.e. the first King of Uisneach. The meeting of Conall with Patrick was already mentioned *supra*. It deserves to be transcribed here in its entirety:

> They progressed as far as *cnoc uachtair Erca* or "upper hill of Erc", which at this time is denominated Usnach. When they came up where should Patrick be but on Usnach's summit, with Dermot son of Cerbhall [Diarmait mac Cerbaill] on his right hand, and on his left Ossian son of Finn, beside whom sat Muiredach mac Finnachta, king of Connacht; by him again was Eochaid *leithderg* king of Leinster, and next to him Eoghan *derg* mac Angus king of Munster's both provinces, who thus [for they sat in a circle] touched the king of Ireland's right hand. Now came Conall mac Néill, laid his head in Patrick's bosom and made genuflexion to him. Dermot the king said: "come hither, Conall"; but he answered: "rather is it in Patrick's presence I will be [to serve him], so that as here on Earth so too in Heaven 'tis he shall be my superior". Patrick made answer: "regal power I convey to thee, and that of thy seed thirty kings shall reign; my metropolitan city and mine abbacy I make over to thee, and that thou enjoy all whatsoever I shall have out of Ireland's five great provinces".[109]

Conall mac Néill is here legitimized by Saint Patrick on the hill of Uisneach, in the presence of the kings of the great Irish provinces, after the members of the southern Uí Néill pledged allegiance to him: from the hand of Patrick, Conall gains royal power over the five Irish provinces. He *de facto* becomes the first King of Uisneach and has claims over the whole of Ireland – a "true" High King indeed. The hill becomes the symbolic royal seat of the dynasty, whose power is legitimated over Mide, the center of Ireland, or even over the whole of Ireland. In this excerpt, it is therefore implicit that a *ríg Uisnig* is an *Ard Rí*: a King of Uisneach is a High King of Ireland.

Undoubtedly, historical facts contradict the episode, which is more difficult to interpret than it seems at first. The author does present Diarmait as a contemporary of Patrick, which is troublesome: it is generally believed that Diarmait mac Cerbaill was in power between 545 and 565,[110] whereas Saint Patrick is thought to have come in Ireland a century earlier.[111] Additionally, some sources present Conall as the grand-father of Diarmait.[112] Finally, according to the *Annals of Ulster*, Conall died in 480.

Such obvious anachronisms are difficult to account for. Why stage a meeting between those three characters and portray Diarmait as king before his own alleged ancestor? If the idea was in fact to establish the supremacy of the Uí Néill dynasty over Uisneach – and more specifically the southern Uí Néill, since Diarmait is the founder of the lineage – why not simply make of Diarmait the central character of this episode? The answer, as could be expected, is manifold.

The Colloquy with the Ancients: Difficulty of Interpretation

The Colloquy with the Ancients is defined by the Rees as a "long rambling narrative in which Caílte recounts to St. Patrick and others of his period of the [adventures] in war and the chase".[113] Annie Donahue brings to our notice the fact that "elements of these tales originating in the oral narrative tradition were crafted into a written literary form by an unnamed ecclesiastic from a monastic scriptorium".[114]

The Colloquy with the Ancients is not a collection of texts with either a historical or a genealogical vocation. The primary motivation of the author(s) was probably not to delineate the power of a particular dynasty in Ireland. Its purpose was rather to influence the Irish customs and mores that were popular at the time of redaction. As noted by Annie Donahue, who alludes to the introduction of the narrative by translators and editors Ann Dooley and Harry Roe:

> Tensions evident between the Irish marriage customs and the prescribed practices of canon law prompt the consideration of this text as "an instructive tool of some subtlety in the effort to reform the social fabric".[115]

It is therefore possible that, by trying to collect a set of oral traditions into one text, the transcribers lapsed into inaccuracy, if not sheer anachronism. The meeting-up of three protagonists that did not live in the same century may simply be a mistake of the redactor(s) of *The Colloquy with the Ancients*, who were apparently quite ill-versed in Irish genealogies.

Be it as it may, the excerpt gives the acute impression that the central element here is Conall being bestowed the title of "first King of Uisneach" by the hand of Patrick. The true political or politico-religions motivations of authors of which nothing is known are impossible to discern.[116] Maybe the desire to praise Conall was very real and stemmed from unknown motives. Maybe the author(s) of the excerpt fashioned their narrative by superposing several anterior traditions, some of which bore within them a will to glorify members of the Uí Néill dynasty.

1.4 Uí Néill and Hagiographers of Patrick

Hagiography of Patrick by Tírechán: Background

Five centuries before the redaction of *The Colloquy with the Ancients*, one of Patrick's hagiographers, Tírechán, also spoke of Conall mac Néill in the most flattering terms. Fortunately, the life of the hagiographer is better known than that of the redactor(s) of *The Colloquy with the Ancients*: his motivations and potential biases are easier to encompass.[117]

At the time Tírechán wrote his Life of Patrick (or *Collectanea*), i.e. the second half of the 7th century, the hagiographer lived in the heart of the territory of the southern Uí Néill, which comprised the provinces of Brega[118] in the east (including the hill of Tara) and "Mide (the 'Middle Country') in the center of Tethbae between the Shannon and the Inny",[119] that is a large part of the central plain of Ireland.

Tírechán: The Uí Néill and Patrick at Uisneach

Tírechán describes an episode which is said to unfold on Uisneach. The following association of Uisneach with the province of sovereignty, Mide, is of course significant:

> Patrick established [a church] in Uisneach in [Mide]. He stayed at Coithrige's Stone, but some of his foreign companions were killed by the son of Fíachu son of Níall; [Patrick] cursed him, saying: "There shall be no king from thy progeny, but thou shalt serve the seed of thy brothers".[120]

"Uisneach, in Mide" becomes the theater of a confrontation between Patrick and the son of Fiachu mac Néill, second King of Uisneach: the saint had established a church on the hill and settled at *Ail na Mireann*, here called *Petra Coithrigi*. *Petra Coithrigi* translates as "the stone of Coithrige" or "the stone of Patrick": Coithrige is another name of the saint. Joseph Loth believes that the stone could originally bear the name of *Ail Coic-rige*, the "stone of five realms", which is in keeping with our knowledge of the mythical division of Ireland.[121] Under the pen of the hagiographer, *Coic-rige* could have become *Coithrige*, i.e. Patrick. Whether the unprovable theory of Loth is accepted or not, it remains obvious that by calling *Ail na Mireann* "the stone of Patrick", Tírechán connects it to the Patrician tradition: the New Faith endorses the mysticism of the place.

The son of Fiachu mac Néill killed the journeymen of Patrick, which leads the saint to curse their direct lineage: the brothers of Fiachu will inherit royal power, therefore becoming the next Kings of Uisneach. The saint therefore establishes his power by choosing who will reign over Uisneach – and perhaps over the whole of Ireland, since a *ríg Uisnig* is an *Ard Rí*; a King of Uisneach is theoretically a High King of Ireland. The lineage of the Uí Néill will continue but the direct descent of Fiachu will not be able to claim the title of King of Uisneach and exert its authority: Conall mac Néill will reign over Uisneach.

Possible Motives of Tírechán: Political

According to hagiographer Tírechán, it is on Uisneach that Patrick establishes his own – not only religious and mystical but also political – power over Irish royalty. The saint is the one who grants royal power to a chosen part of the lineage of the Uí Néill. As opposed to other episodes written down by other transcribers – not the least of which is *The Colloquy with the Ancients* – the story documented by Tírechán is in keeping with the genealogies and annals mentioning the Kings of Uisneach. The sources confirm that Fiachu could not place his descent on the throne of Uisneach (be it a symbolic or a real one) because his clan, *Cenél Fiachach*, was defeated by the Uí Néill of Diarmait. The different documents report that it is indeed the lineage of Conall mac Néill, the brother of Fiachu, which succeeded him.

The question that needs to be addressed is why the hagiographer apparently chooses to endorse *Conall* in his hagiography. Arguably, very little of his life was known to Tírechán, who writes two centuries after the assumed date of the encounter. Nothing is said of the character of Conall in the Irish Annals, except that he died in 480. If the fact that the hagiographer did not know the life of Conall in much detail is accepted, why then present him as a hospitable, honest king who is ready to accept the Christian faith rather than his antagonists?

The episode is complex and ambiguous: the explanation that is required is just as intricate. The southern Uí Néill of Diarmait had several rival clans, the most famous of which are perhaps *Cenél Fiachach*, *Cenél Coirpri* and *Cenél Lóegairi*, founded by three distinct characters, namely Fiachu, Coirpre and Lóegaire. Tírechán has Patrick meet those three clan leaders[122] at three distinct places, i.e. Uisneach, Tailtiu and Tara, which is rather significant as they corresponded to three prominent places of power.

Rivals of the Southern Uí Néill

Cenél Fiachach

The aim of bishop Tírechán was apparently to bolster the descendants of Conall, as opposed to other clans or dynasties, especially that of Fiachu the banned. He therefore emphasizes the power of the "true" southern Uí Néill – the progeny of Conall – at the expense of *Cenél Fiachach*, the dissenting clan of the lineage of Fiachu.

At the time of the hagiographer, the southern Uí Néill of the lineage of Diarmait were in fact the ruling dynasty of the center of Ireland – so much so that, in the mind of Tírechán, the royal power of the Uí Néill in Ireland probably amounted to a hegemony of the southern Uí Néill.[123] By favoring Conall and having the son of Fiachu cursed, the hagiographer accommodated – perhaps reconciled – the political power in place and the religious power he represented – Christianity or, more specifically, its Patrician avatar. The theory according to which Tírechán promoted the southern Uí Néill is made all the more credible that the endorsing of Conall was not made at the expense of the lineage of Fiachu only.

Cenél Coirpri

As early as his first encounter with Conall, who had welcomed the saint with hospitality, the Saint makes the following announcement: "The seed of thy brother shall serve thy seed for ever".[124] The declaration echoes an episode that unfolded a couple of lines prior. When confronting a certain Coirpre,[125] at Tailtiu, during a royal assembly, Patrick had made a comparable warning: "Thy seed shall serve the seed of thy brothers, and there shall be no king of thy lineage for ever".[126]

Coirpre is the founder of his own dissenting clan, *Cenél Coirpri*, excluded from power by the main branch of the southern Uí Néill.[127] Later, Tírechán uses the exact same phrasing to remove Fiachu from power: "There shall be no king from thy progeny, but thou shalt serve the seed of thy brothers".[128]

The three encounters – respectively with Conall, Coirpre and Fiachu – are thus united by the same figure of speech. Simply put, Patrick meets Conall and declares his support for him. He also meets with Coirpre, founder of the dissenting *Cenél Coirpri* and Fiachu, emblematic leader of the dissenting *Cenél Fiachach* and disavow both.

During his meetings with Coirpre and Fiachu (on the hill of Tailtiu and Uisneach respectively), Patrick curses their lineage. In both cases, the episode takes place on a major place of power and perhaps even more eloquently during a royal assembly in the case of Coirpre.[129] In both cases also, the dissenting clans are known to be the enemies of the southern Uí Néill of Diarmait.

Conall, first King of Uisneach and ancestor of the southern Uí Néill comes out victorious in those confrontations. Portraying Conall in such a positive light undoubtedly served a reinforcement of the legitimacy of the dynasty that was still in power at the time Tírechán was writing – the southern Uí Néill.

But the hagiographer goes a step further: he also mentions visits made by Patrick at a couple of places inherently connected with power in Ireland: besides Tailtiu and Uisneach, the saint also visits Tara,[130] heart of royal power and seat of the feast of Tara. There, he meets with Lóegaire mac Néill, Pagan king of Tara and ancestor of yet another clan, *Cenél Lóegairi*.

Cenél Lóegairi

Lóegaire was the king of Tara and thus the alleged High King of Ireland. In parallel, he also held close connections with the province of Connacht.[131] In the hagiography of Patrick by Tírechán, king Lóegaire refuses the New Faith, whereas in the other famous Patrician hagiography – written by a monk called Muirchú– he is said to convert to Christianity.[132] In Muirchú's work, Lóegaire is endorsed by Patrick, whereas in Tírechán's he remains on the Pagan side. In the following passage taken from Tírechán's work, Lóegaire refuses the Christian faith and the emphasis on Pagan rituals and druidism is rather telling:

[Loíguire] could not accept the faith, saying: "My father Níall did not allow me to accept the faith, but bade me to be buried on the ridges of Tara, I son of Níall and the sons of Dúnlang in Maistiu in Mag Liphi, face to face (with each other) in the manner of men at war" (for the pagans, armed in their tombs, have their weapons ready) until the day of *erdathe* (as the druids call it, that is, the day of the Lord's judgement).[133]

The general idea is comparable to the confrontation with Coirpre and the son of Fiachu: since Lóegaire did not accept the Christian faith, his Christian rivals could legitimately claim the kingship of Connacht. Incidentally, what was presented as the "land of Lóegaire" at the beginning of Tírechán's hagiography became the "land of Lóegaire and Conall mac Néill" at the end.[134]

It is therefore possible to interpret the episode as a new attempt at re-inforcing the legitimacy of the southern Uí Néill: the power of Diarmait's dynasty is rightful because it was approved by Patrick; on the other hand, Lóegaire was but another Pagan that would not accept Christianity. His lineage could not possibly rule and could therefore be subordinated to the dynasty of the southern Uí Néill, endorsed by the Christian saint.

Cenél Fiachach, Cenél Coirpri, Cenél Lóegairi

The three visits – at Tara, Tailtiu and Uisneach – where Patrick met with three Uí Néill leaders – Lóegaire, Coirpre and the son of Fiachu – who were ancestors to three dissenting clans – *Cenél Lóegairi, Cenél Coirpri, Cenél Fiachach* – are essential because they corresponded to three notable places of power and three potential enemies of the southern Uí Néill of Diarmait, the ruling dynasty.

Furthermore, Tara, Tailtiu and Uisneach are associated, in Irish tradition, with three Irish festivals which supposedly corresponded to three general assemblies of the men of Ireland – true central places of power, be it po-litical or spiritual.[135] It is hard to believe that Tírechán mentioned those highly symbolic encounters without any specific intent, especially when his account is compared with other hagiographies.

The hypothesis according to which the hagiographer wished to support the dynasty of the southern Uí Néill is more than convincing. His motives, though, are yet to be deciphered: did Tírechán have specific reasons to endorse the southern Uí Néill throughout his work? Or was his choice only about strengthening their power and flattering the ruling dynasty?

Possible Motives of Tírechán: Religious

In the hagiography written by Tírechán, the visits of Patrick are not limited to Tailtiu, Uisneach and Tara. As an evangelizer, Patrick is said to have travelled across the country. The encounters with the protagonists of the Uí Néill are but one obstacle the saint manages to overcome.

The work of Tírechán is actually divided into two parts: one dedicated to the land of the southern Uí Néill, the other to Connacht, which happens to be the hagiographer's birthplace:[136]

> Patrick's journey takes the form of a circuit (*circulus*), *dessel* "sun-wise") as was traditional; it takes Patrick through [Mide], then across the Shannon into Connaught (mainly Roscommon and Mayo), then to the territory of the northern Uí Néill and back to [Mide]. This circuit completed [...], Patrick is made to start on another, this time in a southerly direction, from [Mide] to Leinster.[137]

It seems that Tírechán wanted to include Connacht in the potential territorial claims of the southern Uí Néill: Lóegaire had close connections with the province and associating him with Paganism left open the door for any claim. However, one point is essential and must be addressed: the story told by the hagiographer revolves around the Christian faith before anything. As obvious as it may sound, a hagiography is quite literally the written "life of a saint": Tírechán's main objective was to glorify the work of Patrick and to strengthen the influence of Christianity in Ireland – probably even more than endorsing the political power of a dynasty.

Unlike Lóegaire, Conall is thus presented as accepting the Christian faith by the hand of Patrick – who in return grants him royal power. Turning the ancestor of the ruling dynasty into an ally of Christianity was probably quite convenient for the hagiographer. In addition to reinforcing the hegemony of the power in place, the method consolidated the power – both spiritual and political – of the Christian religion: Patrick granted power to the southern Uí Néill and the southern Uí Néill still ruled at the time of Tírechán. The lineage of Conall deserved the throne because their ancestor was fair-minded and had accepted the New Faith by the very hand of Patrick. Christianity here emerges as victor. But it is Patrick who appears as the true champion in the episodes: he is the one to grant Conall power.

Tírechán and the Politico-religious Hypothesis

A common and quite compelling scholarly theory makes of Tírechán an apostle of his own monastery – Armagh – in a historical nationwide context of rivalries between different monasteries.

It is known that Armagh was the most important monastery of the Patrician tradition: according to the *Annals of the Four Masters*, Patrick founded it in 457 and felt that it was to become "the head and chief of the churches of Ireland in general".[138] Most scholars believe that Tírechán, when writing the life of Patrick, wanted to confirm the influence of the monastery of Armagh – to which he was affiliated – by establishing the limits of his *paruchia*, its sphere of influence: this may explain what led him to undertake an enumeration of the churches that could claim to be of the lineage of Patrick and Armagh.[139]

This idea is not incompatible with other underlying designs – i.e. the will of the hagiographer to support the southern Uí Néill. By cursing the rival dynasties and confirming the power of the dynasty ruling in his time, Tírechán indirectly praises Patrick, *his* saint: the hagiographer spreads his words, comforts the legitimacy of his supporters and confirms the symbolic dominance of his monastery while strengthening the authority of the dynasty in power. Catherine Swift even goes one step further:

> Tírechán was writing the *Collectanea* as a loyal member of the Patrician regnum or kingdom which was headed by the heir of Patrick in Armagh. He was addressing it to a king of Tara who was also a descendant of Conall Cremthainne, and his aim was to claim favour from a dynasty that (so Tírechán informs us) had traditionally supported Patrick's church. He sought such aid because his own kingdom, that of Patrick, was under threat at the time and, in particular, was shrinking in territorial extent [although he did not specify from where these attacks came].[140]

This interpretation is convincing in the sense that it does not deny the importance of the claims of Armagh in the writings of Tírechán and Patrician writings in general. It merely places them in the wider context of political and religious struggles in Ireland. The author goes on to explain that the clans of *Cenél Coirpri* and *Cenél Fiachach* may have been a part of an anti-Patrician alliance which could have prompted Tírechán to write his hagiography.[141]

Aed Mac Bricc and Lommán, Rivals of Patrick?

In this regard, a detail from the hagiography of Patrick is quite persuasive and will connect further the story told by Tírechán to the symbolism and importance of the hill of Uisneach in Ireland.

As we already know, the son of Fiachu is presented as a murderous antagonist and his lineage is cursed by the saint: it so happens that Aed mac Bricc, the saint of the Uí Néill, is often presented as a descendant of Fiachu. As mentioned previously, some genealogies even portray him as his great-great-grand-son.[142]

Cursing the lineage of the son of Fiachu could therefore amount to cursing, or at least undermining the saint Aed mad Bricc, potentially in favor of Patrick or the monastery of Armagh.[143] Notably, the hagiographer of Aed mac Bricc tells us Aed had built his main churches in Killare, at the foot of the hill of Uisneach and later discovered *Ail na Mireann*. It is not hard to imagine those churches coming into conflict with the church supposedly established by Patrick on Uisneach, in Mide;[144] more broadly speaking, the saint of *Cenél Fiachach* was possibly used as a symbol, at one point of history or another, by the alleged anti-Patrician alliance. This theory is unconfirmed but, once again, the idea might have been to consolidate the influence of Armagh while sustaining the power of the southern Uí Néill.

Similarly, the speculation arises that, by denying the character of Lóegaire to be converted,[145] Tírechán's intent was to undermine the saint of the dissenting *Cenél Lóegairi*. This saint was apparently a certain Lommán, of whom very little is known except for the fact that he was associated with the territory of Trim. At the time of Tírechán, Trim was a small kingdom held by the lineage of Lóegaire which had not yet come under the yoke of Armagh.[146]

The question is indeed very complex: it seems impossible to assert that the main objective of Tírechán was to reinforce the influence of Christianity, that of Patrick, of Armagh or of the southern Uí Néill. One theory does not exclude the other though: Tírechán was most likely guided by a host of complementary reasons that all revolved around the maintenance of hegemony – the religious power of Christianity and Patrick, the political power of the Uí Néill and the politico-religious power of Armagh. Within the present discussion, the fact that power is at the core of the symbolism inherent to Uisneach is of course essential: the hill was *a* center of power, possibly *the* center of power in Ireland at one point of history or another.

The "appropriation" of Ireland was not solely political, as might been expected when first considering the Kings of Uisneach and their influence. Thus, the place of the hill in Irish history gradually comes into focus: Uisneach was a remarkable politico-religious and symbolic tool that history has kept exploiting for centuries.

1.5 Stone of Uisneach and Stones of Uisneach

Stones of Uisneach in the Vita Tripartita Sancti Patricii

The confrontation of Patrick with the clan of Fiachu mac Néill can be found in another episode from a hagiography called the *Tripartite Life of Patrick* (*Vita Tripartita Sancti Patricii*). The document is difficult to date but scholars believe it was probably contemporary to Tírechán and, in any case, cannot be subsequent to the 9th century.[147] The details vary substantially from the account of Tírechán and the mention of the hill of Uisneach is rather peculiar:

> [Patrick] came again from Tara till he was in Uisneach. He founded a cloister there. Two sons of Niall, namely, Fiacha and Endar, came against him. Patrick said to them that their children would inhabit that cloister if he should find a welcome with them. They refused and expelled him. "A curse", saith Patrick "on the stones of Uisneach", saith Sechnall. "Be it so" saith Patrick. Nothing good is made of them from that time forward. Not even washing-stones are made of them.[148]

The connection between Tara and Uisneach is here obvious enough and stands as further evidence of the symbolic bonds uniting the two places.

Here, the confrontation no longer opposes Patrick to the son of Fiachu but rather the saint to Fiachu himself, who was accompanied by his brother Enda. The brothers were said to both rule over the surrounding area.[149] The saint's presence was not well-received and Patrick endeavored to curse Fiachu. The attempt provides parallels to the curse of Fiachu's son in Tírechán's work. Here however, a companion of Patrick called Sechnall modifies the sentence *in extremis*: only the stones of Uisneach will be cursed – and thus the lineage of Fiachu is spared, if only by implication. This episode is therefore not about diminishing the influence of a clan rival to the southern Uí Néill nor their lineage: the curse in this telling consolidates the reputation of Patrick and the influence of his *paruchia*.[150]

Interestingly enough, the malediction is cast on the "stones" of Uisneach and not on one single "stone", be it the "stone of division" or that "of Patrick": the use of the plural form does not appear to be a mistake.

Stones of Uisneach in Jocelyn of Furness

At the end of the 12th century, the same episode was told by an English hagiographer of Patrick called Jocelyn of Furness under the following – and rather telling – title: "The Malediction of the Saint is laid upon the Stones of U[i]sneach":

> And with the like intention of building a church, this servant of Christ turned unto a certain very renowned place named [Uisneach]. But two brothers, by name Fiechus and Enda, ruled in those parts; and unto them and unto their offspring the saint prophesied, if they would so permit him, many blessings in this world and in the next; yet not only turned they their ears from his entreaty and from his preaching, but violently expelled him from the place. Then the saint, more grievously taking the hindrance of his purpose than his own expulsion, began to cast on them and on their seed the dart of his malediction. And Secundinus, his disciple, caught the word of his lip, and, ere he could finish, entreated and said unto him: "I beseech thee, my father, that thy malediction be not poured forth on these men, but on the stones of this place!"[151]

Once again, it is Sechnall, the disciple of Patrick – here called Secundinus –[152] who alleviates, or at least deflects the curse by begging Patrick for mercy, although the reason for such greatness of spirit is never addressed. Patrick accepts the demand:

> And the saint was patient, and he was silent, and he assented. Wonderful was the event! From that day forth are these stones found useful unto no building; but if should any one thereunto dispose them, suddenly would the whole work fall down and tumble into pieces. [...]

> whence it hath become a proverb in that country, when at any time a
> stone falleth from a building, that it is one of the stones of Uisneach.[153]

The saint establishes his power over the hill by granting Uisneach otherworldly features: its stones will prove impossible to use for building
structures, whatever structures may be attempted. The hill is not only
Christianized and freed from Pagan influences: it becomes cursed. Such
relentlessness could be explained by a will to demonstrate the power of the
saint: this process is quite common in hagiographies. In a more literally
hegemonic sense, the curse also strips Uisneach from any form of sacredness, thus simultaneously showing the power of the saint and diminishing
the authority of the Pagan. The domination of the Uí Néill was no longer
relevant in the 12th century though, and the idea may rather be to deter or
discredit the generally Pagan aura of the place as it was perhaps still vivid at
the time of writing, rather than to enact a temporal upset.

It would be a mistake to believe that a 12th-century English monk did not
care for Irish political or religious stakes: in fact, the context of redaction of the
Life of Patrick by Jocelyn suggests otherwise. It must be remembered that the
peninsula of Furness, in the south-west of England, maintained close connections with Ireland. Those connections date back to the Norman Conquest
at least.[154] Additionally, it is now established that the Life of Patrick by Jocelyn
was commissioned by Thomas, archbishop of Armagh.[155] Once again, it seems
that this episode was prompted by the desire to reinforce the influence of
Christianity and Patrick over Ireland, but also to consolidate the hold of
Armagh and perhaps adapt the symbolic importance of Uisneach.

The author proceeds as follows: "And [the stones] admit not the heat of
any fire, nor, when plunged into water, do they hiss like other stones".[156] In
other words, because of the curse, the stones of Uisneach could no longer
heat up and, since they remained cold, could not hiss when put in water,
even after being exposed to flames. This reference could be an allusion to
"washing-stones", which have already been mentioned in the hagiography
of Patrick in relation with Uisneach.[157] For A. T. Lucas, those "washing-
stones" refer to centuries-old ablution and cleansing practices that were
supposedly common in ancient Ireland.[158] However, the reference to fire
and water is not necessarily only cultural and historical: it is quite conceivable that this excerpt had a more mystical dimension to it. This mystical
dimension is perhaps not only owed to the Christian tradition, even though
hagiographies indeed abounds with mystic fires, sparks and sacred or holy
waters. This peculiar mention of "stones that do not admit fire" and will
not "hiss" when plunged into water may find its origin elsewhere.

1.6 The Killaraus of Geoffrey of Monmouth

Jocelyn tells us that the stones of Uisneach were cursed by Patrick: they could
not be used to build new structures, they were proverbially associated with

ruins and could not even be utilized as "washing-stones".[159] This curse very distinctly echoes another famous episode which, interestingly enough, is not Irish. Rather, it belongs to another branch of the Celtic culture.

Historia Regum Britanniae

The *Historia regum Britanniae* of Welsh bishop Geoffrey of Monmouth[160] crossed the ages: its influence can still be felt today, notably through the prism of the very popular Arthurian legends and such characters as Merlin or Uther Pendragon. It was redacted in the first half of the 12th century – only a few years prior to the work of Jocelyn of Furness. Chapters 10 to 13 of the eighth volume contain a particularly remarkable episode.

Wizard Merlin is shown conversing with Ambrosius Aurelius (or Emrys Wledig), a warlord of the island of Britain. Aurelius was the contemporary of an Irish king called Gillomanius, who here plays the role of the antagonist. Those pseudo-historical elements place the episode in the 5th century CE: it is very clear though that the word "historical", in the modern sense of the term, does not accurately define the content of the narrative.

The Giant's Dance

Aurelius wishes to erect a monument to the glory of the fallen soldiers buried in Salisbury and seeks the opinion of Merlin.

> "If you are desirous", said Merlin, "to honour the burying-place of these men with an everlasting monument, send for the Giant's Dance, which is in Killaraus, a mountain in Ireland. For there is a structure of stones there, which none of this age could raise, without a profound knowledge of the mechanical arts. They are stones of a vast magnitude and wonderful quality; and if they can be placed here, as they are there, round this spot of ground, they will stand forever".[161]

The *Giant's Dance* – in Latin *Chorea Gigantum* – must be understood as a "circle of Giants", from Latin *Chorea* meaning a round/circle or a dance in a ring. In other words, the *Giant's Dance* refers to a stone circle, famously defined as a circular alignment of standing stones[162] dating back to the Neolithic and/or the Bronze Age.[163]

Killaraus/Killare

Although its exact location is not specified, the name of the hill mentioned in the excerpt, Killaraus in Ireland, is obviously quite striking. It evokes Killare – Cell Aír or, in modern Irish, Cill Áir, genitive Chill Áir. Killare had already been mentioned in the hagiography of Aed mac Bricc: it was the place where the saint had built his first church; Killare/Cell Aír was explicitly said to be found at the foot of the hill of Uisneach. In the 12th century, Giraldus Cambrensis unambiguously mentioned that the stone of *Umbilicus Hiberniae*, the navel of Ireland, could be found in "Kyllari", in Mide.[164] Today, the civil parish of Killare and the constituency of the same name do adjoin Uisneach.[165]

More than anything, the details brought forward by Merlin remind of the writings of Jocelyn and consequently of the hill of Uisneach. Merlin did hold the mystical virtues of the stones of Killaraus in very high esteem:

> They are mystical stones, and of a medicinal virtue. The giants of old brought them from the farthest coast of Africa,[166] and placed them in Ireland, while they inhabited that country. Their design in this was to make baths in them, when they should be taken with any illness. For their method was to wash the stones, and put their sick into the water, which infallibly cured them. With the like success they cured wounds also, adding only the application of some herbs. There is not a stone there which has not some healing virtue.[167]

Jocelyn of Furness and Geoffrey of Monmouth

In the hagiography redacted by Jocelyn of Furness, Patrick curses the stones of Uisneach, which can no longer be used as construction material and do not hiss when heated by fire and plunged in water.[168] Conversely, in Monmouth's telling, the stones of Killaraus would be perfect for the erection of a sacred monument and the "giants of old" used to plunge them into water so as to benefit from their curative virtues. This diametrical opposition cannot be a coincidence and it appears that the purpose of Jocelyn – who writes after Geoffrey of Monmouth – was specifically to discredit the version of the Welsh bishop, probably because it was too ostentatiously imbued with Paganism or at least because it was not compatible with his Christian conception of the world.

As already mentioned, the work of Jocelyn was commissioned by an archbishop of Armagh: it is most conceivable that Jocelyn could not uphold a version that did not correspond with his Christian and Patrician ideology. Furthermore, Jocelyn is known to have used multiple sources – notably hagiographies – when redacting his version of the Life of Patrick. The connection between the monk of Furness and Geoffrey of Monmouth has been established by experts in the field.[169] As a consequence, the hypothesis according to which Jocelyn elaborated on the "curse" of the stones of Uisneach in order to contradict Geoffrey's version and so as to consolidate the power of Armagh at the expense of other saints – or Paganism in general – is quite plausible, and appealing in its neatness.

Confrontation for the Stones of Uisneach

Let us return to the narrative of Geoffrey of Monmouth. The words of Merlin eventually convince Aurelius. He sends his men – led by Uther Pendragon, the future father of Arthur – to Ireland in order to take the stones of Killaraus:

> When the Britons heard this, they resolved to send for the stones, and to make war upon the people of Ireland if they should offer to detain them. And to accomplish this business, they made choice of Uther Pendragon, who was to be attended with fifteen thousand men. They chose also Merlin himself.[170]

The Irish king Gillomanius refuses to give the stones away ("They shall not take from us the least stone of the *Giant's Dance*"),[171] which confirms their symbolic importance in Ireland – or the desire of the author to have his readers believe it, perhaps in order to highlight their excellence. A confrontation follows and is won by Uther: "After the victory they went to the mountain Killaraus, and arrived at the structure of stones, the sight of which filled them with joy and admiration".[172]

Magical Displacement of the Stones of Uisneach

Merlin then dares his men to move the stones ("See whether strength or art can do the most towards taking down these stones"), which they prove unable to do. He therefore uses his magic, which is the only means to move the rocks: their mysticism and sacredness are now evident. Once again, this part of the episode recalls the hagiography of Aed mac Bricc, dated to the 7th or 8th century:[173] the Saint Founder of the churches of Killare moved by his sheer will the giant stone previously identified as *Ail na Mireann*, when his men could not possibly move it themselves. It must be remembered that the stone mentioned in the Life of Aed "withdrew at once to a different place, where it remains to this day and gives cures to the afflictions of all believers".[174]

It appears that the writings of the hagiographer of Aed mac Bricc, those of Jocelyn of Furness and of Geoffrey of Monmouth, echo and complete one another: Uisneach/Killare was indeed a sacred place where a stone (or stones) was/were supposed to hold mystical powers. In the words of Geoffrey of Monmouth, these stones, heated in the fire then plunged in water, even possessed an additional supernatural power: according to Merlin, the stones of Killaraus healed "all diseases" and wounds when they were used alongside with specific "herbs". They held literally *otherworldly* prophylactic virtues, which explains why the wizard had specifically chosen this place.

In the story told by Geoffrey of Monmouth, Merlin uses his magical powers to propel the *Giant's Dance* on Mount Ambrius, near Salisbury.

Aurelius shows great enthusiasm: "He ordered Merlin to set up the stones brought over from Ireland, about the sepulchre; which he accordingly did, and placed them in the same manner as they had been in the mountain Killaraus".[175]

The Irish stone circle is reconstructed faithfully in the south of England. At the end of the 8th volume, Aurelius is even buried within the *Giant's Dance*.[176] Later, the successor of Arthur, Constantine, will also lay at the center of the circle of Salisbury whose English name is finally revealed.

Uisneach and Stonehenge

[Constantine], by the vengeance of God pursuing him, was killed by Conan, and buried close by Uther Pendragon within the structure of stones, which was set up with wonderful art not far from Salisbury, and called in the English tongue, Stonehenge.[177]

The conclusion is clear: according to Geoffrey of Monmouth, Stonehenge, probably the most famous stone circle in history, was constructed with the stones of Killaraus, i.e. Killare, at the foot of the hill of Uisneach. Even if the assertion is not based on any historical ground, the symbolic value of such an assertion cannot be stressed enough: according to Geoffrey of Monmouth, the illustrious stone circle of Salisbury takes its mystical and sacred power from the Irish hill. More than merely its equal, Uisneach is here presented as the ancestor of Stonehenge.

The absence of a stone circle on or in the vicinity of Uisneach today is not surprising.[178] First, two out of the three versions here mentioned clearly state that the stone(s) of Killare were moved – quite far from Uisneach in the case of *Historia regum Britanniae* – which tends to show that, even at the time of redaction, no such stone circle were expected to exist on the Irish hill. Additionally, and this is the essential point, the hagiography of Aed mac Bricc, or the manuscripts written by Jocelyn of Furness and Geoffrey of Monmouth, are not history but rather multiple degrees of myths or mythification: the underlying symbolism is far more important than the narrative detail. Those examples show that the hill of Uisneach has carried a form a sacredness deep within since the dawn of Christianity in Ireland – and probably much before, even if this cannot be demonstrated only by relying on Christian or heavily Christianized documents. They also confirm that the reputation of Uisneach went beyond the borders of Ireland as early as the 12th century at least, which is quite significant.

Assembly at Stonehenge

Once the stones were brought next to Salisbury, Aurelius is more than satisfied with the accomplished work. He decides to gather the members of the Christian sacerdotal class and the people around Stonehenge and crowns himself in front of all:

Aurelius sent messengers to all parts of Britain, to summon the clergy and people together to the mount of Ambrius, in order to celebrate with joy and honour the erection of the monument. Upon this summons appeared the bishops, abbots, and people of all other orders and qualities; and upon the day and place appointed for their general meeting, Aurelius placed the crown upon his head, and with royal pomp celebrated the feast of the Pentecost.[179]

The desire to bring together at Stonehenge all members of society – rulers, members of the clergy and the common man, i.e. "people" –[180] from "all parts" of the island of Britain is obviously crucial: religious, political and productive powers are here gathered in a central, sacred place.

Uisneach, the center of Ireland, saw its stone transported to the location of Stonehenge which, in turn, became the center – the focal point – of Great Britain thanks to a "general assembly"[181] held by the king. The date chosen by Aurelius, as mentioned by Geoffrey of Monmouth, was the Pentecost, which is also quite noteworthy.

Temporality and Myth

The Christian festival of the Pentecost – Whitsun – takes place 50 days after Easter: in Greek, *pentekoste* literally means "fiftieth". As a consequence, it is usually celebrated in May and occasionally in the first half of June.[182] Originally[183] a festival of harvest, the Pentecost commemorates the apparition of "tongues of fire" and their distribution to the Apostles, a symbol of the Holy Spirit resting in each one of them.[184]

This mention is an invitation to question, in a more general sense, the temporality – that is, the place in the year – of the traditions connected to Uisneach and its avatars. The hill routinely appears as a place of transcendence, an otherworldly abode very much suitable for declarations of sovereignty or, more broadly speaking, claims of power. In the same way, a large part of Irish literature seems to connect Uisneach to a specific time of the year, i.e. the end of spring or the beginning of summer – the month of May and the Irish festival of *Bealtaine*. Thus, the mention by Geoffrey of Monmouth of the festival of the Pentecost, at the end of spring, is perhaps not as anecdotal or accidental as it might seem. It could potentially be a distant echo of an old association between Stonehenge – or Uisneach – and the Celtic festival of May: it is conceivable to see the Pentecost as a potential Christianization of *Bealtaine*, a desire to assimilate Pagan customs and possibly myths into the Christian tradition. As will be shown, Uisneach – the hill "out of this world" – was to be celebrated at a specific moment of the year, a transcending period, a moment "out of time", in the words of Françoise Le Roux and Christian Guyonvarc'h.

The documents that have been discussed here do call for a more thorough and profound understanding of the symbolism of the hill, its connection with the "cosmic" and the "transcendent", its relationship with the divine – in plain words, its mythological significance.

The theme of "the center" will be at the core of the Irish mythology of Uisneach: to that extent, the ancient Irish myths will connect with the texts already studied up to this point. Interestingly enough, the symbolisms of fire and water will appear in a variety of forms, to such an extent that an intimate and perhaps original connection between the hill of Uisneach and those "primordial" elements appears to undergird all the other associations. Finally, the connection with the month of May in general and the Irish festival of *Bealtaine* in particular will prove fundamental and literally "essential" as regards the symbolism of Uisneach.

Notes

1   As is well-known, the province of Ulster is now made up of nine counties, three of which are part of Éire; the remaining six constitute Northern Ireland and are attached to the United Kingdom. Leinster, Connacht and Munster are provinces of Éire.

2   Best, R.I. (ed.). 1910. "The Settling of the Manor of Tara", in *Ériu*, IV, 121-72. Guyonvarc'h, Christian-Joseph (ed.). 1980. *Textes Mythologiques irlandais I.* Rennes: Ogam-Celticum, 157-87.

3   "The Settling of the Manor of Tara", *op. cit.*, 147.

4   As mentioned *infra*, transcribers usually place Uisneach in Mide and only occasionally in Connacht. Today, Co. Westmeath is part of the province of Leinster.

5   The term "Meath" is usually used in most English translations of Irish ancient texts and was systematically replaced by "Mide" in this book.

6   Hull, Vernam. 1930. "The Cause of Exile of Fergus mac Roig" in *Zeitschrift für celtische Philologie*, XVIII, 293-8. The episode can be found in other manuscripts, for instance the Glenmasan manuscript: Mackinnon, Donald. 2009 (1904-8). "The Glenmasan manuscript" in *Celtic Review*, I-IV, 217: "they proceeded in that wise to smooth, beautiful Uisneach in [Mide]". All those manuscripts are but variations of one single story, that of *Deirdre*. See chapter II.7.

7   Mythical Cruachan corresponds to Rathcrogan, the – very real – "Fort of Cruachan", Co. Roscommon. See chapter IV.4.

8   "The Glenmasan manuscript", *op. cit.*, 217. The word "smooth" is associated with Uisneach on several occasions: in "The Cause of Exile of Fergus mac Roig" but also a poem of Gofraidh Fionn Ó Dalaigh, dated to the 14th century ("plain of Uisneach, of surface smooth"). Bourke, Angela (ed.). 2005. *The Field Day Anthology of Irish Writing Volumes IV and V: Irish Women's Writing and Tradition.* Cork: Cork University Press, 276.

9   Another parameter may come into play: the character of Fergus is indirectly connected with the hill of Uisneach in the story of Deirdre and the Sons of Uisneach. See chap. II.7.

10   Ryan, Emma (ed.). 2002 (1997). *Annals of the Four Masters.* Cork: Corpus of Electronic Texts, University College Cork.

11   *Ibid.*, M1414.9. See also 1141.13. Additionally, this episode can be found in the *Annals of Connacht* (15th-16th c.); the connection with this "Uisneach, in Mide" is also manifest. Bambury, Pádraig (ed.). 2008 (2001). *Annals of Connacht.* Cork: Corpus of Electronic Texts, University College Cork., 1414.16.

12 Sjoestedt, Marie-Louise. 1940. *Dieux et Héros des Celtes*. Paris: Presses Universitaires de France, 3.
13 See *infra*.
14 *Annals of the Four Masters, op. cit.*, M507.2.
15 Stokes, Whitley (ed.). 1993 (1895-6). *The Annals of Tigernach, Trans. Reprinted from Revue Celtique*. Felinfach: Llanaerch Publishers, T514.3. Both annals were redacted centuries before the alleged battle, which explains the discrepancy in dates (507 and 514 respectively).
16 See Charles-Edwards, Thomas. 2008 (2000). *Early Christian Ireland*. Cambridge: Cambridge University Press, 554.
17 Gwynn, Edward (ed.) 1941 (1903). *The Metrical Dindshenchas*. Dublin: Hodges, Figgis &Co. The first recension of the *Dindshenchas* dates back to the 12th century.
18 *Ibid.*, II, 44-5.
19 Macalister, Robert Alexander Stewart & Praeger Robert Lloyd. 1928-1929. "Report on the Excavation of Uisneach" in *Proceedings of the Royal Irish Academy: Archaeology, Culture, History*, XXXVIII, 69-127, 126.
20 See chap. V.
21 MacKillop, James. 1998. *Dictionary of Celtic Mythology*. Oxford: Oxford University Press, 421.
22 Hamp, Eric. 1974. "Varia" in *Ériu*, XXV, 253-84, more specifically 259-61. See Vendryes, J., Bachallery, Édouard, & Lambert, Pierre-Yves. 1978. *Lexique étymologique de l'irlandais ancien*, IV, 21-2.
23 See *infra*, for example chap. II.1 and 6.
24 http://mistshadows.blogspot.com/2018/06/uisneach-middle-place-that-is-above-or.html?hl= en. The site attributes this etymology to Jürgen Uhlich, Trinity College Dublin.
25 *Ibid.*
26 This hypothesis is favored by Giraldus Cambrensis. See *infra*.
27 Schot, Roseanne. 2011. "From Cult Centre to Royal Centre: Monuments, Myths and Other Revelations at Uisneach" in *Landscapes of Cult and Kingship*. Dublin: Four Courts Press, 87-113, 93.
28 Dames, Michael. 1996. *Mythic Ireland*. London: Thames & Hudson, 196.
29 Macalister, Robert Alexander Stewart (ed.) *Lebor Gabála Érenn* (Book of the Taking of Ireland). 1938 (1932), 1939 (1933), 1940 (1937), 1941 (1939), 1956 (1942). Dublin: Irish Text Society. Here, V, 311.
30 *Dictionary of Celtic Mythology, op. cit.*, 416.
31 Comyn, David & Dineen, Patrick (ed.). 2016 (1898-1908). *Geoffrey Keating. History of Ireland*. Cork: Corpus of Electronic Texts, University College Cork, Book I, 113.
32 O'Rahilly, Thomas Francis. 1946. *Early Irish History and Mythology*. Dublin: Dublin Institute for Advanced Studies, 167, 171, quoted in "From Cult Centre to Royal Centre", *op. cit.*, 92. "there is in fact considerable evidence to demonstrate that, up until at least c.AD500, the midland region comprising Cos Longford, Westmeath and Meath formed part of the ancient province of Leinster". According to the *Dindshenchas*, Mide could even stem from *mí-dé*, "ill smoke", although this explanation is, once again, highly controversial. See "Report on the Excavation of Uisneach", *op. cit.*, 126. Finally, one theory holds that Mide comes from the name of druid Midhe. See *infra*.
33 See chap. I.3-4.
34 Mac Airt, Seán (ed) 1988 (1944). *The Annals of Inisfallen* (MS. Rawlinson B. 503). Dublin: Dublin Institute for Advanced Studies, 167.

35 Meyer, Kuno. 1901. "Brinna Ferchertne" in *Zeitschrift für celtische Philologie*, III, Halle, Max Niemeyer, 41-6.

36 Meyer, Kuno. 1888. "The Wooing of Emer" in *Archaeological Review*, I, London, 68-75; 150-155; 231-235; 298-307: 151.

37 *History of Ireland, op. cit.*, Book I, 153. See also 31 for an association between Uisneach and Mide made by Keating.

38 Stokes, Whitley. 1901. "The destruction of Dá Derga's hostel" in *Revue Celtique*, XXII, 32.

39 "From Cult Centre to Royal Centre", *op. cit.*, 92.

40 In most cases, it was customary to be crowned on Tara; as will be demonstrated, the hill had a very special connection with Uisneach.

41 O'Grady, Standish, (ed.). 1892. *Silva Gadelica*. London & Edinburgh: Williams and Norgate, II, 'XII. Colloquy with the Ancients', 101-264: 158-9.

42 See *infra*.

43 *Ibid.*, 62-3.

44 See *infra* and Bieler, Ludwig (ed.). 2000 (1979). *The Patrician Texts in the Book of Armagh*. Dublin: Dublin Institute for Advanced Studies, 137.

45 See Annex I.5-8. See also chap. V for a more thorough description the site today.

46 See chap. VI.

47 O'Murchadha, Diarmaid. 2005. "A Review of Some Placename Material from Foras Feasa Ar Éirinn" in *Éigse, A Journal of Irish Studies*, XXXV, 81-98: 83.

48 This is the explanation offered by the current owners of the hill of Uisneach. See http://uisneach.ie/history/. This theory stems from the works of O'Donovan who, in 1837, believed that the name came from *Carraig a Chait* (the Stone of the Cat), a derivation of *Carraig Coithrigi* (the Stone of Patrick). O'Donovan, John. 1837. *Letters Containing Information Relative to the Antiquities of the County of Westmeath collected during the Progress of the Ordnance Survey in 1837 (2 vols.)*. O'Flanagan, Michael (ed.). Bray: National Library of Ireland, 41. Local traditions seems to have partially favored this theory. It can for instance be found in this semi-humorous report of the RTE from 1971: https://www.rte.ie/archives/exhibitions/681-history-of-rte/705-rte-1970s/139386-dead-centre-of-ireland/.

49 Those extremely doubtful etymologies were shared by visitors interviewed during the contemporary celebrations of *Bealtaine* on Uisneach in 2017 and 2019.

50 See chap. V.2 and VI.2.

51 *History of Ireland, op. cit.*, Book I, 111.

52 Forester, Thomas (ed.). 2000. *Giraldus Cambrensis. The Topography of Ireland (Topographia Hibernica)*. Cambridge, Ontario: In Parentheses Publications, 66. See *infra* for a similar mention in the *Book of Invasions*.

53 *Lebor Gabála Érenn, op. cit.*, IV, 61-3, poem XLIX of R.1 (First Redaction). See translation of Guyonvarc'h C.-J., *Textes Mythologiques irlandais, op. cit.*, 186 for the phrase [To the stone].

54 *Lebor Gabála Érenn, op. cit.*, IV, 75.

55 See Annex I.5-6.

56 See Dubuisson, Daniel. 2005. *Impostures et pseudo-science: l'œuvre de Mircea Eliade*. Lille: Presses Universitaires du Septentrion.

57 Eliade, Mircea. 1965 (1957). *Le Sacré et le profane*. Paris: Gallimard, 38. Translated from French by Willard R. Trask.

58 *Ibid.*, 38 and 44. See also Le Quellec, Jean-Loïc, Sergent, Bernard. 2017. *Dictionnaire critique de mythologie*. Paris: CNRS Editions, 174.

59 *Le Sacré et le profane, op. cit.*, 39.

60 "The Ash in Tortu—take count thereof!/the Ash of populous Usnech./their boughs fell—it was not amiss—/in the time of the sons of Aed Slane". *Dindshenchas*, *op. cit.*, III, 149. Reportedly, "It fell northward, and reached as far as Granard!", "Report on the Excavation of Uisneach", *op. cit.*, 127.

61 "The Settling of the Manor of Tara", *op. cit.*, 151.

62 For further discussion of the cosmological and royal symbolism associated with sacred trees, see Lucas, A.T. 1963. "The Sacred trees of Ireland" in *Journal of the Cork Historical and Archaeological Society*, LXVIII, 16-54. Watson, Alden. 1981. "The king, the poet and the sacred tree" in *Etudes celtiques*, XVIII, 165-80. Doherty, Charles. 2005. "Kingship in early Ireland", in Edel, Bhreathnach (ed.), *The kingship and landscape of Tara*. Dublin: Four Courts Press, 3-31: 14-7

63 A 17th-century poem written by Fearghal Óg, "The Downfall of the Ó Donnells", mentions the "dark yew trees" of the land of Uisneach without providing further context or explanation. See https://www.bbc.co.uk/history/british/plantation/bardic/poem03.shtml and https://www.bbc.co.uk/history/british/plantation/bardic/bp03.shtml for context.

64 Rees, Alwyn & Brinley. 1988 (1961). *Celtic Heritage, Ancient Tradition in Ireland and Wales*. London: Thames and Hudson, 120.

65 "Chinese, Japanese, Malay, Hindu, Babylonian, Israelite, Arab, Persian, Phoenician, Egyptian, Greek, Italiote, Magyar, Peruvian" and possibly "Scandinavian [and Tibetan]" according to Loth, Joseph, 1915. "L'Omphalos chez les Celtes" in *Revue des Études Anciennes*, XVII-3, 193-206, 193.

66 *Ibid.*

67 See *ibid.*, 174 and *Le Sacré et le Profane*, *op. cit.*, 51-2. See the examples provided for Greece but also the remainder of Europe, including Wales, France, ancient Rome as well as Asia (China, Siberia and India), America (North and South), Africa, Australia and Malaysia.

68 *Dictionnaire critique de mythologie*, *op. cit.*, 123-4, 976-7.

69 See chap. V.2 for a more scientific description.

70 I.e. a spatial reference point used for orientation and the creating of maps.

71 See *infra* for more detail.

72 Schot, Roseanne. 2006. "Uisneach Midi a medón Érenn: A Prehistoric 'Cult' Centre and 'Royal Site' in Co. Westmeath" in *Journal of Irish Archaeology*, XV, 39-71: 45.

73 The enclosure will be described in greater detail in the chapter dedicated to archeology. See Chap. V.2-3.

74 Conceivably, the "column" or original pillar may have been destroyed at a point of history or another, perhaps at the time of the Christianization of Ireland. This idea remains highly hypothetical, all the more so that the Christianization of Ireland was a peaceful process.

75 *Le Sacré et le Profane*, *op. cit.*, 38.

76 "The Settling of the Manor of Tara", *op. cit.*, 153-5.

77 "hisí is cían ó tib dig/dílind ós imlind Usnig". *Ibid.*, 151. See *Textes Mythologiques irlandais*, *op. cit.*, 163.

78 *Textes Mythologiques irlandais*, *op. cit.*, 102.

79 *Celtic Heritage*, *op. cit.*, 347.

80 *Dictionary of Celtic Mythology*, *op. cit.*, 230. Fintan tells us: "By God's doom I am an old man,/I am more unwilling than ever for … /It is long since I drank (?) a drink/of the Deluge over the navel of Uisneach". "The Settling of the Manor of Tara", *op. cit.*, 151. See. *Textes Mythologiques irlandais*, *op. cit.*, 163.

81 See chap. V.2 for this "five-sided" Catstone.

82 "From Cult Centre to Royal Centre", *op. cit.*, 109.

83 *Textes Mythologiques irlandais.*, *op. cit.*, 162.
84 More specifically, those Indo-European kings had, around them, "distributed at the four cardinal points, the functional classes". Those "functional classes" refer to the *sacerdotal*, *military* and *productive* classes – the *clergy*, the *warriors* and the *farmers* – which are pivotal to the controversial approach ("trifunctionality") put forward by Georges Dumézil in the 2nd part of the 20th century: for Dumézil, Indo-European peoples divided their society into three distinct classes which were connected with the ideas of *sovereignty*, *physical strength* and *fecundity* respectively. Cf. the seminal works of George Dumézil mentioned in bibliography. See also the works of some of his followers, first and foremost Bernard Sergent. For instance, Sergent, Bernard. 2005 (1995). *Les Indo-Européens.* Paris: Payot, 355-423, especially 360 for a first, concise definition of "trifunctionality" among Indo-Europeans.
85 Dubuisson, Daniel. 1978. "Le roi indo-européen et la synthèse des trois fonctions" in *Annales. Économies, Sociétés, Civilisations*, 33rd year, I, 21-34, 22. The notion of four cardinal points around a more or less symbolic center is therefore not exclusive to Ireland. Several scholars, including Georges Dumézil, explain that it can be found in Hinduism and on all continents, where it forms the basis of many cosmologies (see Allen, N.J. 1999. "Hinduism, Structuralism and Dumézil" in *Miscellanea Indo-Europea*. Washington: Institute for the study of man, 241-60).
86 See *Early Christian Ireland*, *op. cit.*,15-36, 440-68. Charles-Edwards even claims that "there is no strong reason to think that Niall himself ruled over anything more than an ordinary *túath*". Traditionally, a *túath* is a territory regrouping a few hundreds or thousands of fighters. *Ibid.*, 441.
87 See Byrne, Francis John. 1973. *Irish Kings and High-Kings.* London: Four Courts Press.
88 This is a reference to *Collectio canonum Hibernensis*, a collection of Canon Law from the 7th or 8th c.
89 *Early Christian Ireland*, *op. cit.*, 481.
90 "The Settling of the Manor of Tara", *op. cit.*, 154-5.
91 Noted section 33. Best, R.I., Bergin, Osborn & O'Brien M.A. (ed.). 1954. *Book of Leinster formerly Lebar na Núachongbála.* Dublin: Dublin Institute for Advanced Studies, I., 196-8.
92 Bambury, Pádraig & Beechinor, Stephen (ed.). 2020 (2000). *Annals of Ulster.* Cork: Corpus of Electronic Texts, University College Cork.
93 According to an obscure mention from the *Book of Invasions*, Mael Sechnaill (a descendant of Diarmait and therefore a member of the *southern Uí Néill*) was not only a King of Uisneach but the "proud raper" of the hill: "Máel-Sechlain was dead westward in his house,/the proud raper of Uisnech,/nine rough years after tuneful Brían/he was chief noble over Ireland". *Lebor Gabála Érenn*, *op. cit.*, V, the Verse Texts of Section IX, 555. There is no doubt Mael Sechnaill (son of Mael Ruanaid) and Máel-Sechlain (mac Máeil-Rúanaid) are the same character (AU862.5 and *Lebor Gabala Erenn*, *op. cit.*, V, 551). The character is also associated with the "tree of Banba" and the "summit of the Gaedil", *ibid.*, 553.
94 A detailed genealogy of the Uí Néill (including a distinction between the southern and northern Uí Néill) can be found in *Early Christian Ireland op. cit.*, 601-9.
95 See for example Reeves, William (ed.). 1857. "The life of St. Columba, founder of Hy". Dublin: University Press for the Irish Archaeological and Celtic Society, 382. Occasionally, Conall is presented as the grand-father of Diarmait mac Cerbaill, as Conall was supposed to be the father of Fergus, father of Diarmait. See *Lebor Gabála Érenn*, *op. cit.*, V, 311.

96 *Early Christian Ireland*, *op. cit.*, 294, 603-4.
97 See *infra* and *Textes Mythologiques irlandais*, *op. cit.*, 178.
98 *Early Christian Ireland*, *op. cit.*, 294. The case of the great Irish assemblies will be detailed in chap. III.
99 More precisely "lands stretching from Uisneach to Slieve Bloom and from Birr to the Leinster frontier near Tullamore". *Early Christian Ireland*, *op. cit.*, 554. See also the references from the Annals already mentioned, i.e. *Annals of the Four Masters*, *op. cit.*, M507.2 and *Annals of Tigernach*, *op. cit.*, T514.3.
100 *Early Christian Ireland*, *op. cit.*, 28, 450, 609.
101 *Ibid.*, 609.
102 *Ibid.*, 555, 609. See also "From Cult Centre to Royal Centre", *op. cit.*, 92.
103 The saint is said to have lived in the 6th century but his hagiography was redacted at least 150 years later. Heist, W. W. 1965. *Vitae Sanctorum Hiberniae: ex codice olim Salmanticensi nunc Bruxellensi in Subsidia Hagiographica*. Brussels: Société des Bollandistes. Translated as *Life of Áed Mac Bricc from Codex Salmanticensis* by Kate Peck in 2006.
104 "Killare"/Killar[a]us will be studied later. See chap. I.6 and III.6.
105 *Life of Áed*, *op. cit.*, §25.
106 *Ibid.*
107 See chap. I.6 for a comparison with an episode from the *Historia Regum Britanniae* written by Geoffrey of Monmouth.
108 Donahue, Annie. 2004-5. "The Acallam na Senórach: A Medieval Instruction Manual" in *Proceedings of the Harvard Celtic Colloquium*, XXIV-XXV, 206-15.
109 *Silva Gadelica*, *op. cit.*, II, 158-9.
110 *Textes Mythologiques irlandais*, *op. cit.*, 178.
111 Although controversial, the official date marking the arrival of Patrick in Ireland remains 432.
112 Diarmait is the son of Fergus Cerrbél (see *The Death of Diarmait* whose original title was indeed *Aided Diarmada meic Fergusa Cerrbeoil*, *op. cit.* See also *Lebor Gabála Érenn*, *op. cit.*, V, 311) and Fergus the son of Conall (*ibid.*, V, 373).
113 *Celtic Heritage*, *op. cit.*, 67.
114 "The Acallam na Senórach: A Medieval Instruction Manual", *op. cit.*, 206.
115 *Ibid.* See Dooley, Ann & Roe, Harry (ed.). 2008. *Tales of the Elders of Ireland*. Oxford: Oxford University Press, xxix.
116 "It is not attributed to a specific author in any of the four manuscript witnesses to the work and is normally dated to the twelfth century", *ibid.*, viii.
117 *The Patrician Texts in the Book of Armagh*, *op. cit.*, 35-43.
118 In the *Colloquy with the Ancients*, Patrick does ask for "a well of pure water [in our vicinity here,] from which we might baptize the tuatha of Bregia, of [Mide], and of Usnach". *Op. cit.*, 103.
119 *Early Christian Ireland*, *op. cit.*, 15. See also 554.
120 *The Patrician Texts in the Book of Armagh*, *op. cit.*, 137.
121 "L'Omphalos chez les Celtes", *op. cit.*, 199.
122 Or, in the case of Fiachu, his son.
123 *Early Christian Ireland*, *op. cit.*, 433.
124 *The Patrician Texts in the Book of Armagh*, *op. cit.*, 133.
125 Coirpre is called "Coirpriticus fils de Níall".
126 *Ibid.*, 133.
127 *Early Christian Ireland*, *op. cit.*, for instance 17-20, 446-50, 607.
128 *The Patrician Texts in the Book of Armagh*, *op. cit.*, 137.

129 In a probable deliberate attempt to Christianize the episode, Tirechán placed the encounter on Easter although the assembly of Tailtiu was supposed to be held at *Lughnasa*, in early August.
130 See sections 8 and 12 of the hagiography.
131 In the hagiography written by Tirechán, see the episode where the saint encounters two daughters of Lóegaire at Cruachan, another highly symbolic place of ancient Ireland usually associated with the Otherworld. *The Patrician Texts in the Book of Armagh, op. cit.*, 143-4. As mentioned previously, Cruachan corresponds to Rathcrogan, Co. Roscommon. See chap. IV.3-4.
132 *Ibid.*, 61-122.
133 *Ibid.*, 133.
134 *Ibid.*, 163. See also Swift, Catherine. 1994. "Tírechán's Motives in Compiling the 'Collectanea'" in *Ériu*, XLV, 53-82: 80-1.
135 See *infra*, esp. chap. III.2-3.
136 *Early Christian Ireland, op. cit.*, 11.
137 *The Patrician Texts in the Book of Armagh, op. cit.*, 38.
138 *Annals of the Four Masters, op. cit.*, M457.3.
139 See *Early Christian Ireland, op. cit.*, 10. See also "Tírechán's Motives in Compiling the 'Collectanea'", 54-6 for a summary of previous studies and 60-7 for the relation between Tirechán and Armagh.
140 "Tírechán's Motives in Compiling the 'Collectanea'", *op. cit.*, 81.
141 *Ibid.*
142 *Early Christian Ireland, op. cit.*, 609.
143 Interestingly enough, Tirechán never mentions which son of Fiachu is cursed (see the remark of Charles-Edwards in *Early Christian Ireland, op. cit.*, 28). Fiachu mac Néill had three sons and a certain Crimthand was the grand-father of the saint. Although the hypothesis is intriguing, there is therefore still room for doubt.
144 *The Patrician Texts in the Book of Armagh, op. cit.*, 137.
145 Contrary to the hagiography of Patrick by Muirchú.
146 Later tradition very ostensibly insists on its affiliation with Patrick. *Early Christian Ireland, op. cit.*, 32. In fact, Trim was only attached to Armagh after the 8th century. *Ibid.*, 19.
147 *Ibid.*, 11-2.
148 Stokes, Whitley (ed.). 1887. *The Tripartite Life of Patrick*. London: Eyre and Spottiswoode, 81.
149 See the connection established between Enda and Lóegaire by Charles-Edwards, *op. cit.*, 32. Enda is actually the ancestor of the *Cenél nEndai*, a tribe whose potential rivalry with the main dynasty is not clearly established. *Early Christian Ireland, op. cit.*, 28-30.
150 See MacNeill, Eoin. 1929. "The Origin of the Tripartite Life of Saint Patrick" in *Journal of the Royal Society of Antiquaries of Ireland*, Sixth Series, XIX-1, 1-15 and Etchingham, C. 1993. "The Implications of Paruchia" in *Ériu*, XLIV, 139-63.
151 Swift, Edmund (ed.). 1809. *The Life and Acts of Saint Patrick: the Archbishop, Primate and Apostle of Ireland*. Dublin: Hibernia Press Company, 119-20.
152 See *Early Christian Ireland, op. cit.*, 234.
153 *The Life and Acts of Saint Patrick, op. cit.*
154 Edmonds, Fiona. 2013. "The Furness Peninsula and the Irish Sea Region: Cultural Interaction from the Seventh Century to the Twelfth" in *Jocelin of Furness. Essays from the 2011 Conference*. Shaun Tyas: Donington, 17-44.
155 Flanagan, M.T. 2013. "Jocelin of Furness" in *Jocelin of Furness. Essays from the 2011 Conference*. Shaun Tyas: Donington, 45-66.

156 *Ibid.*
157 *The Tripartite Life of Patrick, op. cit.,* 81.
158 Lucas, A. T. 1965. "Washing and Bathing in Ancient Ireland" in *Journal of the Royal Society of Antiquaries of Ireland,* XCV, No. 1/2, 65-114: 76-84 for water heated up by fire, esp. 77 for Uisneach.
159 See *ibid.*
160 Thompson, Aaron (ed.). 1999. *Geoffrey of Monmouth. History of the Kings of Britain.* Cambridge, Ontario: In Parentheses Publications.
161 *Ibid.,* 133.
162 Among many examples, see Burl, Aubrey. 2000. *The Stone Circles of Britain, Ireland and Brittany.* New Haven: Yale University Press.
163 For the chronology and traditional phases of prehistory (from Early Mesolithic to the Iron Age), see Annex IV.
164 *The Topography of Ireland, op. cit.,* 66.
165 See https://www.townlands.ie/westmeath/killare1/ and https://www.townlands.ie/westmeath/killare2/. Today, the hill is attached to the civil parish of Conry (https://www.townlands.ie/westmeath/conry/).
166 Arguably, uncharted Africa is here used as an allegory of mystery and exotic mysticism.
167 *Ibid.,* 134.
168 *The Life and Acts of Saint Patrick, op. cit.,* 119-20.
169 Birkett, Helen. 2013. "Plausible Fictions: John Stow, Jocelin of Furness and the Book of British Bishops" in *Jocelin of Furness. Essays from the 2011 Conference.* Shaun Tyas: Donington, 91-120.
170 *History of the Kings of Britain, op. cit.,* 134.
171 *Ibid.,* 135.
172 *Ibid.*
173 *Vitae Sanctorum Hiberniae, op. cit.*
174 *Life of Áed Mac Bricc from Codex Salmanticensis, op. cit.,* §25.
175 *History of the Kings of Britain, op. cit.,* 135-6.
176 *Ibid.,* 148.
177 *Ibid.,* 193-4.
178 See chap. V.2.
179 *Ibid.,* 135.
180 Aurelius was a king and a warrior and the "people" here mentioned were, by definition, a part of the "productive" function – a form of "lower class" belonging to neither of the other two classes.
181 See chap. III.6 for a potential parallel with general assemblies of ancient Ireland.
182 Usually a Sunday between 10 May and 13 June. However, the acceptable dates for the celebration of Easter evolved throughout Christian history, which occasionally implied a shift in the celebration of the Pentecost.
183 That is, at least the Old Testament. Jones, Alexander. (ed.). 2000 (1966). *The Jerusalem Bible.* New York: Doubleday. Leviticus 23: 9-17 and Deuteronomy 16: 9-10 for instance.
184 *Ibid.,* Acts 2: 1-4.

2   Uisneach in Irish Mythology

The following chapter references and analyzes a relevant fraction of the mentions of Uisneach in Irish mythology in order to better understand the significance and import of the hill in medieval and possibly prehistoric times.

Although the term will be used repeatedly in the following pages, it should be noted that, strictly speaking, there is no such thing as "Irish mythology". Rather, what is commonly referred to by that name is in fact a palimpsest of Irish mytholog*ies*. The corpus of documents available to us is heterogeneous, both in form and substance; the narratives are frequently complementary but, most often, they tend to contradict one another. Above all, if most Irish myths stem from a branch of the supposedly Celtic traditions, the key point is that the Celts did not transcribe their knowledge: the Christian myths overlaid the Celtic ones, as most documents have been redacted in Irish monasteries since the Early Middle Ages and were therefore Christianized – either on purpose or unintentionally. As a consequence, the references to the Christian world are numerous in this chapter, although it is supposed to deal with a pre-Christian Irish mythology. Scholars widely accept the postulate that the Irish monks did not create those myths and ancient references *ex nihilo*. The idea was to put into writing the oral traditions that had preceded the introduction of Christianity in Ireland while occasionally incorporating Christian elements. This early Irish literature is therefore most precious, provided that the very essence of the myth can be differentiated from the Christian gloss, which is obviously a thorny issue.

The documents analyzed in connection with Uisneach and Irish mythology will confirm the notions developed in the first chapter: the hill at the center of Ireland was a place of power and claim of power. Significantly enough, the political and religious import of Uisneach seems to derive from its older symbolic and spiritual significance.

2.1 The Nemedians: The Druid Midhe

Midhe in the Book of Invasions

The *Book of Invasions* – or *Lebor Gabála Érenn* – is a mythological compilation which goes over the successive waves of mythical invasions of Ireland:

DOI: 10.4324/9781003143161-3

according to the myth, the tribes of Cessair, of Partholón, the Nemedians, the Fir Bolg and finally the Tuatha Dé Danann successively invaded the island. The account is preceded by a pseudo-historical narrative granting biblical origins to the Gaels and ends with the arrival of the Milesians, that is to say Men, in Ireland.

As already mentioned, a redactor of the *Book of Invasions* submitted a specific etymology for the province of Mide. The term "Mide" is said to derive from "the neck" and its segmentation in provinces that was imposed by the alleged High King of Ireland, Tuathal Techtmar.[1] But the author has a second interpretation to offer:

> By Tuathal was each province in Ireland lopped of its head, and so "Mide" was the name given to them, that is "the neck" of every province. Or it is from Mide s. Brith the name comes, *unde dicitur* "Mide".[2]

This mysterious Mide, son of Brith (or Brath), is no other than one of the druids of the tribe of Nemed. According to Keating, he was the first to ever light a fire in Ireland: interestingly enough, this first fire was set ablaze on the hill of Uisneach. The account of Keating unites all the important themes developed in the first chapter of this study and intersperses the ideas of sovereignty, centrality, and that of places "out of the world" and "above of the world". Those themes are assembled in a precise mythological context – the sacerdotal power – and rely on a specific form of symbolism – fire.

Midhe According to Keating

Keating gives a first idea of the substance of the mythological episode and offers a new pseudo-etymology associating the *province* of Mide to the *druid* Mide – or Midhe, a common spelling for the druid employed here-after to avoid confusion:

> It is why it is called [Mide], because that it is from the neck of each province Tuathal Teachtmhar cut it. Or it is why [Mide] is called to it from Midhe, son of Brath, son of Deaghfhath chief druid of the children of [Nemed]; and it is by him was kindled the first fire in Ireland, after the coming of the children of [Nemed]; and hard by Uisneach he kindled it. The children of [Nemed] bestowed on him the "tuath"[3] of land which was there, and from that druid it is called Midhe. And there was not, about that time, of land in [Mide], but the one tuath aforesaid, until Tuathal Teachtmhar put a "meidhe" or neck of every province with it, as we have said.[4]

The first Irish fire is therefore said to have been lit by the Nemedian druid Midhe on the hill of Uisneach; the name of the province of Mide is here connected to that of the druid Midhe, as the character is supposed to have inherited a part of this territory after having lit the fire.

Midhe in the Dindsenchas

The episode is also mentioned in the – much older – *Dindsenchas*. The thesis chosen by the redactor revolves, once again, around the explanation of the origin of the name Mide and the hill of Uisneach – which is not surprising, as the *Dindsenchas* is an onomastics treaty before anything. Fortunately, the redactor does not stop at etymological considerations and grants us with particularly precise details:

> 3. Mid[h]e it was, the ardent son of Brath
> the host-leading son of Deaith;
> for he kindled a mystic fire
> above the race of Nemed, seizer of hostages.
> 4. Seven years good ablaze
> was the fire, it was a sure truce:
> so that he shed the fierceness of the fire for a time
> over the four quarters of Erin.
> 5. So that it is *in return for* this fire in truth
> (it is not a rash saying, it is not a falsehood)
> that *he (Mid[h]e and his descendants) has a right by a perpetual bargain*
> over every chief hearth of Erin.
> 6. So the right belongs to the gentle heir
> of the plain of Mide mirthful and bright;
> even a measure of fine meal with a white pig
> for every rooftree in Erin.[5]

Midhe, druid of the tribe of Nemed, therefore lighted a *mystic* fire: the term could be interpreted as referring to a sacred fire or a fire lit by the alleged powers of the druids. Be it as it may, the fire burned for seven years: this reference to the number "seven" is difficult to interpret. It either could be an echo of a tradition anterior to the redaction of the text – and therefore a relic of Celtic or pre-Christian symbolism – or, on the contrary, an attempt to Christianize the text, as "seven" is a fairly common number in Christian tradition and sacred texts.

This mystic fire was seen from the four corners of Ireland: it is implied further in the text that it was lit on Uisneach[6] and therefore at the symbolic center of the island. As Alwyn and Brinley Rees noted, the idea was undoubtedly that of a "ritual proclamation" of sovereignty on behalf of the tribe of Nemed; this proclamation was made by the druid of the tribe over the whole of the Irish territory, from its center. Furthermore, since Midhe "has a right by a perpetual bargain over every chief hearth of Erin", his tribe gained power and authority over all subsequent Irish fires.

The fire of Midhe could therefore be, symbolically speaking, a sort of original flame, a primordial, sovereign matrix of all ensuing fires. The redactor goes on:

> 7. And they said (no small grief it was),
> the druids of Erin all together,
> "It is an ill smoke (*mi-dé*) was brought to us eastward:
> it has brought an ill to our mind".
> 8. Then Mid[h]e the untiring assembled
> the druids of Erin into one house,
> and cut their tongues (a harsh presage)
> out of the heads of the strong and noble druids.
> 9. And he buried them under the earth
> of Uisneach in mighty Mide,
> and sat him down over their tongues,
> he, the chief seer *and his chief shanachie* [story-tellers][7]

The other Irish druids viewed this flame quite unfavorably: they perhaps understood it as a manifestation of an authority challenging their own. The "ill smoke" (or *mi dé*)[8] coming from the east is a reference to the origins of the tribe of Nemed, which, on several accounts in the *Book of Invasions*, are said to come from the East.

The rest of the story is quite explicit: Midhe gathered the druids of the island in a house,[9] cut their tongues out and buried them on the hill of Uisneach. The druids and the *filid* – or poets, the other eminent members of the Irish sacerdotal class – were the keepers of the oral tradition: cutting their tongue amounted to depriving them of their main power. Joseph Loth even believed that this excerpt implies the existence of an oracle, comparable to that of Delphi, on Uisneach. The theory, though intriguing, remains impossible to demonstrate.[10]

The consequences of such a gesture are extreme. Once again, the science of the druids of *filid* was oral: they did not transcribe their knowledge because confiding science to the material world amounted to tarnishing it and bringing it within reach of the layman. For Midhe, depriving the rival druids of their tongue was a way to symbolically demonstrate his control over the pre-Nemedian culture and society as a whole. This was not a mere way of gaining power and sovereignty: the gesture wiped the slate clean so as to build a fresh new lineage – one that could be liberated from the preceding societies. The erasure permitted Midhe to inscribe new authority onto the palimpsest.

Midhe's victory was total. It found its echo in yet another etymology here developed by prophetess and arch-druidess Gaine, the nurse of Midhe:

> 11. And Gaine said with lamentation,
> before Mid[h]e of the great victory,
> "It is *over somewhat* our house was built,

and hence shall Uisneach be named".
12. Uisneach and mighty Mid[h]e
from which Erin of the red weapons is held,
according as *polished learning relates*,
hence is derived its story.[11]

Thus, Uisneach could signify "over somewhat". The etymological suggestion raises skepticism. It is however not so different from the one that is
favored by a number of scholars – Uisneach deriving from *uss*, "above" and
inne, "the center". In any case, the *Dindsenchas* is far less precious for
etymological impulses than for the substance of the mythological episodes it
recorded. The story's chief import is indeed the significance of the druid
Midhe, his use of fire, and his desire to establish his power over Ireland
from its center.

Midhe and Fire: Points of Comparison

The episode is not the sole instance of the use of fire on Uisneach in Irish
mythology. As already mentioned, in *The Destruction of Da Derga's Hostel*
(*Togail Bruidne Dá Derga*), a "cloud of fire" formed around the hill at
some point of its mythological history.[12] Still in the *Dindshenchas*,
Delbáeth, a sovereign from Munster, is said to have lit a magical fire on
Uisneach, near the lake of Lugh: five streams then appeared.[13]

It is also intriguing to recall that the saint of the Uí Néill – the one that
had erected his main churches at the foot of Uisneach, the one who, thanks
to his powers, had moved *Ail na Mireann* to its current location, the great-
great-grand-son of Fiachu mac Néill – bore the name of "Aed mac Bricc".
And, as it turns out, "Aed" literally means "fire" in ancient Irish.

Kim McCone[14] uses this fact to erect a rickety theory that Aed mac Bricc
might have been a Christianized version of a Pagan deity of fire. The
mention of a hypothetical Celtic male god of fire[15] should always be treated
with caution: its existence has never been firmly established. Additionally,
the name Aed was quite common in ancient Ireland: MacKillop counts not
less than 20 saints and even more kings that bore that name.[16] The Dagda,
one of the most prominent gods of the Irish pantheon, also had a son called
"Aed". Because of this overabundance of characters named Aed, the theories assimilating Aed mac Bricc – or any other mythical or historical
character bearing the name "Aed"– to the themes of fire simply on the
grounds that they are called "Aed" lack substance. They are at the very
least not well supported.

This consideration leads us, however, to pursue the study of the different mythological Irish tribes and their potential connection with
Uisneach. According to the redactors of the *Book of Invasions*, the tribe
of Midhe – the Nemedians – was defeated by yet another mythological
tribe, the Fir Bolg.

2.2 The Fir Bolg and Uisneach

After the tribe of Nemed and before the Tuatha Dé Danann, the tribe of the Fir Bolg is also said to have invaded Ireland. Once again, it is on Uisneach that they chose to divide the island:

> They brought five leaders with them, Gann, Genann, Rudraige, Sengann and Slaine, the five sons of Dela (...). Those men divided Ireland from Uisneach.[17]

> They divided into five, without religion--without a falling for their slender-sided sept--pleasant Ireland, from Uisneach.[18]

According to this version, the five sons of Dela, the leader of the Fir Bolg, were supposed to have divided Ireland into five provinces. This excerpt from the version proposed by Giraldus Cambrensis in the 12th century has already been mentioned:

> five chiefs, all brothers, who were the sons of Dela, and among the descendants of Nemedus, who had taken refuge in Greece, arrived in Ireland, and, finding it uninhabited, divided the country into five equal parts, of which each took one.[19]

A form of appropriation or even a declaration of authority over Ireland is therefore mentioned for the third and fourth Irish tribes – the Nemedians and the Fir Bolg. The fifth and last mythical tribe, the Tuatha Dé Danann, followed the same pattern.

2.3 The Tuatha Dé Danann: The Dagda

Uisneach, House of the Dagda

The Wooing of Étaín (*Tochmarc Etaine*), transcribed in the 9th century, tells us that the Dagda (also called Eochaid), a prominent member of the Tuatha Dé Danann and one of the most important gods of Irish mythology, used to live on Uisneach. This information is already crucial. But the transcriber does not stop there:

> [Midir][20] came to Uisneach of [Mide] in the center of Ireland, for 'tis there that was Eochaid's house, Ireland stretching equally far from it on every side, south and north, to east and west.[21]

Centrality and sovereignty could hardly be expressed in more transparent terms to anyone who understands the implications of the different symbols here used: although the *Book of Invasions* does not mention that the

Tuatha Dé Danann had claimed their authority over Ireland on Uisneach, the fact that the hill bore the name of "Eochaid's house" or "house of the Dagda" implies a form of appropriation that is arguably even more profound.

The mention of the four cardinal points in the episode has led a number of scholars to see a hidden reference to a hypothetical cult of the sun. The argument could have been compelling in the case only east and west had been mentioned. Here, it is obviously the notion of centrality, rather than an allusion to the course of the sun, which is at stake.[22]

This excerpt is of the utmost importance: the Dagda is a major god of the Tuatha Dé Danann; he lives on Uisneach; the hill is his "house". And since the god is considered to be a druid-god and *the* god of druids, this story begs the question of whether Uisneach indeed once corresponded to the Center – either symbolic or factual – of the sacerdotal power in Ireland.

The Dagda, Druid-god: Connection with the Otherworld

> Eochaid Ollathair his name. He was also named the Dagda i.e. good god, for it was he that used to work wonders for them and control the weather and the crops.[23]

The Dagda is said to be quite literally "the good god" (from Irish *dag*, good and *día*, god), or the "god that is able", that can do anything, an archetype of a "polytechnician" – that is, a "pluripotent" – god. The connection he maintained with harvests, crops and the weather tends to associate him to production, fecundity and abundance. Furthermore, he is often called Eochaid Ollathair, the father of all, and is deemed "most divine", a druid-god that is also the god of the druids:

> [He is a] master of the elements, of science (often, sacerdotal knowledge) and also a god of friendship and contracts, of time and weather,[24] of eternity as much as he is a warrior. [...] His main attributes are his club, which kills from one of its end (in this world) and resuscitate from the other (in the Otherworld) and a cauldron of abundance, immortality and resurrection altogether.[25]

A most prominent member of the Tuatha Dé Danann, the Dagda is in fact probably the most important of Irish mythology after Lugh. Importantly, his major attributes are connected to the Otherworld. His club kills and resuscitates: it enables the passage from one world to the other, from the world of the living to the world of the dead and *vice versa*. Placing the house of the Dagda on Uisneach – potentially the cosmic pole of Ireland, the navel connecting the real world to the *sídh* – could therefore prove truly significant, symbolically speaking. The fact that his cauldron was connected to immortality and resurrection illustrates his functions of master of time. Similarly the fact that it is also a cauldron "of abundance" mirrors his role as master of the weather: no abundance or wealth are conceivable without good weather or at the very least conditions that are favorable to agriculture and to the ecosystems humans are trying to manage. Both notions – time and weather – do confront humans with their vulnerability and lack of control: time mirrors man's own finiteness and mortality, weather his powerlessness in the face of elements he can neither grasp nor command.

An echo of these two themes can be found in the two "gates" of the Irish year, the festivals of *Samhain* and *Bealtaine*, respectively at the beginning of the months of November and May of our modern calendar: the two celebrations were – and, in Irish folklore, still are – supposed to be moments of the year that are "out of time", where the world of the living and that of the dead connect. They were pivotal periods for the farmer but also the druid and the warrior.[26] Thus, the fact that, according to a significant number of medieval sources, an assembly – either ritual or secular, either mystic or historical – was held on the hill on Uisneach in connection with the festival of *Bealtaine* is of course noteworthy: the problem will be addressed in detail in the following chapter.

According to several early manuscripts,[27] *Bealtaine* was also the moment druids allegedly chose to light huge fires between which men and cattle were passed, so as to protect them for the coming year. Must we see a connection with the Dagda, master of time, god of druids whose house was on Uisneach – the very hill where the druid Midhe was said to have lit a mystic fire to claim sovereignty for his tribe? The hypothesis is tempting; let us remember, for now, that the implication of the sacerdotal world on Uisneach, already quite vivid thanks to Midhe, is at least reinforced by the association with the Dagda.

The Sons of the Dagda

One last detail must be addressed: according to most mythical genealogies, the Dagda is father to at least three children: Oengus, Aed and Cermait.[28]

Oengus is often presented as a god of youth or even beauty, which does complement the power of his father over time passing. The other son of the Dagda, Aed, has a name which, as already mentioned, literally means "fire": Aed being a very common name in ancient Ireland, though, the etymology should not be considered as particularly telling or even relevant. Cermait is perhaps the most interesting character. He is himself father of Mac Cuill, Mac Cecht and Mac Gréine. It so happens that those three characters – the three grand-children of the Dagda – have a very special place in Irish mythology: they are said to have killed the great god Lugh, also a member of the Tuatha Dé Danann. The episode is all the more remarkable in that it is supposed to have unfolded on the hill of Uisneach, the house of the Dagda.

2.4 The Tuatha Dé Danann: Lugh

Lugh: General Statements

Lugh is, without a doubt, the most important god of Irish mythology. He is a supreme god and his name is notably invoked in modern Irish by that of the festival of *Lughnasa*,[29] celebrated at the beginning of the month of August of our modern calendar and whose name means "assembly" or "gathering of Lugh".

> [Lugh] was euhemerized [...] as a king in the legendary Annals of the *Book of Invasions* and his role has been obliterated by Christianization, except in the archaic narrative of [*Táin Bó Cúailnge*] where he is the leader of the Tuatha Dé Danann. He transcends all functions[30] and classes. This is reflected in his nickname, *Samildanach*, the "polytechnician'" [...] The meaning of his name is "luminous" and [Lugh] is, by definition, a "solar" character.[31]

"Luminous" Lugh is considered by most scholars as the most essential god of the Celtic pantheon: the fact that he is a "polytechnician" – a pluripotent – god is mirrored in his numerous powers and abilities.

Death of Lugh on Uisneach

According to the First Redaction of the *Book of Invasions*, Lugh is supposed to have been killed on the hill of Uisneach, a fact whose significance cannot be stressed enough in the present discussion: "Forty years had Lug, till the three sons of Cermat slew him at Caendruim, that is, in Uisne[a]ch".[32] In Irish mythology, connecting the hill to its most important god is far from insignificant: Lugh died on Uisneach and this confers a primordial importance to the hill of the center of Ireland.

According to tradition, Mac Cuill, Mac Cecht and Mac Gréine were the three slayers of Lugh. They are the sons of Cermait, himself son of the Dagda. In the *Book of Invasions*, the three brothers are also named Sethor, Tethor and Cethor and are married respectively to Fódla, Banba and Ériu, the three eponymous sisters of Ireland or, more precisely, the triple goddess that represented Ireland.[33] The following passage is quite noteworthy:

> The three sons of Cermait [...]: Mac Cuill – Sethor, the hazel his god; Mac Cecht – Tethor, the ploughshare his god; Mac Greine – Cethor, the sun his god. Fotla was wife of Mac Cecht, Banba of Mac Cuill, Ériu of Mac Greine.[34]

The same explanation can be found in the Second – and therefore more recent – Redaction of the *Book of Invasions*.[35] The Third Redaction changes the interpretation dramatically:

The three sons of Cermat son of the Dagda were Mac Cuill, Mac Cecht, Mac Greine. Setheor was the name of Mac Cuill and the sea was his god: Tetheor was the name of Mac Cecht, and the air was his god, with its luminaries, the moon and the sun: Cetheor was the name of Mac Grene, and the earth was his god.[36]

The Third Redaction is almost 700 years posterior to the first manuscripts.[37] It is therefore most likely a rather exotic Christian gloss of Aristotelian inspiration, which is apparently unique. The ancient analogies – i.e. Mac Cuill/hazel, Mac Cecht/ploughshare and Mac Gréine/sun – are of more obvious relevance to this investigation.

In addition to their etymological coherence, one could see in those analogies a form of mythological consistency. In other words, the three attributes each recall of some characteristics of the Dagda – which were indeed numerous. The ploughshare obviously refers to agriculture. The hazel may be connected to the magic of the druids, as it was said to be one of their sacred trees. The case of the sun is substantially more problematic given the multiple interpretations and layers of symbolism that are attributed to the star. Its mention could refer to its path in the sky – that is, to *time* and consequently light as opposed to darkness – to its beneficial influence on crops – that is, to *weather* and thus heat as opposed to cold – or possibly *time* and *weather* combined, i.e. seasons. Additionally, the sun could conceivably signify strength and energy, that same energy that can be found, for instance, in the violence of war-related actions.

Thus, it is possible – though by no means definitely established – that Mac Cecht, Mac Cuill and Mac Gréine could respectively be references to agriculture (the ploughshare), the sacerdotal class (the hazel) and war (the sun?). In other words, Lugh was possibly killed by the hand of three characters representing all parts of society (farmers, priests, warriors): the concept of "triplicity" indeed seems to have been pivotal to the beliefs of the Celts.[38]

Besides, the death of the pluripotent god could not but happen on a very specific place, a place "out of this world" – and incidentally closely connected with the Dagda. Early sources are unanimous: whenever the death of Lugh is mentioned, it is said to have happened on Uisneach, also called *Caen-druim* (or *Coem-druim*), that is the good or beautiful summit.

The *Dindshenchas* is even more specific than the *Book of Invasions* and tells us the causes of the confrontation between the three brothers and Lugh. As always in the *Dindshenchas*, onomastics serves as a pretext to mythological interpretations – and *vice versa*. Here, two etymologies are submitted for Loch Lugborta, which is in all likelihood *Lough Lugh*, the annular pond that lies about the top of Uisneach to this day.[39] The first hypothesis is presented as follows:

[1] Loch Lugborta, whence the name? Not hard to say. A great meeting was held at Caendruim (which is called Usnech) between the three sons of Cermait, the Dagda's son, and Lug son of Ethne, to make peace with

him in regard to their father Cermait, whom he had slain through jealousy about his wife. Now the sons of Cermait, namely, Mac Cuill, Mac Cecht, and Mac Greine, had laid a plot to kill Lug. Mac Cuill thrust a spear into his foot.[40] Then Lug escaped from them by his prowess to yonder lake. There he was killed and drowned; and they say that the cairn which stands on the shore, called the Sidan, was raised over his body:[41] so that cairn is Lug's Grave, and hence come the names Loch Lugborta and Carn Lugdach.[42]

The three brothers supposedly chose to murder Lugh because the god had killed their father Cermait, son of the Dagda. The supreme Irish god was killed and buried on Uisneach during "a great meeting", perhaps the famous *Mórdháil Uisnigh* held on *Bealtaine*. More relevant to the present discussion is the fact that the hill is both the setting of his death and his grave. By being buried on Uisneach, Lugh arguably becomes the ultimate sovereign of the hill, a mythical figure inherently connected to the place. This power, this symbolic dominance over the hill, is all the more effective and legitimate in that it inscribed itself in a strong "family tradition": before him, the ancestors of Lugh maintained close connections with Uisneach.

Uisneach, Hill of Balor

Of course, drawing up a precise genealogy of mythical characters is not an easy task, especially in the context of Irish mythology. However, it is possible to find a number of recurrences by cross-checking the various sources at our disposal, first and foremost the *Book of Invasions* and the *Dindshenchas*.

Cian and Ethniu are said to be the parents of Lugh: Cian is supposed to be the son of the god Dian Cécht; Ethniu the daughter of the god Balor. Both Lugh's grand-fathers, Dian Cécht and Balor, are associated on several occasions with the hill of Uisneach in Irish myths.

In *The Fate of the Children of Tuireann* (*Oidheadh Chloinne Tuireann*),[43] the hill of Uisneach is called the hill of Balor (or rather "Balar", another common spelling of the god's name):

> At this time the Fair Assembly was held by the King of Érinn on Balar's Hill, which is now called Uisneach. And the [Fomoire] had not been long assembled there before they saw the array of a goodly army coming over the plain from the east towards them; and one young man came in the front of that army, high in command over the rest; and like to the setting sun was the splendour of his countenance and his forehead; and they were not able to look in his face from the greatness of its splendour. And he was Lug Lamh-fada [i.e. Lug of the long arms and furious blows] [...] and as bright as the sun on a dry summer's day was the complexion of his face and forehead when he took [his] helmet off.[44]

The Fomorians, a tribe presented as evil and demonic, extorted and despoiled the Tuatha Dé Danann. As noted by C.-J. Guyonvarc'h, "their presence on the hill of Uisneach, called 'hill of Balar' was the first proof of their ascendency over Ireland":[45] just like the Nemedians and the Fir Bolg, the Fomorians followed the tradition of expressing one's hegemony via the hill.

In the excerpt, Uisneach bears the name of the grand-father of Lugh, Balor, who also happens to be the leader of the Fomorians. The hill sees Lugh – at the apex of his divine, solar, luminous power – assist the remainder of the Tuatha Dé Danann, exploited by the awful Fomorians of Balor: later, the god will be killed on that very same hill.

The consequences are profound: the first appearance of Lugh, here presented as a luminous character, takes place on Uisneach. More than a simple appearance, his arrival in fact corresponds to the true "mythological birth" of the character. It may be argued that Lugh was therefore symbolically born on Uisneach, during an assembly, and that he died in a similar context.

Uisneach and Dian Cécht

The bonds uniting Lugh's other grand-father, Dian Cécht, and Uisneach are just as close. According to the *Book of Invasions*:

> [Dian Cécht] made an emetic draught for him, so that he vomited forth three belches from his mouth. Where he drank the draught was in Cnoc Uachtar Archae: and three belches burst forth from his mouth, a cold belch in Loch Uair, an iron belch in Loch Iairn and a … belch in Loch Aininn, and, according to this story, it is thence [the lakes] take their names.[46]

Cnoc Uachtar Archae, or the Top of the hill of Erc, is yet another name of Uisneach.[47] Dian Cécht, medicine-god of the tribe, is therefore said to have disgorged three lakes from the hill. Those three mythical lakes can be associated with three – very real – lakes, to this day still lying in the vicinity of Uisneach: *Loch Aininn* is still a common name of *Lough Ennell*, a lake almost 15 km^2 in area, at the east of the hill; *Loch Uair* refers to *Lough Uail* (or Owel), a 10 km^2 lake that lies at about half a dozen kilometers on the hill's north-east side; the more modest *Lough Iron* can be found at around 6 km on the north-north-east of Uisneach and still bears the name of *Loch Iarainn* in Irish.

The second etymology proposed by the *Dindshenchas* as regards the lake lying on top of the hill of Uisneach uses again the theme of "primordial waters", this time in connection with another character, Delbáeth, and associated with another motif, that of fire. Interestingly enough, the name Delbáeth is often said to mean "fire shape" or "enchanted fire":

[2] Or else the lake was named after Lugaid mac Táil, who was called Delbaeth. For that territory was the place that Delbaeth mac Táil took possession of, when he came northwards out of Munster with his five sons, after being warned by his own daughter to give up his land to her and her husband, Trad mac Tassaig. Then Delbaeth lit a magic fire, and five streams burst forth from it; and he set one of his sons to watch each of the streams [...]. He himself stayed at that spot, and it may be from him that the lake and the place had their name, Loch Lugborta, for till then his name was Lugaid, but thenceforth Delbaeth, that is Dolb-aed, from the enchanted fire.[48]

2.5 Fire, Water, Sídh

Fire and Water: General Statements

The themes of water and fire combined is evidently not an isolated case in Irish mythology. The most prominent example is perhaps that of Balor, the grand-father of Lugh, whose only eye, "poisoned and venomous, dangerous and destructive", "horrible", "dark, sad and red", a "great evil mass" injected with "black blood", could spurt a venom which was a mixture of iced water and fire:[49]

> The "venom" or "poison" gushing out of his eye is described as a liquid that is both icy and burning, both water and fire, two opposite – yet not contradictory – notions: fire and water are fundamental, if not identical elements in druid magic. The primordial water burns and destroys just like fire does: on a theological level, they are similar.[50]

This conception of the world is, among other examples, corroborated by the testimony of Strabo who, in the 1st century CE, makes the following statement: "[Druids][51] assert that the soul is indestructible, and likewise the world, but that sometimes fire and sometimes water have prevailed in making great changes".[52]

Claude Sterckx, who dedicated a whole chapter to the themes of fire and water in his *Eléments de Cosmogonie Celtique*,[53] interprets it as a reflection of the cosmic cycle, a symbol of the "necessary succession of life and death" – all in all a theme of "actualization", or rather of "regeneration". The concept is indeed highly compatible with what is known of *omphaloi*.

Uisneach and the Five Streams

Concerning the second etymology proposed by the *Dindshenchas*, the mystic fire of Delbáeth supposedly generated five streams, which may echo the five provinces of Ireland. Loch Lugborta was so-called because of Delbáeth, as Lugaid mac Táil was one of his names ("Loch Lugborta, for till then his name was Lugaid, but thenceforth Delbaeth").[54] Just like Midhe before him, Delbáeth claimed sovereignty over the hill of Uisneach by lighting a "magic fire" and "and five streams burst forth from it": Uisneach was thus the birthplace, the "center" of those five streams of mystical origin. Once again, sovereignty and "primitiveness" – the navel of Uisneach which gives birth and is at the center – tend to combine. The episode even earned Delbáeth his name, "that is Dolb-aed, from the enchanted fire".[55] His name is all the more interesting that, according to some sources[56], a certain Delbáeth – possibly but not necessarily the same character – was the father of Eithniu, the grandfather of Lugh. It would therefore be tempting to consider that Delbáeth and Balor may be one and the same character – or several facets of the same character. The fact that both individuals deal, each in their own way, with fire and water provides a first argument. Even more peculiar: a "Delbáeth" is presented as the father of Ériu, Fódla and Banba, the three representations of Ireland and incidentally the three brides of Mac Cuill, Mac Cecht and Mac Gréine, the killers of Lugh.[57] If this is indeed the same Delbáeth and if this Delbáeth is an aspect of Balor, this would imply that Lugh was killed by the three husbands – Mac Cuill, Mac Cecht and Mac Gréine – of three daughters – Ériu, Fódla and Banba– of his grandfather – Balor/Delbáeth. To put it differently, Lugh could have been slain by his own "uncles-in-law". Although this speculation does not seem particularly enlightening, it still confirms that all of those characters were connected by blood or marriage – a tragic mythical play indeed.

Uisneach and Primordial Water

At least three other documents clearly state that Uisneach was the source of all rivers of Ireland, or perhaps the world: the *Dindshenchas* itself, a text entitled *This is the Death of Dermot son of Fergus Cerrbeoil* (or simply *The Death of Diarmait/Dermot*; *Aided Diarmada meic Fergusa Cerrbeoil*) and *The Cause of Mongán's Frenzy (Tucait baili Mongáin)*.[58] The latter, which could go back to the 7th century,[59] tells us that, during "a great gathering" on Uisneach in Mide, a "great hail-storm came upon" the hosts: "Such was its greatness that the one shower left twelve chief streams in Ireland forever".[60] In the words of Alwyn and Brinley Rees, "in diverse cosmologies the mountain in the centre of the earth is the source of the world's rivers".[61] In this specific episode, Mongán, his queen and his historian witnessed the apparition, as if by magic, of a "prominent stronghold with a frontage of ancient trees", which they entered. They were welcomed by "seven conspicuous men" in a flamboyant, "marvelous house", which was richly decorated. There, they drank out of "seven vats of wine" and "became intoxicated": "It seemed to them it was not very long they were in that house. They deemed it to be no more but one night. However, they were there a full year".[62]

It is difficult to conclude that this wonderful house was indeed the house of the Dagda – as Uisneach is sometimes said to bear this name, perhaps figuratively. However, the characters do undergo an otherworldly experience and are therefore in touch with the *sídh*. The fact that their experience seems to last one night but actually goes on for a year is not coincidental: as will be demonstrated later, the festival of *Bealtaine*, too, during which the great assembly of Uisneach was in fact supposed to take place, connected the world of the living and that of the dead and was a most important turning point of the year – a moment "out of time".

The *Sídh*

In the Irish context, the Otherworld takes the name of *sídh*. It is the world of the dead and is placed, depending on the source, underground – and is sometimes accessible through specific passages – or beyond the sea. It is inhabited by the people of the *sídh*, which would later become the people of the fairies in Irish folklore. In the *Book of Invasions*, after the defeat by Men, the Tuatha Dé Danann chose to live in the *sídh*. The real world was to be inhabited by humans and the Otherworld by the Tuatha Dé Danann – once again later incorporated in Irish folklore as fairies.

In *The Cause of Mongán's Frenzy* (*Tucait baili Mongáin*), the otherworldly experience of the protagonists is an experience "out of the real world", an experience of transcendence reinforced – or perhaps simply illustrated – by their abuse of alcohol. Roseanne Schot drew a parallel with another text, also probably dated to the 7th century, *The Adventure of Conlae [in the Otherworld]* (*Echtrae Chonlai*).[63]

A certain Conlae/Conle/Connla/Condla Ruad ("the Red") sees a woman on the hill of Uisneach:

> One day Condla the Red-haired, son of Cond, the Fighter of a hundred, was in company of his father on the top of Uisneach when he saw a lady in extraordinary attire [coming] towards him. [...] "I have come", said the lady, "from the Lands of the Living, a place in which is neither death, nor sin, nor transgression. We enjoy perpetual feasts without anxiety; we practice [benevolence] without contention. A large Sid (=mound) is where we dwell, so that it is hence we are called Aés Side" [the people of the mound].[64]

The woman belongs to the people of the fairy and lives, by her own admission, in a great fairy fort.[65] Meeting a fairy – a character of the Otherworld – amounts to transcending the world of the living by getting in touch with the *sídh*, perhaps even the tribe of the gods, the *Tuatha Dé Danann*. To that extent, if the dating of both texts (*The Adventure of Conlae* and *The Cause of Mongán's Frenzy*) are confirmed, it could well be the most ancient examples of Uisneach standing as a place "out of the world", a point of contact between the world of the dead (the *sídh*) and that of the living (i.e. Men, the Milesians of the *Book of Invasions*).

2.6 The Milesians

The Milesians and the Sídh

When the Milesians (or Sons of Míl) landed in Ireland, they were confronted with the Tuatha Dé Danann, whom they eventually defeated. They then shared the world into two parts: the world "above" (i.e., the real world) for Men and the world "below" (the Otherworld) for the Tuatha Dé Danann. Following this partition, the meetings between humans and characters of the Otherworld – i.e. the Tuatha Dé Danann or the fairies of folklore – proved rather scarce: they usually unfold at specific points of space. These points could be places such as Uisneach, obviously, but also Cruachan and other symbolic "gates". The encounters happened most often at specific points in time, mainly *Samhain* and *Bealtaine*, the two lynchpins of the year, around early November and early May.

The *Book of Invasions* describes an important step in the conflict between the Milesians and the Tuatha Dé Danann: the meeting of Men with the three deities Banba, Fódla and Ériu who confront the Milesians on the top of three mountains:

> [The Sons of Míl] landed and came thereafter on to Sliab Mis, where Banba met them, with her druidic and magic hosts in her company. Amorgen asked of her. What is thy name? said he. Banba, said she, and from me is the island named Banba's island. Thereafter they made their way to Sliab Eiblinne, where Fotla met them, and the poet asked of her in like wise, What is thy name? said he. Fotla, said she, is my name, and from me is the island named. They came to Uisnech of Mide, and there found Ériu, and the poet asked of her, What is thy name? She said that it was Ériu, and that from her the island was named.[66]

Thus, men met with Ériu, one of the divine personifications of the island of Ireland on Uisneach, in the province of Mide.[67] The eponymous sovereign goddess of Ireland is in fact a triple goddess, whose three aspects are met over the course of different mythological tales. In other words, Ériu is but one aspect of the triad Fódla/Banba/Ériu who is a single tripartite goddess.

It is of course most remarkable that the "main name of the island is Ériu because the eponymous queen bearing this name has her abode on Uisneach, at the symbolic center of Ireland":[68] Ireland is Éire because Ériu, the personification of Ireland, lived on Uisneach.

The Milesians and Power

Another version, still taken from the *Book of Invasions*, brings a couple of clarifications and mentions some uncertainty:

> They had colloquy with Ériu at Uisnech. She spake thus with them: Warriors, welcome to you. Long have soothsayers known of your coming hither. Yours shall be this island for ever, and no island of its size to the east of the world shall be better, and no race shall be more perfect than your race, for ever. [...] The Book of Druim Sechta says [that] it was Fotla who had converse them in Uisnech.[69]

The episode is confirmed by Keating, who expresses it as follows:

> [The Sons of Míl] proceeded thence to Uisneach in [Mide], where they met Éire. The poet asked her her name. "Éire is my name", said she, "and it is from me that this island is called Éire".[70]

Two out of the three versions tend to believe Ériu was met on Uisneach, which is not insignificant as, once again, it demonstrates the symbolic power of the hill: the goddess gave her name to the island (Ériu/Éire) from its central point. The fact that the Milesians met (or fought)[71] the three aspects of the triple goddess in Ireland on three distinct hills is also noteworthy.

On Uisneach, in Mide, the goddess (or at least one of its aspects) confirmed that the coming of Men was predestined and that their sovereignty over the island would last until the end of time. The power of the Milesians over Ireland was therefore conferred to Men by Ireland itself: this episode must in fact be considered as the ultimate claim of power over Ireland.

The factual domination of Men is here presented under the form of a myth – and a quite heavily Christianized one. The Pagan gods fled underground so as to give way to Men and their unique God. The monks transcribing the *Book of Invasions* did present the Milesians as the legitimate descendants of Japheth, son of Noah and clearly inscribed them in the Christian tradition.[72]

The encounter between Ériu and the Milesians at the top of Uisneach is, of course, most significant. The fact that Christian monks chose to include it in their transcriptions is also quite significant as the encounter is here implicitly presented as the victory of Christianity over Paganism. Still, the substance of the myths is evidently pre-Christian in origin and the episode relies heavily on pre-Christian symbols and traditions: those symbols and traditions arguably remain in the final transcriptions because they were likely to be understood and perhaps accepted by all. The most obvious heathen characteristic of this passage is without a doubt the implication of a triple goddess. Interestingly enough, this "triple" aspect, which could presumptively remind of the tripartite view of Christian theology, is in fact probably the most original – that is, Celtic and Pagan – feature of this episode.

"Triplicity" or "Triplism" as a whole is a recurring theme of Irish mythology. We already know a most distinctive example: Fódla, Banba and Ériu married Mac Cuill, Mac Cecht and Mac Gréine, the three slayers of Lugh. In other words, the three aspects of the triple goddess representing Ireland – one of which even giving its name to Ireland from the top of Uisneach – married the three grand-sons of the Dagda, a powerful member of the Tuatha Dé Danann, and slew the supreme God Lugh on that same hill of Uisneach.

This recurring mythical triplicity may or may not evoke what is sometimes referred to as the "trifunctional hypothesis". Although the theory will not be debated in detail here, let us remember that some researchers[73] believe that Indo-European peoples – which obviously includes the Celts – divided their society into three distinct classes: the *clergy*, the *warriors* and the *farmers*. Those classes were supposedly connected with the ideas of *sovereignty*, *physical strength* and *fecundity*, respectively. According to this theory, the cultural segmentation of Indo-European societies was reflected in their religious and spiritual beliefs: the three functions were arguably applied to deities and heroes, who could therefore be connected with one or several of those functions; the most powerful deities were supposedly linked with all three "functions" and therefore had affinities with the notions of sovereignty, physical strength *and* fecundity. In that case, the three functions made up a whole, a totality whose power was magnified by this segmentation in three functions, three classes. As a consequence, the triads of Celtic gods or goddesses are sometimes said to only refer to one single deity, one that was divided into multiple aspects so as to transcend its powers. Vendryes expressed this idea by defining the concept of "unity in three people" in the Celtic culture.[74] To that extent, a last example taken from Irish mythology – and once again connected to Uisneach – seems quite informative.

2.7 Deirdre and the Sons of Uisneach

General Statements

The three "Sons of Uisneach" are mentioned in a set of documents which stem from one single story, that of Deirdre. The Sons of Uisneach are three brothers called Noíse, Ainnli and Ardan. The origin of the moniker and this affiliation with the hill is never clearly explained in the various texts dealing with the mythological episode: it would of course be tempting to understand it as a potential assimilation of the characters with the Center of Ireland or possibly the world, and even with a symbolism of transcendence and connection between the world of the living and that of the dead.

However, the attempts at interpretation are weakened by the absence of formal proof.

The story of the Sons of Uisneach is mainly found in five different texts, which, in all likelihood, share a common origin and were redacted in a period of time ranging from the 8th to the 15th century: *The Violent/ Tragic Death of the Children of Uisneach* or *The Fate of Children of Uisneach (Oidheadh Chloinne Uisnigh),*[75] *Deirdre,*[76] *The Exile of the Sons of Uisliu (Longes Mac n-Uislenn),*[77] the *Glenmasan manuscript*[78] and *The Cause of the Exile of Fergus Mac Roig (Fochonn loingse Fergusa maic Roig)*[79] can – and should – all be interpreted as different versions of the same story which, for reasons of convenience, will hereafter be called the story of Deirdre.

In the 15th century, the story was compiled into *The Three Sorrows of Storytelling (Tri Truaighe Scéalaigheachta)* alongside with two other texts, *The Fate of the Children of Tuireann (Oidheadh Chloinne Tuireann)*[80] and *The Fate of the Children of Lir (Oidheadh Chloinne Lir),*[81] in slightly modified versions.

This latter transcription later provided material for a fairly large number of Irish writers connected with the *Gaelic Revival* – the famous Irish artistic and to some extent political movements which, at the turn of the 19th and 20th centuries, focused on and revived the Gaelic identity of Ireland. The story of Deirdre and the Sons of Uisneach is sometimes presented, quite rightfully, as the most popular of Irish legends.[82] While it is not possible to provide a comprehensive list of the works inspired by this story, one could mention the *Deirdre* of Samuel Ferguson (1880),[83] of George Russel (1906),[84] William Butler Yeats (1907)[85] and James Stephens (1923),[86] the poem "Avenging and Bright" by Thomas Moore,[87] the *Death of the Children of Usnach* by Ferguson (1887),[88] William Sharp's *House of Usna* (1900), Frederic Herbert Trench's *Deirdre Wedded* (1901),[89] the *Deirdre of the Sorrows* of John Millington Synge (1910),[90] John Coulter (1944),[91] Kenneth Stevens (2017)[92] etc.[93] To those few examples, one could have added the plethora of adaptations in children's literature and in contemporary popular culture.[94]

Obviously, the original version – or at least the most ancient one, as found in the *Book of Leinster (Lebor Laignech)* – is significantly less refined, less beautiful, less "romantic" one might argue, as its modern and contemporary avatars. However, those instances are representative of the major impact the story of Deirdre had on Irish – and in some cases Scottish – culture and identity.

The Story of Deirdre

The story of Deirdre[95] is quickly summarized, even if its significance looms so large: at the birth of Deirdre – the daughter of a high-ranked bard – a druid predicted that she was to become Ireland's most beautiful woman but that a lot of blood would be shed in her name and that three of the greatest Irish warriors would be exiled because of her.

King Conchobar mac Nessa (or Conor) learns about the existence of this beauty to become and decides to raise her in isolation from the world so as to marry her when she is old enough. Deirdre grows up; one day she sees a crow drinking blood on the snow. She therefore prophesizes to her tutor that she will fall in love with a man with hair as black as a crow, skin as white as snow and cheeks as red as blood. The prophecy becomes true when she meets Noíse, Son of Uisneach. They both flee to Scotland, accompanied by the two brothers of the young man, Ainnli and Ardan,[96] the two other Sons of Uisneach.

Conchobar sends Fergus mac Róich, one of the great heroes of Ireland, after them. After a while, Fergus finds Deirdre and the Sons of Uisneach and convinces them to come back in Ireland in exchange of his sincere promise that nothing will happen to them. But, thanks to a ruse, Conchobar manages to separate Fergus from Deirdre and the Sons on Uisneach on their way back to Ireland.

Deirdre and the Sons on Uisneach find shelter in the house of the Red Claw/Branch (Crob Dearg) but are ambushed. Noíse is killed by a spear (or has his head cut) and his two brothers also die. Betrayed by Conchobar, Fergus has failed to keep his promise: he arrives after the battle and goes into exile, out of shame and spite.

Conchobar marries Deirdre but after a year, exasperated by the distant behavior of his spouse, forces her to marry the warrior who killed Noíse. Deirdre cannot handle this cruel ordeal and commits suicide by smashing her skull on a rock or, according to other versions, by using a knife she then throws in the ocean.

Following this episode, a great deal of Conchobar's warriors abandon him to join the rows of Ailill and Medb, two major characters of *The Cattle Raid of Cooley* (*Táin Bó Cúailnge*), Ireland's greatest epic.

Connecting Deirdre and Uisneach

The first striking element is that the connection, in the episode, between the story of Deirdre and the hill of Uisneach is far from obvious. It seems that the three Sons of Uisneach only maintain a distant – and essentially symbolic – relationship with the hill, which, incidentally, is never mentioned directly, and with good reason: most of the narrative takes place in Ulster and in Scotland.

It is notable, however, that the three brothers are presented in a highly favorable light in most versions. They are sometimes called the "three illustrious Sons of Uisneach" and their beauty, courage and reputation are highly praised on numerous occasions.[97] The *Books of Clanranald*, transcribed in the 18th century, is particularly laudatory and explains that the Sons of Uisneach are "powerful heirs presumptive", "fair" and "wondrous".[98] The connection of the three characters with the hill may arguably be considered as a mere distinction, an honorific title supposed to echo their true worth.

Triplism of the Brothers of Uisneach

Out of the three brothers, only Noíse seems to really matter to the plot of the story: it is him with whom Deirdre falls in love and Ainnli and Ardan appear to be mere on-lookers. From all accounts, this process evokes a classic case of Celtic "triplism".

The number three used to have a particular importance in the Celtic culture and traditions: the Celts apparently organized the world with groups of three. The triskelion – often associated with the Celts even though the symbol itself is pre-Celtic – is supposed to reflect this threefold conception of the world: white/grey/black, good/"neutral"/bad, day/twilight/ night, past/present/future, sky/earth/underground etc.[99] It is generally agreed that the "resonant symbolism of the number three runs through Celtic tradition from earliest times".[100]

This peculiar representation of the world is often opposed to dual or "bipolar" conceptions, notably that of Judeo-Christianity.[101] Although a tripartite view of the world applies, nominally, to the Christian creed (the Holy Trinity, the separation between body, spirit and soul etc.), the emphasis is arguably most often laid on a clear-cut dual division between "good and bad", "evil and virtuous", "Christians and heathens" – an opposition which is not as obvious in the tripartite Celtic conception of the world. Perhaps the most convincing example comes from the extensive catalogue of triple deities in the Celtic pantheon, notably goddesses such as the triads Macha, Mórrigan, Badb or Banba, Fódla, Ériu, already mentioned *supra*.

However that may be, it is clear that, in the story of Deirdre, only Noíse truly matters: the two other brothers are, at most, secondary characters, present only to support the character of Noíse. This idea was clearly accounted for by Joseph Vendryes in his seminal article entitled "L'unité en trois personnes chez les Celtes", published in 1935.[102] The author noticed that, most often in Irish mythology, three characters – sometimes three brothers – could bear the same name "to which a distinctive epithet is added, or occasionally names that are closely connected in form or substance".[103] But most often, "one of the three brothers has a name that distinguishes him from the other two. In that case, the latter two have names alliterating with each other or share the same meaning". Vendryes had already noticed the case of the three brothers of Uisneach. In the story of Deirdre, "Ainnli" and "Ardan" do share an assonance, while Noíse, the truly meaningful character, has a distinctive name. Vendryes provides many other examples and arrives at the following – and rather convincing – conclusion:

Only one of them has a clearly defined personality; the other two seem to be but shadows of the first one; they follow him wherever he goes, they tune their behavior to his and play a part in every aspect of [his] life.[104] [...] The dominant feature is the unity of the character, which is marked either by the indivisibility of the personality of the three brothers, or by the fact that one has a defined personality and the two other live, so to speak, in his shadow without distinguishing themselves from him.[105]

Vendryes believed that this "tripling" conferred the character a form of superiority over other men.[106] This hypothesis seems quite convincing in the case of the Sons of Uisneach. As already mentioned, the unparalleled qualities of the three brothers are detailed on many an occasion by the different transcribers and justify the interest of the most beautiful woman of Ireland toward Noíse.

Vendryes also explains that the "tripling" is a "figurative way of indicating the power of a hero".[107] The Sons of Uisneach are nobler, braver and more handsome than most mortals; their might, however, does not seem to be out of the ordinary as they are all killed by one single warrior, Éogan mac Durthacht, who is himself not presented as a particularly exceptional character in Irish mythology. In the case of the Sons of Uisneach, the "tripling" is not so much about power and might as it is about their importance and excellence in comparison with the common run of people – and not necessarily in the context of war.

Triplism: Sons of Uisneach and Slayers of Lugh

Of course, the fact that this tripling must not be understood as a claim of "superior power" for the Sons of Uisneach does not make the idea obsolete for the remainder of Irish mythology. For instance, the killers of Lugh – Mac Cuill, Mac Cecht and Mac Gréine whose name clearly echo one another, as noted by Vendryes – are triple because Lugh is the most powerful god of the Celtic pantheon: one single warrior, even from a divine lineage, could not have overpowered the supreme god.

It may be argued that the two brotherly triads are not as different from each other, mythologically and symbolically speaking: in the *Book of Invasions*, Ainnli, one of the three Sons of Uisneach, is supposed to be one of the sons of Lugh.[108] Consequently, the three brothers of Uisneach could be, by extension, the sons of Lugh, a god that would later be killed by a triad of brothers, Mac Cuill, Mac Cecht and Mac Gréine. The symbolic loop has come full circle: the supreme god of the Celtic pantheon fathers a "unity in triplism" and is killed by this very same "total triplism". The superiority of Lugh over the secular world is confirmed both by the nature of his progeny and his very death.

Black, White, Red

Returning to the story of Deirdre – and still bearing in mind this idea of "total triplism" – the prophecy made by the young girl is interesting to point out: she announced her preceptor that she would fall in love with a man with hair as black as a crow, skin as white as snow and cheeks as red as blood.

The black/white/red triad has been studied by quite a number of scholars specializing in Celtic or, more broadly speaking, Indo-European studies. A parallel is often drawn with the three Indo-European functions and some scholars even consider it as a symbolic representation of the world. For example, Jan De Vries suggests that the three conditions for life in Vedic tradition are fire, water and earth, "respectively symbolized by the colors red, white and black".[109] It is also argued that white could represent the sacerdotal world, red could stand for warriors and black for farmers.[110] This triad of colors may therefore be a representation of unity in triplism, a whole divided in three categories that complete each other. This is, of course, mere conjecture and this intriguing hypothesis has never been confirmed or established once and for all. It is therefore not necessary – and perhaps not preferable – to elaborate too much. In the case of the story of Deirdre, only Noíse has the three physical traits the young woman was looking for, as he is indeed the sole brother with hair as black as the crow, skin as white as snow and cheeks as red as blood, which confirms the secondary nature of the other two siblings.

Symbolism and Importance of the Story of Deirdre

The original and symbolic substance of the story of Deirdre is complex and difficult to grasp. The assimilation of the three brothers to the hill of Uisneach is rather cryptic and very little can be added to the interpretation mentioned earlier: "Son of Uisneach" was most likely an honorific title that was supposed to evoke where the brothers came from or to what they were comparable. The Sons of Uisneach were the sons of the Center of Ireland, perhaps at least partially a symbol of the quintessence of the island, her beauty or her symbolic greatness; only Sons of Uisneach – Sons of the heart of Ireland – were worthy of the beauty of Deirdre.

Whatever the original intention of the symbols, the story left an indelible mark on the cultural history of Ireland. The importance of its role at the time of the *Gaelic Revival*, at the turn of the 19th and 20th centuries, is incontestable. The influence of the Sons of Uisneach can also be felt in many documents dating back to the Middle Ages.

In the 16th century, the *Annals of Loch Cé* mention the Sons of Uisneach twice: the betrayal of Conchobar is considered a reference – an epitome of disloyalty. The author of the reference noted 1582.33 in the Annals thus mentions a historical betrayal that apparently had had no equivalent since the time of the Sons of Uisneach.[111]

From the 14th century, the document entitled *The Death of Fergus Mac Roich* (*Aided Fergusa maic Roig*) tells the story of Fergus after the death of the Sons of Uisneach and, to some extent, is the continuation of the story of Deirdre; Fergus is presented as serving the interests of Ailill and Medb. This episode also echoes *The Cause of the Exile of Fergus Mac Roig* (*Fochonn loingse Fergusa maic Roig*), already mentioned *supra*, where Fergus is shown spending the night on the hill of Uisneach so as to debate over the qualities of the different provinces of Uisneach. Once again, the symbolic loop has come full circle; the one character that had failed at protecting the Sons of Uisneach settles on top of the hill associated with their name so as to make a crucial decision – that of joining the ranks of Ailill and Medb, the two major royal figures of *The Cattle Raid of Cooley*.

The *Táin* itself also references the death of the Sons of Uisneach on two occasions. The perspective chosen by the authors is not so much that of the betrayal – which often stands as the most salient characteristic of the original story – than it is a reminder of the misjudgment and weakness of Fergus: the hero had failed to protect the Sons of Uisneach and Deirdre from the wrath of Conchobar. He therefore had to make up for his mistake. Thus, when it came to finding a proper scout, Fergus was presented as the obvious choice:

> They took counsel who was most proper to seek tidings in advance of the host between the two provinces. And they said it was Fergus, inasmuch as the expedition was an obligatory one with him, for it was he that had been seven years in the kingship of Ulster. And after Conchobar had usurped the kingship and after the murder of the sons of Usnech who were under his protection and surety, Fergus left the Ultonians, and for seventeen years he was away from Ulster in exile and in enmity. For that reason it was fitting that he above all should go after tidings.[112]

Later in the narrative, Fergus has Conchobar at his mercy and is about to kill him. He addresses the crowd:

> "Hearken, ye men of Erin!" cried Fergus; "who opposes a shield to me to-day on this day of battle when four of the five grand provinces of Erin come together on Garech and Ilgarech in the battle of the Cattle-raid of Cualnge?" "Why, then, a gilla [=a young man] that is younger and mightier and comelier than thyself is here", Conchobar answered, "and whose mother and father were better! The man that hath driven thee out of thy borders, thy land and thine inheritance; the man that hath driven thee into the lairs of the deer and the wild hare and the foxes; the man that hath not granted thee to take the breadth of thy foot of thine own domain or land; the man that hath made thee dependent upon the bounty of a woman; the man that of a time

disgraced thee by slaying the three sons of Usnech that were under thy safeguard; the man that will repel thee this day in the presence of the men of Erin; Conchobar son of Fachtna Fathach son of Ross Ruad son of Rudraige, High King of Ulster and son of the High King of Erin!".[113]

Conchobar here clearly reminds the crowd of the past weakness of Fergus, who therefore has no other choice but to try and kill him. Fergus raises his sword and attempts to strike Conchobar three times to get his revenge: according to the symbolism of "triplicity", the warrior therefore tries to get a "total" victory over Conchobar – all the more so that his sword comes from the *sídh*; it is a magic sword from the Otherworld, which can strike the "three fateful blows of Badb", who is one of the aspects of the triple goddess mentioned previously.

The adoptive son of Conchobar stops him and prevents the death of his father: for lack of cutting heads, Fergus ends up "decapitating" three hills:

> Thus it was with that sword, which was the sword of Fergus: The sword of Fergus: The sword of Letè from Faery: Whenever he desired to strike with it, it became the size of a rainbow in the air. Thereupon Fergus turned his hand slantwise over the heads of the hosts, so that he smote the three tops of the three hills, so that they are still visible on the moor in sight of the men of Erin. And these are the three Maels ('the Balds') of [Mide] in that place, which Fergus smote as a reproach and a rebuke to the men of Ulster.[114]

It is quite unfortunate that the name of those three hills have not come down to us. Given the fact that those three hills are explicitly said to be in Mide, and given the – albeit indirect – association of the character of Fergus with Uisneach, it is not unlikely that one of them could actually be Uisneach – although, as often in the case of mythological interpretations, the claim must remain conjecture.

***

Center of Ireland, center of the known world, center of attention and focal point of heroes, druids but also a large portion of redactors and transcribers of Irish mythology, center of religious and royal powers, *Axis mundi* and *omphalos*, outside and above the world: the original symbolism of Uisneach unsurprisingly stems from its geographical position, at the approximate center of the island and overlooking a vast plain. The hill was associated with many deities and the sacerdotal class; it was an "in-between", a vertical hyphen both separating and uniting the world of the living and that of the dead. Uisneach was considered to be a zone of mediation, of passage between the real and the imaginary, between the realm of the humans and the *sídh*, between the Milesians and the Tuatha Dé Danann, men and fairies, a lynchpin of which the druids were the guardians and representatives.

The myths of Uisneach seemed inherently connected to threefold characters, either divine or heroic and, more broadly speaking, to the very idea of "triplism", perhaps in an attempt at reinforcing the symbolic strength of the place. The fact that this "triplism" may or may not echo the Indo-European "trifunctional hypothesis" remains conjectural. The importance of the alleged three "classes" (*sacerdotal, royal* and *agrarian*) that arguably divided Indo-European (and therefore Celtic) societies has yet to be demonstrated in the context of Uisneach.

Clearly, the sacerdotal class, connecting the world of men to that of gods, was at the heart of the symbolism of the hill: the episode of the druid Midhe and his original fire is perhaps the most eloquent example. The pervasiveness of the "royal function" is also beyond question, as shown by the numerous attempts at establishing the dominance of clans – first and foremost the southern Uí Néill and their title of "Kings of Uisneach" – and the desire to glorify the political and religious influence of powerful figures, such as Patrick during his confrontations with the Uí Néill dynasty. Interestingly enough, those two "classes" – warriors and clergy – are both found in what is perhaps the most notorious example of all: the great assembly of Uisneach or *Mórdháil Uisnigh*.

Notes

1　See *supra* and chap. III.
2　*Lebor Gabála Érenn, op. cit.*, V, 311.
3　As mentioned earlier, the term *tuath* refers to a territory. Since this territory corresponded to a specific number of people or fighters, *tuath* is occasionally translated as "a nation", "a people" or "a tribe".
4　*History of Ireland, op. cit.*, Book I, 113.
5　*Dindshenchas, op. cit.*, II, 43-7.
6　See following quote.
7　*Ibid.*, 45.
8　In the early 20th century, Loth already noted that the "*Dindshenchas* is filled with fanciful etymologies". "L'Omphalos chez les Celtes", *op. cit.*, 201.
9　Arguably, this "house" could very well be a figure of speech. Interestingly enough, Uisneach is said to be the "house of the Dagda", one of the major gods of the Irish pantheon. See chap. II.3.
10　"L'Omphalos chez les Celtes", *op. cit.*, 201.
11　*Dindshenchas, op. cit.*, II, 43-7.
12　See *supra* and "The destruction of Dá Derga's hostel", *op. cit.*, 32.
13　*Dindshenchas, op. cit.*, II, 43-7. See chap. II.5.
14　McCone, Kim. 1990. *Pagan Past and Christian Present*. Maynooth: Department of Old Irish, National, 165-6.
15　Brigit, on the other hand, is often said to be a "fire-goddess". See chap. VI.2 for instance.
16　*Dictionary of Celtic Mythology, op. cit.*, 3.
17　*Lebor Gabála Érenn, op. cit.*, V, 147-9.
18　*Ibid.*, V, 181.

19 *The Topography of Ireland*, *op. cit.*, 66. See *infra* for a similar mention in the *Book of Invasions*.
20 Midir was one of the leaders of the *Tuatha Dé Danann*.
21 Bergin, Osborn & Best, R.I. (ed.). 1938. "Tochmarc Étaíne" in *Ériu*, 12, 137-96, 145.
22 "Le Roi indo-européen et la synthèse des trois fonctions, *op. cit.*, 22.
23 "Tochmarc Étaíne", *op. cit.*, 143.
24 The Dagda "control[s] the weather and the crops", *ibid.*
25 *Les Druides*, *op. cit.*, 379.
26 See chap. IV.2-4.
27 See *infra*, esp. chap. IV.2.
28 For instance *Lebor Gabála Érenn*, *op. cit.*, IV, 129. Brigit is also presented as the daughter of the Dagda.
29 The name is also attested in many toponyms, perhaps most famously in Lugdunum, the ancient name of Lyons, France (cf. Lugus).
30 The three functions as defined by Dumézil (i.e. clergy/warriors/farmers). See *infra*.
31 *Les Druides, op. cit.*, 402-3.
32 *Lebor Gabála Érenn, op. cit.*, IV, 125. See also 185.
33 *Ibid.*, IV, 123 (R.1). Another famous triple goddess is Macha, Badb, Mórrigan. See Guyonvarc'h, Christian-Joseph & Le Roux, Françoise, 2016 (1987). *Mórrigan-Bodb-Macha. La Souveraineté Guerrière de l'Irlande*. Fouesnant: Yoran.
34 *Ibid.*, 129 (R.1).
35 *Ibid.*, 153.
36 *Ibid.*, 193-5.
37 See the general introduction of *Lebor Gabála Érenn* for a detailed description of the original manuscripts and their possible dating.
38 See *infra*.
39 See Annex I.1-2 and chap. V.3.
40 A one-legged, one-armed or one-eyed god is a recurring theme of Celtic mythology – as well as of many other mythologies (Lajoye, Patrice. 2006. "Borgne, manchot, boiteux: des démons primordiaux aux dieux tonnants" in *Ollodagos*, 20.2, 211-245 or *Les Indo-Européens*, *op. cit.*, 370-1). Some characters are born with one leg, one arm or one eye: this is for example the case of the Fomoire, the supposedly evil and monstrous mythological Irish tribe. Other deities may lose a leg, an arm or eye, usually in battle – Lugh, for instance. The symbolism of such a mutilation is ambivalent. The power of the maimed god can be greatly increased. On the other hand, this mutilation may prefigure a loss of authority and power, as seems to be the case here.
41 The idea according to which this "Sidan" corresponds to an actual cairn on Uisneach will be discussed *infra*.
42 *Dindshenchas*, *op. cit.*, IV, 279-81.
43 O'Curry, Eugene (ed.). 1863. "The Fate of the Children of Tuireann (Oidhedh Chloinne Tuireann)" in *Atlantis*, IV, 157-240. Occasionally translated as the *Violent Death* or the *Tragedy of the Children of Tuireann* etc.
44 *Ibid.*, 161-3. Trans. E. O'Curry.
45 *Textes Mythologiques irlandais*, *op. cit.*, 133.
46 *Lebor Gabála Érenn*, *op. cit.*, IV, 137, §319.
47 *Ibid.*, IV, 136-7; this name can also be found in *The Colloquy with the Ancients. Silva Gadelica*, *op. cit.*, 158.
48 *Dindshenchas*, *op. cit.*, IV, 279-81.

49 From *Do chath mhuighe tuireadh ann so* in O'Cuív, Brian (ed.). 1945. *Cath Muighe Tuireadh: the Second Battle of Magh Tuireadh*, Dublin: Dublin Institute for Advanced Studies (MS 24 P 9 of the Royal Irish Academy of Dublin). See *Textes Mythologiques irlandais, op. cit.*, 67-9.

50 *Ibid.*, 99.

51 Strabon mentions *vates* (i.e. druids specialized in divination), bards and druids.

52 Hamilton, H.C. & Falconer W. (ed.). 1854. *The Geography of Strabo in Three Volumes*. London. I. Book IV, chapter 4, §4, 294. See Dumézil, Georges. 1963. "Le Puits de Nechtan" in *Celtica*, VI, 50-61.

53 Sterckx, Claude. 1986. *Eléments de Cosmogonie Celtique*. Brussels: Editions de l'Université de Bruxelles, 80-93.

54 *Dindshenchas, op. cit.*, IV, 279-81.

55 *Ibid.*

56 See *infra*.

57 *Lebor Gabála Érenn, op. cit.*, IV, 133. Also *Dictionary of Celtic Mythology, op. cit.*, 33, 175, 192.

58 See chap. III.4.

59 Carey, John. 1995. "On the Interrelationships of some Cín Dromma Snechtai texts" in *Ériu*, 46, 71-92.

60 Meyer, Kuno & Nutt, Alfred (ed.). 1895. *The Voyage of Bran, Son of Febal to the and of the Living*. 2 vols, I: *The happy otherworld*, London: David Nutt, 57.

61 *Celtic Heritage, op. cit.*, 160.

62 *The Voyage of Bran, op. cit.*, 58.

63 Both documents may have been redacted by the same author. "From Cult Centre to Royal Centre", *op. cit.*, 95. The dating of the manuscript is controversial.

64 *The Gaelic Journal, Irislear na elge*, 1882. Dublin: Joseph Dollard, 307 as cited by Schot. See also O'Beirne Crowe, J. 1874. "Mythological Legends of Ancient Ireland. I, the Adventures of Condla Ruad" in *Journal of the Royal Historical and Archaeological Association of Ireland*, Fourth Series, III-18, 118-33: 120 for another translation.

65 Cross, Tom Peete & Slover, Clark Harris (ed.). 1936. *Ancient Irish Tales*, New York: Henry Holt & Co, 488-90.

66 *Lebor Gabála Érenn, op. cit.*, V, 53.

67 See the remark of Alwyn and Brinley Rees in *Celtic Heritage, op. cit.*, 167 on the fact that Irish "founders were almost invariably female".

68 *Les Druides, op. cit.*, 224.

69 *Lebor Gabála Érenn, op. cit.*, V, 77-9. See also V, 35-7.

70 *History of Ireland, op. cit.*, 83-5.

71 The *Lebor Bretnach*, which dates back to the 11th century but is a non-literal translation of a text from the 9th century, explains: "They fought Banba at Sliebh Mis with her hosts,/Faint, wearied;/They fought Fothla at Ebhlinne, murmuring, /Éire at Uisneach". Todd, James Henthorn (ed.). 1848. *Leabhar Breathnach annso sis: The Irish version of the Historia Britonum of Nennius*. Dublin: Irish Archaeological Society, 247.

72 *Lebor Gabála Érenn, op. cit.*, II, 9-125 ("Early History of the Gaedil").

73 See for instance *Les Indo-Européens, op. cit.*: Bernard Sergent, a follower of Georges Dumézil, remains one of the leading researchers embracing the "trifunctional hypothesis" in Europe. Once again, see 355-423, especially 360 for a concise definition of "trifunctionality" among Indo-Europeans. For the Celts, see also, for instance, the works of Alwyn and Brinley Rees mentioned in the bibliography.

74 See section "Triplism of the Brothers of Uisneach" *infra.*
75 Mac Giolla Léith, Caoimhin (ed.). 1994. *Oidheadh Chloinne Uisnigh* in *Ériu,* XLV, 99-112.
76 Hyde, Douglas (ed.). 1899. "Deirdre" in *Zeitschrift für celtische Philologie,* II, 138-55.
77 Hull, Vernam (ed.) reprint. 1971. *Longes Mac n-Uislenn: The Exile of the Sons of Uisliu.* New York: Kraus Reprint. https://celt.ucc.ie//published/T301020B/index.html.
78 "The Glenmasan Manuscript", *op. cit.*
79 "The Cause of Exile of Fergus mac Roig", *op. cit.*
80 O'Curry, Eugene (ed.). 1863. "The Fate of the Children of Tuireann" in *Atlantis,* IV, 157-240.
81 O'Curry, Eugene (ed.). 1863. "The Fate of the Children of Lir'" in *Atlantis,* IV, 113-57.
82 Mathews, P.J. 2009. *The Cambridge Companion to J. M. Synge.* Cambridge: Cambridge University Press, 64. See Hull, Eleanor. 1906. "The Story of Deirdre and the Lay of the Children of Uisne" in *Celtic Review,* 288.
83 Ferguson, Samuel. 1880. *Deirdre: A one-act Drama of old Irish Story.* Unknown. See Suess, Barbara, A. 2003. *Progress & Identity in the Plays of W.B. Yeats, 1892-1907.* New York: Routledge, 127.
84 Russell, George William. 1907. *Deirdre.* Dublin: Maunsel.
85 Yeats, William Butler. 1907. *Deirdre.* London: A.H. Bullen, Dublin: Maunsel &co.
86 Stephens, James. 1970 (1923). *Deirdre.* New York: The Macmillan Company.
87 Moore, Thomas. 1850. *Irish Melodies.* Philadelphia: Lea & Blanchard, 71.
88 Ferguson, Samuel. 1887. *The Death of the Children of Usnach.* Dublin: Sealy, Bryers & Walker.
89 Trench, Herbert. 1901. *Deirdre Wedded: Song for the Funeral of a Boy, Shakespeare, A Charge, & Other Poems.* London: Methuen.
90 Synge, John Millington. 1910. *Deirdre of the Sorrows.* Dublin: Cuala Press.
91 Coulter, John. 1944. *Deirdre of the Sorrows.* Macmillan Company of Canada.
92 Steven, Kenneth. 2017. *Deirdre of the Sorrows.* Edinburgh: Birlinn.
93 A very thorough list can be found here: https://celt.ucc.ie/published/T301020B.html ("Translations and Adaptations").
94 See Fackler, Herbert V. 1978. *That Tragic Queen: The Deirdre Legend in Anglo-Irish Literature.* Salzburg: Institut für Englische Sprache und Literatur.
95 The most common traits of the story, as found in the five texts mentioned above, are hereafter presented. The story of Deirdre and the allusions to the Sons of Uisneach can be found in other ancient documents. Thus, "The Wooing of Emer" by Cú Chulainn alludes to Noíse, Son of Uisneach ("The Wooing of Emer", *op. cit.,* 299), just like Stokes, Whitley (ed.). 1908. "The Training of Cúchulainn" in *Revue Celtique,* 29, 109-52: 139.
96 The spelling of the names varies depending on the versions but the assonance is always preserved.
97 See Stokes, Whitley (ed.). 1887. "The death of the sons of Uisnech" in *Irische Texte mit Wörterbuch.* Leipzig, II-2, 109-84, for instance 161-2, 173. See also Hyde, "Deirdre", *op. cit.,* 145, 153, "The Glenmasan Manuscript", *op. cit.,* 115, 119 etc.
98 Cameron, Alexander, Macbain, Alexander & Kennedy, John. 1894. "The Book of Clanranald" in *Reliquiae Celticae,* Inverness: The Northern Counties Newspaper and Printing and Publishing Company, Limited, II, 149-288, 237.
99 *Les Fêtes celtiques,* *op. cit.,* 170.
100 *Dictionary of Celtic mythology, op. cit.,* 412.

101 See the reference to Vendryes *infra*. See also Green, Miranda J. 1989. *Symbols and Image in Celtic Religious Arts*. London and New York: Routledge, 169-205.

102 Vendryes, Joseph. 1935. "L'unité en trois personnes chez les Celtes" in *Comptes rendus des séances de l'Académie des Inscriptions et Belles-Lettres*, 79th year, III, 324-41.

103 *Ibid.*, 325.

104 *Ibid.*, 327.

105 *Ibid.*, 331.

106 *Ibid.*, 341.

107 *Ibid.*

108 *Lebor Gabála Érenn, op. cit.*, IV, 101.

109 De Vries, Jan. 1942. "Rood, wit, zwart", Volkskunde, cited by Dumézil, Georges. 1946. "'Tripertita' fonctionnels chez divers peuples indoeuropéens" in *Revue de l'Histoire des Religions*, CXXXI-1-3, 53-72, esp. 58.

110 *Ibid.*

111 Hennessy, William M. (ed.). 1871. *The Annals of Loch Cé*. A Chronicle of Irish Affairs from A.D. 1014 to A.D. 1590. Oxford/Cambridge/Edinburgh/Dublin: Longman & Co., Trübner & Co., Paternoster Row; Parker & Co; Macmillan & Co.; A. & C. Black; A. Thom, 1582.33; see also 1581.11.

112 Dunn, Joseph (ed.). 1914. *The Ancient Irish Epic Tale: Táin Bó Cúailnge*. London: David Nutt, 25.

113 *Ibid.*, 354-5.

114 *Ibid.*, 356-7.

3 Uisneach and the Ancient Assemblies

"Great assemblies" were apparently held in ancient Ireland. They were general meetings, which punctuated the year and were usually associated with specific festivals. Transcribers mention three – sometimes four – great assemblies.

The assembly of Tailtiu was a "fair" (*óenach*); the assembly of Tara a "feast" (*féis*), the assembly of Uisneach was usually called a "great assembly" or a "convention" (*mórdháil*). Some sources state that those gatherings were held every year. Others mention a three-year or even a seven-year cycle. In any case, they were held at specific times of the year and were almost systematically connected with the four traditional seasonal festivals of ancient Ireland: *Samhain* at the beginning of the month of November, then *Imbolc*, *Bealtaine* and *Lughnasa*, each one being celebrated three months after its predecessor.[1]

The three (or four) assemblies were *general* gatherings in Ireland, in the sense that they affected the whole of the island and were not limited to a region or a province. They were "national" events, although the term must be used cautiously in the context of ancient Ireland. The existence of interprovincial gatherings affecting the entirety of the territory at a period where there was actually no recognition of a central authority is in itself remarkable – if we accept, of course, that they were indeed historical events.

Françoise Le Roux and Christian-Joseph Guyonvarc'h believed them to be "great calendar meetings", which acted as "political assemblies as well as popular celebrations". They were "characterized by religious ceremonies, feasts, competitions and administrative talks, both provincial and interprovincial".[2] Addressing the case of the fair of Tailtiu, Máire MacNeill explained that it was a "unitive, religious, political and social assembly".[3]

Defining those great assemblies is obviously essential. The central question, however, remains to know whether they were a historical reality or not. Is the existence of great Irish assemblies, and more specifically *Mórdháil Uisnigh*, the convention of Uisneach, confirmed? Could it be that they were late inventions or even myths diffused by different transcribers through centuries?

Before going into further detail, it must be noted that the terms "gathering" or "assembly" are quite ambiguous because of their very broad meaning: this

DOI: 10.4324/9781003143161-4

ambiguity occasionally led to mistakes and misinterpretations, which should be addressed here. Although an "assembly" – *Mórdháil Uisnigh* – was supposedly held on a regular basis on Uisneach, not all assemblies on the hill were "great assemblies". It is in fact *Mórdháil Uisnigh*, the "convention", which came down through the centuries and remains a textbook case of Irish and Celtic studies; this convention was inscribed in a triad (or tetrad) of great periodic assemblies. However, not all large gatherings held on the hill were connected with this set of great Irish assemblies. For example, the first decades of the 12th century saw the holding of at least three highly political or religious gatherings on or around the hill. Those gatherings, however, were by no means "conventions of Uisneach" as we understand them today.

3.1 Conferences and Synods

Peace Conferences on Uisneach

One category of meetings the Irish Annals mention is "peace conferences" held on Uisneach. For instance, according to the *Annals of Clonmacnoise*, compiled[4] in the 17th century, "Connor o'Brian, king of Munster, and king Terlaugh o'Connor" met in 1135 at Avall Keherny, next to Uisneach, "with all the clergie of Mounster" to establish a one-year truce.[5] A couple of years later, in 1141, peace was made on Uisneach between Toirdhealbhach Ua Conchobhair, king of Connacht and Murchadh Ua Maeleachlainn, king of Tara. The meeting also served as an opportunity to exchange the hostages held by both sovereigns.[6]

Those gatherings, which are never presented as a *Mórdháil Uisnigh*, were political above all. Although "all the clergie of Mounster" supposedly accompanied the king – which is a doubtful claim – the meeting had little or no direct connection with the religious world and its symbols: both in 1135 and 1141, the idea was mainly to come to terms with fights and draw up with a pact between rulers. Of course, choosing Uisneach, the symbolic center of Ireland, was not insignificant to that purpose.

The Clergy and the Synod of 1111

The Irish Christian clergy was still quite conscious of the religious or sacred worth of the hill of Uisneach. Thus, at least five distinct sources[7] mention a great synod organized on Uisneach in 1111. The *Chronicum Scotorum*, compiled in the 17th century, presents the gathering as follows:

> The great synod of Uisnech in the same year and in that synod the diocese of the men of Mide was divided between the bishop of Cluain moccu Nóis and the bishop of Cluain Iraird i.e. from Clochán an Imrim westwards to the bishop of Cluain moccu.[8]

The *Annals of Loch Cé* (16th century) go into greater detail:

> A synod of clerics at Fiadh-mic-Aenghusa, in Uisnech, including Cellach, comarb [successor] of Patrick, and including Maelmuire Ua Dunain, i.e. the noble senior of Érinn, with fifty bishops, vel paulo plus, with three hundred priests, and with three thousand students, together with Muirchertach Ua Briain, attended by the nobles of Leth-Mogha, to impose rules and good customs on all, both laity and clergy.[9]

The *Annals of Ulster*[10] explain that 300 priests, 3,000 clerics "with fifty bishops or a little more" gathered: their objective was "to enjoin uprightness and good conduct on everyone, both laity and church".

The 1111 synod of Uisneach was therefore, as could be expected, an exclusively Christian event with no apparent connection to the Pagan past of the hill. Yet the choice of Uisneach for the holding of a synod still raises questions: was the place chosen for reasons of convenience, for example the relative proximity to Dublin and the central position of the hill? Or were those reasons more symbolic – an attempt at Christianizing a place known for its connection with Paganism? Or even a desire to connect with the symbolism of the center?

Without better insight and knowledge of the protagonists and their affinity with the Pagan world, it is quite difficult to tell – although it is even harder to believe all this happened by accident. Of course, the hill of Uisneach was a convenient meeting place as it is relatively accessible, easy to climb and as its size enables the meeting of thousands of people. But a multitude of similar places exist in Ireland and many are more suitable for the holding of such events. Other parameters most likely came into play, first and foremost the idea of centrality, be it geographic and/or symbolic.

The peace conferences held on Uisneach were connected with "rulers" – warriors and kings; the synod of 1111 with the religious world. Neither types of gatherings should be mistaken, however, with the convention of Uisneach. At best, they inscribed themselves in its indirect continuity, capitalizing on the sacerdotal and royal value of *Mórdháil Uisnigh* and the Irish periodic assemblies. Those assemblies were indeed mentioned by a large number of sources, of more or less ancient origin.

3.2 Mórdháil Uisnigh According to Keating

Tuathal Techtmar, Founder of Mórdháil Uisnigh

According to the pseudo-historical Irish tradition – which was redacted *a posteriori* of the facts mentioned and which relied on unknown, missing or doubtful sources – the alleged High King Tuathal Techtmar was said to be the founder of the convention of Uisneach, *Mórdháil Uisnigh*, and, more broadly speaking, the creator of the province of Mide and the other periodic great assemblies of Ireland. In the case of Tuathal, the first sources were compiled from the 7th century onward.

Tuathal has already been mentioned on several occasions here: the mythical High King was said to rule in the 2nd century CE. He is associated with the doubtful etymologies connecting Mide to a "neck".[11] The idea re-emerged in the 17th century thanks to Keating,[12] who described in detail the appropriation of some parts of Irish provinces by Tuathal so as to create Mide.[13]

In a very detailed account, Keating makes of Tuathal Techtmar not only the creator of Mide but also the founder of the ancient Irish assemblies. The author explains extensively what led the king to establish the periodic gatherings of Tlachtga, Uisneach, Tailtiu and Tara.

Assembly of Tlachtga on Samhain

Keating starts by indicating that, once Mide was created, King Tuathal built a fortress on a hill that lay in a portion of Mide which corresponded to Munster before the new territorial division. The assembly of Tlachtga was to be celebrated at the time of the festival of *Samhain*, at the beginning of November:

> Now, when Tuathal had put these four parts together and made them into one territory called [Mide], he built therein four chief fortresses, that is, a fortress in each of the portions. Accordingly he built Tlachtga in the portion of Munster which goes with [Mide]; and it was there the Fire of Tlachtga was instituted, at which it was their custom to assemble and bring together the druids of Ireland on the eve of *Samhain* to offer sacrifice to all the gods. It was at that fire they used to burn their victims; and it was of obligation under penalty of fine to quench the fires of Ireland on that night, and the men of Ireland were forbidden to kindle fires except from that fire; and for each fire that was kindled from it in Ireland the king of Munster received a tax of a screaball, or three-pence, since the land on which Tlachtga is belongs to the part of Munster given to [Mide].[14]

The author therefore tells us that the assembly of Tlachtga was intimately connected with fire and the sacerdotal world; Keating mentions unspecified sacrifice to unspecified gods and explains that all fires were to be extinguished in Ireland. As a matter of fact, the festival of *Samhain* was – and remains – closely connected with fire. Although the mentions of sacrifices are too vague and isolated to be completely credible, the essence of the assembly of Tlachtga seems to correspond to what we know of the celebration of early November.[15]

The hill where the assembly was held was in all likelihood the hill of Ward, which raises to 90 meters only in the County of Meath, around 50 kilometers east-north-east of Uisneach (~53°37'30"N/6°53'10"W), less than 20 kilometers west of Tara and half a dozen kilometers on the south-west of Tailtiu. Recent excavations ("The Hill of Ward Project", University College Dublin)[16] indicate the presence of a fort – or more specifically several successive forts – on the top of the hill. Today, only the vestiges of a stone enclosure remain; they were originally part of a complex of three enclosures, which partially overlapped and were placed within a much wider enclosure, about 200 meters in diameter.

Convention of Uisneach on Bealtaine

But let us return for now to the narrative depicting the endeavors of Tuathal Techtmar. Keating goes on:

> On the portion he had acquired from the province of Connaught he built the second fortress, namely Uisneach, where a general meeting of the men of Ireland used to be held, which was called the Convention of Uisneach, and it was at *Bealltaine* that this fair took place, at which it was their custom to exchange with one another their goods, their wares, and their valuables. They also used to offer sacrifice to the chief god they adored, who was called Beil; and it was their wont to light two fires in honour of Beil in every district in Ireland, and to drive a weakling of each species of cattle that were in the district between the two fires as a preservative to shield them from all diseases during that year; and it is from that fire that was made in honour of Beil that the name of *Bealltaine* is given to the noble festival on which falls the day of the two Apostles, namely, Philip and James; *Bealltaine*, that is *Beilteine*, or the fire of Beil. The horse and the trappings of every chieftain who came to the great meeting of Uisneach were to be given as a tax to the king of Connaught, as the place in which Uisneach is belongs to the part of the province of Connaught given to [Mide].[17]

Tuathal Techtmar therefore established *Mórdháil Uisnigh*, the convention of Uisneach, six months after the assembly of Tlachtga, on the occasion of the festival of *Bealtaine*, celebrated at the beginning of the month of May of our modern calendar. To some extent, the convention could have taken the form of a fair (*óenach* or *aonach* in Irish) where goods were exchanged and taxes were collected. But it is mainly the mention of sacrifices to a god named Béil or Bel that attract attention: fires were said to have been lit by druids to honor him and the gathering is here presented as closely connected with the sacerdotal world. The fact that Uisneach is identified as belonging to an ancient part of Connacht – "ancient" as in "prior to its incorporation to Mide by Tuathal" – seems to back up that claim, since Connacht was the province of Science, knowledge and, by extension, of erudition and the educated.

Fair of Tailtiu on Lughnasa

The third fortress built by Tuathal bears the name of Tailtiu (or Taillte), and is associated by Keating with Ulster:

It was here the fair of Taillte was held, in which the men of Ireland were wont to form alliances of marriage and friendship with one another. And a most becoming custom was observed in that assembly, namely, the men kept apart by themselves on one side, and the women apart by themselves on the other side, while their fathers and mothers were making the contract between them; and every couple who entered into treaty and contract with one another were married.[18]

Keating tells us later on that this assembly took place on *Lughnasa*, the festival corresponding to the beginning of August in our modern calendar. No mention is made here of druids, kings or even warriors: for Keating, the gathering of Tailtiu was before anything a fair (*óenach/aonach*).[19] The main themes of the assembly – or at least the main theme underlined by the pseudo-historian – were those of exchanges and contracts, which could arguably connect it to the third function, as described by Dumézil. Bernard Sergent briefly outlined the three functions as such:

> The initial discovery [of Dumézil] makes it possible to define, roughly speaking, the *first function* (first, because it is superior to the other two, and is usually cited first in the enumerations) as being that of *sovereignty*, magical and religious power, thought; the *second* is that of muscular and *physical strength*, which applies mainly, but not exclusively, to the concept of war; the *third* function is more multifaceted, it is linked with *fecundity, agriculture, human masses, seduction* in the sense of *reproduction*.[20]

A fair is, by definition, the occasion to exchange goods, notably in an agricultural context. If one follows the aforementioned definition, fairs logically connect with the third function. Additionally, in his description of the fair of Tailtiu, Keating tells us about marriages, established or confirmed at the fair: marriages are but a projection, a natural continuity of the process of seduction[21] and reproduction. This arguably tends to confirm the overall predominance of the third function at the fair of Tailtiu: fecundity and the "human masses" – the people – as opposed to clergy and rulers, which are never alluded to in the description of Keating.

Feast of Tara on Samhain

Finally, Keating identifies the fourth fortress built by Tuathal as that of Tara. An assembly was held every three years only, in the wake of the gathering of Tlachtga, which was but its "prelude". The assemblies of Tlachtga and Tara were therefore held on the occasion of the same festival, *Samhain*. The assembly of Tara is described as a feast:

The fourth royal fortress, Tara, is situated in the part of Leinster given to [Mide], and there the Feis of Tara was held, every third year after the sacrifice had been offered to all the gods at Tlachtga (as we have said) as a prelude to that royal assembly called the Feis of Tara, at which they were wont to institute laws and customs, and to confirm the annals and the records of Ireland, so that the ardollamhs might inscribe all that was approved of them in the Roll of the kings, which was called the Psalter of Tara; and every custom and record that was in Ireland that did not agree with that chief book were not regarded as genuine. [...] I shall only give here the custom that was instituted at the Feis of Tara regarding the placing of the nobles and warriors for meals in the banquet-halls when they met for a feast.[22]

The royal fortress was the setting of a royal assembly: laws, customs, annals and genealogies were discussed at Tara around a banquet where nobles and warriors eat following well-established rules. The predominance of "warriors" and their interests at the feast of Tara – the second function – is beyond question.

Synthesis of the Elements Provided by Keating

The description of Keating could be summarized as follows. According to the historian, Tuathal Techtmar erected four fortresses corresponding to four gatherings. Those four assemblies were celebrated in connection with three of the four seasonal Irish festivals: Tlachtga and Tara at *Samhain* in November, Uisneach at *Bealtaine* in May, and Tailtiu at *Lughnasa* in August. Only *Imbolc*, the festival of early February, is not associated with an assembly by Keating.

The assembly of Uisneach was a convention; the religious aspect prevailed. The fact that Uisneach belonged, according to Keating, to Connacht rather than Mide does connect the hill to the sacerdotal function – as Connacht was supposedly the province of Science, that is, in the broad sense, the knowledge kept by the druids.

The assembly of Tailtiu was a fair; it relied mainly on exchanges and partnerships. The assembly of Tara was a *royal* feast. The nature of the assembly of Tlachtga is not specified – it is neither presented as a fair, nor a feast, nor a convention. However, it is indirectly connected with two other assemblies: Tara, because it was purportedly held on the same day and Uisneach, because of the recurrence of fires, either extinguished or lit.

It is therefore possible to present the Irish assemblies, or rather *Keating's description of the Irish assemblies*, as follows:

	Tlachtga	*Uisneach*	*Tailtiu*	*Tara*
Festival	*Samhain*	*Bealtaine*	*Lughnasa*	*Samhain*
Date	November	May	August	November (every three years)
Salient features	Tributes + Sacrifices + fires extinguished	Tributes + Sacrifices + fires lit	Alliances + Exchanges	Laws, rules, genealogies
Name	–	Convention *Mórdháil Uisnigh*	Fair *Aonach Taillten*	Feast *Feis Teamhrach*
Province mentioned	Munster (south)	Connacht (west)	Ulster[23] (north)	Leinster (east)
Mythical province	Mide (center)			

In Keating's account, Tlachtga is linked with Tara because it was but its pre-lude, its complement and was held at the same time of the year; it was also connected with the convention of Uisneach through its rituals and salient features.

However, the question of the credibility of those assertions and, more generally speaking, the trustworthiness of Keating's arguments remain. As always with the author, it is necessary to take a step back and compare his assertions with older sources. Fortunately, the historian is not the only source – and certainly not the oldest – dealing with this ancient Irish assemblies.

3.3 Mórdháil Uisnigh: Alternative Sources

Most of the alternative sources – that is, alternative to Keating and in most cases anterior to the pseudo-historian – do not mention four but rather three distinct gatherings: the assembly of Tlachtga is usually not mentioned, either deliberately or not. Many scholars tend to present the Irish assemblies as follows[24]:

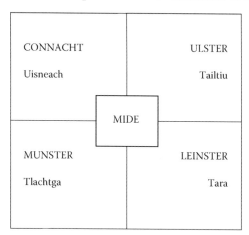

However, most authors fail to mention an important detail: this table describes the vision of Keating, and exclusively that of Keating as the assembly of Tlachtga is absent from the other sources. Additionally, since Keating presents Tlachtga as an introduction to Tara, it would be possible to merge the two bottom rows and obtain a sort of triad of assemblies. Alwyn and Brinley Rees went one step further and speculated a possible north/south divide: according to the authors, the assemblies of the north could represent summer – as the gatherings of Uisneach and Tailtiu were held in May and August – and that of the south, winter – the assemblies of Tara and Tlachtga being held on *Samhain*, which marked the beginning of winter.[25]

Those speculations are interesting but impossible to prove and we should focus on the essential: the sources anterior to the 17th century do not mention Tlachtga and actually favor a triad of assemblies. Better still: Keating himself occasionally fails to refer to Tlachtga.

Irish Ordeals

The *Irish Ordeals*, which go back to the 14th century, confirm the existence of three great assemblies in Ireland and use the three denominations mentioned earlier, i.e. "feast", "fair" and "convention":

> Three preeminent assemblies used to be held at that time, namely the Feast of Tara on Allhallowtide (samhuin) —for that was the Easter of the heathen, and all the men of Erin were at that meeting, helping the king of Erin to hold it—and the Fair of Tailtiu at *Lammas*[26] (im lu[g] nusadh), and the Great Meeting of Uisnech on May Day (a mbeall-taine). Seven years lasted the preparation of the Feast of Tara, and still at the end of seven years then used to be a convention of all the men of Erin at the Feast of Tara, and there they would determine a jubilee, namely, the Rule of Seven Years from one Feast of Tara to another.[27]

The frequency of the assemblies of Tailtiu and Uisneach is not addressed by the author. The feast of Tara is here presented as being held every seven years whereas it said to be annual in at least two other narratives (*The Wasting Sickness of Cúchulainn* or *Serglige Con Culainn*[28] and the *Birth of Aedh Sláine* or *Genemain Aeda Sláne*[29]) and Keating himself believed it was held every three years.[30] The issue is difficult to settle. Most of all, it must be remembered that those sources are mainly mythological or, at best, pseudo-historical: asserting at this point that the Irish assemblies were, from a historical point of view, annual or not would be perfectly out of place. Since the ancient Irish "thought their history in mythical terms",[31] it is necessary to discriminate between historical and mythological considerations, although both make a substantial contribution to our understanding of the matter.

The Book of Rights

The following gloss can be found in the *Book of Rights* (*Lebor na Cert*), redacted in the 14th and 15th centuries:

> The seat of the King of the Oirghialla [is] next the seat of the King of Éire, at Taillte and at Uisneach and at the feast of Samhain [at Teamhair or Tara] and the distance [between them] is such that his sword would reach the hand of the King of Éire.[32]

Oirghialla (or Airgialla) was, together with Ailech and Ulaid, one the three primitive kingdoms of the north of Ireland. The territory of Airgialla spread along a line starting at *Lough Foyle* and reaching the mouth of river Newry; it included the modern counties of Armagh and Monaghan as well as parts of the counties of Louth, Down and Fermanagh.[33] The crucial point from this extract is the joint mention of three assemblies at Tailtiu, Uisneach and Tara: the presence of the King of Ireland and such a prominent king as that of Oirghialla conferred a major importance to the three assemblies. Generally speaking, redactors usually associated Uisneach with the sacerdotal class. However, since the sacerdotal and royal powers were closely connected – notably, in the Celtic tradition, through the figure of the druid – an occasional assimilation of Uisneach to warriors and kings does not contradict this formulation. This connection also appears in a manuscript dating back to the 9th century,[34] which was edited and translated by Myles Dillon in his "Taboos of the Kings of Ireland".

Taboos of the Kings of Ireland

> Séts after his place has been proclaimed [?]
> in Uisneach of mead-rich [Mide]
> in every seventh fair year
> from him to the king of wholesome Uisneach. [...]
> Payment for their seats in Uisneach Mide every seventh year, and upon his accession, is due from each of these kings to the king of [Mide], and the same amount is due from each provincial king in Ireland.[35]

The manuscript indicates that the kings of Ireland therefore had to "purchase" their seat, i.e. their right to rule, on Uisneach every seven years. No assembly or convention is mentioned here; additionally, the seven-year recurrence is unique in the case of the gathering of Uisneach: as often, the sources are quite contradictory. Another example taken from the *Book of Rights* is very much along the same lines: it features the only reference to a potential assembly of Uisneach on Easter – not *Bealtaine* – together with explicit mentions of Tara and Tailtiu.

> Those are the severe tabus of the high king
> of the province of the Branch-red House;
> if he be used to do those things,
> he will never succeed to Tara.
> Among the lucky things of the great king
> of Ulaid are to spend Easter at Caendruim,
> to have his stewards in Tailtiu of the triple rampart,
> and that Emain shall harbour his daughters.[36]

This passage is difficult to interpret on a number of counts. The visit of a king to Caendruim – another name[37] of Uisneach, as already pointed out – on Easter is here presented on a positive light but the very mention of the Christian festival is surprising. It could be argued that this was an attempt at Christianizing the festival of *Bealtaine* as the dates and symbols inherent to both celebrations were quite compatible.[38] However, although Caendruim is Uisneach, the name in itself also reminds of Tara, called *Druim cain* in the *Dindshenchas*: this obviously does not make things any simpler. Though not surprising, Tara and Uisneach have "opposite" – perhaps complementary – alternative names: the two hills are quite definitely the "two kidneys in a beast"[39] to borrow the words of *The Settling of the Manor of Tara*. Additionally, the inclusion of Tara and Uisneach in the "Tailtiu/Tara/Uisneach" triad of assemblies confirms, once again, the bonds uniting the two hills.

Contradictions of Keating

This triad of assemblies can also be found in the writings of Keating. Although the historian commonly mentions the existence of four distinct assemblies, another extract from his *History of Ireland* may seem surprising:

> The following are the other conditions which Fionn son of Cumhall attached to the degrees in bravery which each one was bound to obtain before being received into the Fian. The first condition: no man was received into the Fian or the great Assembly of Uisneach, or the Fair of Taillte, or the Feis of Tara, until his father and mother and clan and relatives gave guarantees that they would never demand any retribution from anyone for his death, so that he might look to no one to avenge him but to himself.[40]

How to account for the absence of the fourth gathering, that of Tlachtga? Here, the Irish assemblies also appear quite dangerous and, once again, the question of the historicity of Keating's assertions arises: were the three assemblies of Tailtiu, Tara and Uisneach so perilous that anyone taking part in them had to prove that their family would not avenge their death? No other account seems to corroborate that claim, at least in early Irish literature.

In order to address those issues, we must first consider that, in this extract, Keating does not put forth general truths: this passage is supposed to be an account of the life of Finn and his tribe. Although the work of Keating is a *"History" of Ireland*, it is quite clear that we are here dealing with mythology disguised in history. It also appears that the historian was in fact inspired by a text entitled *The Enumeration of Finn's People (Airem muintri Finn)*,[41] first transcribed in the 12th century.[42]

3.4 Mythological Aspects of Mórdháil Uisnigh

The Enumeration of Finn's People

The author of *The Enumeration of Finn's People* remains unknown. The document describes the tribe of Finn (or Fionn), its members, its power, its initiatory rituals and traditions. Fionn mac Cumhaill is the main hero of the Fenian Cycle. Much in the same manner as the other great hero of ancient Ireland, Cúchulainn, there is no doubt that he was a mythological, and by no means historical character. The analogy with Keating's version is striking:

> Of such not a man was taken into the Fianna; nor admitted whether to the great Gathering of Usnach, to the convention of Taillte, or to Tara's Feast; until both his paternal and his maternal correlatives, his tuatha and kindreds, had given securities for them to the effect that, though at the present instant they were slain, yet should no claim be urged in lieu of them: and this in order that to none other but to themselves alone they should look to avenge them.[43]

There is little doubt that Keating drew his inspiration from this text – or conceivably an unknown auxiliary version of the manuscript, now missing.

Unfortunately, *The Enumeration of Finn's People* also fails to explain this interdiction applying to the members of the tribe of Finn. Perhaps it was dictated by a will to soothe flared tempers or to quell fears: those general meetings were supposedly highly political; gathering rival tribes – and potentially quick-tempered leaders – was perhaps considered risky. This is, of course, mere conjecture as, once again, those texts cannot be considered as historical accounts. Noting that a 12th-century document mentions the three great Irish assemblies is already significant enough. It is possible to go back even further in time as the three Irish assemblies are referred to in several other medieval manuscripts. Once again, the mythological nature of those manuscripts is beyond doubt: this implies that no conclusion regarding the historicity of the assemblies can be drawn from their study. Perhaps the most interesting trait of those documents is the association of the assembly of Uisneach with the death of Lugh and arguably his symbolic birth.

The Fate of the Children of Tuireann

This extract from *The Fate* or *the Tragedy of the Children/Sons of Tuireann* (*Oidheadh Chloinne Tuireann*) has already been quoted *supra:*

> At this time the Fair Assembly was held by the King of Érinn on Balar's Hill, which is now called Uisneach. And the [Fomoire] had not been long assembled there before they saw the array of a goodly army coming over the plain from the east towards them.[44]

The face of Lugh is "as bright as the sun on a dry summer's day": the god, here presented as the leader of the group, has a face shining so much that it is blinding. On two occasions, the text associates Uisneach to two other places where great assemblies were held:

> Pity your journey from Tara,
> And from Tailltin of the pleasant plains,
> And from great Uisneach of [Mide];
> There is not an event more pitiful.[45]

> Hold upon thy Brest and upon thy shoulder
> These heads, thou manly champion,
> That we may from off the water see
> Uisneach, Tailltin, and Tara.[46]

A connection with the site of the potential fourth assembly, Tlachtga, is even perceptible:

> Ath Cliath, and the smooth Brugh with thee,
> Freamhainn, Tlachtga along with them,
> The Plain of Lifé [Liffey], the dewy Magh Breagh
> And the mountains around the fair green of Tailltin.[47]

The question of the actual value and significance of this fourth assembly remains. Here, Tlachtga is simply coupled with a mention of Tara. This is coherent if one accepts Keating's interpretation, which implied that the assemblies of Tlachtga and Tara were connected, with the first standing as an introduction to the latter.

However, the text called *The Fate of the Children of Tuireann* poses a problem: it can only be found in fairly recent documents, dating from the 18th and 19th centuries, even though this claim must be qualified:

> The language used is modern Irish [...] but it is obvious that the transcription was coupled with a modernization of the text, if one considers the numerous archaisms, almost all of whom date back to

middle-Irish. This stands as a typical example of a very late transmission of an ancient narrative.[48]

Be it as it may, no document prior to Keating and the 17th century confirms the connection between *four* potential assemblies or even four places associated with four assemblies.

Thus, *The Colloquy with the Ancients*, dating back to the 12th century – just like *The Enumeration of Finn's People* – only seems to acknowledge Tara, Uisneach and Tailtiiu. The clothing prescriptions here detailed are unique:

> Special and gorgeously-coloured apparel it was that men practiced to take into the gathering of Taillte, into the great convention of Usnach, to the Feast of Tara; and none cared for raiment other than such as those women had made.

The famous *Dindshenchas*, whose first recension also dates back to the 12th century, also confirms the existence of only three assemblies: Tara, Uisneach and Tailtiu.

The Dindshenchas

Many assemblies and gatherings are cited in the *Dindshenchas* but never Tlachtga's, although the *place* is mentioned on several occasions.[49] Furthermore, the assemblies of Tara, Uisneach and Tailtiu are alluded to several times: they are presented as key federative events. To that extent, Tara and Tailtiu are called "land[s] of assembly"[50] and are mentioned first in a long list of place-names. Similarly, the gathering of Tailtiu is described in great detail.[51]

The *Dindshenchas* mentions a gathering in connection with Uisneach twice. The assembly is first associated with the start of a short epic – or "kingly adventure", to quote from the text – where the protagonist visits several mythological places and bring back treasures from them:

> Well I fared on a glorious adventure
> from the assembly in [...] cold Usnech;[52]
> much sea and much land were traversed
> by the king's son, on that gallant journey.[53]

The hero notably brought back "the shirt of fierce Lugh",[54] which, from a mythological perspective, is a particularly glorious find.

The second extract mentioning an assembly at Uisneach in the *Dindshenchas* is also connected to Lugh. The death of the god took place during a "great meeting" on Uisneach:

> A great meeting was held at [Uisneach] between the three sons of
> Cermait, the Dagda's son, and [Lugh], to make peace with him in
> regard to their father Cermait, whom he had slain.[55]

In this passage, already quoted *supra*, the assembly is presented as an occasion to establish peace between the several gods attending, which confirms
the sacred nature of the hill and of the gatherings that were supposedly held
on it. Better yet, the allusion to peacemaking represents a form of *mediation*,
from Latin *medius*, "middle". The term is, in itself, appropriate as it is quite
representative of the idea one might have of the hill "in the middle". Here,
this "mediation", this peacemaking, is jeopardized by the plot conceived by
the grand-sons of the Dagda: they want to take advantage of the occasion to
avenge the death of their father Cermait, killed by the hand of Lugh. Lugh,
the supreme god, is therefore slain on Uisneach, during the convention of
Uisneach: he is drowned in the lake bearing his name.

In both cases, the assembly convened on Uisneach is but the stage for the
mythological play unfolding – or starting – there. Unfortunately, the stage
itself is not well-documented, to say the least. The description of what was
supposed to be a great annual event is not even laconic: it is virtually non-
existent. Fortunately, other mythological texts are not as short on detail. In
that vein, the richest and most complete document perhaps remains *The
Death of Diarmait/Dermot*, usually dated between the 15th and 17th
centuries.[56]

The Death of Diarmait

The character of Diarmait is quite well-known: the king, who supposedly
ruled in the 6th century, founded the southern Uí Néill dynasty and his
mythological and pseudo-historical importance is beyond doubt. As a King
of Uisneach, his connection with the hill is also evident. The story of the
Death of Diarmait tells of his arrival to power, his hegemony over Ireland
("[his] tribute, and discipline, and law prevailed in Ireland generally"),[57]
and his death. It is structured around the three Irish assemblies: first, that of
Uisneach, then Tailtiu and finally Tara. Diarmait is presented in an extremely favorable light, which is reminiscent of the many political manip-
ulations in favor of the southern Uí Néill mentioned earlier:

> For a long period Dermot reigned in Ireland; neither came there in
> those times a king that was grander, that was more revered, or that in
> figure and in face, in wisdom, in speech, in royal rule, was more
> excellent than he.[58]

At the beginning of the story, Tuathal Máelgarb is said to reign all over
Ireland: Tuathal Máelgarb – which should not be confused with Tuathal
Techtmar, the alleged creator of the province of Mide and the great

assemblies – was said to be a king of Tara in the 6th century. He was most of all a member of the *Cenél Coirpri*, a tribe dissenting from the southern Uí Néill.[59] This may explain why it is claimed, in the very beginning of the text, that Diarmait would become king by the will of God:[60] once again, the idea is obviously to establish the supremacy of the southern Uí Néill over its rivals.

Once in power, Diarmait made a point to hold the great Irish assemblies, first and foremost that of Uisneach on the festival of *Bealtaine*:

> By Dermot and by the men of Ireland the great congregation of Usnach is held now at *Bealtaine*; for at that time Ireland's three high gatherings were these: the congregation of Usnach, at *Bealtaine*; the convention of Tailite, at Lammas; the feast of Tara, at *Samhain*; and whosoever of the men of Ireland should have transgressed these, the same [I say] that should have violated this their ordinance, was guilty of death.[61]

The connection between the three assemblies is confirmed. Later, an episode is set during the assembly of Tailtiu at the time of the festival of *Lughnasa* (identified as *Lammas-tide*)[62] and Diarmait holds the feast of Tara.[63] The symbolic weight of the three assemblies is considerable: "transgressing" their rules amounted to being "guilty of death", even if the exact meaning of such a transgression and the reasons for such severity are not elucidated by the author. Rather, he chooses to elaborate on another episode, which is just as valuable:

> The [king and cleric], repaired to Uisneach, joined the congregation of the men of Erin and there they were for a fortnight. In which meeting a mighty thirst [i.e. drought] afflicted them; so that their human were in strait peril, and their four-footed perished largely. Then they had recourse to Kieran, to find them succour. Kieran made prayer, and there came then a wet [i.e. Rain] that in token of the miracle left twelve main streams in Ireland.[64]

Kieran, a cleric whose powers recall those of the druids, therefore creates "twelve main streams in Ireland" from Uisneach so as to quench the thirst of men and beasts. The episode appears in another legend which had been transcribed centuries before.

The Legend of Mongan

The Legend of Mongan actually refers to a group of five texts, including *The Cause of Mongán's Frenzy* (*Tucait baili Mongáin*). The manuscript is usually dated to the 12th century but some scholars believe the most ancient versions goes back as far as the 9th or possibly the 7th century.[65] As noted by Roseanne Schot, this dating would make it the oldest available reference to the assemblies in Ireland and one of the first to insist on the central aspect of the hill of Uisneach, in Mide. The text is here reproduced in its entirety:

Findtigernd, Mongán's wife, besought Mongán to tell her the simple truth of his adventures. He asked of her a respite of seven years. It was granted. Then that period arrived. The men of Ireland had a great gathering at Usnech in Meath, the year of the death of Ciaráen, the son of the carpenter, and of the slaying of Túathal Maelgarb, and of the taking of the kingship by Diarmait. The hosts were on (the hill of) Usnech. A great hail-storm came upon them there. Such was its greatness that the one shower left twelve chief streams in Ireland for ever [/from then until Judgement Day]. Mongán with seven men arose and went from the cairn aside, and his queen and his shanachie [reciter of lore] Cairthide, son of Marcán. Then they saw something, a prominent stronghold with a frontage of ancient trees. They go to it. They went into the enclosure. They go into a marvelous house there. A covering of bronze was on the house, a pleasant bower over its windows. Seven conspicuous men were there. Within the house there was a marvelous spread of quilts and covers, and of wonderful jewels. Seven vats of wine there were. He became intoxicated. It was then and there that Mongán sang the "Frenzy" to his wife, since he had promised he would tell her something of his adventures. It seemed to them it was not very long they were in that house. They deemed it to be no more but one night. However, they were there a full year. When they awoke, they saw it was Rathmore of Moy-Linny in which they were.[66]

Let us go over the main elements shedding light on the importance of Uisneach. A great assembly of the men of Ireland on Uisneach is attested: the hill is explicitly mentioned and the direct reference to the province of Mide confirms the symbolic centrality of the place. Just as in *The Death of Diarmait*, the episode is set at a period where Diarmait took power from the hands of Tuathal Máelgarb. However, it is clear that the tone of this excerpt is much more neutral. Diarmait is not presented as necessarily good or great of a king, the character of Kieran is not truly a part of the story and there is no mention of royal power bestowed by divine grace. The magic of Kieran is here replaced by unleashed forces of nature: the 12 rivers of Ireland were created by a "great hail-shower" and the streams were supposed to last forever or "until Judgment Day".[67]

The precision regarding the number "12" is equivocal. It could either be a Pagan reference and suggest a connection with Celtic triplism – increased fourfold – or echo Christian references, for example the 12 Apostles. The mention of "12" is confirmed in *The Death of Diarmait*, which is posterior to *The Cause of Mongán's Frenzy* and is just as Christianized. On the other hand, an episode of the *Dindshenchas* similar in many respects only mentions five original streams. The author who had connected the name of Loch Lugh/Lugborta – the lake of Uisneach – to the death of Lugh has another interpretation to offer:

LOCH LUGBORTA [...]

[2] Or else the lake was named after Lugaid mac Táil, who was called Delbaeth. For that territory was the place that Delbaeth mac Táil took possession of, when he came northwards out of Munster with his five sons, after being warned by his own daughter to give up his land to her and her husband, Trad mac Tassaig. Then Delbaeth lit a magic fire, and five streams burst forth from it; and he set one of his sons to watch each of the streams [...] He himself stayed at that spot, and it may be from him that the lake and the place had their name, Loch Lugborta, for till then his name was Lugaid, but thenceforth Delbaeth, that is Dolb-aed, from the enchanted fire.[68]

The mention of a number – whether 5 of 12 – is of course symbolic. Geographically speaking, the 5 or 12 largest rivers of Ireland are not substantially different from the ones immediately following them in any classification, be it by size, length or flow. In the case of the *Dindshenchas*, the five streams seem to echo the five provinces of Ireland, which is possibly a sign that this version is more ancient.

Another major difference between those various extracts must be highlighted. The rivers materialize thanks to a prayer in *The Death of Diarmait* and are the consequence of a hail-storm in *The Cause of Mongán's Frenzy*. But it is the magic (druidic?) power of fire that creates the five rivers of the *Dindshenchas*. Although it is difficult to tell, this detail might indicate the degree of Christianization of each of those texts – *The Death of Diarmait* probably being the most Christianized and the *Dindshenchas* the most ostensibly Pagan.

In the *Dindshenchas*, the mention of a magic fire on Uisneach is somewhat reminiscent of the episode of the fire of the Nemedian druid Midhe and the combination of the themes of fire and water recalls the character of Balor, grand-father of Lugh.

The Cause of Mongán's Frenzy ends with the arrival of the protagonists in a "prominent stronghold with a frontage of ancient trees" in which they spend a year "out of time", placed under the sign of transcendence: the protagonist quite literally get out of the tangible world. This dwelling has already been mentioned *supra* and a possible analogy with the house of the Dagda, although still debatable, is at least intriguing, if hardly definite.

Generally speaking, it is clear that all those accounts mentioning an assembly of Uisneach are not historical, or at least cannot be interpreted as such today. All the episodes are steeped in mysticism: the notions of primordial waters, magic fire, symbolic center and transcending proclamation of sovereignty succeed to one another and combine, to the point that the reality of the convention of Uisneach becomes quite questionable. Some scholars even believed it has never existed, in historical terms at least.

3.5 Historicity of Mórdháil Uisnigh

As Viewed by D.A. Binchy

In the end, we must acknowledge that most sources that mention the assembly of Uisneach are either extremely laconic, untrustworthy (the *Irish Ordeals*, the gloss of the *Book of Rights*), or infused with mythological references. The description made by Geoffrey Keating is unique in its eloquence and precision. For instance, no document anterior to the 17th century corroborates the fact that two fires were lit at the convention of Uisneach and that sick people or animals were passed through them for protection. The fact that those fires were lit in honor of a hypothetical god call Bel seem even less substantiated – not to mention ritual sacrifices to this allegedly supreme god of whom somehow nothing is known.[69]

Actually, not even the least exotic elements that are mentioned by Keating in connection with the conversion of Uisneach – the exchange of goods and valuables, taxes paid to a king of Connacht whose authority over Uisneach remains to be established – are actually mentioned by more ancient authors in such a specific and transparent manner.

This lack of sources anterior to the time of Keating led some scholars to reject the very existence of the convention of Uisneach. The article of D.A. Binchy entitled *The Fair of Tailtiu and the Feast of Tara*,[70] is notorious. His main argument was that, except for Keating and the mythological texts, no credible element confirms the historical existence of the convention.[71] Binchy believed that *Mórdháil Uisnigh* was a late invention of pseudo-historians "in quest for a third item to set beside the Fair of Tailtiu and the Feast of Tara". In his opinion, it was first presented as a religious gathering because of the "aura of ancient sanctity", which persisted around Uisneach and was later "expanded into a commercial mart, possibly by Keating himself".[72]

Although Binchy's arguments are reasonable, his conclusion is rather dubious: in his own words, the assembly "can be quickly disposed of".[73] He suggests that because the convention of Uisneach is not confirmed from a historical perspective in early Irish literature, studying or investigating it would be pointless. This view is indefensible for a variety of reasons.

The convention of Uisneach, as described by Keating, is precious because, even if its historicity is unconfirmed, it sheds light on Irish myths and possibly the ancient Irish conception of the world. His writings must be mentioned and analyzed – provided that their substance and interest are understood – precisely because the pseudo-historian inscribed himself in a tradition of "mediators of myths".[74] Le Roux and Guyonvarc'h go one step further: they reject the term of "pseudo-historian" and make of Keating a full-fledged *fili*, an Irish poet whose role was to transmit ancient knowledge. This idea seems consistent with what is known of his character and his writings.

Furthermore, ignoring the convention of Uisneach is unacceptable from a methodological perspective. History and myth are intimately bonded: humans produce myths and legends in a historical context that is their own. Understanding their myths and legends sheds light on their time and potentially their lifestyle.

> [There is something] that D. Binchy did not even began to consider precisely because it was unconceivable from his perspective: he never contemplated the idea that the mythical facts of medieval Ireland might be the echoes of the religious, political and social organization of pre-Christian Ireland.[75]

The argumentation of Binchy is flawless and deserves recognition: it is indeed impossible to confirm that the convention of Uisneach was a historical event, at any given point of history, which is quite noteworthy. However, the importance given to the convention in insular mythology is noteworthy in itself. It implicates almost inevitably the "religious, political and social organization of pre-Christian Ireland" or, perhaps more cautiously, in the Ireland of the Early Middle Ages. Everything is history and everything leads to history: this includes myths, which are the product of individuals framed in their own historical context and civilization.

Finally, although it is impossible to confirm the reality of *Mórdháil Uisnigh*, the hypothesis of an actual – in the sense of "historical" – assembly on the hill at one point in time or the other is still quite appealing. As noted by Roseanne Schot:

> While the lack of any historical references to an assembly having taken place at Uisneach prior to the twelfth century[76] might well be of relevance, it is worth recalling that [...] such events are rarely mentioned in the early medieval annals [apart from *Óenach Tailten*, the pre-eminent assembly in early Ireland presided over by the king of Tara at Lugnasad].[77]

Of course, this simply means that the holding of a convention of Uisneach was not an *impossibility*, which is a first step. It is conceivable to go further and mention three convincing reasons that quite plausibly make the convention a historical *possibility*.

First, apparently similar cases of an assembly "at the center" can be found outside of Ireland, especially in the areas influenced by the Celtic culture. Second, the convention as described by Keating is highly compatible with what is known of the mythology connected to the hill and, most of all, to the tradition of the festival of *Bealtaine*, supposedly the "fixed period of the year"[78] when the assembly was held. Finally, the archaeological finds could corroborate a number of specific points mentioned in the *History of Ireland* as regards the convention.

The last two points deserves in-depth study: each will be addressed separately in the next two chapters. Let us dwell for now on comparative analysis: some similarities with the convention of Uisneach can be found among other Celtic nations. Brittany, Wales, the Isle of Man, Scotland and even England provide interesting examples.

3.6 Similarities Outside of Ireland

England: Killaraus/Stonehenge

Geoffrey of Monmouth connected Killaraus/Stonehenge to Killare/Uisneach and did allude to a general assembly. The extract quoted *supra*[79] mentions messengers fetching members of the clergy in "all parts of Britain" and the holding of a "general meeting": Aurelius gathered the clergy and crowned himself king in front of all people. Many themes developed in this passage recall the assembly of Uisneach: the term "general meeting" is also the one used by Keating to describe the Irish convention; the symbolic and mytho-logical prevalence of the sacerdotal class at Uisneach is also beyond doubt, especially whenever the assembly is mentioned. Even the crowning of Aurelius in itself reminds us of the Irish hill: we remember the long list of Kings of Uisneach and the possible importance of the "crowning at the center" in Indo-European cultures even though, in Irish mythology and pseudo-history, this royal center is often placed at Tara rather than Uisneach.

Geoffrey of Monmouth never clearly indicated that Killaraus/Stonehenge might have been at the center of any geographical expanse or territory: gathering the members of a community at a specific point does not ne-cessarily mean this point is the "center" of the said community. However, the assembly clearly took place inside the "Giant's Dance", the stone circle of Stonehenge. In other words, the gathering was supposedly held within the circle of stone, i.e. at its *center*.[80] Finally, as mentioned before, placing the gathering at the Pentecost could reflect a much older tradition: the Irish festival of *Bealtaine*, in early May, was the date chosen for the holding of *Mórdháil Uisnigh* and was intimately connected with the druidic tradition – as, according to Keating at least, the druids allegedly made sacrifices to the hypothetical god Bel during the convention.

Julius Caesar himself tells us that the druids "are engaged in things sacred, conduct the public and the private sacrifices, and interpret all matters of religion".[81] The Roman leader is even more specific:

> [The Druids] assemble at a fixed period of the year in a consecrated place in the territories of the Carnutes, which is reckoned the central region of the whole of Gaul. Hither all, who have disputes, assemble from every part, and submit to their decrees and determinations. This institution is supposed to have been devised in Britain, and to have been brought over from it into Gaul; and now those who desire to gain a more accurate knowledge of that system generally proceed thither for the purpose of studying it.[82]

Gaul: Locus Consecratus *of the Carnutes*

This famous *Locus Consecratus*, the "consecrated place" has never been precisely identified. Because it belonged to the territories of the Carnutes, it may have corresponded to the approximate geographical center of "Gaul", perhaps of "Gallia Celtica" or any other territory or territories which considered themselves as part of a unified nation – which is of course extremely hard to tell in the case of pre-Romanized Gaul(s).[83]

Unfortunately, the "fixed period of the year" is similarly shrouded in mystery. According to Caesar, the meeting was sacerdotal before anything and held in a place where druids submitted people "to their decrees and determinations". We know that the convention of Uisneach was, like the other Irish assemblies, supposed to be held on a "fixed" date, i.e. the festival of *Bealtaine*, and was associated with the power of the druids: this introduces a veneer of similarity. Although the documents connecting *Mórdháil Uisnigh* to the sacerdotal world do not particularly underline the role as "judges" of the druids, it is, however, one of their attributes and we remember that one of the etymologies proposed for *Ail na Mireann* is "the rock of judgments". In Keating's account, rather than stressing the notion of judgment, the emphasis is laid on their knowledge of rituals, notably sacrifices, and their connection with the royal power, mainly when they proclaim the sovereignty of such or the other figure. Those two ideas – proclamation and judgment – are not dissimilar: they make the symbolism of the convention of Uisneach and that of the sacerdotal assembly of the Carnutes at least conceptually compatible.

Finally, the idea of a "consecrated place" recalls of the concept of a place "out of the world", which is so evident for Uisneach as for the other potential *Axis mundi* and *omphalos*: it brings us, once again, to the world of the sacred and the sacerdotal class.

For the Gauls, the concept of a "sanctuarized" center seems to have existed. Jean-Louis Brunaux even tells us that one of the most "common names[84] in the Celtic world was *Mediolanum*, which literally means 'the plain of the middle', in other words the central place of meeting" and could be the origin of a great deal of toponyms today.[85] The term *Mediolanon* is sometimes translated as "full-center":

> This "full-center", often situated high up and in a fringe location, is a term of religious geography that Xavier Delamarre connects to *medio-gardaz, "the enclosure of the middle" of the Germanic peoples, cf. v. norr. miôgarô, got. midjun-gards, intermediate "world" or place between the world above and the world below.[86]

Furthermore, the very notion of central sanctuary can be found in the Gaulish word *Medionemeton*,[87] literally the "sanctuary of the middle". Incidentally, this term could be derived from *Mediolanon* but also

Mediomatrici, i.e. "those who come from *medio-materes*", the "mothers of the world of the Middle", that is "situated between the world above (*Albio-*) and the world below (*Dubno-*).[88]

Jean-Paul Savignac tells us that the sources and rivers of Gaul "were the focus of a cult of 'Mothers'. They were very popular deities and gave their name, *Matrona*, the [divine] Mother"[89] to a great deal of streams and of course to the *Mediomatrici* – those who live "between Mothers" or "between Worlds". In 1915, Joseph Loth already connected the word *Medionemeton* to the Irish "Mide".[90]

This is all quite close and similar to what we know of Uisneach, in Mide: the sacred Irish center situated "between worlds" was, according to some mythological texts, the sources of the main rivers of Ireland and its association with female deities has been demonstrated. Although this does not definitely confirm that the (alleged!) supreme druidic assembly in the forest of the Carnutes was similar to the (alleged!) convention of Uisneach, the number of coincidences does add up and seems to connect the Irish and Gaulish areas and, by extension, the Celtic world as a whole.

As noted by Loth, *Medionemeton* could relate to old Irish "Mide". But Savignac tells us about another connection: old Breton "med". The existence of a Breton *omphalos* comparable to the Irish *omphalos* could strengthen the hypothesis of a central sanctuary and potentially a sacerdotal general assembly in Gaul: to that extent, the stone of Kermaria is perhaps the best candidate.

Brittany: Kermaria

Today, the stone of Kermaria, also called the baetyl or baetylus of Kermaria, is preserved at the National Archaeological Museum of Saint-Germain-en-Laye, next to Paris. It was discovered in 1897[91] in the south of Finistère, near Pont-l'Abbé[92] and could date back to Iron-Age Armorica, perhaps more precisely the 4th or even 5th century BCE.[93] Kermaria is a "complete truncated pyramidal cone":[94] the stone is composed of four rectangular faces, its edges are rounded and its top flattened.[95] It stands at 83 centimeters in height and the four faces are engraved on their upper surface. Most of the research that has been conducted on Kermaria so far relate to archaeological studies. Some scholars noted correspondences with a potential *omphalos* and the comparison is indeed appealing. The description found in a paper published in 2003 is rather persuasive:

> Kermaria, the famous stele of Pont-l'Abbé has a pyramidal shape [...]; its baseplate is smooth and stands above a frieze of chained S or "cresting waves". The four faces are adorned with four square panes, engraved with various motifs and topped with meanders; there is a cross engraved on its rounded top.[96]

The cross engraved on the top is X-shaped: it remains difficult to interpret, although its simplicity and lack of embellishment or adornment implies that it probably was not engraved for the sole purpose of ornamentation. The cross could either denote the sacredness of the stone – the sacred top being held by the four sides of the *omphalos* stone – or a desire to divide the stone in four parts corresponding to the four sides. The symbols that can be found on the four visible faces of Kermaria are highly symbolic indeed. Thus:

-on side 1: a swastika,

-on side 2: a mirror composition of two related motifs made from a Saint-Andrew's cross *pattée* or a square the sides of which are cut out in the shape of a semi-circle or a V,

-on side 3: 4 mistletoe leaves or tears

-and on side 4: a "windmill sails" or blade motif.[97]

The authors of the paper tell us that those motifs were quite common in Europe, especially "at the end of the first Iron Age or the beginning of the Second" and were found "on various media but always on exceptional objects, both in terms of symbolism and richness of ornamentation",[98] for instance on vases, weapons, outfits or statues. Their conclusion is that those motifs had "a very strong symbolic dimension" and hypothesize that they were "used only for the decoration of objects or costumes belonging to the elite, of which they were one of the markers, perhaps the emblems".[99]

The possible presence of mistletoe leaves may denote a connection with the Celtic sacerdotal class, as suggested by a famous, albeit controversial, quote from Pliny the Elder.[100] The recurrence of the number four in the motifs of the stone of Kermaria are perhaps even more intriguing: we can find symbols with four branches (swastika and quadruple motif)[101] on sides 1 and 2, four leaves or tears on side 3, a "windmill sail" motif (which is actually composed of four contiguous squares in which the diagonal was traced) on side 4; but also four sides in all, placed under a top on which a cross was engraved, dividing the said top in four sections. This all could conform to a desire to divide the world in four parts, each represented by one side of the stele and perhaps symbolically placed under the top of the stone, its pinnacle and center – above and "beyond" the four sides.

The division in a "quaternary rhythm, both in conception and orna-mental composition" has been observed before:

In addition to its pyramidal form and its rounded angles, the rhythm is [marked] by the presence of the cross engraved on top of the stone, at the "symbolic junction of the two great orthogonal axes around which the universe was supposed to be structured".[102]

Kermaria does look like an *omphalos*, perhaps even a sacred stone of division that implied the establishment of center evolving around four distinct parts. The "cresting waves" that can be found at the bases of each side are also worth noting and may substantiate that claim. It is, of course, possible to consider them as mere artistic ornamentation. However, they could also be interpreted as referring to the ocean, perhaps the Otherworld, which was often believed to be "beyond the sea" in Ireland and other Celtic cultures.[103] For Loth, the cresting waves of Kermaria could even relate to snakes and remind of the serpents of Delphi.[104] Although the interpretations of Loth can sometimes be a little outdated, this hypothesis is quite appealing: the *omphalos* of Delphi was perhaps the most distinctive and renowned of the Western world. It is tempting to connect Delphi with Uisneach and potentially with Kermaria: the monumental work carried out by Bernard Sergent regarding the connection between the Greeks and the Celts allows us to envisage analogies between the two civilizations.[105]

Loth was the first scholar who tried to establish a possible connection between Uisneach – which, oddly enough, he sometimes calls "Ushriagh Hill" – Delphi and Kermaria.[106] He also noticed a potential correspondence with the stone of Turoe, today in Co. Galway, whose conception was also quadripartite. This latter comparison was later revived by several authors but did not prove fruitful, notably because of the lack of information as regards the stone of Turoe but also because the stones of Kermaria and Turoe "have not a single decorative motif in common".[107]

However, the elements connecting the stone of Kermaria with the notions of *omphalos* and that of "division" are numerous and the comparison with Uisneach is tempting. Unfortunately, without any historical context – or even a geographical one, as the stone may have been displaced before its discovery – it is impossible to back up this theory. Furthermore, it is evidently impossible to claim that any assembly, ritual or not, was held around the Breton stone. Hopefully, some other examples from the Celtic world are more convincing.

The potential candidates to being the *omphalos* of the different Celtic nations are numerous. It will of course not be relevant here to make an inventory of "Celtic" stone circles or standing stones: first, it must be remembered that stone circles and standing stones are not originally Celtic; rather, their erection predates the Celts, who later incorporated them into their own set of traditions. Second, and perhaps more importantly, a standing or pseudo-phallic stone or a stone circle does not necessarily imply the idea of a center or "navel" of the world. Finally, Uisneach is not famous and relevant only because of the presence of a stone: it is also a hill, which is essential, and its symbolism was probably connected to both the concept of *omphalos* and that of *Axis mundi*.

If the field of investigation is limited to hills or mountains whose importance or "centrality" is attested in ancient traditions and which included one or several stones or monuments, the list of candidates becomes much more exclusive. Additionally, Uisneach was connected to a specific time of the year, i.e. the month of May, perhaps spring or summer in general: by adding the parameter of "temporality", the places that are potentially comparable to the Irish hill in the insular Celtic world can be counted on the fingers of one hand.

Isle of Man: Tynwald

In the case of the Isle of Man, one could think, like Alwyn and Brinley Rees before us, of Tynwald Hill. Strictly speaking, Tynwald is not a hill: it is but a four-meter-high mound, which was apparently built using earth taken from the different parishes of the island. From its top, judgments have been made and laws have been created from "time immemorial": the Manx parliament still bears the name of Tynwald and claims to be the oldest parliamentary body in the world, uninterrupted for a thousand years. The statement is more mythical than historical. The oldest mention of judgment on Tynwald dates back to the early 15th century.[108] A mention of a gathering "of all men of Man" at Tynwald so as to establish peace can be found, however, in the *Chronicles of Man*, dated to the 13th or 14th century.[109] The most common theory attributes the creation of the mound to Vikings, between the 10th and 13th centuries. Some scholars have argued that the sacredness of the place could date back to the Bronze Age or even the Neolithic period.[110] Finally, the name "Tynwald" may mean "place of assembly" or "local assembly". To that extent, it could be comparable to the many Thingwall, Dingwall or Tingwall that can be found in Scotland for instance and that may be as many *Mediolana*.[111]

Alwyn and Brinley Rees chose to compare Tynwald with Tara: the Irish hill was indeed commonly associated with judgments and laws in ancient Ireland.[112] However, we must bear in mind that the assembly of the Carnutes supposedly took place at the "consecrated place" at the center of Gaul – or of an unidentified Gallic territory – where controversies and disagreements were settled by the druids. Similarly, the etymologies connecting *Ail na Mireann* to a "rock of judgment" may once again constitute an interesting argument. The fact that the mound of Tynwald was erected with soil coming from the four corners of the island does associate it with the idea of centrality, especially as tradition tells us that it was built as close to the center of the island as possible.[113] Finally, the existence of two May fairs (on 1 and 18 May) that find their counterpart on 1 and 18 November seem to confirm the inscription of the mound of Tynwald[114] in the Celtic calendar tradition, i.e. the festivals of *Bealtaine* and *Samhain*, as early as the 18th century at least. One fair held in May next to Tynwald could not have proved sufficient to establish such a connection; as will be demonstrated later, May fairs were extremely numerous in Europe and were not necessarily connected with the Celtic tradition. On the other hand, the fact that the fair held in May was repeated six months later, in November, tends to inscribe the tradition into the Celtic year, as *Bealtaine* and *Samhain* were its two most significant festivals. Those fairs remind us of the description of *Mórdháil Uisnigh* made by Keating, who explained that the convention was also a fair where "it was their custom to exchange with one another their goods, their wares, and their valuables".[115] Of course, the account of Keating is doubtful and unique, which remains problematic.

Although, the sources are occasionally deficient – either because they are unreliable or because they are too scarce – relating Tynwald with Uisneach seems appropriate: the numerous points of comparison raise questions and arguably constitute a solid foundation for further study, provided that new evidence comes to light.

Scotland: Arthur's Seat?

As regards Scotland, things are further complicated by the great deal of names beginning in *Medio-* that could potentially be references to ancient "centers". They are particularly numerous along the east-west axis between the firth of Forth and that of Clyde.[116] Additionally and as mentioned earlier, the toponyms resembling Tynwald – like Dingwall or Tingwall for the Shetlands – may have played a role as places of assemblies. In either circumstance, the importance of such places appear to have been local only: the systematic lack of proof regarding their possible "national" or "general" dimension prevents any further comparison with Uisneach. It must also be noted that toponyms either starting in *Medio-* or connected with "Tingwall" do not usually refer to hills or heights.[117]

We must therefore look elsewhere for a potential equivalent of Uisneach in Scotland and Arthur's Seat, in Holyrood Park, seems a reasonably well-suited candidate. The 250-meter hill dominates Edinburgh. Arthur's Seat is sometimes assimilated to Camelot, the seat of the king Arthur's court, although the hypothesis has never been demonstrated. Today, popular beliefs still hold that the mountain is the body of a dragon that fell asleep after having eaten the surrounding cattle: the story is reproduced in a variety of versions in tourist brochures and other websites boasting the interest of Arthur's Seat and its ascent.

Regarding a potential comparison with the symbolism of Uisneach, it must be noted that, strictly speaking, Edinburgh does not lie at the geographical center of Scotland – although it does stand at the approximate center of the Central Lowlands. It may also be argued that the city has been situated for quite a while at the heart of Scotland in social, economic and political terms, perhaps also arguably on a symbolic level and in the collective imagination – although this is debatable. Arthur's Seat is actually a fortified hill, both mentioned in ancient documents and folkloric tradition. An in-depth analysis of Arthur's Seat would lead us too far afield. However, one local tradition – confirmed since the 18th century at least – is worth mentioning: young girls were supposed to wash their face in dew on Arthur's Seat on "*May Morning*", i.e. the morning of the first of May:

> On *May Day* in a fairy ring,
> We've seen them round St. Anthon's spring[118]
> Frae grass the caller dew-straps wring,
> To wet their ein,
> And water clear as crystal spring.
> To synd them clean.[119]

This custom is here associated with a "fairy-ring", which can either be an artificial stone circle or a natural occurrence connected by local tradition to the Otherworld.[120] Washing one's face or hands in dew for good luck or purification purposes was extremely common for girls in a large number of European traditions – especially in Celtic, Germanic and Scandinavian countries – almost always in relation with the month of May: this point will be addressed in the following chapter.

The presence of a fort on Arthur's Seat, its conceivable symbolic centrality, its association with May rituals and the world of the fairies could be the first elements indicating a potential symbolic and ritual correspondence between the Irish and the Scottish hills.[121] The fact that the Scottish parliament of Holyrood is today situated at the foot of Arthur's Seat is an amusing – but noteworthy – coincidence. Today, a so-called re-enactment of *Bealtaine* – *Beltane* in its anglicized version – is still held every year at Calton Hill, in close proximity of Holyrood and Arthur's Seat.[122] Interestingly enough, this contemporary Scottish *Beltane Fire Festival* most likely served as a source of inspiration for the creators of the new *Bealtaine Fire Festival* of Uisneach, as will be demonstrated later.[123] All those elements call for a more thorough comparative analysis; an Arthurian or a Scottish studies scholar will hopefully tackle this issue soon enough.

Wales: Pumlumon

The last case to be examined here is that of Wales, which is detailed in a full chapter of *Celtic Heritage* ("Chapter VIII: the five peaks").[124]

Ancient Wales was traditionally divided into five provinces: Bangor in the north-west, St. Asaph in the north-east, Llandaf in the south-east and St. David's in the south-west. The fifth province was Gwrtheyrnion, the territory of Gwrtheyrn, king of Britain at the time of the Saxon invasion. That fifth territory was situated between river Severn and river Wye, respectively first and fifth longest rivers of the whole island of Great Britain. The Severn and Wye spring from mount Pumlumon (752 meters), also called *Plynlimon* or *Plinlim[m]on* in their anglicized versions. Incidentally, Pumlumon lies at the approximate center of Wales and the territorial subdivision (*commote*) stretching west of the mountain is called

Perfedd, "the middle". Furthermore, Alwyn and Brinley Rees mention that the mountain stands next to the point where the provinces and dioceses of the north-west, north-east and south-west met. The name Pumlumon could mean "the five peaks/hills", perhaps the "five banners" or "five chimneys". Eric Hamp proposed an alternative etymology, deriving Pumlumon from *pump* (five) and *llumon* as a compound of *Lüd* +*mon*, that is "peat-ash".[125]

The similarities between the hill of Uisneach and Pumlumon are striking. The Welsh mountain is central; it is associated with the number five; it stands close to the limits of territorial subdivisions which revolve around it;[126] finally, it is the origin of streams, which delimit the central territory. This obviously connects it with the Irish mythological traditions, which mention the magical or miraculous creation of the main rivers of Ireland on Uisneach but also with the Gallic notion of *Mediomatrici* – "between mothers" – the Gallic rivers associated with the cult of *Matronae*.

It is therefore tempting to believe "Pumlumon in Gwrtheyrnion" was to Wales what "Uisneach in Mide" was to Ireland. Several elements are missing for the demonstration to be perfectly convincing: the mountain does not play a major role in Welsh mythology, to say the least; no ancient monument, either natural or artificial, on top or on the sides of Pumlumon was deemed significant enough to have been noticed or described in detail by scholars; its inscription in the Celtic temporal cycle – i.e. the association of the hill with *Calan Mai*, the Welsh equivalent of *Bealtaine* – has yet to be demonstrated, either in ancient Welsh tradition or in modern and contemporary folklore. However, one mythical Welsh narrative, although it does not directly mention Pumlumon, does allude to a "central point" of the isle of Britain in the temporal context of *Calan Mai*.

Great Britain: The Ford of the Ox?

The Adventure of Lludd and Llefelys (*Cyfranc Lludd a Llefelys*) can be found in the compilation of the *Mabinogion*, usually dated between the 12th and 14th centuries. Joseph Loth believed the redaction of this specific episode to date back to the 13th century, though he estimated that the substance of the story was much more ancient.[127]

In *The Adventure of Lludd and Llefelys*, Lludd, king of the island of Britain, calls for his brother Llefelys, king of France: three plagues were unleashed onto his realm and he needs his help. The first "plague" is an evil race, the Coranmeit, a magical and demonic people that has often been presumed to be the fairies.

> The second plague was a scream that was heard every *May Eve* above every hearth in the Island of Britain. It pierced people's hearts and terrified them so much that men lost their colour and their strength, and

women miscarried, and young men and maidens lost their senses, and all animals and trees and the earth and the waters were left barren.[128]

The third plague is embodied by a giant who steals all the food of the royal court, except that consumed on the first night of the year, namely *Calan Mai.*

As a consequence, the last two plagues were connected to the night of the first of May and the first strongly suggests the fairies, often associated with the Tuatha Dé Danann in Ireland, whose connection with early May is transparent.[129]

Llefelys considers that the second plague, the "scream of the first of May" is uttered by a dragon who is attacked by another dragon "of a foreign race". To get to the bottom of the matter, Llefelys offers Lludd the following advice:

> When you get home, have the Island measured, its length and breadth, and where you find the exact centre, have that place dug up. And then into that hole put a vat of the best mead that can be made, and a sheet of brocaded silk over the top of the vat, and then you yourself keep watch. And then you will see the dragons fighting in the shape of monstrous animals. But eventually they will rise into the air in the shape of dragons; and finally, when they are exhausted after the fierce and frightful fighting, they will fall onto the sheet in the shape of two little pigs, and make the sheet sink down with them, and drag it to the bottom of the vat, and they will drink all the mead, and after that they will sleep. Then immediately wrap the sheet around them, and in the strongest place you can find in your kingdom, bury them in a stone chest and hide it in the ground, and as long as they are in that secure place, no plague shall come to the Island of Britain from anywhere else.[130]

In order to protect the isle of Britain from invasions, the two dragons had to be trapped at the center of the island. The ruse was to be put into action right after their confrontation, on *Calan Mai.*

Lludd follows the advice of his brother: he has "the length and breadth of the Island measured"[131] and manages to trap the dragons.[132] The central point is identified by Lludd as "Rytychen". Loth believed that Rytychen (or Rhyd-Ychen) was Oxford, in both cases, the "ford of the ox[en]", a suggestion that is now accepted and featured in most recent translations. This choice of "Oxford" as a central point seems rather peculiar: "Oxford is central only from west to east, starting at the mouth of the Severn and moving on to London".[133] It may simply be indicative of the size and shape of the kingdom at the time of redaction – perhaps not even in historical terms but in symbolic terms or according to the redactor only. Today, Oxford stands indeed at the approximate middle-point of modern England, considered on its east-west axis.

The Adventure of Lludd and Llefelys is interesting in many respects: first and foremost, it connects a potential "center" of the island of Britain – or England – to the beginning of the month of May, which is, of course, reminiscent of Uisneach: the "center of Ireland" was indeed celebrated at (or at least connected to) the very same time of the year. However, it still proves quite useless in the study of possible assemblies at a center-point – or even of the symbolism of central hills or monuments in Britain and the Celtic world: no mountain or hill connected to Rytychen/Oxford is ever mentioned in the narrative.

* * *

Locus Consecratus in Gaul, Kermaria in Brittany, Tynwald, in the Isle of Man, Arthur's Seat in Scotland, Stonehenge (or Oxford!) in England, Pumlumon in Wales: the comparisons with the different potential central points of the Celtic world – or of regions influenced by the Celtic tradition – proved rather fruitful, although by no means completely demonstrated and established; the sources are either too scarce, too biased or too recent. As for the notion of "assemblies", it can only be found in connection with Stonehenge, the *Locus Consecratus* of Caesar and in Tynwald,[134] respectively at the time of the Pentecost, a "fixed period of the year" and the month of May. The month of May is also mentioned in the traditions or myths connected to Arthur's Seat, the "ford of the ox" and Pumlumon.

It is therefore possible to remark a recurrence, perhaps a pattern, that has already been noticed in connection with Uisneach: the importance of "time" and the place in the year of the traditions connected to the center. Quite often, a "specific date" (the beginning of the month of May) and a specific celebration (*Bealtaine* or its more or less direct equivalents)[135] are mentioned.

The study of the apparent connection between time and sacredness in relation to Uisneach therefore proves necessary. This analysis will of course shed light on the potential historicity of the convention of Uisneach. Perhaps even more interestingly, it will prove crucial in our understanding of the symbolism traditionally conferred to the hill.

Notes

1 See chap. IV.6.
2 *Les Druides, op. cit.*, 410.
3 MacNeill, Máire. 1962. *The Festival of Lughnasa.* Dublin: Comhairle Bhéaloideas Éireann, 288.
4 More specifically, this version of the Annals is a translation to English of Irish Annals now missing and probably dating back to the 15th century.
5 Murphy, Denis (ed.). 1896. *The Annals of Clonmacnoise, being annals of Ireland from the earliest period to A.D. 1408.* Dublin: Royal Society of Antiquaries of Ireland, 194.

6 *Annals of the Four Masters, op. cit.*, M1141.13.
7 *Annals of Tigernach, op. cit.*, T1111.7 ("The great synod of Uisneach in this year"); *Lebor Gabála Érenn, op. cit.*, V, section IX, Roll of the Kings, Poem CXXXVI, 413 ("The great Synod before the two sons of Oengus", "at a place called Fiad-mic-Oengusso, somewhere near Uisnech Hill in Co. Westmeath, to make certain regulations concerning public morals"). See *infra* for other references.
8 Hennessy, William M. (ed.). 1866. *Chronicum Scotorum: A Chronicle of Irish Affairs*. London: Longmans, Green, Reader, and Dyer, CS1111.
9 Hennessy, William M. (ed.). 1871. *The Annals of Loch Cé*. Oxford: Longman & Co, LC1111.6.
10 *Annals of Ulster, op. cit.*, U1111.8.
11 *Lebor Gabála Érenn, op. cit.*, V, 311.
12 *History of Ireland, op. cit.*, Book I, 111 and 113.
13 *Ibid.*, section III.
14 *Ibid.*, Book I, Section XXXIX, 247.
15 See chapter IV.
16 https://www.ucd.ie/archaeology/research/how.
17 *History of Ireland, op. cit.*, Book I, Section XXXIX, 247-9.
18 *Ibid.*, 249-51.
19 For further detail, see the seminal work of Máire McNeill: *The Festival of Lughnasa, op. cit.*
20 *Les Indo-Européens, op. cit.*, 360.
21 Arguably, the same argument could apply to the "friendship" and the "contracts" mentioned by Keating, which are but other forms of partnership.
22 *Ibid.*, 251-3.
23 The Rees explained the association made by Keating between Tailtiu and Ulster by the fact that Tailtiu was also a mythological character, i.e. the queen of the Fir Bolg, who were closely connected with the province. *Celtic Heritage, op. cit.*, 164.
24 See for example Les Druides, op. cit., 220.
25 *Celtic Heritage, op. cit.*, 163-6. This north-south/Summer-Winter division could at least partially echo the Indian tradition.
26 *Lammas* or *Lammas-Tide* corresponds to the festival of Lughnasa. See *The Festival of Lughnasa, op. cit.*
27 Stokes, Whitley (ed.). 1891. "The Irish ordeals, Cormac's Adventure in the Land of Promise, and the Decision as to Cormac's Sword", in *Irische Texte mit Wörterbuch*, 4 vols, III: 1, Leipzig, 183-221: 57-8 and 217.
28 "The Ultonians had a custom of holding a fair every year, which lasted the three days before Samhain [the first of November], the day of Samhain itself, and the three days that followed it"; the fact that the fair is indeed the assembly of Tara is clearly mentioned in the narrative. Dillon, Myles. 1953. "The Wasting Sickness of Cú Chulainn" in *Scottish Gaelic Studies*, VII, 47-88.
29 "Tara's Feast at every samhain", *Silva Gadelica, op. cit.*, II, 88.
30 *History of Ireland, op. cit.*, 57-8.
31 Sjoestedt, Marie-Louise. 1940. *Dieux et Héros des Celtes*. Paris: Presses Universitaires de France, 3.
32 Dillon, Myles (ed.). 1962. *Lebor Na Cert. The Book of Rights*. Dublin: Irish Text Society: 73. Version from the Book of Lecan, note L, 1416-8, as mentioned page xxi.
33 See *Dictionary of Celtic Mythology, op. cit.*, 11.
34 Bhreathnach, Edel. 1995. *Tara: a select bibliography*. Dublin: Royal Irish Academy, 8.

35 Dillon, Myles (ed.). 1951-2. "Taboos of the kings of Ireland" in *Proceedings of the Royal Irish Academy: Archaeology, Culture, History, Literature*, LIV, 1-36, 22-5.
36 *The Book of Rights, op. cit.*, 131.
37 See also Binchy's remark on the confusion between Tara and Uisneach: Binchy, D.A.. 1955-8. "The Fair of Tailtiu and the Feast of Tara", in *Ériu*, XVII-XVIII, 113-38: 113
38 See *infra* and for the Christianization of *Bealtaine* and its connection with Easter see Armao, Frédéric. 2002. "De Beltaine à Pâques" in *Etudes irlandaises*, XXVII-2, 29-43.
39 "The Settling of the Manor of Tara", *op. cit.*, 163-4.
40 *History of Ireland, op. cit.*, 331-5.
41 *Silva Gadelica, op. cit.*, II, 99-101.
42 Wyatt, David R. 2009. *Slaves and Warriors in Medieval Britain and Ireland: 800 - 1200*. Leiden: Brill, 76.
43 *Silva Gadelica, op. cit.*, II, 99.
44 "The Fate of the Children of Tuireann (Oidhedh Chloinne Tuireann)", *op. cit.*, 161-3.
45 *Ibid.*
46 *Ibid.*
47 *Ibid.*
48 *Textes Mythologiques irlandais, op. cit.*, 105.
49 *Dindshenchas, op. cit.*, I, 39, III, 441, IV, 187-91, 243.
50 *Ibid.*, I, 29, 37, 39.
51 *Ibid.*, IV, 149-63. "A fair with gold, with silver, with games, with music of chariots, with adornment of body and of soul by means of knowledge and eloquence. A fair without wounding or robbing of any man, without trouble, without dispute, without reaving, without challenge of property, without suing, without law-sessions, without evasion, without arrest. A fair without sin, without fraud, without reproach, without insult, without contention, without seizure, without theft, without redemption: No man going into the seats of the women, nor woman into the seats of the men, shining fair, but each in due order by rank in his place in the high Fair.", etc. *Ibid*, 151.
52 The mention of "cold Uisneach" is enigmatic and can also be found in *Lebor Gabála Érenn, op. cit.*, IV, 75 as mentioned above.
53 *Ibid.*, III, 121.
54 *Ibid.*, 123.
55 *Dindshenchas, op. cit.*, IV, 279-81.
56 *Silva Gadelica, op. cit.*, II, 76-88.
57 *Ibid.*, 80.
58 *Ibid.*, 78.
59 *Early Christian Ireland, op. cit.*, 607.
60 "That is a matter for God". *Silva Gadelica, op. cit.*, II, 78.
61 *Ibid.*, 78.
62 *Ibid.*
63 *Ibid.*, 84.
64 *Ibid.*, 78.
65 *Ibid.*, 203. See "Landscapes of Cult and Kingship", *op. cit.*, 95 and 111.
66 *The Voyage of Bran, op. cit.*, 57-8.
67 See for instance Hull, Vernam E. 1930. "An Incomplete Version of the Imram Brain and four Stories concerning Mongan" in *Zeitschrift für celtische Philologie*, XVIII, 409-19.

68 *Dindshenchas*, *op. cit.*, IV, 279-81.
69 See chap. IV.4 for further discussion about Bel.
70 Binchy, D.A.. 1955-8. "The Fair of Tailtiu and the Feast of Tara", in *Ériu*, XVII-XVIII, 113-38.
71 As mentioned earlier, the references from the *Book of Rights* are due, according to Binchy, to a mistake on the part of the glosser, who confused the assembly of Uisneach with that of Tara.
72 *Ibid.*, 115.
73 *Ibid.*, 113.
74 *Les Fêtes celtiques*, *op. cit.*, 25.
75 *Ibid.*
76 Even the references to those assemblies in the 12th century are dubious, as noted previously.
77 "From Cult Centre to Royal Centre", *op. cit.*, 112.
78 See Caesar's remark on the assembly of the Carnutes *infra*.
79 See "Assembly at Stonehenge".
80 See also *infra* the remarks of the "full-center" of the Gauls.
81 *The Gallic Wars*, *op. cit.*, VI, §13.
82 *Ibid.*
83 Le Roux and Guyonvarc'h also note that "the four most powerful nations of Gauls are also the most central ones: Carnutes, Bituriges, Arvernes, Eduens", which is perhaps not coincidental. *Les Druides*, *op. cit.*, 220.
84 Joseph Loth, commenting the work of Alfred Holder, mentions the existence of forty-two Mediolana "almost all of which in the Gallic territory". "L'Omphalos chez les Celtes", *op. cit.*, 195.
85 Brunaux, Jean-Louis. 2005. *Les Gaulois*. Paris: les Belles Lettres, 79-80.
86 Savignac, Jean-Paul. 2014 (2004). *Dictionnaire Français-Gaulois*. Paris: La Différence, 88-9.
87 "L'Omphalos chez les Celtes", *op. cit.*, 194. See also *Dictionnaire Français-Gaulois*, *op. cit.*, 88-9, 239, 269-70, 299-300, 311.
88 *Dictionnaire Français-Gaulois*, *op. cit.*, 88-9.
89 *Ibid.*, 238.
90 "L'Omphalos chez les Celtes", *op. cit.*, 194, quoted in *Dictionnaire Français-Gaulois*, *op. cit.*, 239.
91 Daire, Marie-Yvonne & Villard, Anne. 1996. "Les Stèles à décors géométriques et curvilignes. Etat de la question dans l'Ouest armoricain", in *Revue Archéologique de l'Ouest*, XIII, 123-56: 136.
92 Waddell, John. 1982. "From Kermaria to Turoe?" in Scott, B. G. (ed.), *Studies on Early Ireland*. Essays in honour of M. V. Duignan. Belfast, 21-8.
93 Villard-le Tiec, Anne, Cherel, Anne-Françoise & Le Goff, Elven. 2003. "Aspects de l'art celtique en Bretagne au Vᵉ siècle avant J.-C." in *Supplément à la Revue archéologique du centre de la France*, XXIV, 221-36: 226.
94 "Les Stèles à décors géométriques et curvilignes", *op. cit.*, 146.
95 See https://musee-archeologienationale.fr/phototheque/oeuvres/betyle-de-kermaria_calcaire_sculpture-technique.
96 "Aspects de l'art celtique en Bretagne au Vᵉ siècle avant J.-C.", *op. cit.*, 226.
97 *Ibid.*
98 *Ibid.*
99 *Ibid.*, 227.
100 As often when it comes to Roman authors dealing with the Celtic culture, the line between historical reality and inventions or adaptations is rather thin and unclear. "The Druids—that is what they call their magicians—hold nothing

more sacred than mistletoe and a tree on which it is growing, provided it is a hard-oak. Groves of hard-oaks are chosen even for their own sake, and the magicians perform no rites without using the foliage of those trees, so that it may be supposed that it is from this custom that they get their name of Druids, from the Greek word meaning 'oak'; but further, anything growing on oak-trees they think to have been sent down from heaven, and to be a sign that the particular tree has been chosen by God himself. Mistletoe is, however, rather seldom found on a hard-oak, and when it is discovered it is gathered with great ceremony, and particularly on the sixth day of the moon (which for these tribes constitutes the beginning of the months and the years) and after every thirty years of a new generation, because it is then rising in strength and not one half of its full size. Hailing the moon in a native word that means 'healing all things', they prepare a ritual sacrifice and banquet beneath a tree and bring up two white bulls, whose horns are bound for the first time on this occasion. A priest arrayed in white vestments climbs the tree and with a golden sickle cuts down the mistletoe, which is caught in a white cloak. Then finally they kill the victims, praying to God to render his gift propitious to those on whom he has bestowed it. They believe that mistletoe given in drink will impart fertility to any animal that is barren, and that it is an antidote for all poisons. So powerful is the superstition in regard to trifling matters that frequently prevails among the races of mankind". Rackham H., Jones, W,H.S. & Eichholz, D.E. (ed.). 1949-54. *Pliny's Natural History*. London: William Heinemann, XVI, 95.

101 See "Les Stèles à décors géométriques et curvilignes", *op. cit.*, 144-5 for the difficulty in interpreting those motives.

102 "Les Stèles à décors géométriques et curvilignes", *op. cit.*,144, quoting Kruta, V. 1985. *Les Celtes en Occident*. Paris: Ed. Atlas, 111. The authors make a connection with the stone of Cape Clear, Ireland.

103 Gaignebet, Claude. 1987. "A la Pêche aux Enfants", in *Civilisations*, XXXVII, No. 2, Ethnologies d'Europe et d'ailleurs, 35-41.

104 Loth, Joseph. 1914. "La croyance à l'omphalos chez les Celtes" in *Comptes rendus des séances de l'Académie des Inscriptions et Belles*, LVIII-5, 481-2.

105 Sergent, Bernard. 1999. *Celtes et Grecs. I, Le livre des héros*. Paris: Payot and 2004. *Celtes et Grecs. II, Le livre des dieux*. Paris: Payot.

106 "La croyance à l'omphalos chez les Celtes", *op. cit.*, 481-2 and "L'Omphalos chez les Celtes", *op. cit.*, 205.

107 "From Kermaria to Turoe?", *op. cit.*, 25.

108 McDonald, Russell Andrew. 2007. *Manx kingship in its Irish sea setting, 1187-1229: king Rǫgnvaldr and the Crovan dynasty*. Dublin: Four Courts Press, 174.

109 "A meeting was held of all the people of Man at Tynwald". Munch, P.A (ed.). 1874. *Chronica Regvm Manniae et Insvlarvm. The Chronicles of Man and the Sudreys from the Manuscript Codex in the British Museum. I.* Douglas: The Manx Society, years 1225 to 1249.

110 Broderick, George. 2003. "Tynwald: a Manx cult-site and institution of pre-Scandinavian origin?" in *Cambrian Medieval Celtic Studies*, XLVI, 55-94.

111 Fellows-Jensen, Gillian. 1993. "Tingwall, Dingwall and Thingwall" in *North-Western European Language Evolution*, XXI-XXII, 53-67. For potential similarities with Þingvellir/Thingvellir in Iceland see Mehler, Natascha. 2015. "Þingvellir: A Place of Assembly and a Market?" in *Journal of the North Atlantic*, spec. VIII, 69-81.

112 *Celtic Heritage, op. cit.*, 171.

113 *Dictionary of Celtic Mythology, op. cit.*, 418.

114 Feltham, John. 1798. *A Tour through the Island of Mann in 1797 and 1798.* R. Cruttwell, 172. See also Rhys, John. 1901. *Celtic Folklore, Welsh and Manx.* Oxford: Clarendon Press, 1901 and Moore, A.W. 1994 (1891). *The Folklore of the Isle of Man.* Felinfach: Llanerch Publishers. However, "Tynwald Fair Day" was celebrated on *Midsummer*, which could be explained by the Scandinavian influence. See chap. IV.6.

115 *History of Ireland, op. cit.*

116 Rivet, A.L.F. & Smith, Colin. 1979. *The Place-Names of Roman Britain.* London: Batsford Ltd, 'Medionemetum' and 'Mediolanum'. Quoted in Griffin-Kremer, Merrie-Cozette. 1999. *May Day in Insular Celtic Traditions.* PhD thesis. Brest: Université de Bretagne Occidentale, 944.

117 The presence of a "standing stone" on the shores of Lake Tingwall, on Mainland, Shetlands, must be noted. Tingwall is indeed situated at the approximate center of the island.

118 Original footnote: "St. Anthony's Well, a beautiful small spring, on Arthur's Seat, near Edinburgh, and a favourite resort of the youth of the city for the purpose of gathering *May Dew*, as described".

119 Fergusson, Robert. 1773. *Poems.* Edinburgh: Walter & Thomas Ruddiman, 32-3.

120 In this case, it is perhaps a natural circle caused by the proliferation of a mushroom. See Wollaston, William Hyde. 1814. "On Fairy-Rings" in *Abstracts of the Papers Printed in the Philosophical Transactions of the Royal Society of London,* I, 260-1.

121 On the mountain, there are also cliffs called "Salisbury Crags". Those could remind us of Geoffrey of Monmouth and the stones of Uisneach, which were supposed to have moved to Salisbury. However, the "Salisbury" mentioned by Monmouth is clearly that of Stonehenge: the toponym is quite common.

122 See *infra.*

123 See chap. IV.5 and VI.3.

124 *Celtic Heritage, op. cit.,* 173-85.

125 "Varia", *op. cit.,* 256-8.

126 However, the Rees explain that Pumlumon is situated next to the point where only three out of the four Welsh territories met.

127 "L'Omphalos chez les Celtes", *op. cit.,* 195.

128 Davies, Sioned (ed.). 2007. *The Mabinogion.* Oxford: Oxford University Press, Kindle Edition, chap. "Lludd and Llefelys".

129 Dumézil believed the three plagues corresponded to the three functions. Dumézil, Georges. 1955. "Triades de calamités et triades de délits à valeur trifonctionnelle chez divers peuples indo-européens" in *Latomus,* XIV, 173-85.

130 *The Mabinogion, op. cit.*

131 *Ibid.*

132 He did not bury them at the central point of the island or on Pumlumon, the central point of Wales, but in the mountainous region of Snowdonia, in northwestern Wales. For Loth, "in the primitive version, the chest was probably buried at the central point precisely, as it was deemed safer because of its religious character." ("L'Omphalos chez les Celtes", *op. cit.,* 196). This idea is interesting but remains to be demonstrated.

133 *Ibid.,* 196.

134 The idea of an assembly of the "five Royal tribes" at Pumlumon is an interesting hypothesis yet to be demonstrated.

135 *Calan Mai,* Easter and Whitsun are only but a few examples.

4   Time and Sacredness: *Bealtaine*

Discussing the festival of *Bealtaine* and the other three "Celtic" festivals in a detailed and comprehensive manner would not be relevant here: the subject of the Irish or Celtic calendar year is so rich and essential that each of the four seasonal celebrations can support a whole book on their structure, ritual, and importance. Other authors have already undertaken this task, most famously in *The Festival of Lughnasa* by Máire MacNeill, which remains unmatched to this day, both thanks to the pioneering ideas of the author and the abundance of information presented. MacNeill coupled the analysis of medieval texts with the study of modern folklore. Her methodology opened new horizons and actually initiated an entirely new field of research.

Very few writers have tried to cover the case of the four festivals in one single book and even fewer followed a rigorous approach: only a handful of those attempts are actually useful to the academic study of the festivals. The most convincing probably remains *Les Fêtes Celtiques* (*The Celtic Festivals*) by C.-J. Guyonvarc'h and F. Le Roux, published for the first time in 1995. The two scholars specialized in philology and history of religions respectively. This synergy frequently proved complementary but had the shortcoming of focusing their work mainly on ancient traditions, while ignoring or discounting modern and contemporary aspects. As opposed to Máire MacNeill, who compiled hundreds, if not thousands, of folkloric customs connected with the celebration of *Lughnasa* and tried to connect them with ancient beliefs, the two French authors preferred to summarize the folkloric corpus in a few lines or even turned the folkloric customs into mere footnotes, rendering them inert, yet still essential. Ideally, four distinct books – each dedicated to one of the four Irish seasonal festivals and each tracing back their history, from their origin to the contemporary celebrations – would greatly improve our knowledge and understanding of those celebrations. This long and tedious effort would be particularly important to, and shed an original light on a whole field of Irish and pan-Celtic cultures.

> The study of festival is most fruitful in preparation for the study of myths, because it is in festivals that the religious actions and thoughts are the most closely connected.[1]

DOI: 10.4324/9781003143161-5

More than a simple preparation for the study of myths, the study of festivals is arguably an end in itself: it casts light not only on civilizations, their conception of the world, social stratification and societal stakes but also on their imaginary and symbolic corpus as well as their very interpretation of the space and time they invent for themselves. This is all the more true for Uisneach, which cannot be understood without taking into consideration its place in the year: the hill only took – and takes – its full significance on *Bealtaine*.

Time and space are connected, both in terms of symbolism and the sensitive world. A celebration of Uisneach on *Bealtaine*, a festivity connecting a specific place to a specific time was perhaps as much about *celebrating hic et nunc* as it was about *transcending* this "here" and this "now".

As already mentioned on several occasions, the Irish year used to be divided into four parts – four seasons – each beginning with a specific festival:

> It is one of the great facts of the Celtic past and the strength with which it was rooted in consciousness and has survived to this day is remarkable. The four feasts were identified (when and how we cannot tell) with November first, February first, May first, and August first of the Julian calendar.[2]

More specifically, the festival of *Samhain* was apparently celebrated around the beginning of the month of November, *Imbolc*, the beginning of February, *Bealtaine* in early May and *Lughnasa* in early August. Of course, those dates are late adjustments to our Julian, and later Gregorian calendars. The Celts used a luni-solar calendar and the original celebration dates probably varied: this point will be addressed later.

It is generally believed that the year started on *Samhain*, with the winter season. This seems consonant with the statement made by Caesar according to which the Celts – more specifically the Gauls – had a peculiar way of dividing their days and seasons:

> All the Gauls assert that they are descended from the god Dis [Pater], and say that this tradition has been handed down by the Druids. For that reason they compute the divisions of every season, not by the number of days, but of nights; they keep birthdays and the beginnings of months and years in such an order that the day follows the night.[3]

Nights first, days second: in a similar manner, starting the year on *Samhain* amounted to starting the year with the darkest season of all, winter, followed by the brighter seasons of spring and summer. As surprising as it may sound to a contemporary ear, the ancient Irish (and probably Celtic) winter started on or around the first of November – or the corresponding date in their ancient calendar. Spring began on or around the first of February, summer on or around the first of May, fall on or around the first of August. Although this preference may seem confusing, it will be demonstrated as perfectly coherent in the last pages of this chapter.

In both medieval texts and more recent customs, the world of the dead – the Otherworld or *sídh* – and the world of the living almost literally came into contact on *Samhain* and on *Bealtaine.* The two festivals were considered to be the two "gates" of the year, two turning points[4] that were very often connected with each other; a custom or a belief associated with *Samhain* usually – although not systematically – found a counterpart or equivalent on *Bealtaine.* Likewise, a number of mythological episodes retail events set on either one of the two festivals and seem to more or less directly correspond with each other.

The festival of *Bealtaine* – which will be our main focus here as Uisneach was most prominently involved on that date – seemed to have important implications on all members of societies, i.e. rulers, members of the clergy and farmers. Just like *Samhain, Bealtaine* was threefold or, by extension, a "total" celebration; this was all the more true when the celebration of May was associated with the hill of Uisneach. Both ancient and modern sources are considered hereafter, their study shedding light on the potential evolution of the celebration through centuries, as well as on the symbolism of Uisneach and possibly some aspects of *Mórdháil Uisnigh.*

4.1 Background

Bealtaine marked the beginning of the summer season and was celebrated in early May. In modern Irish, *Lá Bealtaine* literally means "the first day of May" and *Bealtaine* refers to the whole month. In English, the festival is often translated by *May Day.* This is not an accurate translation, as *May Day* and *Bealtaine* were (and remain) two specific celebrations,[5] with distinct origins, which most English and Irish speakers seemed or seem to ignore.

As already mentioned, the original celebration of *Bealtaine* together with the three other festivals were not connected to the Julian calendar: evidence suggests that the festivals are thousands of years old and that the Celts used a luni-solar calendar. The adaptation to the months of May, August, November and February is a relatively late one, although "when and how, we cannot tell" and probably never will be able to.

The idea of a "first" of May – and a first of August, November and February – is also problematic. Often, in modern folklore, it is the night *between* 30 April and the first of May that actually mattered. Sometimes, the local clergy attempted a Christianization of the celebrations and imposed the first Sunday of each month as their celebration date. Finally, things became even more complicated in 1752, when the United Kingdom adopted the Gregorian calendar; at the time, the British calendar was eleven days late compared to Catholic countries, most of which had embraced the reform as early as 1582. The adoption of the Gregorian calendar created a discrepancy in the dates of festivals and a part of the population chose to keep the ancient dates. As noted by Máire MacNeill:

> The folklore attaches great importance to the right day for celebrating a festival. The unit of time with which a festival is identified is regarded as having an inherent solemnity, and it is important to know exactly when to observe it in order to enjoy its efficacy [...]. The idea that its place in the yearly round could be changed or regulated by an Act of Parliament was something so strange as to be almost inconceivable.[6]

As a consequence, some Irish celebrations were held on 11 or 12 May/ August/November/February instead of the first. This led to a duplication of the celebrations and induced a sense of confusion among Irish people themselves. Occasionally, the refusal to adopt the new dates was a deliberate attempt at obfuscation stemming from the rejection of the British rule. The festivals respectively called *New May Day (Lá-Bealtaine-Ure)/Old May Day (Sean-Lá-Bealtaine)* then arose in Ireland, *New May Day* being held on 1 May and *Old May Day* on 11 or 12 May. Others believed that *Bealtaine* was to be celebrated on 8 or 9 of May, some on the second Sunday of the month, the last Sunday of April, the first Sunday of May (if it was not Whitsunday) or on 20 or 21. Actually, it seems that, in Irish folklore, the festival could be celebrated at any time of the month, especially during its first half. This flexibility is important to bear in mind; today, the *Fire Festival* held on Uisneach at the beginning of May is also celebrated on a flexible date.[7]

Up to the beginning of the 20th century, the rural Irish population considered that summer was supposed to begin on *Bealtaine*, as attested by the folkloric traditions collected by the *Irish Folklore Commission*.[8] Each of the four Irish festivals was considered to be a "quarter-day" marking the beginning of a season. Occasionally, Irish folklore mentions a twofold division of the year: *Samhain* and *Bealtaine* were sometimes said to play the role of "half-year days" respectively marking the beginning of a six-month winter and summer.

The contradictory idea that either two great seasons of six months or four seasons of three months existed is also found in medieval texts. Thus, in *The Wooing of Emer (Tochmarc Emire*, version III), the hero Cúchulainn addressed beautiful Emer and made the following statement:

> For two divisions were formerly on the year, viz., summer from *Beltaine* (the first of May), and winter from *Samuin* to *Beltaine*. Or *sainfuin*, viz., *suain* (sounds), for it is then that gentle voices sound, viz., *sám-son* "gentle sound". To *Oimolc*, i.e., the beginning of spring, viz., different (ime) is its wet (folc), viz the wet of spring, and the wet of winter. [...] To *Beldine*, i.e. *Beltine*, viz., a favouring fire. [...] To *Brón Trogaill*, i.e. *Lammas-day*, viz., the beginning of autumn.[9]

This extract confirms a division of the year, either in two or four seasons, although the social or symbolic repercussions of such a division is not explained by the Irish hero. This idea is further confirmed by the *Senchus Mór*, a famous collection of Irish ancient laws,[10] which corroborates the holding of seasonal feasts: "[For] the great cauldron of each quarter [...] which is used for the preparation of feast every quarter of a year".[11] This laconic mention proves that the division of the year in four parts and the holding of quarterly festivals dates back to the 14th century at least. A cauldron was used in each case in order to prepare the said feast, although the precise function of this cauldron is hard to grasp: why does a collection of laws mention it in such terms? What was its role and what were the laws relating to it? Those questions must remain unanswered. The fact that the cauldron was the main attribute of the Dagda, god of druids and master of time, may or may not be connected with this short note.

Fortunately, another document is significantly less concise and enables us to understand the fact that this division had repercussions on the profane world, namely the agricultural world – which is not surprising.

4.2 Bealtaine and Farmers

Notion of Seasons

The two main versions of the *Second Battle of Mag Tuired* (also commonly noted *Magh Tuireadh* or *Moytura*) are usually dated to the 15th and 17th centuries, respectively. Those late transcriptions must not deter us from the main point: "the substance is infinitely more ancient than the form".[12] The text was probably transcribed for the first time in the 9th or 10th century and most scholars believe that the "substance" is essentially pre-Christian.

The *Second Battle of Mag Tuired* details a confrontation we are now familiar with: that opposing the Tuatha Dé Danann led by Lugh to the Fomorians, led by his grand-father Balor. One extract seems of particular relevance. Bres the Beautiful is put to the test by Lugh for his poor conduct. Lugh looks for a reason to spare him and Bres proposes the following:

> "Tell your Brehon [judges] that for sparing me the men of Ireland shall reap a harvest in every quarter of the year". Said Lugh to Moeltne: "Shall Bres be spared for giving the men of Ireland a harvest of corn every quarter?". "This has suited us"; saith Maeltne: "the spring for ploughing and sowing, and the beginning of summer for the end of the strength of corn, and the beginning of autumn for the end of the ripeness of corn and for reaping it. Winter for consuming it".[13]

This excerpt therefore confirms the existence of a notion of "quarter-days", or at least four distinct seasons, in the ancient Irish system: it also associates the division with the agricultural production. Bres proposes a harvest at each quarter of the year but the offer is rejected by druid Maeltne, who is satisfied with the traditional system: plowing and sowing in spring, growth in summer till fall and harvest at the beginning of winter. This pattern is perfectly logical and consistent with the cycle of nature and the sedentary agricultural societies; it has persisted and could even be found in modern Irish traditions, once again associated with the seasonal festivals. As *Bealtaine* marked the beginning of summer, it was a most significant celebration for the farmer and proved a major turning point of the year, regarding both pastoral and agricultural activities.

Regulation of the Rural World: Crops

The 1947 manuscripts of the *Irish Folklore Commission* tell us that, in most parts of Ireland, all crops were to be in the ground before *Bealtaine* – or, when the informant was Anglophone, before *May Day*:

> Farmers were always anxious to have their seeds in the earth before *May Day* as the real growth commenced about that date.[14]
>
> Potato crops should all be planted by *May Day*.[15]
>
> People tried to have corn and potatoes planted before *May Day* but in late season up to Old *May Day* (12th May) is considered early enough].[16]
>
> [*May Day* is the latest date on which spring crops should be sown].[17]
>
> The "old barley" always sown on the 12th (Old *May Day*) or about it.[18]

Bealtaine was not only a "time boundary". The festival – and especially its "ancient version", *Old May Day* – was considered auspicious, as it was a lucky day for sowing. The festival also marked the beginning of the gathering of sea-weed,[19] sometimes called "May seaweed", for instance, along the coast of Co. Kerry.[20] On *Bealtaine*, the fishing seasons of the "May mackerels" opened.[21] Finally, as an informant from Co. Kerry tells us: "[*Old May Day*] is the usual starting time for turf-cutting in hilly and exposed country districts".[22] In Co. Donegal, "They would try to cut all their turf between the two Mays", i.e., between *May Day* and *Old May Day*.[23]

Regulation of the Rural World: Cattle

The most popular, and perhaps the most significant custom of *Bealtaine* was not connected to crops but to farming. The feast was the day chosen to neuter animals (lambs, pigs or calves)[24] but most of all to start transhumance. In some rural areas, the tradition lasted up to the second half of the 20th century:

There was a systematic moving of cattle on *May Day* to rough pasture.[25]

> The people used to drive the cows to the bogs or mountains on May when the sun would rise and while the dew was still on the ground and then they would bring them back to be milked in the evening. They were put into the [...] milking field and would get cabbage while being milked. [...] Cattle and sheep were sent on grass for six months.[26]

Bealtaine often represented the beginning of a pastoral cycle which was marked by the return of the cattle six months later. Summer grazing started on *Bealtaine* and was supposed to end on *Samhain*: the festivals were indeed "quarter-days" or perhaps more appropriately "half-year days". The tradition was observed in every rural part of Ireland: in the 1947 *Irish Folklore Commission* collection alone, about 100 independent allusions to a transhumance starting on *Bealtaine* are mentioned – a number that should be compared to the two hundreds informants involved in the survey.

There is no question that the festival played the role of a time boundary which was known and recognized (sometimes up to this day) by both Irish cattle owners and farm laborers: a large number of activities were supposed to start or end on that specific date. Furthermore, *Bealtaine* traditionally marked the moment of the year when accounts were settled and contracts were renewed.

Regulation of the Rural World: Settlements

Thus, in modern rural Ireland, the festival was connected to financial settlements and agreements: "[*May Day* is the beginning of every bargain and agreement]".[27] This notion is of course all the more interesting when compared with the statement of Keating according to which the convention of Uisneach was the moment chosen to settle debts and pay taxes, notably to the king of Connacht.

More broadly speaking, the idea of renewing contracts in May seems to be quite ancient in Ireland. According to the *Senchus Mór*, the month of May was the occasion to break up marriages:

> One-ninth of his (*the man's*) increase, and of his corn, and of his bacon *is due to the woman* if she be a great worker; she has a sack every month she is *with him* to the end of a year,[28] i.e. to the next May-days, for this is mostly the time in which they make their separation.[29]

Therefore, it was apparently customary, in ancient or early medieval Ireland, to divorce during the month of *Bealtaine*, or at least to end what may be assimilated to a "marriage settlement". Another manuscript associates the ancient festival to the theme of marriage. A king of Tara who wanted to marry the daughter of the king of Offaly promised a substantial dowry, namely 80 cows – 40 to be given immediately and 40 on the following first of May.[30] Out of context, the reference seems rather anecdotal, if not cryptic. However, it takes on a new dimension when compared to the statement of the *Senchus Mór*: in all likelihood, the beginning of the month of May was a time of the year that was closely connected to settlements and marriages. Unions were celebrated, divorces were pronounced and, in some case, marital contracts were renewed.

Along these same lines and the idea of "contract renewal", it was customary in modern rural tradition to pay rent for one's land – especially pasture land – or one's dwelling at the beginning of May:[31] "Farmers generally dressed in their Sunday clothes on *May Day* as they had to meet their landlords to pay their rents".[32] Most of the leases were six-month agreements, which implies that the second payment or the renewal of contract was due on *Samhain*.

To that extent, *Bealtaine* and *Samhain* were "Gale Days",[33] the day on which rent was due. The custom is mentioned as early as 1576 by Sir Henry Piers: "At *May Day*, commonly, the Irish captains and lords use to bargain and compound with their tenants".[34] The tradition which was still customary in rural parts of Ireland in 1947 was therefore not recent. There is every reason to believe that it had its heyday at the time of the Plantations of Ireland in the 16th and 17th centuries. To that extent, *Bealtaine* was also connected with job hunting and employment: in the Irish rural world, the first of May was a hiring day. Both in the case of servants and even more frequently of farmers, the hiring was supposed to last for six months, that is until *Samhain*: "Day for hiring of farm laborers, from the 1st of May to the 1st of November".[35] In a village of Co. Westmeath situated in the district of Rathowen, men and women gathered at a corner of a specific street from 5AM every first of May;[36] in the Parish of Barr na Cuaile, Co. Leitrim, young boys and girls in want of a job carried a white stick in their hand in order to be noticed by potential employers.[37] Additionally, many hiring fairs were held throughout the country: it is during those meetings that the chance to get a job until *Samhain* was at its peak.

Hiring fairs were actually but one of the two types of "profane" or "secular" May gatherings – that is, gatherings devoid of any sacred dimension, the other being cattle fairs. Since Keating specifically mentioned that the ancient convention of Uisneach on *Bealtaine* was a fair "at which it was their custom to exchange with one another their goods, their wares, and their valuables", a more in-depth study of modern traditions connecting fairs with the arrival of *Bealtaine* seems relevant.

Secular Gatherings of May: Hiring Fairs

At the time of the folkloric collections carried out by the *Irish Folklore Commission* – the 1930s for the *Schools' Collection* and 1947 for the specific case of the festival of *Bealtaine* – hiring fairs were still very much a reality in some parts of Ireland. They were mainly popular in the north of Ireland – Ulster.[38] Manuscript *NFCS 962* (i.e. *National Folklore Collection, Schools' Collection*, number 962) gives a detailed account of the fairs of Co. Cavan:

> The biggest fairs of the year are held in Blacklion on 22nd May, and 19th November, these are the two hiring fairs, and boys and girls who are looking for work, go to these fairs and are hired by men who require help on their farms on in their homes. On fair days there are a lot of things sold on the street, and old clothes too.[39]

Once again, the coupling of the months of May and November is apparent: it was indeed very common as regards hiring and cattle fairs. The hiring fair of Blacklion and the neighboring towns of Balieborough and Kingscourt (held on 17 May and 17 November) were still popular at the beginning of the 20th century[40] but soon fell into oblivion. The system was archaic and inadequate, and progressively died out and was discontinued everywhere in Ireland.

Some fairs were simply more popular than others. Thus, the great fair of Letterkenny, Co. Donegal, was held on 12 May, on *Old May Day*. Farmers from the neighboring counties of Derry, Antrim and Tyrone visited the fair in order to find a job for the following six months.[41] It took the name of "Rabble(s) Fair", as a probable reference to both meanings of the term, i.e., "a disorganized or disorderly crowd of people" or "the lowest class of people".[42] It was the most important hiring fair of the year. Still in Ulster, the hiring fairs of Co. Armagh stood out: they were held all around the county at the beginning of the month of May, August, November and February, a fact which confirms the traditional division of the year and the notion of quarter-days. Employment usually lasted for three months, occasionally six when the secondary fairs – that of February and August – were not held.[43]

The popularity of those hiring fairs among the "rabble" was perhaps not only owed to the possibility of finding a job: they also provided an opportunity to meet up and have fun. In 1833, the authors of the *Ordnance Survey Memoirs of Ireland, Parishes of Co. Donegal* recommended the abolition of those fairs, especially that of Clady, on 16 May and 16 November. According to them, the fairs only benefited to the owners of public houses and caused fights and all kinds of excesses.[44]

The fact that those Irish fairs were mainly to be found in the north and north-east of Ireland led some scholars to believe they were an English invention that was introduced in Ireland in the Late Middle Ages, namely during the reign of Edward III, in the 14th century, or after. According to P. Logan:

> Like so many Irish fair customs, the hiring fair may be derived from an act of the English parliament passed during the reign of Edward III.

This act, called the Statute of Labourers, declared that magistrates must fix the wages of farm labourers and the rates must then be made known to all those concerned. This was done at what were called Statute Sessions, held about 1 May or in the autumn. When the employers and the workers of the district assembled to learn what the fixed rates were, they met and made their agreements, and so the hiring fair began.[45]

It is therefore possible that the hiring fairs persisted in Ulster because the English influence was more prominent and lasted for a longer period in the north of Ireland. However, even though they are rarer, the Irish fairs did exist outside Ulster up to the first half of the 20th century. Once again, some of them were festive events, as this description of Kilmacthomas, Co. Waterford tends to show:

> [*Bealtaine*] It was a fair day – hiring fair. Men and women, boys and girls marched to Kilmacthomas to be hired for a year's work. According as each was hired he, or she, received a shilling which sealed the contract. The workers kept this day as a holiday or day of recreation and enjoyment and held dances in the village during the entire day, the music being supplied by travelling fiddlers who made sure to be present for the occasion and by pipe-players. A collection was made among the crowd for the musicians – the hat was sent round and the collection often reached as high as £3 or £4.[46]

The hiring fair of New Ross, Co. Wexford, was one of the most popular in all Ireland.[47] This fair, known locally under the name "old May fair of New Ross" was held on 3 May and its creation dates back to the 13th century at least: a fair in Rosbercon, Co. Wexford, from 2 to 5 May, stopped being organized in 1286 because of the success of the fair of New Ross.[48] Since the *Statute of Labourers* dates back to 1351 only, the theory of Logan seems rather doubtful. Of course, the English law probably strengthened the importance of May hiring fairs in Ireland but it is clear that they already existed before the law was passed.

The modern fair of New Ross lasted until the beginning of the 20th century and is particularly well-documented. It is not necessary to go into much detail for the present discussion: only the details that offer useful information in connection with the potential convention of Uisneach are discussed below. The fair of New Ross was the biggest hiring fair of the south-east of Ireland; hiring was made for six months or a year. Boys and girls who wished to find a job gathered on the fair field of the *Irishtown* district. Some informants mentioned that the meeting was supposed to take place at the "Long Stone", without providing more information:

> Girls and boys who could milk carried a spancel. The girls in their bright and flashy coloured frocks and hats paraded up and down the

fair sometimes by themselves sometimes accompanied by the boys. More often they stood against walls in groups talking. [...] The girls were usually dressed in the most gaudy colours. For weeks before the 3rd of May each girl would be getting ready. Hats with all the colours of the rainbow in feathers and flowers and ornaments decorated the girls' heads.[49]

Hiring took place according to the usual protocol: after settling the terms, a shilling was exchanged and sealed the transaction; occasionally, both parties spat on their palms and shook hands. As often, the hiring fair of New Ross was associated with a great cattle fair, which was the farmers' last opportunity to do business before the beginning of the transhumance.

Secular Gatherings of May: Cattle Fairs

Cattle fairs were extremely common in Ireland up to the mid-20th century. They could take place at any time of the year although the largest and most popular events were held in connection with any of the four seasonal festivals. The resemblance with the description of *Mórdháil Uisnigh* by Keating is remarkable:

> [Local fairs] are always held in the towns. [...] If a person buys and sells he has to pay toll. There is a man standing on the street. When you are coming home from the fair he asks you for the toll. When an animal is sold, luck-money is generally given. [Sixpence is generally given for a sheep, a shilling for a pig, and two shillings for cattle and horses]. [Animals are marked with chalk, sometimes mud]. When a bargain has been made, the buyer and the seller strike hands. Sometimes they spit on their hands before striking.[50]

The description here offered of the fair of Nenagh is perfectly representative of Irish modern cattle fairs, up to the mid-20th century. Giving luck-money[51] and spitting "on their hands before striking" were common rules. Depending on the fair, the livestock sold varied between bovines, sheep, horses or other animals likely to be of interest for farmers and ploughmen.

Just like hiring fairs, the cattle fairs – and more specifically those held in May – saw the holding of festive events occasionally leading to various excesses. The fairs of Bective, Co. Meath, were held on 1 November and 16 May, the latter being both a sheep fair and a hiring fair. Bective was renowned for its festivities: at the end of the 19th century, no less than 30 tents were dedicated to the confection of "punch" and the selling of whiskey. People danced, played music and attended different performances. But the most striking feature of the meeting held at Bective was undoubtedly its faction fights:[52]

"Ribbon men"[53] visited the fair. [Party divided into two parties. One called the Bees and the other the Billy Smith's]. If they had any ill-feeling against one another in the parties they had a word which was called a "Code Word" when they were drinking. One of the Bees would say 'the moon is rising already' and out they'd be with sticks and stones to fight with the Billy Smith's.[54]

A comprehensive study of the manuscripts of the *Schools' Collection* relating to the counties of Kerry, Galway and Meath shows that the tradition of faction fights during fairs is completely absent from the first two counties and quite common in the third.[55] Scholars such as Kevin Danaher have also noticed that those faction fights were closer to being an "extreme sport", often caused by an excessive consumption of alcohol, than actual ritual customary fights.[56] The confrontations could prove lethal. They were sometimes associated with other sporting and playful activities called *May Games*, which were usually much more composed and organized. Those *May Games*, the most famous of which took place in Dublin – more specifically Finglas and Donnybrook – were often associated with other May customs, namely the very ritualized traditions of *May Bushes* and *May Poles* which, as will be demonstrated later, most likely stem from Anglo-Norman traditions.

The examples that we have just reviewed suggest that the account of Keating regarding *Mórdháil Uisnigh* is credible. The author mentioned that "it was their custom to exchange with one another their goods, their wares, and their valuables" and the idea is quite in tune with what is known of modern May fairs in Ireland. However, this comparison must be handled with care.

First, the antiquity of the holding of fairs and their association with ancient festivals is hard to establish. Holding a fair in May (or on the first of May) is not proof of its relationship with the festival *Bealtaine* and its inherent symbolism; as noted by MacNeill, it is likely that, in most cases, the date was chosen mainly for practical purposes.[57] Similarly, the recurring correspondence of fairs to four quarter-days does not on its own constitute proof of their affiliations with four ancient festivals. It is at best an element substantiating the hypothesis according to which the Irish year was divided into four equal parts – or two six-month seasons.

One last crucial element must be taken into account: the Anglo-Norman influence. Although the fair of New Ross was, for instance, anterior to the *Statute of Labourers* of Edward III, this does not mean that the ensuing impact of the law was nil. Additionally, this does not contradict the possibility that the fair of New Ross was actually created by Anglo-Normans at the time of the first invasions, namely the 12th century – as the Norman implantation at New Ross took place at an early stage of Irish history. It is in fact quite conceivable that many Irish fairs owed their existence to the Anglo-Norman influence. The flourishing trade in Western Europe was already stimulated by the holding of large fairs in the 12th and 13th centuries. They were so influential and significant that, in theory, only a royal charter could allow their creation.

Two hypotheses should be considered: first, the Normans that had already settled in Ireland could be at the origin of all the known Irish fairs, notably in the areas where their influence was the most pronounced; according to this hypothesis, the Normans created most, if not all of the medieval May fairs in Ireland and the Irish embraced them. An alternative hypothesis could be that, at their arrival in Ireland and in the following centuries, the Normans claimed authority on already-existing ancient Irish fairs, adapted them and injected new traditions inspired by their own culture.[58] Although both hypotheses are compelling, none is completely above criticism or even verifiable: a clear and specific mention of a cattle fair or a hiring fair associated with *Bealtaine* and anterior to the Norman invasions would have sufficed, yet is not known to exist. Still, the Irish May fairs were extremely numerous and scattered over all the island, which is sufficient enough for the present discussion. The cattle fairs in the large urban centers of the east and north of Ireland were sometimes associated with *May Games* and various customs, mainly the *May Bush* – i.e., an adorned bush carried in procession. They were occasionally part of a set of fairs, as a second one was often held in November and even a third and a fourth fair corresponded to the other two quarter-days. To that extent, they actively participated in the traditional division of the agricultural year into four distinct parts – a division that is therefore clearly demonstrated in modern Irish folklore.

On the other hand, nothing indicates that those fairs were anterior to the Anglo-Norman invasions. As a consequence, when Keating described the convention of Uisneach as a fair, he could as well be inspired by cattle or hiring fairs held in his day. If this were so, the irony of the situation is rather striking: Keating became a proponent of Anglo-Norman traditions imported in Ireland during the Middle Ages while being convinced he was perpetuating an ancient Irish custom – unless of course, as is sometimes argued, Keating had access to ancient manuscripts now lost which did mention a fair at Uisneach. For lack of proof, this argument must be swept aside: the notion of "fair" at the convention of Uisneach is impossible to establish in historical terms, despite the fact it was compatible with was is known of the "space" and "time" in question.

Rural Beliefs and Superstitions

In modern Irish rural tradition, the beginning of the month of May was connected with a large number of extremely strong beliefs, all linked with the fact that *Bealtaine* marked a period of transition. The festival embodied the beginning of summer, a pivotal period of the year where the temporality and mortality of human beings were emphasized and where the themes of fear and hope were intimately intertwined: fear of bad crops or diseases affecting beasts and humans; hope of a full granary, radiant health and fat cattle. The notion of fear also extended to the private sphere, more specifically to the love life of rural Irish people: on *Bealtaine*, marriage divination was common and it was customary to try and guess the name or face of one's future partner, especially for women. The most renowned of those customs was the use of *May Dew*, whose importance was central according to many informants. Thus, young girls or women got up quite early on the morning of the first of May and washed their face in dew: not only was it supposed to make them beautiful and give them a good complexion for the following year – or even bring good luck and ward off diseases – but the first name that they heard afterwards was supposed to be that of their future husband.[59]

Most of all, on *Bealtaine*, the obsession of the cattle owners and farm laborers was to preserve their wealth – crops, dairies or beasts – for the following year. To that extent, starting transhumance on *Bealtaine* was not only customary: it was a way to bring good luck. As the informants of the *Irish Folklore Commission* tell us:

Lucky to move cattle to rough pasture [on *Bealtaine*].[60]

Summer grazing until November. [...] If [animals] turned to pastures on 1st May they never took cold or disease.[61]

Young calves put out for the first time on *May Day* would not get a cold.[62]

Starting transhumance on *Bealtaine* was more than a simple agricultural tradition. It was a superstition that aimed at bringing prosperity and luck on both cattle and farmers. The beginning of transhumance was sometimes associated with very specific purification rituals:

In south Co. Wicklow it used to be the custom to drive the cows out to the fields on *May Morning* with a stick cut from a mountain-ash tree. It was said that this would prevent losses of stock for the year.[63]

But the prophylactic custom of *Bealtaine* that was most common in Ireland clearly reminds us of the account given by Keating for the convention of Uisneach. Farmers lighted up two large fires and passed their cattle between them. Occasionally, the custom continued well into the 20th century. Let us mention three of the most telling examples that can be found in the *National Folklore Collection*:

The driving of milking cows through the gap of fire: in the year 1883 I worked on the farm of one Thomas Barron whose place was situated in the Parish of Butlerstown near Waterford City in the Townland of Knockeen. Thomas Barron kept fifty milking cows. Every year, on the night of *May Eve*, the cows were driven into a field adjoining those in which they were to spend the night. After supper Mr. Barron and his men (farm hands) went out, made a gap in the fence through which the cows could pass to their night quarters. This gap was then filled with withered grass and furze which were then set alight. All the men then armed themselves with sticks, rounded up the cows and forced them through the gap of fire into the fields where they were to spend the night. I, myself, took part in this driving of the cattle through the gap of fire on *May Eve* during my years of service with Mr. Barron. The driving of the cattle was a custom there. The reason for this practice: it was believed that such a driving [...] was powerful to prevent those who worked charms from taking the produce of the cows. The practice has long since died.[64]

On *May Eve* bonfires were lighted at the crossroads. Horses and cattle were driven through the flames as this was considered very lucky. Burning sticks from the fire were carried three times round the fields to bring luck to crops. [...] Michael Clooney who lives near Ballycuddy cross states that his mother, who is now dead, saw them. The custom was carried on 60 or 70 years ago. All the people gathered and helped to light the fire. Each farmer brought his herd of cattle to the place where the fire was lighted. In turn each farmer's cattle were driven through the bonfire three times. Then a stick, taken out of the fire, was carried round their fields, in the hope of causing the crops to grow well.[65]

After milking time on the evening of *May Day* the cattle were driven into a field and allowed to graze. Later they were transferred to another field which was to be their night quarters, but when this transfer was being made the cattle were driven through fire. A gap was made; a bonfire was kindled in this gap; then, men armed with sticks forced the animals through the gap of fire. This was supposed to ward off harm from the cattle for the coming year.[66]

The tradition of the passing of cattle between the *Bealtaine* fires was conducted by the farmers themselves and not a member of the sacerdotal class, either Christian or Pagan.[67] Here, those examples clearly demonstrate that driving cattle between two fires was understood as a way to protect them for the following year. Accordingly, those fires were by no means joyful bonfires and had very little to do with *Midsummer* bonfires for example.[68] In the case of *Bealtaine*, the informants mention two (and not just one) prophylactic fires between which cattle were driven so as to purify or protect them. Similarly, the customs of dancing around the fire(s) – so common in relation with bonfires of Saint John – are not documented and never mentioned in the 1947 collection of the *Irish Folklore Commission* in relation with the festival of May.

The *Bealtaine* custom seemed to epitomize the fears of the farmer: it echoed the general belief in rural Ireland, up to the beginning of the 20th century, that the month of May – and *Bealtaine* in particular – was a particularly dangerous period. First of all, regarding weather and health: although the rains of May and of *Bealtaine* were welcomed as they were believed to be profitable,[69] a disease contracted in May was particularly dreaded, either for beasts or humans. According to some informants, colds were supposedly the most dangerous of the year. Thus, the elderly were quite apprehensive of the arrival of the month, as the slightest health concern could prove lethal.

However, as exemplified by the testimonies found in the folkloric collections of the early 20th century, it was undoubtedly the influence of the Otherworld, which the farmers feared the most on *Bealtaine*: witches and fairies were the chief figures of the *sídh* and focused the attention of a fraction of the rural world.

Witches

On *Bealtaine*, the fear of witches was exacerbated. It was on the morning of the first of May or in the night between 30 April and 1 May that, according to popular belief, the witches performed their most evil deeds. People believed that they visited forts, swamps and, generally speaking, any remote place in order to gather and prepare their future wrongdoings. This fear led to an almost absolute ban for people to get out on *May Eve* or *May Night*: that night considered to be "more 'lonesome' than the darkest November night".[70]

Those witchcraft practices were usually believed to be carried out by women, not men. Accordingly, a great deal of traditions associated the sight of an unknown woman next to one's house or field as an evil omen. Meeting a red-haired woman was particularly unwelcome, as red hair was thought to be a devilish attribute.[71] Spells cast on *May Night* mainly revolved around stealing milk, butter or, more figuratively speaking, wealth or luck (i.e. "fortune") of farmers and farm workers. Cattle – first and foremost dairy cows – were to be preserved from this "evil influence". The belief was so common that some priests actually condemned magic butter-stealing in their sermons of May up to the end of the 19th century at least.[72]

As *Bealtaine* marked the beginning of transhumance, the farmers were anxious to protect their cattle from the evil influence of witches on *May Night*. Some locked their stables and stayed at home until the next morning; others started transhumance during the night of *Bealtaine* so as to stay close to their animals during this crucial time of the year.[73] In all cases, under no circumstances were the cattle supposed to be left alone.

Many informants also mentioned the transformation of Irish witches into "milking-hares" on the morning of the first of May: people believed those hares could be seen sucking on the udder of cows left alone in the fields, which meant that the witch (turned into a hare) was stealing the fortune (i.e. wealth or luck) of the animal's owner.[74] As noted by an informant from Co. Cork, "People usually watched the cattle all night in case the 'milking hare' would visit them during the night".[75] As a consequence, the presence of a stranger on a farmer's field on *Bealtaine* was viewed negatively, although the belief in "milking-hares" was not the sole reason.

Witches were in fact believed to steal wealth and luck using a wide array of – very peculiar and very creative – spells and charms: milking a cow, stealing a spancel, being the first to drink from the well or spring of a farm on *May Morning*,[76] stealing dew from the field of the owner (for instance by dragging a piece of cloth or a rope on the ground) or simply chanting spells. The list is far from exhaustive.

To this quick inventory must be added the belief according to which giving fire in any form – flames, embers, burning coal, incandescent pieces of turf or even a burning pipe – on *May Morning* amounted to giving away one's luck. For this reason, farmers and farm laborers avoided giving or lending anything. Strangers asking for that type of service were often considered to be – male or female – witches. People also generally avoided being the first to light their fire on the morning of *Bealtaine* because, according to popular belief, the witches could take away the fortune of the first house that had smoke coming out of its chimney. Some testimonies are even more peculiar: throwing a carrion or a rotten egg on a neighbor's field was sometimes said to be a sure way to steal his crops, kill his cattle or bring ill luck.[77] In a similar manner:

> Some [witches] were said to go to graveyards and remove an arm and hand from some lately buried corpse. This dead hand was one of the most potent charms known to witchcraft. It played an important part in the taking of butter.[78]

According to the informants, this "dead hand" was either to be placed under the churn[79] or used to stir the milk during churning.[80] In some cases, it was supposed to be put on the udders of the cows so as to mimic milking.[81]

This belief in magical theft – of fortune, butter or milk – on *Bealtaine* practiced by (usually female but occasionally male) witches was extremely strong. It continued well into the 20th century. On 3 May 1902, a certain William Murphy was even sentenced to three months in jail "on the charge of having unlawfully entered the lands and premises of John Russell, of Coolepoorawn, Ballyporeen, for the purpose of performing an act of witchcraft on the latter's cattle".[82]

One of the most ancient, if not the oldest mention of magic theft in Ireland, dates back to the 12th century and actually includes a reference to milking-hares. In his *Topographia Hibernica*, Giraldus Cambrensis tells us:

> It has also been a frequent complaint, from old times as well as in the present, that certain hags in Wales, as well as in Ireland and Scotland, changed themselves into the shape of hares, that, sucking teats under this counterfeit form, they might stealthily rob other people's milk.[83]

As noted by Giraldus, the belief was by no means not exclusive to Ireland; the fear of witches and the belief in milking-hares at the beginning of May appeared in many European countries – from Great Britain to Scandinavia (the Swedish *mjölkhare* being particularly common), from France to Germanic countries (and the famous *Walpurgis*) but also in Central and Eastern Europe. Under these circumstances, it is impossible to consider the belief in witches and milking-hares to be a purely Celtic or Irish tradition. Although the reference made by Giraldus Cambrensis is rather old, it is still posterior to the Norman invasion of Ireland. Additionally, the island already maintained strong cultural and commercial relationships with the isle of Great Britain and most parts of Europe before the 12th century.

The idea according to which the belief was introduced or at least reinforced over the centuries through different contacts with other cultures – Vikings or, later, Anglo-Normans – is all the more compelling because it is in Ulster that the tales of milking-hares were the most popular. It is quite likely that this pan-European superstition found a most fertile ground in Ireland, where the fears connected to the month of May were particularly strong and where the figure of the witch was already known, in one form or the other. The detailed study of divine (or divinized) figures related to old women or "hags" – for example, the famous Gaelic Cailleach – would take us too far from the point. However, it is clear that the very idea of a woman with supernatural powers who was able to steal butter, milk or fortune is consistent with what is known of *Bealtaine*: the festival was the point of the year which symbolized the passing from winter to summer, where the fear of a bad season was at its pinnacle and where the worlds of the *profane* and the *sacred* – the world of men and the Otherworld – were supposed to conflate.

Fairies

The second category of individuals or rather "beings" that were feared in early May was even more symptomatic of those two worlds colliding: up to the mid-20th century at least, fairies were particularly feared on *Bealtaine* by cattle-owners, farm laborers and rural Irish families.

The fairy people as imagined by the Irish farmers at the dawn of the 20th century have nothing in common with their idealized modern and contemporary counterparts. In Irish folklore, the fairies (in Irish *sheehogue*, *sídhéóg,* or *sióg*) were a people on their own, with both female and male individuals, who dwelled in the Otherworld, the *sídh*.[84] They were said to look like humans except for a couple of important details: they had the size of a young child and were supposed to have supernatural powers. Traditionally, the month of May was the "month of the fairies";[85] they were particularly active during the first three days of the month and especially on the first of May, the eve of *Bealtaine* (or *May Eve*) or the night between 30 April and 1 May (*May Night*).

The fairy people was supposed to live either underground, "beside a large stone or rocks",[86] beyond the ocean or in what is referred to as forts or *rátha* (sg. *ráth*), i.e. circular stone or earthen walls used as fortification.

According to a nearly universal belief in rural Ireland, the fairies changed their abode in early May. They moved "from fort to fort, changing from winter quarters to summer".[87] They then settled in their new summer quarters until the following first of November, which marked a new "moving" and therefore a renewed fear: most believed that the "Good People", as they were often called, did not like to be disturbed during their peregrinations.

Meeting a fairy on *Bealtaine* was an ill omen: it was considered a dangerous encounter with the *sídh* – a world so important in the traditions connected with Uisneach – which could potentially lead to kidnapping or death. The folkloric collections of the 1930s and 1940s are filled with alleged apparitions of fairies on *Bealtaine* and even more frequently on *May Eve* or *May Night*. People firmly believed that it was possible to see them riding horses, going to war and doing some hunting. Meeting them while they were dancing in the fields, playing Gaelic football or hurling was seemingly even more common. According to popular belief, the fairies could abduct people on *Bealtaine*, either by means of a magic wind which could carry people away to the Otherworld or, for instance, by trying to have them eat their otherworldly food, which one had to refuse. Children were particularly prone to disappearing on *Bealtaine* and, once back from the *sídh*, they were "changed": they had become *corpán sídhe* ("bodies of fairies/of the Otherworld), or *changelings* in English. Once again, the belief was not unique to Ireland: for instance, French folklore, like many others, is filled with mentions of "*changelins de mai*":[88] the body of the child seemed intact but his/her soul was different to the point that mothers could not even recognize their own offspring. In general, the Irish *changelings* were supposed to die some time after their coming back from the Otherworld.

For that very reason, it was strongly recommended never to sleep outside on *May Night* or *May Eve*, especially for children, as they were more likely to be kidnapped. Those customs and superstitions are probably the most abundant and richest of any May tradition; only one last example will be mentioned, as it is particularly striking and representative.

At her arrival on the island of Aran, at the beginning of the 20th century, a nurse found that superstitious customs were deeply rooted in the everyday life of its inhabitants. According to her testimony, modern medicine was virtually unknown and the fairies were held responsible for most diseases. For instance, in order to protect a baby from hypothetical fairy abductions, people would place "a piece of butter mixed with some other substance in her mouth immediately after the birth of her offspring". The author adds with a touch of humor that "no matter how vigilant the nurse may be, directly her back is turned advantage is taken to effect this, for they think that failure renders the woman liable to be kidnapped on the following *May Morning*".

She goes on to detail a most extraordinary medical visit:

> I visited a small boy with a tuberculous knee. [...] I advised hospital treatment but the mother would not hear it. The first pain was felt on 'May Eve' consequently cure was hopeless. The fairies are believed to change their residence on this day, and frequently to snatch children met on their way. They must accordingly have taken her boy, and substituted this other, and how could she think of getting back her own? She did not protect him sufficiently and must accept the inevitable; and now she seemed patiently resigned to it, despite the fact that I had the child afterwards [...] recovered. The 'May Eve' superstition is specially dreaded in the case of cattle. They have great faith in putting a cross on the cow, and go out early on that morning to plaster the poor animal with her own excrement – a large Roman cross on the right side. This is believed to protect it from all subsequent harm for that year. This is also the case with horses.[89]

This excerpt is perfectly representative of the rural Irish "May beliefs" of the 19th and early 20th centuries: the *fear* of the ill influence of the Otherworld was at its peak; conversely, the *hope* to counter evil spells and ill-fortune at that pivotal period of the year did exist. The folkloric collections brim with prevention methods and other conjuration strategies that could protect people from fairies, witches and, more broadly speaking, the *sídh* and its ominous influence.

Counter-spells

It is not necessary here to feature a comprehensive list of the methods envisaged to protect from the evil eye on *Bealtaine*, although a quick mention of the most common practices could shed light of the symbolic substance of such beliefs. Sometimes May flowers (usually but not necessarily hawthorn flowers) were used to decorate the house – especially the kitchen, the threshold or the window sills – the stables and the barns, which were tidied up for the occasion; the flowers were supposed to honor the fairies,[90] for whom a little food, water, milk or even alcohol was left. Those flowers were occasionally put on small twigs or branches that were then stuck on a manure pile, next to the house. In other cases, the cow horns or tails and horses harnesses were adorned with flowers to protect them. The May flowers were often replaced with red ribbons and pieces of cloth as it was said to be the color of the Otherworld and the fairies in general.

Some plants, for example nettles, were picked on the morning of *Bealtaine* and were supposed to have healing or protection powers against fairies and witches, although no tradition was universally accepted among Irish farmers. Placing a four-leaf clover on the cows' head, rubbing their udders with "some herb" during milking, poking farmed birds with a hazel stick, spilling milk on a white hawthorn bush, and so forth. To each informant its own custom: many were unique and representative only of a *local* tradition. Only one feature seems to emerge from this profusion of practices: the use of mountain-ashes. The fact that rowans do flourish in May and their flowers are red may explain this popularity. On many occasions, folkloric manuscripts mention of counter-spells which consisted in circling the churn with a branch of rowan tree, churning butter with a rowan twig, placing a piece of mountain-ash bark on the handle of the milking pail, etc. The idea was always to protect people, beasts and goods from the evil influence of the fairies or from magical theft and witches.

For the same reasons, lending, giving or borrowing anything on the morning of *Bealtaine* was avoided: this symbolically amounted to giving away one's luck, usually for a whole year. As mentioned before, the superstition was quite popular in relation with fire and its derivatives, but also for farm and obviously *dairy* products. Giving or lending milk or butter on *Bealtaine* was completely unconceivable, especially when churning was taking place – although people usually refrained from churning on the morning of the first of May for the same reason. If a farmer decided to churn on *Bealtaine* anyway, a set of counter-spells were possible and the same conjurations sometimes served to protect cattle or family members. Quite often, masses were said: priests visited farms during the month of May so as to protect cattle from diseases and evil spirits. Cattle and crops were blessed in the name of Mary, which is not surprising as, in the Catholic tradition, the month of May is dedicated to the figure. Holy water – or better still, Easter water, i.e. water blessed on Easter and stored – was sprinkled on people, beasts and dwellings. If the priest was not able to come on site, the farmer could pray himself in the name of the Father, the Son and the Holy Ghost on *May Eve* or *May Day*, as a way to protect himself from milk-stealing practices or fairies.

It was common to place a pinch of salt in the butter or milk that was given away to a stranger or even directly in the churn in order to get the stolen "fortune" back. Occasionally, blessed salt was given to cattle on *May Morning* and at the local spring well, the animals and crops were sprinkled with salt.

Iron was also symbolically very powerful: it was customary to place an iron horse – or any other object made of iron – in the local private wells to be protected from thieves. One way to uncover the person who stole the butter was to boil ten pins in milk or to hammer nails to the churn. According to some informants, the ban on giving away or lending anything on *Bealtaine* was particularly strong regarding iron objects, especially in the case of plowshares, coulters or any other object related to farm or soil work. For this reason, blacksmiths were believed to be mystical and occasionally supernatural figures: this is not surprising as, symbolically speaking, blacksmiths master fire and the transmutation of metals; the symbolic power of blacksmiths is common to a great number of cultures, including that of the Celts. In Irish folklore, some people believed that third-generation blacksmiths had the power to expose the people who had magically stolen butter in May, which is arguably a remnant of this symbolic significance.

Fire(s) *and the Folklore of* Bealtaine

Iron was a naturally potent tool to counter spells but was actually even more efficient when associated with fire. The most effective way to expose a thief consisted in placing a piece of iron (especially, once again, a coulter or plowshare) in the hearth until it was red-hot: the thief subsequently experienced excruciating burning pain until the owner decided to take the piece of iron out of the fire.

The place of fire in the folklore of *Bealtaine* was indeed central – and, to some extent, the idea can also be found in the description of the convention of Uisneach made by Keating. In both cases, the element is presented as a most efficient purifying or protective tool.

As already mentioned, popular belief held that giving away fire or being the first to light up the hearth on *Bealtaine* led to the loss of milk and butter production for the benefit of an ill-intentioned thief until the following month of May: as a consequence, farmers took great care that no smoke would come out of their chimney before their neighbors'. For the same reasons, the first fire of the day was occasionally blessed. In other cases, the first fire was to be lit up using firestones or fueled with branches of rowan tree picked up the day before, which prevented any "mystical use" of the fire. Often, farmers would place a burning coal under or in the churn to counter the spells.

Farmers believed lighting one's pipe with a burning piece of turf brought good luck when tillage began on the first of May: the beneficial effect of the fire of *Bealtaine* was transmitted to the soil and farm work through the piece of ember. Even ashes coming from the combustion of a fire of *Bealtaine* were considered useful. In Co. Donegal, a handful of ashes were thrown on cows before transhumance to protect them from spells; the rump of milking cows was rubbed with ashes for the same reason. Cleaning up the ashes of the first fire was considered unlucky: people advised not to throw them away for fear that luck would leave the house with them.

Several accounts of "magical theft" end up with the cremation of the "tools" used by the thief – ropes, tethers or any object that could be dragged on the ground to collect *May Dew*. Similarly, dead animals found on one's land had to be burnt in order to counter the spells. It is also said that burning bales of rowan on the four corners of a field or using the fire of the morning of *Bealtaine* was a sure way to get rid of fairies.

This last practice leads us to the most common conjuration practice of all, i.e., lighting up fires and driving cattle (or in rarer instances, people) between those fires to protect them for the following year:

> Two large fires were lighted[91] and the cattle driven three times between them. Some prayer or invocations were used. The object was to preserve the cattle from the evil eye of the fairies.[92]

According to another informant, children could also benefit from the custom: "On *May Eve* fires were lighted and children and cattle were passed through them for purification".[93] Manuscript S.456 of the *Schools' Collection* from Co. Kerry directly connects the tradition of kindling fires to milk and butter-stealing: "The milk-houses were guarded by big bonfires and when the milk-man had finished milking he would make the sign of the cross with the froth of the fresh milk".[94]

Is it possible to consider that such customs authenticate Keating's testimony and his mention of huge purifying fires at the convention of Uisneach? The correspondences do confirm that the symbolic value of that period of the year remained unchanged from the time of the historian at least up to the folkloric collection of the *Irish Folklore Commission*. They do not, however, confirm the antiquity of such traditions: after all, if Keating mentions large purifying fires, it is perhaps simply because the custom was known and carried out by Irish farmers in his own time and not necessarily because it existed at the time of pre-Christian Celts.

For now at least, we can only conclude that the testimony made by Keating is not incompatible with the symbolism of *Bealtaine*: both medieval documents and modern folklore confirm that the festival was – for the farmer and the Irish "rurality" – a turning point of the year with high symbolical stakes and strong mystical implications. On *Bealtaine*, people were reminded of their own mortality: the celebration marked the passing of time accompanied by its procession of fears – death and disease, loss and destruction.

The study of the festival in relation with farmers and more widely speaking "the common people" proved that *Bealtaine* used to combine the fear of the Otherworld to the hope of countering its evil deeds. An analysis of the impact of the festival on other more prominent members of society (warriors and rulers, including the clergy) will lead us further back in time and confirm that the account made by Keating does seem to follow a millennial tradition: the sources connected to farmers can mainly be found in modern folkloric accounts and fairly recent tradition but those associated with the clergy and warriors are much more ancient.

4.3 Bealtaine and Warriors

Of all members of society, it is arguably with warriors and the global notion of "physical strength" that the connections with *Bealtaine* are the least obvious.[95] The importance of the festival is clearly attested as regards the agricultural world and the sacerdotal sphere but the examples connecting the celebration with warriors, heroes and kings – in their dimension of "supreme fighters" more than their quality of sovereign – are usually relegated to background detail. In most cases, they are connected to either one of the two other "classes" (i.e. the clergy or farmers) in such a way that the festival appears only indirectly related to war and warriors.

Let us consider the example of the *Finn's Poem on May-Day* that can be found in the *Boyish Exploits of Finn* (*Macgnímartha Finn*), dated to the 12th century – although it was probably composed before, perhaps in the 9th century.[96] As already mentioned, Finn is the central character of the Fenian Cycle: he was a hero and a warrior but also a *faíth*, that is to say a prophet. In other words, Finn is connected with magic and divination, which makes him a character on the borders of the warrior and the sacerdotal worlds. In fact, *Finn's Poem on May-Day* was supposed to have been written by the hero while trying to master the art of poetry and perfect his knowledge of lyricism. This connected him with another social category, that of the *filid*, the Irish poets, traditionally associated with the druidic function and the sacerdotal world.

The extract is so useful and informative that it is here reproduced in its entirety. The hero here recites a poem praising *Cétemain*, which is but another name of *May Day* or *Bealtaine*.

1 *Cétemain* [*/Bealtaine*], fair aspect, perfect season; blackbirds sing a full lay when the sun casts a slender beam.
2 The hardy vigorous cuckoo calls. Welcome to noble summer: it abates the bitterness of storm during which the branchy wood is lacerated.
3 Summer cuts the stream small; swift horses seek water; tall heather spreads; delicate fair foliage flourishes.
4 Sprouting comes to the bud of the hawthorn; the ocean flows a smooth course; [summer] sends the sea to sleep; blossom covers the world.
5 Bees of small strength carry bundles in their feet, blossoms having been reaped; the mountain, supplying rich sufficiency, carries off the cattle.
6 Woodland music plays; melody provides perfect peace; dust is blown from dwelling-place and haze from lake full of water.
7 The strenuous corncrake speaks; the high pure cataract sings of joy from the warm water; rustling of rushes has come.

8 Swallows dart aloft; vigour of music surrounds the hill [?]; soft rich fruit flourishes; ...

9 ... ; ... the hardy cuckoo sings; the trout leaps; strong is the swift warrior's ...

10 Men's vigour thrives; the excellence of great hills is complete; fair is every spreading wood, and every great woody plain.

11 Delightful the season: winter's harsh wind has departed; woodland is bright; water fruitful; peace is immense; summer is joyous.

12 A flock of birds settles on land where a woman walks; there is noise in every green field through which a swift bright rivulet flows.

13 Fierce ardour and riding of horses; the serried host is ranged around; the pond is noble in bounty and turns the iris to gold.

14 The frail man fears loudness; the constant man sings with a heart; rightly does he sing out '*Cétemain* [/*Bealtaine*], fair aspect!'[97]

Most of Finn's rhetoric is based on the beneficial aspect of the season opened by *Bealtaine*; summer is nice, generous and fecund. Some references do recall certain traits of the Irish season featured in folkloric collections and ancient sources: this "mountain, supplying rich sufficiency", which "carries off the cattle", obviously reminds of the beginning of transhumance on *Bealtaine*. The mentions of flowers are numerous, although they are never attached to any specific custom and do not necessarily seem to be inherently mystical or symbolic. Finally, the two mentions of "hills" are unfortunately too cryptic: how to interpret this "excellence of great hills" that was "complete"? Finn – or rather, the author of the manuscript – seems to refer to the importance of unspecified places on *Bealtaine* and it is unclear whether this is a reference to "great hills" in general or to a more specific location. Similarly, should we understand the "vigour of music" that "surrounds the hill" as a flight of poetry (the "music" of the woods) or an allusion to specific art-based practices or even assemblies on hills where music could have played a part?

Fortunately, other lines are much more explicit, for instance, when Finn refers to the warriors. The hero tells us that, on *Bealtaine*, the vigor of men was significantly increased – an idea found in the incomplete mention: "strong is the swift warrior's". Better still, Finn explains that, at the beginning of May, men prepared for battle once again: "Fierce ardour and riding of horses; the serried host is ranged around".

The Warrior

As implied by *Finn's Poem on May-Day*, the festival apparently marked the beginning of war-related activities. However, the poem does not make clear whether this reference was a general statement pertaining to all warriors in Ireland or if, on the contrary, it was a simple allusion to the imagined customs of the mythical tribe of Finn, the Fianna.

In a late text entitled *The Pursuit of the Gilla Decair and his Horse* (*Tóraighecht in ghilla dhecair ocus a chapaill inso*),[98] the author comments on the lifestyle of the tribe of Finn:

> For thus it was that [Finn and the Fianna] used to pass the year: from *Beltane* to *All-hallows* in hunting and in deeds of venery; from *All-hallows* to *Beltane* again in the prescribed keeping of all Ireland.[99]

The explanation is clear but, regrettably, was only redacted in 1765.[100] Once again, the text refers to the Fianna and *not* Irish warriors as a whole: *The Pursuit of the Gilla Decair and his Horse* is by no means historical commentary. The same idea can be found two centuries earlier under the pen of Tadhg Dall Ó hUiginn, a poet from the second half of the 16th century:

> They are entitled—what an achievement—from November to summer to quarter their steeds and their hounds from house to house on the plain of *Teathbha*.[101]

The three documents that connect the start of war-related activities at the time of the festival of *Bealtaine* are therefore dated respectively to the 12th, 16th and 18th centuries – although *Finn's Poem* may have been composed much earlier. In all three cases, the connection with Finn or his tribe is obvious. Does that necessarily imply that only the Fianna were (mythically) supposed to spend summer "in hunting and in deeds of venery" and, during winter, to be "in the prescribed keeping of all Ireland" and "to quarter their steeds and their hounds from house to house"? Could the referenced tradition be but a mythological whiff, therefore impossible to apply to Ireland in general and non-mythological warriors in particular?

Several other sources confirm a division of the year from *Samhain* to *Bealtaine* and from *Bealtaine* to *Samhain* while insisting on the fact that the active seasons spanned, in ancient or medieval Ireland, from May to November and was counterbalanced by a season of rest or retreat, winter, from early November to early May.

Thus, two documents seem to indicate that the Irish poets, the *filid*,[102] practiced their art in winter, which corresponded to the time they were lodged by the "men of Ireland". This essentially means that the Irish spent their winter at rest while listening to the works of the *filid* and would start their – war-related – activities in summer. To that extent, in the 17th century, Keating made the following observation:

> And about that time nearly a third of the men of Ireland belonged to the poetic order, and they quartered themselves from *Samhain* to *Bealltaine* on the men of Ireland.[103]

This division was already present in an episode taken from *The Legend of Mongan* which, as already mentioned, could date back to the 7th century:

> Mongan was in Rath Mor of Mag Linne in his kingship. Forgoll, the poet, came to him. [...] Each night the poet told Mongan a story. His repertoire was so vast that they continued from *Samain* to *Beltaine*.[104]

This could mean that *filid* would rather practice their art in winter than summer.[105] However, "from *Samain* to *Beltaine*" (*O Samhain go Bealtaine* in Irish) is actually an expression that refers to something which drags on interminably. It is therefore possible that this sentence was a mere figure of speech meant to glorify the erudition of *fili* Forgoll.

As a consequence, the example of *filid* lacks consistency: Keating is not trustworthy enough, and the episode from *The Legend of Mongan* is too ambiguous. This is quite unfortunate since proving that the *filid* actually "quartered themselves" in winter would back up the supposition that Irish warriors – and not only mythological figures – did fight in summer and rest from *Samhain* to *Bealtaine*. This would confirm a division of the year in two parts: summer as an active season, placed under the sign of war and "vigor", in the words of *Finn's Poem*; winter as an inactive season, dedicated to resting, poetry and the telling of epics.

By chance, one last example is much more credible and confirms the association of the month of May with the resumption of war-related activities: the *Book of Rights* (*Lebor na Cert*) even makes it a royal prerogative.

The King

The *Book of Rights* indeed mentions that one of the five prerogatives of the king of Connacht was to go to Maen-mhagh, a plain in modern-day Co. Galway, on the morning of the first of May. The cause of this royal privilege is unknown: it is of course possible to imagine that it was linked to a long-forgotten custom or ritual; when put into context, the law also seems to echo the resuming of war-related activities.[106]

One of the five prerogatives of the king of Munster is also worth noting: "The cattle of Cruachan at the singing of the cuckoo".[107] The description of the privilege is concise, to say the least. According to tradition, the singing of the cuckoo is associated with the beginning of summer and therefore with *Bealtaine*; additionally, Cruachan, i.e., Rathcrogan (the "Fort of Cruachan"), was believed to be one of the passages between both worlds.[108] o'Donovan explains the mention as follows: "looting the plain of *Rath Cruacha[i]n* and taking the cattle of the king of Connacht at the beginning of summer was considered most likely to be successful and the king of Munster was pressured to do it".[109] Starting a battle or war-related activities – for example looting – "at the singing of the cuckoo" was a privilege and was considered lucky to succeed: the association with the beginning of the summer season bode well for its success. Those different mentions seem to confirm – at least in part – the association of the festival of *Bealtaine* with the start of war-related activities.

Concurrently, the *Book of Rights* also tells us that the Irish kings and their subjects had to follow certain rules on the day of *Bealtaine* – which actually remind us of settlements and payments that were to be done at the convention of Uisneach, according to Keating. The farm animals, mainly dairy cows, and other precious goods used as currency had to be given to the king precisely on *Bealtaine*. Hereafter are transcribed three of the most telling passages:

> The stipend of the King of noble Aine
> From the king of Caiseal of the terrific sword,
> His shield and his bright sword,
> Thirty cows each *Bealltaine*.[110]

> The Privileges of the King of Cruachain: [...] six times fifty milch-cows, three times fifty hogs, three times fifty cloaks from the Luighne every *Bealltaine*, and three times fifty oxen.[111]

> There are due of the Luighne without fault,
> As a supply for the residence,
> Seven times fifty milch-cows hither
> To be brought every [*Beltaine*].
> Thrice fifty bull-like hogs
> To be brought every Samain, thrice fifty super cloaks
> To the King of [Cruachain].[112]

The last two examples deal with the same protagonists: according to the version in prose, all exchanges had to be done on *Bealtaine*. On the other hand, the authors of the versified version chose to divide payment into two parts: half of the transactions were moved to *Samhain*. As always in this type of ancient document, the versification implies a late addition[113] and must be considered as a gloss subsequent to the prose version. Originally, payments were to be done on *Bealtaine* exclusively.

Perhaps more intriguing are the royal prohibitions concerning water. The *Book of Rights* begins with the seven "restrictions and prohibitions of the King of Éire".[114] The sixth one is of particular interest: it was clearly established that the king was in no way allowed "to go in a ship upon the water the Monday after *Bealltaine*".[115] Similarly, the king of Ulster could in no circumstances swim eastward in the waters of *Loch Feabhail* on the day of *Bealtaine*.[116]

Those royal prohibitions seem at first quite difficult to interpret. It is always possible to conjure up the influence of a forgotten superstition, perhaps of a mythological episode or some local legends. However, this fear of waters or the ocean and the prohibitions ensuing could as well be a reminiscence of the *sídh*, which is often believed to be "beyond the ocean". Since *Bealtaine* was the moment when the world of the dead and that of the living collided, it seems quite logical that the element was dreaded at that time of the year.

In Irish folklore, the fear of the sea is verified at the beginning of May: in coastal areas, mermaids were supposed to appear and their influence was comparable with that of the fairies.[117] Well into the 20th century, meanwhile, fishermen from the west coast of Ireland refused to set sail on *Bealtaine*. Apparitions of specters or legendary characters are mentioned on the shores of certain Irish lakes[118] and it was not rare to see a ship belonging to the "Good People" sailing on *May Night*.

A tale told in Irish in manuscript 1096[119] of the *Irish Folklore Commission* explains that three rocks, situated off the island of Owey – which is itself off the coast of Arvanmore – were actually the ships of three kings who, a long time ago, came to invade Ireland. Balor, king of Tory, turned the three vessels into stone in order to protect his sovereignty. Every 7 May, the three rocks were seen sailing toward the isle of Tory. Legend holds that in case they succeeded in reaching Tory without being seen by anyone, they would destroy the island and subsequently wreak havoc in Owey and Arvanmore.

The story is obviously steeped in mythological references, which mainly revolved around the central character of Balor in Irish mythology, his connection with *Bealtaine* and his link with water and fire. Most of all, we already know that one of the names of Uisneach was "the hill of Balor". Another informant tells us that an extraordinary island appeared every year on *Bealtaine* between the isles of Owey and Arvanmore. It was filled with birds and covered with beautiful trees; its inhabitants were "a diminutive people" – an obvious reference to the fairies – who could be seen cultivating the land.[120]

According to another local legend,[121] three small islands next to Dursey Island "sailed" very early on the morning of *Bealtaine* to Fastnet Rock – off Cape Clear, about 50 kilometers east of Dursey – and went back soon after. Today, those three small islands bear the evocative names of *Bull*, *Cow* and *Calf*. Finally, another informant[122] tells us that the Rock of Fastnet itself moved southward and disappeared at the horizon on *Bealtaine*, before sunrise, and returned to its place in the same morning.

All those beliefs relative to Irish rocks and islets are essentially similar: islands or groups of islands appear, disappear or move on *Bealtaine*. Although the exact origin of those tales remains a mystery, they are probably reminiscent of the belief according to which the Otherworld, the *sídh*, was "very far [beyond the seas] west of Ireland".[123] This obviously invites us to contemplate the importance of the *sídh* on *Bealtaine* and especially the connection it held with the most important representatives of the clergy in ancient Ireland, namely the druids.

4.4 Bealtaine and the Clergy

The Druids and the Fire of Bel

Except for the purely mythological documents and the writings of Keating, only two documents clearly connect the members of the sacerdotal class to the festival of *Bealtaine*. *The Wooing of Emer* has already been mentioned on several occasions: Kuno Meyer believed it dates back to the 10th century. The explanation given by Cúchulainn is reproduced hereafter *in extenso*:

> Beldine, i.e. Beltine, viz., a favouring fire. For the druids used to make two fires with great incantations, and to drive the cattle between them against the plagues, every year. Or to Beldin, viz., Bel the name of an idol. At that time the young of every neat were placed in the possession of Bel. Beldine, then Beltine.[124]

Cormac's Glossary (Sanas Cormaic) elaborates on approximately the same ideas. At the entry word *Bealtaine*, the manuscript, which is also dated to the 10th century, gives the following definition:

> *Belltaine*, "May-day" i.e. *bil-tene* [fire of Bel?] i.e. lucky fire, i.e. two fires which Druids used to make with great incantations, and they used to bring the cattle [as a safeguard] against the diseases of each year to those fires [*in marg.*] they used to drive the cattle between them.[125]

Therefore, only the etymological explanations differ: *Bealtaine* supposedly means "favoring fire" or "the young of every neat [placed] in the possession of Bel" in *The Wooing of Emer* and "lucky fire" or possibly "fire of Bel" in *Cormac's Glossary*.

The fragments seem to imply that Bel was an ancient god to whom the festival of *Bealtaine* was dedicated. However, no references to this god appear anywhere else in Irish mythology: our knowledge of an hypothetical god named Bel is limited to what the two 10th-century manuscripts tell us; in fact, this reference in the two manuscripts might simply be an allusion to a Canaanite god named Ba'al.[126]

According to another tempting explanation, "Bel" could be an Irish equivalent of the continental god Belenos (or Belenus), a name of the Gaulish Apollo, who was venerated in a territory stretching from the north of Greece to Tyrol, the north of Italy.[127] He was also known in Great Britain – even more so than in Gaul, where the traces of his worship were mainly concentrated in modern-day Aquitaine and Provence.[128] The archaeological elements related to Belenos confirm that he was essentially a god assimilated to the cult of water. It is possible that he was considered, at one point of history or another, as a solar god, although this could very well be due to the influence of Apollo, who tends to be confused or assimilated to the god: this led to the ensuing popularity of a deity called Apollo-Belenos.[129]

Understanding the true nature of Apollo is not an easy task. The "luminous" deity was often associated with agriculture, although Apollo, son of Zeus, was also a protective god – for instance of cattle – and a medicine god. The bow was one of his attributes and could unleash epidemics. Furthermore, he was one of the main gods of divination; he was consulted, *inter alia*, in Delphi where he delivered Oracles through the Pythia.[130] Apollo was therefore an ambivalent god: a protective figure on the one hand but an avenging and dreadful warrior on the other. According to Caesar, the Gaulish Apollo – that is, in all likelihood, Belenos or one of its avatars – was essentially worshipped for his ability to "ward off diseases".[131] It is also interesting to bear in mind that Apollo was supposed to come from "beyond the north"; every fall, the god withdrew for three months in Hyperborea and came back for spring. Finally, the *Thargêlia*, celebrating Apollo and Artemis, were held on the sixth and seventh days of the month of *Thargêliôn* of the Athenian calendar, which corresponds to the end of May: it was an agrarian festival whose purpose was to secure good crops via miscellaneous offerings; young people hung olive branches from the doors of their house to circumvent famine.[132] A sheep and a pig were apparently offered as a sacrifice on the first day of the celebration. Originally, two men were also sacrificed; garlands made of figs were tied around their neck before they were lapidated, their bodies burnt and their ashes spread at sea or on the fields so as to fertilize them.[133]

All those elements make the blended figure Apollo/Belenos/Bel rather appealing: most seem compatible with at least one aspect of the festival of *Bealtaine*: agriculture; ambivalence (protection and vengeance) connected to the concept of fear and hope on *Bealtaine*; purification and prophylaxis; cycle of the Otherworld and the Hyperboreans; month of May and spring; offerings and potentially sacrifices; divination; and finally, of course, the mention of Delphi, whose correspondences with Uisneach have already been noted.

However, caution is still advisable: Apollo is one of these pluripotent gods whose attributes were so numerous that it is quite easy to find similarities and points of comparisons. Most of all, if Bel indeed existed, the fact that it completely disappeared from the Christian transcriptions of Irish mythology remains unsolved: whereas the documents at our disposal describe the mythical life of Lugh, the Dagda and many others in great detail, Bel is not even mentioned. Perhaps the Christian monks considered that the character could not be featured in their transcription because of the possible sacrifices made in his honor, as the practice proved too ostensibly Pagan and opposed to the ideals of the New Religion.[134] Yet this overlooks the fact that many controversial Pagan deities were described and included in the Christian transcriptions, including for instance "Balor of the evil eye", later assimilated to the demon Baal or even Beelzebub or Bel (/zebub) – although this mythological comparison and etymological theory have long been discarded. Nothing proves that the Christian monks actually selected the information they wanted to share with their contemporaries: since even ostensibly Pagan figures were included in Christian transcriptions, most scholars believe the selection and "censorship" in Irish Christian manu-scripts was minimal.

The mention of large fires on *Bealtaine* in *Cormac's Glossary* and *The Wooing of Emer*, whether they were consecrated to Bel or not, is by far more conclusive: *Bealtaine* is presented as an essentially sacerdotal festival; the druidic fire is the key element of the celebration.

The medieval sources do present fire as the ultimate druidic element: "the druids [were] masters of fire and it was the fire of the most powerful druid, the one whose magic was the most efficient which prevailed".[135] The fire of *Bealtaine* was a purifying, prophylactic fire and therefore, in essence, it was beneficial, as frequently emphasized by the authors and transcribers. To that extent, it was, symbolically speaking, very powerful and "mystical" by nature. Both *Cormac's Glossary* and *The Wooing of Emer* underline the fact that the fire or fires were to be lit "by incantation". This belief justifies on its own the prophylactic and healing qualities of the druidic flames: as could be expected, the mentions of fire do not refer to any kind of medical treatment, in the modern and scientific sense, but rather to a ritual pur-ification connected to the world of the sacred and the religious.

Although the druids disappeared gradually in the centuries following the Christianization of Ireland, the tradition of the *Bealtaine* fires remained. This is also suggested by the modern folklore of the festival: Irish farmers did light huge fires through which they passed their cattle to preserve them from dis-eases, fairies and "stealing" for a whole year, well into the 20th century. Those supernatural fires could find their symbolic source in a specific mythological episode: the "mystic fire" of Midhe, lit on the top of the hill of Uisneach, the first flame ever lit in Ireland and the origin of all ensuing fires. Yet the cor-respondence is not exact: first, the fire of Midhe is a "single" fire and not two fires acting as "gates" through which people or cattle could pass for protec-tion. Secondly, the documents relating to Midhe never mention that the epi-sode took place on *Bealtaine*. But if no date is explicitly mentioned in the texts at our disposal, the assimilation of the mythical tribe of Nemed – of which Midhe was the druid – but also of most mythical tribes of Ireland with the beginning of the month of May could be a first indication.

Mythical Ancestors, Gods and the Sídh

According to the various mythological sources at our disposal, the Irish gods were members of the mythological tribe of the Tuatha Dé Danann. Tradition holds that the tribe took possession of Ireland in "time im-memorial", with the Tuatha Dé Danann, led by Lugh, establishing their supremacy thanks to their victory over the tribe of the Fir Bolg, described in *The First Battle of Mag Tuired* and over the Fomorians, the evil creatures defeated in *The Second Battle of Mag Tuired*.

However, according to the redactors of the *Book of Invasions*, the Tuatha Dé Danann were not the first tribe to set foot in Ireland. As already pointed out, five distinct tribes[136] are usually mentioned: the tribe of queen Cessair, the tribe of Partholón, the Nemedians, the Fir Bolg then the Tuatha Dé Danann, ultimately defeated by the Milesians, i.e., men. The tribes are presented as the descendants of Japheth, son of Noah, which reminds us that the *Book of Invasions* was composed in a monastery. The first part of the book is entitled "From the Creation to the dispersal of the nations" and is almost exclusively dedicated to the Flood account. It is a relatively faithful transcription of the Biblical episode that can be found in the Genesis, with one notable difference: the beginning and the end of the Flood are almost systematically associated with the beginning of the month of May. As noted by Macalister:

> The month of May is named in the Irish text: the Hebrew and all the versions say 'the second month'. On the hypothesis that the Creation took place at the Vernal Equinox, April would be the first complete month, and so May would be the second. That the biblical months were lunar was hidden from the compilers.[137]

The theory is convincing although one could rightly wonder why the Irish monks insisted so much on this specific episode and its correspondence to the month of May when most other episodes – either Biblical or from Irish mythology – developed in *Book of Invasions* are usually not related to modern calendars. Perhaps the period of the year was important enough, symbolically speaking, for the transcribers and their contemporaries. The association of mythical episodes to the month of May does not end there: most Irish mythical tribes were said to have arrived in Ireland at the same period of the year. Cessair reached the Irish shores three hundred years before Partholón but in the very same month:

> On a Tuesday [Partholón] reached Ireland, upon the seventeenth of the moon, on the calends of May. Or on the fourteenth. [...] Or further, it is on the sixteenth of the age of the moon in the month of May that Partholón took Ireland, and in the fifth unit of the moon of the same month that Cessair took Ireland.[138]

The tribe of Cessair was wiped out in a week following a mysterious disease. As it turns out, the tribe of Partholón met with the same fate and was struck with a plague precisely on the calends of May. It is therefore possible to consider that, very much in the same manner that the Flood was supposed to start and end in May, the tribes of Cessair and Partholón were decimated in the same month.

No specific date is mentioned for the tribe of Nemed and the Fir Bolg are said to have come in Ireland on the calends of August. On the other hand, the tribe of the great Irish gods, that of the Tuatha Dé Danann, did land in Ireland at the beginning of the month of May:

> And they came to Ireland, on Monday, the kalends of May, in ships [and vessels].[139]

> On Monday in the beginning of the month of May, to be exact, [the Tuatha Dé Danann] took Ireland.[140]

> The seventeenth, a Tuesday,
> was found the battle-plain of warrior men,
> they took, in an attack on the land,
> on the kalends of May in the solar month.[141]

The mythological tale of the *The First Battle of Mag Tuired* had already placed the arrival of the Tuatha Dé Danann on the first Monday of May:

> Then those warriors gathered their fleets to one place till they had three hundred ships under way. Thereupon their seers, Cairbre, Aed, and Edan asked the chiefs of the host in which ship they should sail, recommending that of Fiachra. The chiefs approved and went on board. Then they all set sail, and after three years and three days and three nights landed at wide Tracht Mugha in Ulster on Monday of the first week in May.[142]

Later, the idea was taken up by Keating:

> Concerning the Tuatha Dé Danann, they, having spent seven years in the north of Scotland, came to Ireland; and, on their coming to land, Monday Bealtaine in the north of Ireland, they burn their ships, so to certify that, this rann was composed:

> Each warrior of them burned his ship,
> When he reached noble Éire:
> It was a grave decision in his state [?]
> The vapour of the ships being burned.[143]

The First Battle of Mag Tuired narrates the confrontation opposing the Fir Bold, then masters of the island, and the Tuatha Dé Danann. The manuscripts date back to the 14th, 15th and 16th centuries but the episode is already mentioned in the 11th century. The tribe of the supreme Irish gods left a deep impression on the Fir Bold on that famous "Monday *Bealtaine*":

Now it was reported to the Fir Bolg that that company had arrived in Ireland. That was the most handsome and delightful company, the fairest of form, the most distinguished in their equipment and apparel, and their skill in music and playing, the most gifted in mind and temperament that ever came to Ireland. That too was the company that was bravest and inspired most horror and fear and dread, for the Tuatha De excelled all the peoples of the world in their proficiency in every art.[144]

The Fir Bolg, who had landed in Ireland "on the Calends of August" – the festival of *Lughnasa* – are therefore attacked by the Tuatha Dé Danann, who had arrived "on the Calends of May" – the festival of *Bealtaine*. The episode inscribes the confrontation of two traditions: the tribe of *Lughnasa*, so to speak, against the tribe of *Bealtaine*.

Furthermore, the battle takes place after "six weeks of the summer, half the quarter";[145] placing a confrontation on such a specific date cannot be coincidental. Most scholars chose not to comment this passage and the few who did could not find any good reason for this specification. In *Textes Mythologiques irlandais*, Christian-Joseph Guyonvarc'h made the following comment: "Since the beginning of summer is the festival of *Bealtaine*, on the first of May, the date here mentioned is 15 June, which is not significant in the Celtic calendar".[146] It is true that 15 June does not correspond to any remarkable Celtic or Gaelic celebration. Since *Bealtaine* was a mobile feast, it may however be possible to consider this reference to "six weeks of the summer" as an allusion to the summer solstice.[147] Most of all, a *First Battle of Mag Tuired* taking place "six weeks" after *Bealtaine* implied that it took place six weeks before *Lughnasa*, precisely at "half the quarter" as mentioned in the original text. In other words, the confrontation between the two tribes is placed by the authors or by the transcribers precisely halfway – at the "just midpoint" – between the two celebrations associated with each of the two tribes.

Cessair, Partholón, Tuatha Dé Danann and then the Milesians:[148] most of the invaders of Ireland arrived on the island on the first of May or what was referred to as the "week of *Bealtaine*". The recurrence could be partially explained by a desire to inscribe the Celtic tradition in the Christian world. Since the Flood was supposed to have taken place on the second month of the year – which the Irish monks believed to be the month of May – having the mythological tribes of Ireland arriving precisely at the same time of the year connected them with the Biblical episode.

However, the hypothesis is not fully satisfying. Although it is possible to believe in an occasional adaptation of the insular tradition, such a manifest and homogenous Christianization of pre-Christian myths seems unlikely. The Christianization of Ireland should not be imagined as an organized, coherent nation-wide endeavor. The association of the Tuatha Dé Danann with the month of May appears in at least three different texts or compilations, which themselves were declined in multiple versions and redacted in very different places and times. Moreover, the hypothesis by no means explains the confrontation opposing the Fir Bolg – assimilated to *Lughnasa*– to the Tuatha Dé Danann – assimilated to *Bealtaine* – that has just been demonstrated and which was supposed to take place at "half the quarter".

We therefore have every reason to believe that the assimilation of the Irish mythical invaders with "the month of May" – or its equivalent in the Celtic calendar – does have pre-Christian roots. Moreover, it is quite likely that only the association of the Tuatha Dé Danann with *Bealtaine* was actually really significant in the original myth: out of the five mythical tribes, only the tribe of Dana is of central importance in Irish mythology; the other four seem to exist merely to prepare for the arrival of the tribe of the Irish gods.

D'Arbois de Jubainville, one of the first Celtic scholars of the modern era outside of Britain and Ireland, believed that *Bealtaine* was a festival dedicated to a god of death. According to this theory, which springs from a most debatable interpretation of the etymology of *Bealtaine*,[149] the festival celebrated the Tuatha Dé Danann as ancestors (albeit *indirect* ancestors) of the human race and was connected to a cult of the dead.[150] The hypothesis could be supported by the fact that the festivals of May worldwide tend to be associated with a cult of the dead as well as the insistence of the redactors of the *Book of Invasions* to connect the mythical arrivals to that specific month. However, the theory is manifestly unsustainable, first because the etymology proposed is groundless and also because the Tuatha Dé Danann are never presented as the ancestors of men but rather the tribe of Irish gods, separate and distinct from men. On the other hand, the bond uniting the tribe of Dana to the Otherworld cannot be overlooked.

Although it cannot be considered as an echo of a potential cult of the dead, it is possible to see in this recurrence of the month of May a reference to the Otherworld: it is perhaps precisely because the month of May – or even more precisely the festival of *Bealtaine* – is intimately associated with the *sídh*, the world of the dead and the gods (the Tuatha Dé Danann) that this time of the year was so common in the myths attached to the mythical tribes of Ireland. For this reason also, a certain number of mythological episodes – for example those describing the death of Lugh – were set on *Bealtaine* and, better still, on the hill of Uisneach: the hill clearly appears as a *spatial* hyphen between two worlds which is venerated at *Bealtaine*, a *temporal* hyphen between those same two worlds. Similarly, this could explain why a fairly large number of ritual assemblies took place at the beginning of the month of May in Ireland through ages: Uisneach was not an isolated case.

Ritual Assemblies

It is possible to divide the gatherings potentially connected with *Bealtaine* into several distinct categories – although, once again, it would be pointless to try and provide an exhaustive list of such gatherings. As will be demonstrated, many aspects found in those meetings share similarities with the various celebrations held on Uisneach, past or present.

Hundreds, if not thousands of sacred/holy wells and springs were – and still are – visited in May in Ireland. It is probable that, in the 18th and 19th centuries, almost every parish had its own well-associated with a pilgrimage or a gathering in May. However, a "May pilgrimage" does not necessarily imply a connection with *Bealtaine*. In the vast majority of cases, the wells could be visited throughout the month and especially during the last two Sundays of May. Those wells usually bore the name of *Tobar Muire*, i.e., the "well of Mary" and were obviously connected with the veneration of the Virgin; in most cases, the association lasted into the present day.

It would be both impossible and irrelevant to try and prove that each and every one of those sources or wells were originally Pagan springs linked with *Bealtaine* and later taken over by Christianity to benefit the cult of Mary: in most cases, the *Toibreacha Muire* and the wells associated with patron saints can be found next to ancient parish churches or Christian cemeteries: the possibility that they were sacred *because* of their connection with Christian sites cannot be ruled out. However, in other cases, it is still possible to perceive a more ancient origin. For example, the source of Dromtariffe – literally the "ridge of the bull – in Co. Cork was to be visited on 6 May: according to a local proverb, the pilgrimage marked the beginning of summer, which confirms a direct connection with *Bealtaine*. Still in Co. Cork, *Tobarín na Súl* was – and still is – visited on the first of May: pilgrims bring offerings and tie them to the branches of the tree overlooking the well. As is often the case of sacred or holy wells, the votive items can take many forms and shapes, from the most common – pieces of paper on which the wish or vow is written, small jewels, rosaries, picture of deceased people, colored ribbons, cloths and rags of any kind – to the most improbable – headbands, automotive air fresheners, advertising key-rings etc. The main idea is to drop or hang a personal object with little to no monetary value. The well is said to cure eye afflictions when its water is drunk or applied on eyes: *Tobarín na Súl* literally means "the little well of the eyes".

In other cases, the sacred water sources were not mere wells but entire lakes: for instance, *Lough Fergus* in Co. Clare and *Glendalough* in Co. Wicklow both knew gatherings at the beginning of May during which the cattle were put to the water so as to protect them for the following year.[151]

Finally, perhaps the most convincing example is that of *Cathair Crobh Dearg* on the border of Co. Kerry and Co. Cork, whose most salient features only will be mentioned hereafter.[152] *Cathair Crobh Dearg* refers to a stone enclosure, about 50 meters in diameter. A statue of the Virgin Mary and an altar built at the beginning of the 20th century can be found within the enclosure as well as two megaliths at its center and a holy well in a smaller adjacent enclosure. In the distance, the two *Paps of Anu* – two twin mountains owing their name to their evocative shape – overlook the site. *Cathair Crobh Dearg* is visited at the beginning of May by pilgrims who still make the "Christian rounds" to this day: they follow a precise circuit in or around the enclosure while reciting prayers and making small votive offerings. The water of the holy well is said to protect and cure humans, cattle and horses for a whole year when drunk in May. Up to the 19th century, cows were made to spend the night within the enclosure so as to protect them from diseases and other "evil influences", i.e. fairies. The importance of the *Paps of Anu* is confirmed in folklore, both modern and contemporary: some farmers still recite prayers from *Cathair Crobh Dearg* while looking at the distant twin mountains named after Anu, which is but another name of Ana/Dana. The connection of the Pagan goddess with the site is obvious: the *Paps* bear her name and the site is celebrated on *Bealtaine*, which is the date of the landing of her tribe, the Tuatha Dé Danann, in Ireland. Additionally, the three sons of the Dagda, who killed Lugh on *Bealtaine*, had three wives: the most ancient versions of the *Book of Invasions* tell us that they were "Badb and Macha and Anand of whom are the Paps of Anu" (R1)/"Badb and Macha (the Morrigu) and Anann of whom are the Two paps of Ana" (R2).[153]

The connection with the ancient festival of *Bealtaine* is undeniable and the Christianization of the site quite clear: time erased all traces of the in-fluence of the Pagan/druidic clergy in the modern and contemporary cus-toms connected to *Cathair Crobh Dearg* and the Christian clergy took over the traditions. To that extent, a sermon preached on 1 May 1925 by a local priest is quite significant:

> The pagan danger is now past. Paganism is dead, or rather all the best elements in it have been absorbed into Christianity. It would therefore be criminal negligence on our part to allow this storied stream of age-old enthusiasm to perish … It is most fitting that the Festival is held on the first day of Our Lady's month, for the Mother of God, in the person of Dana, has been worshipped here for hundreds of generations.[154]

The study of the other categories of ritual assemblies in early May is far less conclusive, in the sense that they are harder to connect with ancient Pagan traditions and the festival of *Bealtaine*. Some have argued that funerary sites were visited in early May by pilgrims, a theory that is not confirmed by the comprehensive study of the *Irish Folklore Commission* manuscripts of 1947: at best, folkloric traditions refer to apparitions of fairies in early May in cemeteries, which is not surprising but does not fall within the scope of "ritual assemblies". May pilgrimages in cemeteries are usually mentioned only because they are connected with a holy well, which is itself worshipped in May, as in the case of the cemetery of Kilsarcon, Co. Kerry for instance.[155] The same observation can be made for assemblies and pilgrimages on heights; although extremely numerous in connection with the month of August, they remained fairly rare in relation with the festival of *Bealtaine*. Of course, a certain number of hills do bear the name of *Cnoc Na Bealtaine, Beltany Hill* or *Summerhill*. But those places were usually visited at *Lughnasa* in modern folklore: young people picked flowers and berries, danced, rejoiced and had fun while eating and drinking together.[156] Those joyful events were *a priori* out of the question in early May as the period was closely connected with the anxiety of the rural world: in May, the wheat granaries were still empty, the cattle still not fat enough and the crops had yet to grow. Summer weather was also yet to come, despite the fact that *Bealtaine* marked the beginning of the season – which naturally induced a fear of a potentially unfruitful summer for farmers. And this is indeed the main difference between the celebration of the festival in rural and in urban areas: the former were steeped in apprehension and fear when the latter were joyful events, which were all about dancing, rejoicing and celebrating the beauty of summer. In Irish urban centers – especially in the north and east of the island – *May Bushes, May Queens, May Babies, May Pole* dances, *May Games* and sports were so many frivolous occasions to enjoy oneself and must be distinguished from the ancient Celtic *Bealtaine* celebration.[157]

However, assemblies on "heights" – note the quotation marks – did exist in connection with *Bealtaine*. William Wilde, a prominent folklorist and incidentally the father of Oscar, describes perhaps the most interesting example as follows:

> It was not unusual, some fifteen or twenty years ago, to bleed a whole heard of cattle upon a *May Morning*, and then to dry and burn the blood. We have more than once, when a boy, seen the entire of the great Fort of Rathcrogan, then the centre of one of the most extensive and fertile grazing districts of Connacht, literally reddened with the blood thus drawn upon a *May Morning*. [...] In some districts, and particularly during hard times, some of the blood thus drawn used to be mixed with meal, boiled into a posset and eaten by the herds and the poor people. But many of these ceremonies, having been either laughed at or positively interdicted by the more educated Roman Catholic clergy, are fast falling into disuse.[158]

Rathcroghan is Ráth Cruachan: at the heart of Co. Roscommon, the site was one of the centers of Irish royalty. According to tradition, it was the royal seat of legendary queen Medb and her husband Ailill, king of Connacht. Rathcrogan is the place where the plot of *Cattle Raid of Cooley* starts. It stands at the approximate center of an 800-hectare site comprising about 50 – mainly funerary – monuments built or created over centuries: the most ancient date back to prehistoric times.

Rathcrogan now looks like a small rounded hill or actually a rather unimpressive rise, about six meters in height. It is actually an artificial and nearly circular mound which is often described as a major funerary site where a great number of warriors were buried. It is frequently described as "a magic place with an entrance to the Otherworld",[159] i.e., a place connecting the world of the living and that of the dead and obviously reminding both of Uisneach and *Bealtaine.*

Ráth Cruachan means the "fort of Cruachan", a term that may derive from *crúach,* "a hill or mound". According to John Waddel,[160] Cruachan may therefore signify "the people of the hill" or "of the mound". Although this was possibly a tribal name, the denomination of "people of the hill" is intriguing as it clearly reminds of the fairies. This association is compelling on two counts at least.

First, it may first explain the custom of the bleeding of cattle on Rathcrogan, at least from a folkloric perspective. The forts were the dwellings of the fairies and the fairies were connected, in modern folklore, to *Bealtaine;* the modern folkloric custom was probably a prophylactic ritual justified both by the symbolism of the festival and the otherworldly influence of fairies.

Moreover, if one accepts that the tradition indeed had ancient Pagan origins, the fairies therefore become directly associated with the world of the dead; in other words, and symbolically speaking, the world of the fairies and that of the dead were but one. This implies that the fairies themselves were not a distinct race of "fairy people" but rather constituted a modern projection of deceased ancestors or deities: as mentioned by a folkloric informant, "the fairies are the Tuatha Dé Danann".[161] As a matter of fact, there is no doubt that Irish folklore and Celtic mythology were connected, although a number of nuances, mentioned hereafter, must be taken into account.

4.5 Influences and Confluences

How Celtic were the ancient four seasonal celebrations? How Celtic, and indeed how Irish were the old festival of *Bealtaine* and its modern equivalent? For most scholars, the fact that *Bealtaine* was part of a set of four celebrations and that those celebrations were originally Celtic is largely taken for granted.[162]

However, the ancient – perhaps original – festival of *Bealtaine* must be distinguished from its modern and contemporary equivalent. This recent avatar was the subject of profound mutations, to the point that what is now called *Bealtaine* in Ireland must be understood as a very specific version of the original Celtic *Bealtaine,* and for good reason: during the last two millennia, Ireland witnessed multiple waves of invasions and a complex canvas of influences – either Christian, Germanic, Scandinavian, English, Norman and even indirectly Roman – which necessarily left their marks on the Irish culture and, by extension, on the very substance of the festival of May.

In other words, the ancient Irish festival of *Bealtaine* seems "Celtic" in essence, notably because close equivalents can be found in a number of countries, which were strongly influenced by the Celtic civilization, both from a cultural and a linguistic point of view. Scotland, Wales and the Isle of Man all seem to know an equivalent of *Bealtaine* in their ancient and more modern traditions. Nevertheless, the modern Irish festival of *Bealtaine* is a sort of patchwork of different traditions: it is the prolongation of the ancient Celtic festival but, due to the contacts with various cultures throughout centuries, it has integrated many aspects which did not – could not – originally exist in the most ancient version of the Irish celebration.

An in-depth analysis of the Celtic "confluences" of *Bealtaine*, i.e., the common points between the many celebrations of May in Celtic countries, would take us too far from our point. Similarly, it is not necessary here to catalogue the entirety of potential influences that have transformed the substance of the original Celtic *Bealtaine* in Ireland. Let us simply mention the essentials: apart from a few minor details, the celebrations of the beginning of the month of May were virtually identical – including the use of prophylactic fires – in many "Celtic countries". In the Isle of Man, it took the name of *Laa-Boaldyn*, in Scotland, the barely anglicized name of *Beltane* and in Wales, it was famously called *Calan Mai*.

In the Isle of Man and Scotland, the points of comparison are limited for the most part to modern and contemporary folklore – with a few notable exceptions, such as the ancient sacredness of Tynwald. The case of Wales is much more informative and eloquent, and for good reason: medieval sources are still available for consideration and do confirm the importance of the date in Welsh mythology. The episode of Lludd and Llefelys has already been mentioned and is rather compelling. The confrontation between Gwyn and Gwythyr is also noteworthy: the two characters were condemned by Arthur to fight "every *May Day* forever from that day forth until Judgement Day",[163] an ordeal sometimes interpreted as a symbolic confrontation between winter and summer. We should also mention Taliesin, one of the most prominent figures of Welsh mythology, presented as either a druid, a soothsayer, a counsellor or a renowned poet of Wales: most of all, he is said to have been born on 29 April and was found three days later in a fisherman's net.[164] Finally, the story of Pwyll and Rhiannon is often very rightly cited as proof of the importance of *Calan Mai* in Welsh myths: the narrative describes an annual confrontation between summer and winter – respectively represented by Hafgan, whose name means "white summer" and Arawn, a king of the Welsh Otherworld; most of the important events of the episode take place after a one-year delay, meaning that almost everything takes place on *Calan Mai*. The white mare of

Rhiannon – a female character often compared with Gaulish Epona or Irish Macha– gives birth "every night of the Calends of May",[165] therefore substantiating the importance of *Calan Mai* in Welsh mythology and probably in its symbolic corpus. The comparison Epona/Rhiannon/Macha is also compelling:[166] the deity was a funerary goddess connected with agrarian fertility, a Gallo-Roman *matres.* In other words, her attributes were intimately linked with the Otherworld and the notion of abundance, two essential themes of both *Bealtaine* and *Calan Mai.*

Still in the supposedly "Celtic" context, the case of Gaul and later France is considerably more complex, mainly because most of its territory was so heavily Romanized for centuries – Brittany included and perhaps above all. It is therefore extremely difficult to discriminate between potentially Celtic traditions and other influences that modified the customs and beliefs of Gaul, then France. Some celebrations that were very popular in the Roman, then Gallo-Roman worlds, probably influenced the Gaulish and Breton traditions. Amongst other examples, one could think of the Roman Lemuria (9, 11, 13 May, where dead people were supposed to haunt the living), the Floralia (end of April-early May, where Flora, goddess of flowers, was celebrated), the Parilia (21 April, where shepherds purified their flock) and the Ambarvalia (29 May, where pasture lands were purified by fire).

Given the similarities between those Roman festivals and what we know of the Irish festival of *Bealtaine*, it is quite clear that all those May celebrations probably had a common ancestor. From a more general perspective, the curious reader can consult the exquisitely rich – and perhaps inextricable – *Folklore français* of Arnold Van Gennep.[167] The obvious conclusion to be drawn from this phenomenal folkloric compilation is that the situation of France, a country which stands at the crossroads of Europe, generated a great disparity in beliefs: almost all May customs, potentially Celtic or not, are mentioned in some part of the country or the other: from *May Queens* to the worship of saints protecting crops or animals – for example, the famous Ice Saints[168] of 11, 12 and 13 May – from the veneration of holy wells to weather superstitions, from marriage divination to cattle fairs, from fertility rituals to witchcraft, from the importance of *May Dew* to the ritual protection of dairy, from – although quite rare – purifying fires to *May Poles*, from *Green Men* (*"les feuillus"*) to *May Babies*, from *May Games* to processions etc. The folklore of France was markedly protean and noticeably manifold. Studying this folklore could not possibly lead to a fuller comprehension of the origins of traditions and their alleged "Celticism": on the contrary, the ideal candidate for the study of the origin of traditions would be a region influenced by as few cultures as possible – precisely the opposite of modern-day France.

Obviously, in France, Ireland and just about anywhere else in Europe and the Western world, every ceremonial event became even more complex at the arrival of the New Religion: as already mentioned, *Bealtaine* and its other Celtic equivalents were at least partially Christianized either by being adapted to "a Sunday in May", to Easter or possibly the Pentecost; the similarities between those celebrations were underlined and utilized – voluntarily or not – by many Irish monks and transcribers. Christianization is a process, not an event: it unfolded in the long term. It is therefore not surprising to observe, in the Irish folklore of *Bealtaine,* that the Virgin Mary was and still is omnipresent, that the water of the sacred wells was often replaced by holy water or Easter water, that *Bealtaine* was to be celebrated on a Sunday, preferably Whitsunday etc.

Last but by no means least, the influence of English "May traditions" in Ireland – and therefore indirectly the influence of Germanic, Norman and Scandinavian cultures – must be addressed here.

In England, *May Day* was a very popular celebration. The famous *May Fairs* left their marks and are remembered in a large number of toponyms, not the least of which being the area of Mayfair in London, which takes its name from a fair held at the turn of the 17th and 18th century near Piccadilly.

The story of the festival in England could be the subject of a whole book in itself:[169] in turn established then abolished and rehabilitated, *May Day* occasionally took the name of *Rodmas* (the "Feast of the Cross") or was adapted to the Feast of Sts. Philip and James (3 May); some constants of its symbolism can be found in the English celebration of *Saint George's Day* (23 April) or *Saint Mark's Day* (25 April). The theme of "vegetation" together with the plethora of associated festive customs were without a doubt the most prominent characteristic of the celebration in England: far from being a festival of fear and hope, *May Day* was a joyful celebration.

In England, *May Poles* were erected and sometimes adorned with *May Bushes,* which were themselves decorated with flowers, ribbons and other colorful items. Children turned and danced around the pole, usually holding in their hand a festoon or long band of fabric whose other extremity was attached to its top. *Jacks in the green* (*May Bushes* arranged in the form of a cone) were sometimes erected. Just like about anywhere in Europe, *May Queens* were elected among young girls of the neighboring area and some babies were named *May Babies* and were occasionally carried in procession. In some cities, *May Games* were organized: it was the occasion for young men to prove their strength and skills. The "collective" *May Bush*[170] was in some cases carried in procession through the streets of the city or town and followed by children who danced joyfully, sometimes begging the passers-by for a coin or two.

Those traditions were known, widespread and celebrated everywhere in England, first and foremost in urban centers. They could also be found in most places in Europe and some customs even crossed the ocean and survived to this day – mainly the *May Pole* traditions which are still fairly widespread in some parts of North America. However, it must be noted that those customs were less common in the "Celtic" areas of Europe than in the rest of the continent. Although the *May Bushes, Queens, Babies* and *Games* did exist in Ireland, they were almost exclusively found in large Irish cities or in Ulster – in other words, in the areas where the influence of England, and later Britain was the strongest. The ancient mythological Irish texts never mention customs even remotely resembling those May traditions: there is no doubt that the *May Day* customs mentioned in the last few paragraphs are late imports to Ireland and have no original connection with the ancient Celtic celebration of *Bealtaine.*

The terms of *Bealtaine* and *May Day* are therefore not interchangeable, or rather *should not* be interchangeable in the context of an academic study: one refers to an ancient Celtic celebration and its Irish prolongation, the other to the English version of an ancient festival, which was probably heavily influenced by Germanic and Scandinavian cultures. But this is not the end of the matter.

First, the festivals of *Bealtaine* and *May Day* both were held at the same time of the year. However, it is important to note that *Bealtaine* was a festival based on a fearful hope that the summer season will unfold in a positive manner, whereas *May Day* was a joyful festivity, to that extent comparable to *Midsummer/Saint John's Eve.* Although both *Bealtaine* and *May Day* celebrated the same yearly event – the arrival of summer – they did it in opposite (perhaps at best *complementary*) ways. *May Day* and *Bealtaine* could be the two sides of the same ancestral celebration which evolved in different manners throughout centuries and places: one was based on the joy to see summer arriving, the other on the fear of this moment of passage. Complementarity does *not* suggest that they are not distinct celebrations though.

The second part of the problem is that *Bealtaine* actually means "the first day of May" in Irish, just like *May Day* refers to the first day of the month in English. In 20th-century Ireland, both terms became interchangeable, depending on the native language of the speaker. *Bealtaine* was considered a translation of *May Day* and *vice versa.* But *May Day* is only a translation of *Bealtaine* "in form", not "in substance", as both words originally referred to two distinct celebrations – or at least two distinct ways of celebrating the same event. At the beginning of the 20th century, the informants of the *Irish Folklore Commission* did not draw any distinction between the two terms: when the informants wrote in Irish, they used the term *Bealtaine* in their descriptions of the local customs. When their native language was English, the term *May Day* was chosen whereas, quite often, the celebrations they were describing related to the Celtic Irish festival of *Bealtaine* and not to *May Day* traditions imported from England.

The original Celtic festival of *Bealtaine* is therefore not easy to understand: grasping the substance of the celebration amounts to embracing the whole history of Ireland – perhaps even of all Europe.

Thus, the similarities that can be found between the English *May Day,* some aspects of the Irish *Bealtaine,* the Germanic *Walpurgis* and the

Scandinavian *Valborgsmässoafton* are striking to the point that assessing where the "influence" starts and where the "confluence" ends proves almost impossible. The Germanic and Scandinavian celebrations do seem to combine almost every idea previously reviewed in an apparently anarchic way, so much so that asserting which of those celebrations influenced the others is perhaps an insurmountable task.

In Sweden, on *Valborgsmässoafton*, people welcomed the summer with huge bonfires – today, usually replaced by fireworks – lit up on hills and they used to dance around them; some ritual confrontations between opposing characters embodying summer and winter were quite common; the milking-hare and witches were known and feared. In Central Europe, *Walpurgis* focused on the potential danger of witches and their "Sabbath". But the Germanic tradition also included many joyful and festive events, such as the customs of *May Bushes* and *May Poles* (*Walperbäume* and *Walpurgismaie*) detailed by George Frazer in his famous *Golden Bough*.[171] However, it is interesting to note that the idea of purification or prophylaxis through two large fires is almost completely absent from those two great traditions: in Central and Northern Europe, fear and conjuration focused on the character of the witch more than on the notion of time passing or rural and agrarian weaknesses – diseases of the cattle and insufficient crops.

Surprisingly, one must turn to Eastern Europe to find traditions including those notions. *Saint George's Day* or *Gergiovden* – celebrated between 23 April and 6 May because of the adaptation to the Gregorian calendar – was popular in modern-day Romania, Bulgaria or even Hungary up to the beginning of the 20th century and in some cases today. The undead and ghosts were feared at that time of the year: for the anecdote collector, this did not escape the attention of Bram Stoker, who had Dracula meet Jonathan Harker for the first time on 5 May, after an old woman had told the solicitor that it was the eve of *Saint George's Day*: "Do you not know that to-night, when the clock strikes midnight, all the evil things in the world will have full sway?"[172]

It is also most remarkable that the traditions connected to *Gergiovden* on the one hand and to the first of May on the other were significantly different in Eastern Europe. On the first May, people elected *May Queens* and *Babies* – especially in the Protestant communities of Hungary – and enjoyed themselves; on *Gergiovden*, they protected the cattle, usually thanks to a fire that was supposed to ward off diseases and in some cases animal sacrifices: for instance, in Bulgaria, lamb sacrifices were common up to the beginning of the 20th century.[173] To that extent, the dichotomy between *Gergiovden* and the first of May in Eastern Europe seems similar to that opposing *Bealtaine* to *May Day* in Ireland: it undoubtedly implies a difference in origins. *Gergiovden* and *Bealtaine* seem connected and arguably shared the same common (Celtic?) origin, while the traditions of *May Day* in Ireland and the rest of Europe substantially differ.

4.6 Calendar Justification

Bealtaine *and* Midsummer

The complexity of May traditions in Europe is also amplified by the discrepancies and delays in their time of celebration, often induced by popular confusion. Thus, some customs connected to the beginning of the month of May were – and sometimes still are – occasionally celebrated on *Midsummer* (*Saint John's Day* in their Christianized version) in association with the summer solstice. This is particularly true for the Scandinavian tradition. The custom of kindling a huge bonfire and in some place jumping over the fire for amusement purposes or to keep the evil eye away was known across Europe. In Ireland, the custom is virtually absent of the *Gaeltachtaí*, the region where the Irish language was predominant: in those areas, only *Bealtaine* fires – i.e. the two fires meant to purify and protect, as opposed to the joyful single *Midsummer* bonfire – were known. Similarly, Saint John's Eve fires were quite rare in Scotland before the contemporary era.

Let us be perfectly clear: the celebrations of the summer solstice – including *Midsummer* and *Saint John's Day* customs – are not Celtic in essence. Nowhere in Celtic mythology, nowhere in the modern folklore of the *Gaeltachtaí* and more generally of Ireland was the summer solstice of particular import. At best, the European folklore of *Midsummer* was influenced by the Celtic traditions of May and *vice versa* so that the festivals became mixed up: the importance of *Midsummer* in the Scandinavian tradition and the Scandinavian influence over Great Britain and Ireland from the first Viking raids of the 8th century onward are probably not irrelevant to this popular confusion and mutual influence.

In Irish mythology and more generally in early Irish texts, the emphasis is laid on the four celebrations that we have come to know very well – *Samhain, Imbolc, Bealtaine* and *Lughnasa* – but never directly to the summer solstice.[174] Additionally, the name of *Midsummer* is in itself quite telling and must be questioned: how come a festival celebrated between 19 and 25 June – or 24 June precisely for *Saint John's Day* – became known under the name of *Mid/summer?*

The Juste Milieu*: The Just Midpoint*

Many hypotheses have been put forward to rationalize the dates – quite exotic and seemingly unjustified – of the four Irish celebrations. Some believed that 1 November, February, May and August originally corresponded to the dates of solstices and equinoxes: because of the very gradual change in inclination of the rotation axis of the Earth, the first of May could have corresponded to the spring equinox about 25,000 years ago. According to this theory, the Celtic celebrations originally marked equinoxes and solstices:

the association with the modern calendar was a mistake, a confusion induced by what is referred to today as the "precession of the equinoxes" or "axial precession". However, the fact that the Celtic celebrations were actually created at that specific time of history, 25,000 years ago, remains to be proven; furthermore, this theory fails to explain why the original celebrations did not gradually follow the discrepancy induced by the axial precession of the Earth, year after year: in other words, nothing explains why the four celebrations – if they were indeed originally celebrations of the solstices and equinoxes – did not continue to correspond to the solstices and equinoxes at the time of their adaptation to the Julian calendar.[175]

A number of scholars also tried to relate the Celtic festivals to the heliacal rising of Sirius or the Pleiades in the observable sky of the Northern hemisphere but similarly failed to persuade: no clear connection was ever established. Finally, others believed that the Irish festivals were based on agriculture and farm life more than on celestial movements. Their idea was that the essential character of the Celtic calendar was pastoral before anything and was adjusted "not to the solar year but the agricultural and pastoral year, i.e. the beginning and end of agrarian and farming labor".[176]

But if the Irish festivals were connected "neither to solstices nor equinoxes"[177] and were exclusively agrarian and pastoral, how can we account for the mythical, symbolic and later folkloric importance of the dates? Was the beginning of the months of May and November chosen to celebrate *Bealtaine* and *Samhain* only by convention? Did the first mythical inhabitants of Ireland land on the island in the beginning of May solely because the date corresponded to the reopening of agricultural activities? Did the characters of the Otherworld meet with humans on *Bealtaine* and *Samhain* simply because the festivals marked the beginning and the end of transhumance? Even more absurd: was Lugh killed on *Bealtaine* because the date matched the departure of the herds to pastures?

This is all very unlikely: a reference to astronomy seems necessary because, from a cultural point of view, an astronomical justification is a justification of divine origin.[178] This reference could explain the choice of specific dates for the celebration of the great festivals and amplify their symbolic significance. For this reason, it appears very likely that the calendar that inspired the dates of celebration of the Irish festival was neither purely agrarian nor simply astronomical but rather "astro-agrarian": it took from the agricultural symbolism while relying upon an astronomical justification.

The festivals were indeed calculated according to the equinoxes and solstices: however, they did not originally correspond to those solstices and equinoxes but rather to a mid-point between those solar events. Although the solstices and equinoxes take place around 21 June, December, March and September of our contemporary calendar, they are obviously not fixed events: for purely physical reasons – the eccentricity of the terrestrial orbit first and foremost – the date of those astronomical phenomena vary from one year to another. The fluctuations were even stronger before peoples understood that the revolution of the earth around the sun does not last 365 days precisely and leap years were introduced. By taking those fluctuations into account, we can see that the 1 November, February, May and August are placed approximately 45 days before and after the solstices and equinoxes following or preceding.

With those facts in mind, it is persuasive that the idea was to place the four festivals halfway between the solstices and equinoxes. Because the calendar of the Celts was luni-solar, we can even conjecture that the Celtic festivals were celebrated at a remarkable position of the moon that was closest to the temporal "halfway" between solstice and equinoxes. More simply put, as the days of the Celts supposedly followed their nights,[179] it is possible to assume that the New Moon immediately following each solstice and equinox originally corresponded to each of the four festivals.

The four Irish festivals are therefore the festivals of the *"juste milieu"*, the "just midpoint", in the words of Donatien Laurent, who has planted the seeds of this interpretation. They most likely corresponded to remarkable positions of the sun: *Bealtaine* was the linchpin, the midpoint between the spring equinox and the summer solstice. This entails significant symbolic consequences. Since the festival celebrated the beginning of summer, we are left with a Celtic summer – or, to be more cautious, an Irish summer – which included the months of May, June and July, whereas our current calendar has it last from 19–22 June to 21–24 September, depending on the year.

The difference is of utmost importance: in the current system, summer arguably corresponds to the hottest period of the year, while the ancient Irish summer corresponded to the most "luminous" three months, i.e. the months with the longest days of the year. In the contemporary calendar, summer begins on the solstice and days start becoming shorter immediately after the very first day of summer. Conversely, in the ancient Irish system, *Bealtaine* opened the most luminous period of the year. Although the celebration of the solstice is not Celtic in essence, the very name of "*Midsummer*" may show the influence of the Celtic division of the year on the English tongue and so many other European languages:[180] *Midsummer* is never directly mentioned in Celtic mythology[181] and in the folklore of the *Gaeltachtaí* but the solstice did represent the midpoint of the Celtic summer, i.e., *Mid/summer* – just like, it must be added, it represents a midpoint between the spring and the autumn equinoxes, which some traditions[182] believe to be a six-months summer.

Samhain was a New Year's festival and marked the start of the Celtic year[183] but also the beginning of the period where the days became shorter. *Imbolc* corresponded to the beginning of spring, the season where the length of days grew; a fall season starting on 1 August therefore seems less surprising as it opened the period where the length of days decreased the most – and the terms "spring" and "fall" are, to that extent, quite eloquent. The principle could be summarized as follows:

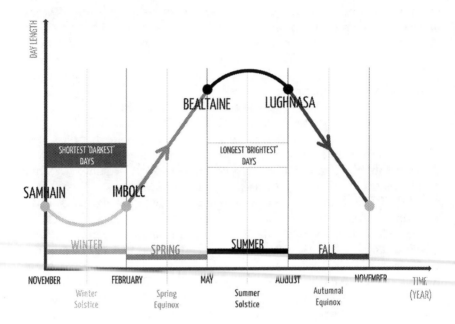

The system is elegantly logical, and rationally ordered. It is also extremely powerful from a symbolic point of view: the importance of the date from a mythological perspective appears clearer and influences our perception of the symbolism of Uisneach. *Bealtaine* and *Samhain* were the two gates of the solar year as they echoed the luminous and beneficent influence of the star. The place of *Bealtaine* in the Irish calendar justifies both the mythological episodes reviewed *supra* and its rural and agricultural implications. Since the festival inaugurated the clearest, most luminous time of the year, the simple decision to associate a hero, a tribe or a god, to attach a specific place – a tumulus, a hill, a mound – or to put to practice a ritual or custom on that very date amounted to placing this hero, this tribe, this god, this place, this custom into the temporal cycle of a "sacred" natural order.

The system thus deciphered also explains why, according to the various traditions at our disposal, the "tangible world" and the Otherworld met on *Bealtaine* and *Samhain*: the astronomical cycle – and therefore, for the sacerdotal class, the divine cycle – collided with the agricultural world. The immutable sacredness of nature, the eternal rhythm of seasons on which humans have no grasp and influence met with the "profane" secular world and its many physical constraints. On *Bealtaine*, the idea was, quite literally, to "come into the light".

Moreover, this explains why it was on *Bealtaine* that the hill of Uisneach took on its full meaning. Time and space were evidently connected: *Bealtaine* was a moment of passage marking the beginning of the luminous season, a temporal in-between symbolizing the lynchpin between the dark and the luminous; similarly, Uisneach was a sacred hill, the Irish *Medionemeton*, a spatial in-between, a tool of mediation between up and down, between the world of humans and the *sídh*. For the Irish sacerdotal class, *Bealtaine* perhaps transcended time, and Uisneach space: celebrating this specific place at this specific time was a way to transcend the world and connect the material to the immaterial – an attempt arguably at the core of any spiritual or religious endeavor.

Just like Uisneach was an intermediary, a spatial midpoint, center and axis of the world, *Bealtaine* was an intermediary, a temporal midpoint embodying the passage between winter and summer, between the world of the dead and that of the living. Since the druids were the intercessors between the secular and the sacred worlds, between the human and the spiritual, they were almost necessarily connected to Uisneach and *Bealtaine*: in the true sense of the term, the druids were the "mediators" *on* the midpoint hill precisely *at* the midpoint of the year.

Most of the elements mentioned by Keating in his description of the convention of Uisneach are attested or are at least highly compatible with what is now known of the symbolic substance of the time and place of the assembly. However, the picture is more nuanced. The payments on *Bealtaine*, just like the exchange of goods, seem to echo certain ancient mentions taken from the *Book of Rights* and do remind of the Irish May fairs – but those fairs could as well be a late import from the Anglo-Norman tradition. The kindling of great purifying fires can be found both in modern folklore and medieval texts; nevertheless, Keating could have been inspired by the folkloric customs still popular at his time. The mentions of the god Bel – and its possible assimilation to Belenos – are far from conclusive since the god is not mentioned anywhere else in Irish mythology. Finally, the idea that the "fortress" of Uisneach was built by Tuathal Techtmar is everything but historical and seems to be at best a mythification of facts, at worst an invention, pure and simple.

One might well ask to what this "fortress of Tuathal" on which Keating insists so much actually refers to: today, the visitors who climb Uisneach only find a few ruins, barely visible and not the least impressive. Nonetheless, the various archaeological excavations that have been conducted for over a century reveal a certain degree of correspondence, some of which will deepen our perspective and improve our understanding of the site.

Notes

1 Hubert, Henri, quoted in *The Festival of Lughnasa, op. cit.*, viii.
2 *The Festival of Lughnasa, op. cit.*, 1.
3 *The Gallic Wars op. cit.*, VI, §18.
4 Armao, Frédéric. 2013. "La Charnière de mai: Beltaine, fête celtique ou fête irlandaise?" in *Ollodagos*, Institut des Hautes Etudes de Belgique, Brussels, XXVIII, 61-128.
5 See *infra*.

6 *Ibid.*, 21.

7 See chap. IV.6.

8 For the 1947 collection of folkloric data related to the festival, see manuscripts from the *National Folklore Collection* (*Main Collection*) noted NFC *1095*, *1096* and *1097*.

9 Meyer, Kuno. 1888. "*The Wooing of Emer*" in *Archaeological Review*, I, 68-75; 150-5; 231-5; 298-307. See page 232.

10 It was supposedly compiled as early as the 5th century (the *Annals of the Four Masters* dates back to 438) on the orders of Saint Patrick. Of course, this statement is quite doubtful: the most ancient manuscripts apparently date back to the 14th century. However, the original text or ideas were undoubtedly much more ancient and the Pagan origin of most of these laws is usually accepted.

11 O'Donovan, John (ed.). 1865. *Senchus Mór, Ancient Laws of Ireland*. Dublin: Longman, Roberts and Green, 135.

12 *Textes Mythologiques irlandais, op. cit.*, 88.

13 Stokes, Whitley (ed.). 1891. "The Second Battle of Moytura" in *Revue Celtique*, XII, 52-130, 306-8: 107.

14 NFC *1096* (Galway), 24-30.

15 NFC *1096* (Antrim), 351.

16 NFC *1096* (Donegal), 402-4.

17 NFC *1097* (Longford), 147-53. See also NFC *1096* (Galway), 65-9.

18 NFC *1096* (Antrim), 352-9.

19 For example NFC *1095* (Kerry), 15-25.

20 NFC *1095* (Kerry), 49-71.

21 *Ibid.*

22 NFC *1095* (Kerry), 6-9.

23 NFC *1096* (Donegal), 476-81.

24 NFC *1096* (Galway), 31-40.

25 NFC *1095* (Limerick), 293-300.

26 NFC *1095* (Clare), 187-94.

27 NFC *1095* (Cork), 108-16.

28 The month of May is here associated with the end of the year which implies that *Bealtaine* was a New Year's festival. However, Irish tradition generally holds that *Samhain* – not *Bealtaine* – marked the beginning of the year.

29 O'Donovan, John (ed.). 1869. *Senchus Mór, Ancient Laws of Ireland*. II. Dublin: Longman, Green, Reader, and Dyer, 391.

30 See Lucas, A.T. 1989. *Cattle in Ancient Ireland*. Kilkenny: Boethius Press, 232.

31 The questionnaire of the *Irish Folklore Commission* counts dozens of examples; the custom was common throughout Ireland but, once again, predominated in the rural areas.

32 NFC *1097* (Kildare), 161-4.

33 Perhaps from "*gabelle*", a tax on commodities. In the *Gaeltachtaí*, the term *Gombeen Monday* was used to refer to the first Monday of May, when rent was due. NFC *1096* (Galway), 70-7.

34 Piers Baronet, Henry. 1576. *State Papers, Ireland, Letter to the Privy Council*. Quoted in Danaher, Kevin. 1972. *The Year in Ireland*. Dublin: Mercier Press, 86.

35 NFC *1095* (Clare), 201-5.

36 NFC *1097* (Westmeath), 91-8.

37 NFC *1096* (Leitrim), 166-7.

38 Obviously, the term "Ulster" must not be confused with "Northern Ireland". The counties of Cavan, Monaghan and Donegal are part of the province of Ulster but are attached to the Republic of Ireland.

39 *NFCS 962* (Cavan), 228 (i.e., manuscript 962 from the *National Folklore Collection, Schools' Collection*, page 228).

40 More precisely in the 1930s and 1940s, at the time of the manuscripts of the *Schools' Collection* and the *Bealtaine* questionnaire.

41 *NFC 1096* (Donegal), 431-4, 437-9, 440-51. Other similar fairs were held in Strabane and Millford, among other examples, always on 12 May and 12 November.

42 https://www.merriam-webster.com/dictionary/rabble.

43 *NFC 1096* (Armagh), 312-4.

44 Day, Angelique & McWilliams, Patrick (ed.). 1990-7 (1834-6). *Ordnance Survey Memoirs of Ireland.* Dublin: Institute of Irish Studies.

45 Logan, Patrick. 1986. *Fair Day, the Story of Irish Fairs and Markets.* Belfast: Appletree Press, 121.

46 *NFC 1095* (Waterford), 322-8.

47 The sources relative to the following description of the fair of New Ross include *NFC 1097* (Laois; mentioning Co. Wexford), 195-202 and (Wexford), 219-26.

48 Holton, Karina. 2001. "From Charters to Carters: Aspects of Fairs and Markets in Medieval Leinster" in *Irish Fairs and Markets, Studies in Local History.* Bodmin: Four Courts Press, 37.

49 *NFC 1097* (Wexford), 219-26.

50 From *NFCS 534* (Tipperary), 142, 234, 236.

51 Or *luck-penny.*

52 Ritual faction fights must not be mistaken with fights caused by the abuse of alcohol which were common during the festivities linked with the fairs of May. To that extent, see Connel, Paul. 2001. "Slaughtered like Wild Beasts; Massacre at Castlepollard Fair" in *Irish Fairs and Markets, Studies in Local History.* Bodmin: Four Courts Press, 143-63.

53 Men wearing colorful ribbons on their clothes.

54 *NFCS 687* (Meath), 68-9.

55 Bective: *NFCS 708* (Meath), 240-3. Barristown: *NFCS 685* (Meath), 99. Ardamagh: *NFCS 708* (Meath), *op. cit..* See also *NFCS 710* (Meath) for the parish of Nobber.

56 Danaher, Kevin. 1964. *In Ireland Long Ago.* Dublin: Mercier Press, 123-7.

57 *The Festival of Lughnasa, op. cit.,* 288-9.

58 See *Fair Day, op. cit.,* for the establishment of fairs in Ireland.

59 The tradition had many possible variations and was absolutely not exclusive to Ireland. The use of *May Dew* was extremely popular in Great Britain and Ireland but also almost everywhere in continental Europe.

60 *NFC 1096* (Donegal), 456-7.

61 *NFC 1096* (Monaghan), 377-84.

62 *NFC 1096* (Donegal), 456-7.

63 *NFC 1097* (Wicklow), 240-2.

64 *NFC 1095* (Waterford), 319-21.

65 *NFC 1097* (Laois), 203-8.

66 *NFC 1095* (Waterford), 322-8.

67 The appropriation by "common people" of a task traditionally devolved to spiritual leaders is not particularly surprising: the Christian clergy could not possibly assimilate a tradition which was so obviously Pagan. Arguably, the farmers who were attached to the custom had no other choice but to do without them.

68 This point will be addressed in greater detail later.

69 "A wet May and a dry June (makes) the farmer whistles a (merry) tune"; "A wet/leaky May and a dry/dropping/sultry June make the farmer whistle a merry tune"; "Wet May and dripping June/Puts all things in tune". *NFC 1095* (Cork &

Kerry), 29-35, *NFC 1096* (Sligo), 134-6, (Leitrim), 146-9, 150-6, (Cavan), 300-11, (Armagh), 312-4, (Donegal), 458-60, *NFC 1097* (Longford), 153-6. The storms of May were sometimes called the "Cuckoo storms" and were believed to be lucky. *NFC 1096* (Donegal), 413-28, 486-90.

70 *NFC 1095* (Cork), 130-6.

71 In the Middle Ages, tradition held that red-haired men and women had come too close to hell, which burnt their hair. Foxes were often feared because of their color, which was considered evil, and Christian tradition sometimes held that red squirrels were incarnations of the devil. Of course, in Irish tradition, the color red was supposed to be the color of the Otherworld, both in folklore and mythology, which is not insignificant.

72 *NFC 1095* (Tipperary), 242-5.

73 *NFC 1097* (Meath), 49-50, (Laois), 195-202 for instance.

74 See Armao, Frédéric. 2016. "Les Superstitions du lièvre-trayeur en Irlande" in *Babel-Civilisations & Sociétés*, Univ. Toulon, XI, 23-40.

75 *NFC 1095* (Cork), 125-9.

76 Especially when the spring was situated next to the boundary between several farms, as "boundary water" was believed most potent.

77 *NFC 1095* (Tipperary), 276-80. *NFC 1095* (Limerick), 307-11. *NFC 1095* (Tipperary), 248-51, *NFC 1096* (Sligo), 130-3. *NFCS 415* (Kerry), 12 for example.

78 *NFC 1096* (Leitrim), 150-2, that can be found in *NFC 1096* (Fermanagh), 335-41.

79 *NFC 1096* (Leitrim), 146-9.

80 *Ibid.*, *NFC 1097* (Westmeath), 59-66.

81 *NFC 1096* (Leitrim), 146-9.

82 Westropp, Thomas Johnson. 1902. "Bewitching" in *Journal of the Royal Society of Antiquaries of Ireland*, XXXII (XII of the 5th series), 265.

83 *The Topography of Ireland, op. cit.*, 46.

84 The term *banshee* (a female spirit) comes from Irish *bean sídhe*, i.e. "woman from the land of the fairies" or "woman of the hill".

85 The belief was so common that an informant of the *Schools' Collection* declares: "You all know May is the month of the fairies", *NFCS 26* (Galway), 190. The month of November was the other period of the year when the activity of the fairies was at its peak.

86 *NFC 1097* (Wexford), 235-9.

87 *NFC 1095* (Clare), 201-5.

88 For French folklore, see the monumental work of Van Gennep, Arnold. 1999 (1937-58). *Le Folklore français. II. Cycles de mai, de la Saint-Jean, de l'été et de l'automne*. Paris: Robert Laffont.

89 Hedderman, B.N. 1917. *Glimpses of my Life in Aran, part I*. Bristol: John Wright and Sons Ltd., 105-6.

90 Occasionally, the custom is associated with the Virgin Mary. This of course reminds us of the fact that, in Catholic tradition, the month of May is traditionally dedicated to the Virgin.

91 According to a proverb, someone "between two May fires" is either in trouble or simply considered as rather perplexing. *NFC 1095* (Kerry), 49-71 *NFC 1096* (Donegal), 391-8, 413-28.

92 *NFC 1096* (Cavan), 295-9.

93 *NFC 1095* (Clare), 187-94.

94 *NFCS 456* (Kerry), 287.

95 That is, if we follow the division of Indo-European societies proposed by Georges Dumézil, i.e. the clergy, the warriors, the farmers. See *supra*.

96 Murphy, Gerard. 1955. "Finn's Poem on *May-Day*" in *Ériu*, XVII, 86-99, especially 87-8. The text can be found in a manuscript from the 15th century: *Laud. 610, f. 118 sq.* (Oxford).

97 "Finn's Poem on *May-Day*", *op. cit.*, 89-91.

98 *Silva Gadelica, op. cit.*, II, 292-311.

99 *Ibid.*, 292.

100 *Ibid.*, xii.

101 Knott, Eleanor (ed.). 1922. *The Bardic Poems of Tadhg Dall Ó Huiginn (1550-1591)*. London: Irish Texts Society, XXIII. "To Cú Chonnacht Maguire", 39.

102 A *fili* was mainly a "druid specialized in all magical practices of divination and all fields of intellectual activity" (*Les Druides, op. cit.*, 390). In medieval texts, "the term refers to erudites [...] well-versed in traditional poetry and 'literature'". (*Ibid.*, 439).

103 *History of Ireland, op. cit.*, III, section IX, 79. Keating probably refers to the 7th century. *Les Fêtes celtiques, op. cit.*, 41.

104 *Textes Mythologiques irlandais, op. cit.*, 204.

105 *Les Fêtes celtiques, op. cit.*, 41.

106 "To be on Maen-mhagh on *May Morning*, but so as that he goes not over upon Dar-mhagh". O'Donovan, John (ed.). 1847. *The Book of Rights*. Dublin: Celtic Society, 5.

107 *Ibid.*

108 Uisneach and Cruachan are united in a rather unique Irish tale mentioned by Eugene O'Curry in 1873 and commented by the Rees. In this tale taking place on *Halloween* – the modern prolongation of *Samhain* – the three "chief arti- facts" of Ireland are said to the crown of Brionn, hidden by the Mórrigan in the well of Cruachan, the *fidchell* (a board game) of Crimthann "which was brought from the secret recesses of the sea and hidden in the Rath of Uisneach" and the crown of Loegaire in *Síd Findacha* in Ulster. *Celtic Heritage, op. cit.*, 300. O'Curry, Eugene. 1873. *On the Manners and Customs of the Ancient Irish*, Dublin: Williams and Norgate, III, 202-3.

109 *Book of Rights, op. cit.*,16-7.

110 *Ibid.*, 87.

111 *Ibid.*, 97.

112 *Ibid.*, 103.

113 See for instance, *Lebor Gabála Érenn, op. cit.*, I, introduction.

114 *The Book of Rights, op. cit.*, 4.

115 *Ibid.*, 4 and 11.

116 Loch Feabhail is in fact *Lough Foyle*, the estuary of River Foyle. *Ibid.*, 249.

117 See for instance *NFC 1095* (Clare), 187-94 and O'Sullivan (Ó Súilleabháin), Seán. 1974. *Folklore of Ireland*. London: B.T. Batsford, 116.

118 For example, O'Donoghue of the Glens was said to be seen riding a gray horse on *May Morning* on the shores of Lake Killarney. *NFC 1095* (Kerry), 6-9.

119 *NFC 1096* (Donegal), 413-28.

120 *NFC 1096* (Donegal), 475-81.

121 *NFC 1095* (Cork), 83-94.

122 *NFC 1095* (Cork), 80-2.

123 *Les Druides, op. cit.*, 281.

124 *"The oldest version of Tochmarc Emire"*, *op. cit.* This interpretation does not seem to be based on any rational argument.

125 O'Donovan, John. 1868. *Cormac's Glossary*. Calcutta: the Irish Archaeological and Celtic Society, 19.

126 Williams, Mark. 2016. *Ireland's Immortals. A History of the Gods of Irish Myths*. Princeton: Princeton University Press, 81 (footnote 35), 287-8.

127 For instance, according to Tertullian, "Every province and city has its proper gods, as Syria the god Ashtaroth, Arabia has Disares, Bavaria Belinus, Africa the Celestial Virgin, and Mauritania their kings. Now these provinces (if I mistake not) are under the Roman jurisdiction, and yet I do not find any of the Roman gods in worship among them." Reeve, William (ed.) 1907 [?]. *The Apology of Tertullian*. London: Griffith, Farran, Okeden & Welsh, 81-2. See Duval, Paul-Marie. 1993 (1957). *Les Dieux de la Gaule*. Paris: Payot, 77.

128 Gourvest, Jacques. 1954. "Le Culte de Belenos en Provence occidentale et en Gaule" in *Ogam*, VI, 1954, 256.

129 *Ibid.*, 260.

130 See for instance *Les Dieux de la Gaule, op. cit.*, 32, 76-8 and 101.

131 *The Gallic Wars, op. cit.*, VI, §17.

132 See *Celtes et Grecs. II, op. cit.*, 86-97, esp. 86-7. The first part of the book (23-368) is dedicated to a fascinating comparison between Lug and Apollo.

133 Smith, Williams. 1973. *Dictionary of Greek and Roman Antiquities*. London: Milford House. Camps-Gaset, Montserrat. 1994. *L'Année des Grecs, la fête et le mythe*. Paris: Annales Littéraires de l'Université de Besançon, 60-2.

134 A fanciful theory popularized at least as early as the 18th century made of Bel a version of the demon Baal or even Beelzebub/Bel-zebub.

135 *Les Druides, op. cit.*, 165.

136 Occasionally seven, depending on the version. See *Lebor Gabála Érenn, op. cit.*, introduction.

137 *Ibid.*, I, 218-9.

138 R.2 and R.3. *Ibid.*, III, 5.

139 R.2. *Ibid.*, IV, 139.

140 R.3. *Ibid.*, IV, 203.

141 *Ibid.*, IV, 257.

142 Fraser, J. (ed.). 1916. "The First Battle of Moytura" in *Ériu*, VIII, 1-63: 19.

143 *History of Ireland, op. cit.*, 213.

144 "The First Battle of Moytura", *op. cit.*, 21.

145 *Ibid.*, 31.

146 *Textes Mythologiques Irlandais, op. cit.*, 43.

147 See chap. IV.6 the remarks on *Midsummer* and the calendar justification of the Celtic festivals.

148 R.2. *Lebor Gabála Érenn, op. cit.*, V, 59. Similarly, R.3. *Ibid.*, V, 71.

149 *Bealtaine* is said to stem from the infinitive *beltu, genitive *belten, dative *beltin, preserved in old Irish in *épeltu*, "death"=*ate-belatu. Arbois de Jubainville, Henri D'. 1884. *Cours de Littérature celtique*. Paris: Ernest Thorin Editeur, II, 243.

150 See also Arbois de Jubainville, Henri D'. 1879. *Le Dieu de la mort et les origines mythologiques de la race celtique*. Troyes: Dufour-Bouquot.

151 See Westropp, Thomas J. 2000. *Folklore of Clare*. Ennis: Clasp Press, 57-9. Meehan, Cary. 2002. *The Traveller's Guide to Sacred Ireland*. London: Gothic Image Publications, 314-7 and Rodgers, Michael, Losack, Marcus. 1996. *Glendalough, a Celtic Pilgrimage*. Harriburg: Morehouse Publishing, 199.

152 For the mythological aspects connected to the site, see Armao, Frédéric. 2018. "Dá Chích Anann: mythes et rituels associés aux 'Seins de Dana'" in *Ollodagos*, Institut des Hautes Etudes de Belgique, Brussels, XXXIII, 157-217; for contemporary folklore, see Armao, Frédéric. 2017. "Cathair Crobh Dearg: From Ancient Beliefs to the Rounds 2017" in *Estudios Irlandeses, Electronic Journal of the Spanish Association for Irish Studies*, XII.2, 8-31.

153 *Lebor Gabála Érenn, op. cit.,* IV, 123.
154 Cronin, Dan. 2001. *In the Shadow of the Paps.* Killarney: Crede, Sliabh Luachra Heritage Group, 38.
155 See for instance *NFCS 445* (Kerry), 288.
156 Obviously, see the monumental work of *Festival of Lughnasa* de Máire MacNeill, *op. cit.*
157 See chap. IV, 5-6.
158 Wilde, William R. 1995 (1852). *Irish Popular Superstitions.* New York: Sterling Publishing, 32.
159 Waddel, John. 2000 (1998). *The Prehistoric Archaeology of Ireland.* Dublin: Wordwell, 347. See also 347-58.
160 *Ibid.,* 348.
161 *NFCS 697* (Meath), 352.
162 The terms "Celtic" and "Celts" are hereafter used in the very broad, traditional and historical sense of the term, i.e. pertaining to and issued from the civilizations of Hallstatt and La Tène, whose cultural and linguistic influence persisted mainly but not exclusively in populations living in Britain, Ireland, Britany and Galicia. For a more refined definition, see for instance Sergent, Bernard. 2013. "Préface" in *Les Nations Celtiques et le monde contemporain. Babel-Civilisations & Sociétés.* Toulon: Université de Toulon, VIII, 17-20.
163 *The Mabinogion, op. cit.,* 207.
164 *Textes Mythologiques irlandais, op. cit.,* 151-2.
165 *Ibid.,* 217.
166 See Gricourt, Jean. 1954. "Epona – Rhiannon – Macha" in *Ogam,* VI, 25-40, 75-86, 137-8, 155-68, 165-89, 269-72. Dumézil, Georges. 1954. "Le Trio des Macha" in *Revue de l'Histoire des Religions,* CXLVI, 5-17 and Guyonvarc'h, Christian-Joseph & Le Roux, Françoise. 2016 (1987). *Mórrigan-Bodb-Macha. La Souveraineté Guerrière de l'Irlande.* Fouesnant: Yoran.
167 Van Gennep, Arnold. 1998 (1937-58). *Le Folklore français. I. Du berceau à la tombe, cycles de carnaval - Carême et de Pâques* and 1999 (1937-58). *II. Cycles de mai, de la Saint-Jean, de l'été et de l'automne.* Paris: Robert Laffont.
168 Interestingly enough, the Breton saints protecting crops were mainly celebrated in May and November. Stany-Gauthier, J. 1953. "Les Saints Bretons protecteurs des récoltes et des jardins" in *Arts et traditions populaires,* 1st year, IV, 307-21.
169 See for instance Hutton, Ronald. 2001. *The Rise and Fall Of Merry England: The Ritual Year 1400-1700.* Oxford: Oxford Paperbacks.
170 What is here referred to as the "collective" *May Bush* must not be confused with "individual" *May Bushes,* also called "*May Branches*", i.e. a small decorated branch usually planted in a manure heap. See *infra.*
171 Frazer, James. 1996 (1922). *The Golden Bough.* London: Penguin Books, 149-52 for instance.
172 Stoker, Bram. 1994 (1897). *Dracula.* London: Penguin Books, 13.
173 MacDermott, Mercia. 1998. *Bulgarian Folk Customs.* London: Jessica Kingsley Publishers, 217-22. See also Buhociu, Octavian. 1957. *Le Folklore Roumain de Printemps.* PhD Thesis. Paris: Université de Paris, 213-5.
174 Some very rare exceptions do exist but are for the most part indirect references to the solstice, for example *The First Battle of Mag Tuired* which supposedly took place after "six weeks of the summer".
175 Bernard Sergent used a compelling argument on several occasions: "the existence of [*Lughnasa*] in Gaul is confirmed by the decisions taken by L. Munatius Plancus when he founded the Roman colony of Lyons in -43, i.e. Romanized the Celtic Lugudunum and instituted the first meeting of Consilium

Galliarum on the 1st of August. [...] Since the gap between the [four festivals] and the [four solar events] stayed the same between the 1st century BCE (Lyons was founded by Plancus in -43) and the Early Irish Middle Ages [...] this gap was necessarily a voluntary choice and by no means an accident." Sergent, Bernard. 2004. "Le Sacrifice des femmes samnites" in *La Fête, la rencontre des dieux et des hommes. Actes du 2e Colloque international de Paris "La fête, la rencontre du sacré et du profane"*. Paris: L'Harmattan, 274.

176 *Un Aspect du cycle de mai en Europe occidentale, op. cit.,* 22.

177 *Ibid.,* 23.

178 See *Le Sacré et le profane, op. cit.,* chap. II.

179 *The Gallic Wars, op. cit.,* VI, §18.

180 *Mittsommerfest, Mezza estate, Midzomerfeest, Midsommar* very clearly share the same etymology.

181 Once again, *The First Battle of Mag Tuired* is said to have taken place after "six weeks of the summer", i.e. after about 45 days, a figure similar to the calculation mentioned above. This implies that the Battle symbolically took place at the summer solstice (six weeks after *Bealtaine*, which was not originally celebrated on a fixed date).

182 This division of the year in two halves can be found, for example, in Gaul, India and Iran. See Duval, Paul-Marie & Pinault, Georges. 1986. *Recueil des Inscriptions gauloises. Vol. III: les calendriers (Coligny Villards d'Héria).* Paris: CNRS Editions, 405.

183 Summer followed winter just like days followed nights.

5   Uisneach: Archaeological Data

The historiography of the archaeological studies of Uisneach is almost two centuries old, although the laconic and very approximate mentions of the 19th century are of relatively little help. John O'Donovan did visit Uisneach on 12 September 1837[1] as part of the *Ordnance Survey of Ireland* investigations, whose purpose was to map the Irish territory, but his remarks remained anecdotal. *Ail na Mireann*, which he referred to as the "Cat's Rock" rather than the *Catstone*, is mentioned but the sparse etymological[2] or historical comments of the scholar do not hold water. O'Donovan, for example, believed that the stone was split on purpose: research established that the "broken" aspect of *Ail na Mireann* is clearly due to erosion. However, the precision of the first maps that were produced following this visit is remarkable: the curious reader should explore the website of the *Ordnance Survey*, which has the distinctive – and quite inspirational – feature of storing all the maps currently available, from the manuscript representations of the 1830s to the most recent satellite images.[3]

The following decades saw a number of scholars taking an interest in Uisneach; the rudimentary technologies and fallacious preconceptions of the time prevented those studies from being truly conclusive. Thus, the theories according to which Uisneach could have been a royal cemetery,[4] a fortified city[5] or an ancient palace[6] must be discarded for a host of reasons discussed hereafter.

It took another few decades before excavations were actually carried out on Uisneach: between 1925 and 1931, Robert Macalister and Robert Praeger dedicated nine weeks to the study of the site.[7] For the first time ever, the excavations were driven by a truly scientific approach, although the conclusions of the scholars are questionable in many respects, as they still exhibit biases of their age and their methodology remained quite rudimentary. Be that as it may, the investigations of Macalister and Praeger are a milestone in the history of Uisneach.

Finally, after almost 80 years of scholarly neglect, the work performed by Roseanne Schot finally provided a more accurate picture of the nature of the site. The archaeological investigations, consisting of geophysical and topographical surveys and palaeoenvironmental investigations, were

DOI: 10.4324/9781003143161-6

carried out between 2002 and 2014. Although some of the hypotheses arising from these studies remain to be confirmed, most theories and ideas presented hereafter are owed to her investigations, to whom we are much indebted. Similarly, a number of elements theorized by Macalister and Praeger in the early 20th century are still relevant and actually prove quite useful and convincing.

5.1 Topography and Salient Features

It does not seem necessary here to dwell on the geological origin of the hill – which usually serves as an introduction to most archaeological studies.[8] As noted by Macalister and Praeger, Uisneach is best defined as a "low, broad hill with its summit broken into three or four rounded eminences",[9] and remains one of the highest limestone hills of the vicinity.[10] Michael Dames, whose analyses are often controversial, still gives a fairly accurate description of the place:

> Seen from any direction or distance the Hill of Uisneach fails to dominate. It stands discreetly tucked in among undulating countryside. The summit rises 181 meters[11] above sea level, but is less than 80 meters above the nearby valley road from Athlone to Mullingar. Nor is the Hill's form memorably compact. Lobes run north, south and west, while three or four swellings compete with the "real" hilltop for preeminence.[12]

The hill does look like a succession of more or less prominent rises; the upper part of Uisneach resolves to a relatively flat and broad plateau where two small swells of similar height rise to form summits – the eastern summit and the western summit, the latter being *stricto sensu* the highest point of the hill.[13]

The terrain is undulating to the point that it considerably reduces general visibility: in other words, it is never possible to fully take in the hill at one glance, all the more so because the "true" (Western) summit (occupied by the monument known as *Saint Patrick's Bed*) is relatively distant from the other points of interest at the site, i.e. *Ail na Mireann* and the "fort" of Rathnew. This conjoined ringfort is arguably not as grandiose and impressive as some of the renowned royal forts and enclosures elsewhere in Ireland.[14] The "relatively inconspicuous character of the largest prehistoric monuments at Uisneach" led Roseanne Schot to believe that, originally, the site was dedicated to spiritual and religious matters more than political ones. This idea echoes the apparent neutrality – or "detached centrality" – of the province of Mide:

> The relatively inconspicuous character of the largest prehistoric monuments at Uisneach seems to diminish their effectiveness as material

expressions of earthly power, and could very well reflect the ritual exclusivity and political "detachment" claimed for the site in the early literature. All things considered, the possibility that Uisneach was more a religious than a political centre in later prehistory, and only later emerged as a *bona fide* "royal site", cannot be easily dismissed.[15]

The theory according to which Uisneach was originally a religious and sacred place rather than a political one is indeed quite appealing. The general configuration of Uisneach seems compatible with the notion of *Mediolanum* as envisaged by Loth: the "sacred and central" hill was an accommodating place of union which enabled the gathering of many. In spite of the hilly, undulating nature of Uisneach, the hilltop is flat and large enough to correspond to Loth's definition of a *Mediolanum*, i.e. "a united place, freed from any natural obstacle, where meetings and religious cere-monies [were held]".[16] Today, the contemporary gathering of *Bealtaine* on Uisneach still takes place on that plateau.

From both its foot and its summit, a striking feature of Uisneach is the verdant, green aspect of the site. This idea of lush vegetation and greenery resonates with one of the poems of Tadhg Dall Ó Huiginn who, in the second half of the 16th century, called the hill "green-swarded Ushnagh" before mentioning its "bright meadows" and "fields.[17] Obviously, the green color is by no means rare in the Irish landscape; still, the fact that Uisneach is watered by a large number of streams probably established and nurtured its distinctive verdure. Few trees, lots of shrubs and small vegetation: the soil of the hill has not been exploited for the growth of crops[18] since the early 20th century at the very least.[19] However, its large fields are still used as pasture land. The archaeological investigations unearthed cattle remains dating back to the end of the Iron Age and the Early Middle Ages, which confirms that the practice is ancient.[20]

All scholars studying the topography of the hill noted the central position of Uisneach in relation with the rest of Ireland, which is of course not sur-prising. The idea according to which a large portion of the central plain of Ireland can be observed from the top of Uisneach is accepted by all, despite the fact that other hills tend to block the horizon on its north and east sides.[21] Macalister and Praeger mention that "landmarks in no less than twenty counties are to be identified from the summit".[22] Presumably relying on their own observations, they also state that fires lit up on Uisneach could poten-tially be seen from a quarter of Ireland. The archeologists even went so far as to imagine a system in which "[the hills upon the horizon] could relay the message of the beacon as far as the sea-coast" in "most directions".[23] The theory is intriguing, as it obviously recalls the idea that all fires in Ireland were to be lit from the fire of Uisneach. It remains purely hypothetical though, as no medieval text or modern folkloric account can substantiate it.

The hill itself occupies an area of about 4 km[2]. It is situated in the parish of Conry and the townland of Ushnagh Hill but also covers parts of Clonownmore, Kellybrok, Lockardstown, Mweelra, Rathnew and Togherstown.[24] As noted by Roseanne Schot, the very shape and expanse of the hill is "a natural boundary to a complex of monuments". Better still, "this natural boundary may have been formalized in early pre-history through the erection of a series of standing stones, which sur-round the hill from the north-west around the south-east at a distance of 1-2 km".[25] The antiquity of Uisneach's veneration seems therefore con-firmed, although "early prehistory" is a vague and fluctuating timeframe and Schot was rather cautious in her statement: standing stones indeed have a very long history of use, making them very difficult to date with precision.

The monuments of Uisneach are numerous and of a varied nature. Macalister and Praeger established a first list in 1929.[26] Today, about 40 sites have been identified on and around the hill.[27] About 20 significant monuments are situated on the summit plateau of Uisneach, apparently ranging in date from the Neolithic or early Bronze Age[28] – i.e. from around 5,000–4,000 years ago – to the medieval period.[29] The tumuli, barrows, megalithic tomb(s) and the various enclosures vouch for an occupation of the site over the long term, which is believed to extend back at least 5,000 years. The antiquity of Uisneach's social importance and of its sacredness is beyond doubt, although its origins are not verifiable; similarly, the precise age of many of the monuments has yet to be clearly established.

The various items found on site during the excavations of the 1920s are very significant, providing information on both the chronology and nature of activity at the site. Macalister and Praeger organized the 120 discovered items into distinct categories.[30] Their classification is based on the material of the items, i.e. objects made of stone (whetstones, querns, quartz pebbles, crucibles etc.), of "bone and horn" (mainly needles and small utensils), bronze (pins and small jewels), iron (the most numerous: rings, buckles, rudimentary tools, nails, pins, knives, plates, fibulae, horseshoes, small rods and bars …) as well as many more small and perhaps irrelevant finds, such as a silver penny from the 13th century.[31] Macalister and Prager explain the absence of valuable items by a – hy-pothetical – abandonment of the site at an unspecified date or a possible succession of lootings throughout centuries.[32]

One of the most interesting artificial monuments of Uisneach is the conjoined ringfort of Rathnew, a figure-of-eight shaped enclosure: it is one of the largest constructions on the hill. On the western summit – the highest point of the hill – one can find another monument which played a pivotal role: *Saint Patrick's Bed*, a probable ancient megalithic tomb.

The topographical overview of Uisneach is still incomplete, though. Before turning to human constructions, two natural phenomena of re-markable importance must be scrutinized: *Ail na Mireann* and *Lough Lugh*, both mentioned in the medieval literature of Ireland.

5.2 Ail na Mireann

The Rock of Uisneach

The rock of Uisneach – or more appropriately the *rocky conglomerate* or *erratic boulder* – still lies on the south-west side of the hill, about 300 meters from its top, 30 meters below the western summit. As already mentioned, it is a subspherical conglomerate of approximately five meters in length on each edge, that dates back to the last ice age; the carboniferous limestone conglomerates are common in the surroundings, although they are usually smaller and less impressive than *Ail na Mireann*.[33] They are all made of the same crumbly limestone rock which gives the stone of Uisneach its gnarled and "knotted" appearance. The older interpretations[34] which assumed that its fragmentary state was owed to the hand of man are no longer accepted: *Ail na Mireann* is not an artificial "cromlech" built in "time immemorial".

Incidentally, the numerous fractures of the rock form a sort of tunnel underneath the stone. The passage follows an east-west axis. An adult can easily crawl under the stone and go through the structure. Some imagined that the tunnel could have been used for "rites of passage" or ceremonies based on the idea of rebirth.[35] No direct testimony, past or present, confirms this hypothesis.

The Natural and the Artificial

Ail na Mireann is therefore a natural rock in the sense that nothing indicates it was modified by man. Nonetheless, the site excited the imagination of many. For example, in *Stars, Stones and Scholars*,[36] Andis Kaulins recently proposed that an ancient map of celestial constellations was engraved on *Ail na Mireann*. Although the author struggles to show that this celestial map (following mysterious patterns and – hypothetical – eroded ring-marks) used to be engraved on the boulder, it is quite clear that the hypothesis is a complete fabrication. The author seems to invent fallacious arguments as he puts pen to the paper, although he does struggle to prove his initial intuition with a certain degree of confidence. His argumentation borders on wishful thinking and the book as a whole is hardly worth the weight of the paper it was printed on. Its online equivalent, http://megaliths. co.uk/, is a most instructive example of misinformation. Hopefully, it will be studied in the years to come for what it is: an interesting archetype of pseudo-scholarly reinvention which reflects the curiosity of a certain type of Celtic enthusiast for a culture allegedly shrouded in mystery.

Apart from a hole on the top of *Ail na Mireann* – which was apparently used to hold a flag pole[37] – human modification of the conglomerate is not manifest, to say the least. It is most of all the earthen enclosure circling the stone of Uisneach, which suggests an ancient veneration of the site.

Enclosure of Ail na Mireann

Because of erosion, the earthen enclosure is now barely noticeable. It is about 20 meters in diameter.[38] No entrance nor gap is visible.[39] In 1915, Loth already mentioned its existence; the curator of the National Museum of Dublin apparently told him about the presence of "several large debris that seem to form a circle around" *Ail na Mireann*.[40] Macalister and Praeger more accurately define the enclosure as a "shallow bowl-shaped depression with a raised ring-like edge"[41] circling the stone. *Ail na Mireann* lies "a little south of the middle point" of the enclosure. The conclusion of the authors is twofold: first, the conglomerate is of natural origin *but* was already noticed in ancient times. The second conclusion is much more conjectural: the enclosure supposedly conferred the site an approximate shape of an *"umbilicus"* which could suggest that *Ail na Mireann* was an omphalos comparable to that of Delphi. Roseanne Schot believes the idea to be an "obvious possibility".[42] It is perhaps more prudent to remain suspicious of any preconceived idea ("*Ail na Mireann* is a navel") correlated to enigmatic discoveries: after all, a stone in the middle of an earthen bank can *be* or *represent* many things, including a "symbolic navel" indeed.

Although the site is unique and the enclosure has not been excavated, archaeologists believe the enclosure may have been built between the late Neolithic period and the first millennium BCE, possibly even in the Early Middle Ages.[43] In other words, the antiquity of the monument remains quite hazy, ranging from a period starting four-five thousand years ago to the 8th century CE, which makes interpretations uncertain and thwarts any form of comparative study.

Earthen Circle, Stone Circle?

The enclosure may also remind of the "stone circle" supposedly sur-rounding *Ail na Mireann* in Geoffrey of Monmouth's account; the author indeed mentioned that the stones of the circle of Salisbury were placed by Merlin "in the same manner as they had been in the mountain Killaraus", a summit identified *supra* as being but another name for Uisneach. Quoting Lappenberg, Loth also tells us that "on the summit [of Uisneach stood] a gigantic stone called the navel of the earth; it was surrounded by smaller rocks".[44] This mention suggests that *Ail na Mireann* may have been sur-rounded by a stone circle at one point in its history. Unfortunately, there is every indication to believe that this was a mistake of Lappenberg, since the author quotes a source that actually does not mention Uisneach. Furthermore, the earthen enclosure of *Ail na Mireann* in no way resembles the stone circle of Stonehenge. It is actually made of earth taken from the vicinity of the conglomerate, not of stone pillars or megaliths. From a purely morphological perspective, the earthen circle "shares affinities with a diverse group of ritual and funerary monuments that includes embanked enclosures and some forms of barrow".[45] However, this is apparently unique in Ireland as no other rock of glacial origin is surrounded by such an enclosure on the island:

> The construction of the enclosure around the stone clearly marks it out as a place of special significance, and may have been driven by a desire to enhance, contain and control the stone's potency and meaning.[46]

Surrounding a stone with a large enclosure unquestionably implies that the stone was "of special significance" – although the enclosure is impossible to date with precision, which means that we do not know at what time of history the stone actually became significant. On the other hand, the "desire to enhance, contain and control the stone's potency and meaning" seems a more conjectural idea. Surrounding *Ail na Mireann* with an enclosure was rather evidently a way of "enhancing" its symbolic importance but nothing proves that this enclosure was about containing or controlling its alleged potency. An earthen enclosure perhaps simply suggests that the stone was most likely sacred and, symbolically speaking, important: the rest is a matter of interpretation.

Original Importance

On this matter, Macalister and Praeger first raised a most crucial question: was *Ail na Mireann* sacred because it stood on Uisneach, or was Uisneach sacred because of *Ail na Mireann*?

Joseph Loth believed that it was the presence of the conglomerate on the hill of Uisneach that actually made the essence of the place: for him, *Ail na Mireann* truly was the omphalos of Ireland around which the symbolism of the hill had developed.[47] However, an argument articulated by Macalister and Praeger is quite compelling: if *Ail na Mireann* was really at the origin of the veneration of the hill, why was no significant construction or monument – for example a sanctuary – constructed in the vicinity of the conglomerate? The largest enclosures, the main forts and burial monuments were all built hundreds of meters from the stone.[48]

Shot and colleagues believe that Uisneach was not about its stone only; in their view, *Ail na Mireann* is, together with *Lough Lugh*, one of the two "conspicuous natural features to inspire the perception of Uisneach as a 'place apart' from early prehistory onwards".[49] The theory is quite convincing: *Lough Lugh* is certainly another remarkable feature of the site, both because of its shape and its location, as will be shown *infra*.

However, the question of the "original significance" of the site seems impossible to settle. Perhaps it was simply not ever posed in such straightforward terms. The origin of the sacredness of a place does not necessarily rely on emotional criteria only – such as the impressive aspect of a stone or a lake for example. In the case of Uisneach, other criteria, perhaps more rational in essence, may have had their importance: the fertility of the land; the ability to see and be seen from the top of the hill; its potentially strategic location (at one point in history or another, at least); the size of the plateau which enabled the gathering of many; and, most of all, its approximately central position on the island. All those characteristics may have led to the creation of a first site – either royal, war-related, religious or funerary, as discussed *infra*. Given the fertility of the land, the first original utilization of the hill was perhaps mainly secular in nature: there is a possibility that farm activities predate any other spiritual or symbolic significance of Uisneach. Subsequently – or simultaneously, we may never know – the conglomerate of Uisneach and possibly *Lough Lugh*, as well as the outstanding fertility, the centrality and the general configuration of the site may have contributed to the *mystique* and the symbolic position conferred to the hill. Be it as it may, the place in history of Uisneach was most likely justified by a host of reasons which completed each other rather than by a monolithic cause.

5.3 Lough Lugh and Water Sources

Description of Lough Lugh

The lake of Lugh, or *Lough Lugh*, is still very much a topographical reality of the hill of Uisneach: until recently, it was even used as a water supply for cattle.[50] The pond is oval in shape and occupies a modest 3,800 m^2 area with a diameter varying from 60 to 80 meters. Today, a floating isle – or peninsula, depending on the seasons and years – of vegetation occupies about half of its surface. Despite the fact that the islet reaches a thickness of up to 1.5 meter, walking on it is not advised: today, unauthorized access is prohibited. The islet is actually quite recent. It was not featured on a watercolor painting depicting the lake – and a cottage now gone – which dates back to the 1820s or 1830s. In her detailed study of the site, the team led by Roseanne Schot indicated that *Lough Lugh* may disappear under vegetation in the coming years if nothing is done to manage growth through regular maintenance.[51]

Uisneach and its surroundings are fed by many streams and springs. The Rath River flows just south and west of the hill.[52] It is a tributary of the Inny, whose name derives from Eithne,[53] a mythological figure usually described as the daughter of Balor and mother of Lugh, which is perhaps not coincidental.[54] The River Inny is itself tributary to *Lough Ree* and the Shannon. The hill of Uisneach is also surrounded by larger lakes, including *Lough Ennell*, five kilometers to the east, *Lough Owel*, half a dozen kilometers to the north-east, not far from the smaller *Lough Iron*. Those three lakes have already been identified *supra* with the mythological lakes Aininn, Uail and Iarainn which Dian Cécht was said to have vomited from Uisneach.

Lough Lugh lies on the central plateau of the hilltop, between the two summits of Uisneach.[55] However, it is by no means the sole water source visible on Uisneach, although it is obviously the most elevated and most apparent.

Tobernaslath

There are two other springs on the southern side of the hill, namely Saint Patrick's Well and *Tobernaslath* (*Finnleascach*, the "white rimmed well"). The latter lies at the bottom of a natural hillock on which a prostrate pillar-stone lies. As already mentioned, excavation might provide evidence of whether it originally stood upright, although it certainly cannot confirm what the specific symbolic significance of the stone (the cosmic pillar of Uisneach?) was.[56]

The sacredness of the place is reinforced by that fact that, in olden times, the top of the mound was surrounded by an earthen enclosure, 35 meters in diameter, similar to that circling *Ail na Mireann*. This could support the proposal that there used to be both a sacred "cosmic pillar" on Uisneach (the pillar-stone of *Tobernaslath*?) and a sacred navel (*Ail na Mireann*); but, once again, a specific archaeological study dedicated to the pillar and its surroundings is missing for this hypothesis to be truly conclusive.

Saint Patrick's Well

As for the spring called Saint Patrick's Well, Macalister and Praeger do mention its existence and specify that it supplied a copious amount of "good water", but did not apparently possess "any special sanctity at present".[57] On the other hand, during his visit in 1837, O'Donovan did not mention Saint Patrick's Well, although the scholar explained that local tradition knew of a well of that name which had run dry.[58] This could be explained by the topographical configuration of the area: according to Schot's team, it is possible that water sources appeared and disappeared through the centuries, including in the area of Saint Patrick's Well.[59] Another significant water source does exist today on the southern side of Uisneach: the sizeable pond has the particularity of being nameless, which implies either that it is quite recent or that no significant symbolic or traditional custom is attached to it.

Importance of Lough Lugh

The fact that Uisneach brims with wells, springs and other notable water sources had obvious symbolic repercussions. Many ancient Irish ceremonial centers were intimately connected with the presence of ponds or small lakes, such as *Loughnashade* at Navan (Co. Armagh) or *Dá Chích Anann* and the well of *Cathair Crobh Dearg* in Co. Kerry. The abundance of water on and around Uisneach, coupled with the central aspect of the hill, probably provided its reputation as a primordial source of Irish waters.[60] The fact that *Lough Lugh* does not seem connected to any river or spring at first glance possibly consolidated the symbolic potency of the place. The pond is likely fed by a hidden stream flowing underground or perhaps water filtering through limestone, as suggested by the local plants.[61] Ancient populations, who lacked this sort of scientific insight, may have believed the lake to spring as if by magic – yet another reason to see the mark of the Otherworld.

Origin and Evolution

From a strictly scientific perspective, the origin of *Lough Lugh* is quite clear now, notably thanks to the investigations conducted by the authors of "Reflections on a Lake: a Multi-Proxy Study of Environmental Change and Human Impacts at *Lough Lugh*, Uisneach, Co. Westmeath":

> The pollen and chironomid records indicate a Late Glacial origin for the lake, and this is supported by a radiocarbon date of 8349-8236 cal. BC from a hazelnut shell at 170 cm depth.[62]

This implies that the pond was formed before the arrival of the first human population in Ireland. Although *Lough Lugh* seems to be a natural feature of Uisneach, the question of whether or not the lake was modified by man was tackled by a couple of recent archeological papers. Archaeologists do mention a "hiatus", an anomaly in the succession of sedimentary layers of the lake; between three and seven meters of organic deposits are missing in the sedimentation of the last 10,000 years. Two hypotheses prevail:

> A cognate desire to maintain *Lough Lugh* as an open-water "ritual" pond may have provided an impetus for the removal of surface vegetation and lake sediment in antiquity, although, given the obvious importance of water as a resource, economic considerations could also have played a role.[63]

The author clarifies her second hypothesis as follows:

> Archaeological evidence for the presence of cattle and other domesticates at Uisneach during the later Iron Age and early medieval period, and the use of *Lough Lugh* as a watering-hole in modern times, suggests that (intermittent?) cleaning out of the lake to improve water access for livestock might also provide a viable explanation for the hiatus in the sediment record.[64]

A subsequent 2015 study indeed established that "the lake was most likely dug out in the past in order to restore open water conditions", possibly in the 11th century AD.[65] Following this "hiatus", the presence and impact of humans continued[66] and were confirmed by sedimentary studies: since medieval times, humans have never stopped maintaining connections with *Lough Lugh* although, of course, the nature of those links remains to be identified. Whether this landscaping and cleaning out were done for sacred or secular reasons is not verifiable: what actually matters is that the site was never left unattended and in a wild state, which tends to imply a (continuous?) occupation or use of the site at least from the 11th century AD onward. On the other hand, "the possibility that sediment from Lough Lugh was deliberately removed in prehistory to create an open water ritual pond"[67] may suggest a more ancient origin of what could be considered as an archeological monument in itself and not only a natural lake.[68]

Just as in the case of *Ail na Mireann*, there are no ancient constructions *per se* that could confirm the existence of an antique royal or sacred residence in the immediate vicinity of *Lough Lugh* . It must be noted, however, that the lake lies at a very approximate center of the different points of interest of the hill: the actual summit of Uisneach is situated about 250 meters west of the pond and the second highest peak – or rather mound – about 200 meters east; the conjoined ringfort at Rathnew was built 200 meters to the south-east of the lake; *Ail na Mireann* and *Tobernaslath* are a little farther, i.e. 500 meters at the south-west and south-south-west of *Lough Lugh* respectively. This gives the – rather vague – impression that the *lough* lies at the geographical, and therefore perhaps symbolic center of the whole. The recent archaeological investigations that were carried out focused on a better understand the origins and development of the lake: their purpose was not necessarily to look for offerings and artefacts, which would have required an entirely different methodology, and the investigators did not find specific offerings or even ruins of ancient monuments. The sacred nature of the lake was not confirmed: although the conclusion is tempting, it is not possible, to this day, to assert that *Lough Lugh* was ever used for rituals.[69]

In the 1830s, the occupants of the cottage then built on the western shore of the pond described the area north of *Lough Lugh* as being "the site of an old burying ground"[70] but no archeological data confirms the statement. On the other hand, the two summits of Uisneach – connected by an imaginary line, the approximate middle of which is *Lough Lugh* – seem to be funerary sites indeed.

5.4 The Summits of Uisneach

Eastern Summit: Burial Mound of Lugh?

The eastern summit is surrounded by "a substantial, probably rock-cut, ditch whose fill may contain significant quantities of burnt material":[71] the ditch of this monumental enclosure is about two meters wide, 200 meters in diameter and almost adjoins *Lough Lugh* on its eastern shore. A four-meter gap on its east-north-east side probably corresponded to an entrance.

This enclosure is the largest monument on Uisneach and is dated by Schot to the end of the Prehistoric period. Its impressive size vouches for a probable sacred character of the eastern summit. Most of all, a 1.7 meter high and 20 meter diameter earthen mound stands at the center of the enclosure. In 1929, Macalister and Praeger reported that, from hearsay, "this mound had been violated in comparatively recent times, [and a] cist had been found within it; but if so, it was utterly demolished".[72] A cist is a stone-lined grave, usually rectangular (or square) in form. The statement therefore suggests that the Easter summit of Uisneach was a prehistoric tumulus.[73]

Roseanne Schot goes even further and identifies it as Carn Lugdach, which is said to be the burial mound raised in Lugh's honor.[74] The *Dindshenchas* does imply that the grave of Lugh adjoined the lake:

> the cairn which stands on the shore, called the Sidan, was raised over his body: so that cairn is Lug's Grave, and hence come the names Loch Lugborta and Carn Lugdach.[75]

As mentioned before, the enclosure surrounding the eastern summit almost touches the shore of *Lough Lugh*; the probable megalithic tomb known as *Saint Patrick's Bed*, on the western summit, is much more distant. It is therefore conceivable that the mound of the eastern summit was considered to be a site dedicated to Lugh, perhaps even the symbolic resting place of the god. The true origin of the prehistoric tumulus remains unknown but this comparison was, from a symbolic perspective, most important.

Western Summit: Saint Patrick's Bed

From its very modest 182 meters in altitude, the western summit is the actual culminating point of Uisneach: the structure called *Saint Patrick's Bed* can still be found on the top of the hill today.

Just as in the case of Saint Patrick's Well, the reference to the saint in the toponym is quite generic: nothing must be inferred from this very common denomination, although the importance of Uisneach in the hagiography of Patrick by Tírechán might initially have suggested otherwise. It is of course always possible that the name was inspired by the Christian Life of the Saint and his famous *Petra Coithrigi*; but it is just as likely – and perhaps much more – that this naming was merely coincidental and stemmed from the popularity of the saint in Ireland.

Saint Patrick's Bed was already noticed in 1837 by O'Donovan. He reported that the locals complained the site had been violated: a triangulation pillar[76] had recently been placed on top of the monument by the *Ordnance*

Survey and a great quantity of stones was allegedly moved or taken away.[77] As a matter of fact, the current aspect of the monument is far from reminiscent of a megalithic tomb, which it probably was. For the untrained eye, *Saint Patrick's Bed* is today but an anarchic heap of a few dozen big rocks. Fortunately, archaeological studies give a more detailed account of the site:

> The monument presently consists of a low, subrectangular cairn (max dimensions 9.2 m n-s by 5 m e-w) delimited to the north and west by a setting of stone uprights. Two discontinuous arcs of stones form a "court-like" feature to the west.[78]

Better still, surveys have revealed several other remarkable monuments next to the summit, including a tumulus on its northern side, an artificial mound on its southern side and the below-surface remains of two enclosures, 23 and 35 meters in diameter, respectively: they surrounded *Saint Patrick's Bed* and both used to be delimited by wooden fences.[79] These discoveries confirm once again the importance and sacredness of the place. The two enclosures around *Saint Patrick's Bed* provide an interesting counterpoint to the mound of the eastern summit and its gigantic enclosure. Roseanne Schot explains the interest of such constructions as follows:

> The overall arrangement is reminiscent of the palisade trenches identified in pre-tomb levels at Tara (Mound of the Hostages) and Knowth and ostensibly links Uisneach with a select group of multi-period ceremonial sites in Ireland where structural activity pre-dating the construction of a megalithic tomb is attested.[80]

She therefore identifies Uisneach as a sacred burial ground: *Saint Patrick's Bed* was a megalithic tomb and the burial mound of the eastern summit was perhaps dedicated to Lugh.[81] The archaeologist's idea is that the hill was actually a prehistoric necropolis later used as a royal site.[82] The absence of visible signs of veneration, funerary rites, offerings and most of all the lack of human remains in both *Saint Patrick's Bed* and the burial mound of the eastern summit are worth noting – although *Saint Patrick's Bed* is yet to be thoroughly excavated.

Imagining a necropolis with no body or offering is surprising but by no means unsustainable. Macalister and Praeger did mention a cist that was stolen and, more generally speaking, contemplated the idea of a systematic looting of the site at an undetermined date: this could be a reasonable first explanation.

It is actually quite conceivable that Uisneach was originally (or, perhaps more cautiously *at an early period*) a necropolis. Interestingly enough, most of the "ritual attention", all the sacredness of the place was later focused on another monument:

In fact, the only human remains recorded from Uisneach were found, not in a burial monument, but in the ditch and internal area of the penannular enclosure underlying the conjoined ringfort of Rathnew.[83]

5.5 Rathnew

In the 16th century, the poems of Tadhg Dall Ó Huiginn mentioned a "fort like that of famed Ushnagh, which the Hound of the Feats subdued".[84] The first poem of the collection compiled and edited by Eleanor Knott is un-equivocal: Uisneach was considered as one of "Ireland's capitals" but at the time, its castle, a "darling of kings", was already but a ruin:

> Ushnagh's castle, darling of kings, hath been brought to such a state that it is a sorrowful omen to watch over the fair, modest contours of her bright countenance. Ireland's capitals have been defiled, one after another; a garment of weeds invests each keep, the white rampart of every castle is become a trench.[85]

The "castle" here mentioned is most likely the conjoined ringfort of Rathnew – also referred to as the *figure of eight* – which is now only a fort in name: time and erosion have done their work. Apart from the occasional unevenness of the ground, a couple of stones scattered here and there, and irregular earthen ramparts, nothing indicates the – alleged – past splendor of the place.[86] Fortunately, the most extensive excavations made in the last hundred years were carried out at the ringfort of Rathnew, which is exceptionally well documented from an archaeological perspective.

For a long time, Rathnew was believed to conceal ancient graves. Macalister and Praeger proved that this was not the case. They also pointed out that the site was quite difficult to study as it was erected in several phases and changed significantly over time. The structure is the most complex to be found on Uisneach and also the largest – aside from the monumental ditched enclosure around the eastern summit. Roseanne Schot, who studied Rathnew at length, summarizes the essential elements as follow:

> The site occupies a commanding position on a prominent rise (175 m above sea-level) on the south-eastern cusp of the [eastern summit of Uisneach], and boasts extensive views, particularly to the south and east. It is bivallate and consists of a large, subcircular enclosure (hereafter the "Eastern Enclosure"), with a smaller, semicircular enclosure conjoined to its western side (hereafter the "Western Enclosure"). (...) Excavation within the interior of the enclosures led to the discovery of a variety of features, including the remains of several houses, two souterrains and, most remarkably, a large ditched

enclosure associated with an earlier phase of activity, pre-dating the bivallate earthworks. Other evidence of occupation in the form of areas of paving, burning, pits and post-holes, and large quantities of animal bone was also uncovered.[87]

Macalister and Praeger believed Rathnew experienced four periods of settlement and was built between before the 3rd century CE. Schot, whose account is more scientific and objective, theorized three distinct phases of construction only (notated from I to III). Based on the structural remains and objects found on the site, she suggests an occupation of the site starting in the Iron Age[88] (if not before) and possibly continuing up to the 13th century. The construction of the fort *per se* is believed to have taken place in the 7th or 8th century CE.[89]

The structural phases called "phase II" and "phase III" correspond with the construction and occupation of the conjoined fort. "Phase I" is more ancient and is represented by a series of enclosure ditches, trenches, pits and other features, which contribute greatly to our comprehension of the history of the site.

Sanctuary of Rathnew (Rathnew I)

The first structural phase is ancient but still quite difficult to date: Schot suggests the end of the Iron Age and more specifically a period ranging from the 3rd and 5th century CE. Its most obvious feature is a ditch of about 50 meters in diameter, 1.2 meter deep at most and between 1.2 and 3 meters wide. A three-meter wide entrance on its eastern side gives it a distinctive penannular or "omega" shape.[90] The trench is doubled by a line of stones for around 25 meters on the southern side; Macalister and Praeger believed it to be the remnant of a wall that originally circled the site. At the time of the excavation, the enclosure ditch was filled with earth and sediments that had accumulated over centuries.

Within the enclosure, the excavators discovered a number of pits and post-holes whose purpose appeared to vary, based upon their contents: wood charcoal, ashes, or even animal bones. They mention two rectangular pits in particular, of about 1.5 to 2.5 meters on either side, which were aligned with the entrance of the site:

> At the bottom of each there was a thick bed of ashes, intermingled with stones of moderately large size, and with many animal bones. The latter were in great quantities immediately above the ash-beds; they were unburnt.[91]

Except for a small metal knife, no significant object was found. Those small pits may have been holes enabling the erection of large posts. Given their morphological configuration and the presence of what could be considered as offerings, Schot tends to see similarities with "Iron Age sanctuaries in Britain and on the Continent, which are commonly associated with chthonic offerings".[92]

Two other circular pits of approximately the same dimensions (1.2 meter in diameter) are also aligned with the entrance, 12 meters to the west. They were also filled with charcoal – but not ashes – and were blocked by flat stones at the time of the excavation. According to Macalister and Praeger:

> the half-burnt appearance of the deposit suggested that a fire had been kindled, and then suddenly quenched by pouring water or soil over it. Mingled with the clay and charcoal in the pit was a quantity of animal bones, not burnt; and in the northern pit there were also about a dozen quartz pebbles, of about the size and shape of an average potato, and displaying no trace of the action of fire. (...) They must have been collected and placed with intention [and] must have been brought from a considerable distance.[93]

The exact function of those small stones remains a mystery. It is possible they were offerings connected with an unknown ritual. The fact that those two holes were aligned with the rectangular pits and the entrance in an east-west orientation also suggests an ancient ritual activity.

Within the enclosure, seven other pits, probably intended to support posts, are also recorded by Macalister and Praeger; two of those holes were filled with ashes.[94]

Several other trenches and pits could be found outside of the enclosure, in the immediate proximity of the main trench. The archaeologists mention in particular a 1.8-meter wide pit "close to the Rampart, which contained at the bottom black earth, ashes, many bones, large and many small stones".[95] Four other holes, some of which contain traces of combustion, are also mentioned in an approximate east-west alignment. The easternmost hole was placed next to a small ash-bed. Another much more significant ash-bed could be found on the south-south-west side of the main trench: it was filled – and even overflowing – with ashes and visible traces of combustion.

The archaeologists noted six different layers in this ash-bed, from the surface humus to a gray and brown clay layer with unburnt bones and coal: except for the surface layer, all strata contained animal bones. The fourth stratum corresponded to a thick layer of black ash and completely calcined bones. Macalister and Praeger reached the following conclusion:

> The appearances were strongly suggestive of a sanctuary-site, in which fire was kept burning perpetually, or kindled at frequent intervals; and of animal sacrifices offered in this fire.[96]

The archaeologists indicate that the bones found in this ash-bed substantially differ from those found elsewhere during the excavations.

Macalister and Praeger did uncover a considerable quantity of bones in or next to Rathnew: bones or teeth of "Ox, Sheep, Pig, Horse, Red Deer, Dog or Wolf[97], Cat, Fox, Rabbit, Irish Stoat, Hedgehog, Frog, and several kinds of birds" were unearthed.[98] In most cases, those bones were fragmentary, partially burnt or cooked. In the opinion of the archaeologists, a great number of feasts had taken place on the site throughout its history. Conversely, the bones found in the great ash-bed did not seem to belong to animals killed for their meat:

> Bones naturally in contact were found together, which shews that whole carcasses, or at least limbs and other large portions containing more than one bone, were committed to the flames with the flesh still upon them.[99]

The authors never explicitly mention the species to which those bones found in the ash-bed belonged, unfortunately. From their account, it is possible to infer that they most likely were bovines. Of course, the idea of potential animal sacrifices is compelling, given what is known of the festival of *Bealtaine* on the one hand and the description of *Mórdháil Uisnigh* on the other.

The discovery of human remains during the excavations is not remotely as conclusive: two adult skeletons – a young man and an older woman – were found in an east-west alignment within the enclosure, more specifically halfway between the rectangular pits and the two circular holes blocked with flat stones. However, no potential offering or object of any kind was discovered next to them. The analysis of the remains following the 1929 excavations suggested that they dated to the early 19th century only.[100] Unfortunately, the scientific methods used at the beginning of the 20th century cast doubt on this dating, but since the skeletons are now missing, we will probably never know is the conclusions were correct or if, on the contrary, the remains were more ancient. Apart from those two skeletons, only one fragment of a child's skull, a piece of a long bone (also belonging to a child) and the epiphysis of a thigh bone were uncovered. This is, of course, far too little to jump to any conclusion regarding a potential ritual significance of the place, especially since these fragments have not been dated. The history of Uisneach stretches over thousands of years; as time passes, the probability for injuries grows exponentially, and not all bones are broken on purpose, not all wounds are made for ritual purposes.

This still confirms that the enclosure is not an ancient cemetery or, given that the two bodies discovered are *a priori* only two hundred years old, an ancient funerary site. The most adequate term to encompass this "phase I" of Rathnew is indeed, as suggested by Macalister and Praeger, a "sanctuary". The morphology of the site and the presence of animal sacrifices on the one hand and traces of feasting on the other, leave little doubt as regards the symbolic and ritual importance of the place: "Phase I" Rathnew was a ceremonial enclosure dating to the end of the Iron Age[101] whose ritual significance seems compatible with what we know of the festival of *Bealtaine*.

Whether or not this sanctuary of Rathnew was associated, at some point of history or another, with the "house of the Dagda" or the "house" where Midhe cut the tongue of his rivals remains a matter of conjecture.

Some of the artifacts found within the enclosure – such as bronze pins and other brooches, fragments of metal and fibulae – date back to the 6th or 7th century.[102] As mentioned before, Roseanne Schot goes further and suggests a date somewhere between the 3rd and 5th centuries CE for the construction of this Phase I, a theory that does match the archeological evidence as well as our knowledge of Irish history.

Ringfort of Rathnew (Rathnew II): General Statements

Today, the "fort of Rathnew" consists of a earth and stone enclosure divided into two parts and is better defined as the "conjoined ringfort of Rathnew": the Eastern Enclosure is the larger of the two and has a subcircular shape; the Western Enclosure is a C-shaped annex contiguous to its left side.[103]

This double ringfort corresponds to the second major phase of development of the site, denoted Phase II. This Phase II of Rathnew was built in an east-west alignment and has a very distinctive *figure-of-eight* shape. The enclosure of Phase I is contained within the Eastern Enclosure of Phase II. The enclosures of Phase I and of Phase II are quite obviously off-centered, and no deliberate geometrical correspondence is evident at first glance. However, a closer look shows a "[deliberate effort] to incorporate the older monument within the new".[104]

The current site is in an advanced state of deterioration; the *figure of eight* is now but a seemingly chaotic heap of semi-buried rocks surrounded by earthworks. Macalister and Praeger noted the presence of a ruined cottage in a close-by field, which probably dated back to the late 18th or early 19th century: the authors believed that stones of the fort were used to build the cottage, which may have contributed to the disfigurement of the site. The theory requires qualification, however: as already mentioned earlier, the poet Tadhg Dall Ó hUiginn made a reference to the ruins of what he called "Ushnagh's castle" in the 16th century. It is possible that the last standing stones of the *figure of eight* were used to build the adjoining farmhouse but the ringfort of Rathnew – which most likely corresponds to this "Ushnagh's castle"– was already critically damaged and probably in ruins at the time of Ó hUiginn.

Macalister and Praeger believed that the Western Enclosure was more recent than the Eastern one, which was later refuted by Schot's investigation: she holds that both enclosures were built at the same time and that the double aspect of the *figure of eight* was planned from the start.[105]

Eastern Enclosure

With an inner diameter of about 65 meters, the Eastern Enclosure is more than twice as large as the Western one – which itself varies between 30 and

35 meters in diameter. The enclosure takes the shape of a (now ruined and semi-buried) stone-revetted rampart, sometimes reaching as much as 3.5 meters in height/depth. It is circled by a 2.5-meters deep trench on more than half of its circumference, from the north-west to the south-east.[106]

The entrance to the enclosure lies on its eastern side, in a similar fashion to that of Phase I, although the two entrances do not precisely align. It "consists of a well-defined gap in the inner rampart", which was "revetted with large blocks of stone, between which lay, at right angles, the remains of several stone 'steps'".[107]

Excavators made several interesting finds within the Eastern Enclosure. As already mentioned *supra*, the bodies of the young man and the elderly woman may or may not date back to the early 19th century, as suggested by Macalister and Praeger. In the north-western quadrant of the enclosure, "a small single-chambered souterrain, some 11 m in length"[108] may be ascribed to Phase II, as suggested by Schot, but its precise role or function remains unknown. Finally, the enclosure also contains a wide range of other secondary structures – isolated post-holes, lines or heaps of stones, small ash-beds etc.– which will not be described here in detail so as to focus on the most striking feature of the Eastern Enclosure: the presence of what archaeologists called the *Eastern House*.

This *Eastern House* is the most important and visible structure of the enclosure. It was the first site to be thoroughly excavated by Macalister and Praeger. It is placed slightly south of the center of the Eastern Enclosure. The *Eastern House* is a group of "compartments and chambers [contained] within a more or less circular wall of earth".[109] The wall is about one meter high and three meters thick at the base and is "faced on one or both sides with dry-stone masonry". The whole structure is a little over 13 meters in diameter and was later described as "rather like a complex souterrain".[110]

Once again, the entrance to the House was situated on its eastern side: it was accessible through a three-meter long passage paved with flat slabs and bordered by stones; "just outside where the pavement begins there are two well marked post-holes for the door-posts".[111] Macalister and Praeger believe that the *Eastern House* was originally covered with a conical thatched roof, a hypothesis that Schot thinks plausible, especially when considering the configuration of the several post-holes uncovered by the archaeologists.[112] Still on the eastern side of the structure, the "traces of a powerful fire underlying the foundation" were uncovered during the first excavations. The bed of ashes continued "along the inside of the circumference northward for a total length of" over 8 meters, "including the breadth of the entrance passage, and running under the foundation of the enclosing wall".[113] The authors believed this peculiar use of fire indicated a sort of "foundation rite". Inside the *Eastern House*, Macalister and Praeger also uncovered a thick layer of blackish-gray soil "containing animal bones, fragments of charcoal and occasional pockets of ashes".[114]

Later, during what Schot calls the phases 2 and 3 of the construction of the *Eastern House* – not to be confused with Phases II and III of Rathnew as a whole – some elements were added to the structure. This included two annex chambers roughly measuring 4 m by 2 m, auxiliary entrance passages, structural changes and additions made to the south-eastern side and subsequently even more entrances and new – notably poorly constructed – chambers, as well as a passageway connecting two rooms and several other walls.[115]

Finally, several objects were unearthed – both from the Eastern House and the site as the whole – by the archaeologists between 1925 and 1928. Those objects unfortunately failed to shed light on the specific function of the site or even to give an idea of its antiquity: the piece of whetstone found at the bottom of one chamber, the fragment of skull mentioned *supra*, the spear (or coulter?) and the knife potentially dating back to the 8th–11th centuries did not prove conclusive in establishing with any certainty the date of construction of the *Eastern House*. The discovery of a silver penny depicting King John of England or Henry III – and therefore dating to the 12th–13th centuries – was of no more help, especially since it probably came from a different stratigraphical horizon.

Western Enclosure

The C-shaped Western Enclosure is significantly smaller – 37 meters on its north-south axis, 30 meters east-west – and adjoins the eastern structure. Just like the Eastern Enclosure, it is surrounded by a trench and is enclosed with two ramparts, which were originally covered with large stone blocks. A two-meter wide entrance lies at the southern side of the structure.

Several elements uncovered during the excavations within the enclosure are remarkable. Macalister and Praeger found a stone pillar (1.3 × 0.8 × 0.4 m), approximately at its center; it rested on two other smaller stones, in a disposition similar to that of a dolmen. However, the authors believed it was a mere coincidence[116] and did not jump to any conclusion regarding its potential ritual significance. Aside from this pillar and several stone fragments and post-holes, it is once again the presence of a structure, the *Western House*, that caught the attention of the archaeologists.

This *Western House* is divided into two smaller structures: the Upper Chamber and the Souterrain. The Upper Chamber was almost completely destroyed by erosion but was of subrectangular form (about 5 m on each side). It is situated slightly to the south-west of the center of the Western Enclosure. An opening in the ground led to the Souterrain, whose walls were studded with various holes and recesses. One of those recesses "seems to have been used as a fire place. It was filled with clay in which were mingled charcoal and ashes". As noted by Macalister and Praeger, "when the fire was burning it seems inevitable that the Upper Chamber was full of smoke".[117]

Finally, outside of the *Western House*, two post-holes were identified as the probable foundation of a shed, or at least an annex structure now gone, which leaned against the main structure.

Ringfort of Rathnew: Alterations (Rathnew III)

The several additions to the different structures during what Schot calls "Phase III" are, for the most part, limited to the details. Thus, a small rectangular stone structure – about 6×3 m – was added inside the *Western House*: traces of combustion were found in its center. It was most likely a hearth, which potentially indicates that the rectangular structure was used as a home. Similarly, a roadway leading to Rathnew was probably constructed at that time. The other notable additions are detailed as follows by the Irish archaeologist, to whom scholars owe so much:

—the levelling of the ramparts and backfilling of the fosse along the south side of the Eastern Enclosure (in line with the roadway);

—the remodelling of the putative Phase II boundary "wall" between the Eastern and Western Enclosures, the southern portion of which was deflected from its original course (adjoining the inner bank of the Eastern Enclosure) to conjoin with the western bank of the roadway; the so-called "Outwork", at the southern junction of the enclosures, may also have been constructed at this time;

—the division of the eastern part of the enclosure into several small, subrectangular fields (long axis east-west) defined by a series of drystone walls, which abut the Phase II ramparts and the *Eastern House*.[118]

Those additions and remodelling raise questions and, more broadly speaking, it seems reasonable to wonder what the different structures of the "fort of Rathnew" were truly used for. Phase I of Rathnew most likely corresponded to a sanctuary where fire seemingly played a role and which was probably constructed between the 3rd and 5th centuries CE. The same questions of interpretation and dating are much more difficult to answer for Phases II and III: evidence is scarce and we have no choice but to settle for hypotheses.

Rathnew: Interpretation and Dating

Although the objects found in Rathnew do not completely elucidate the purpose and history of the conjoined ringfort, most of the artifacts can be dated from a period spanning between the early centuries of the first millennium CE and the 13th century – mainly between the 7th and 11th centuries. The two oldest items are a stone ball and a key. The decorated sandstone ball was found at the northeast of the penannular enclosure and measures 5 centimeters in diameter. It is very similar to the carved balls that can often be found in Scotland and that are usually dated between the Neolithic period and the end of the Antiquity: their purpose remains a mystery, or perhaps more accurately, there is no consensus over their precise function. It is still unclear whether they were used for a ritual or a purely functional reason. The key dates to the 2nd–4th centuries CE. Roseanne Schot notes that it is "of the same type and date as a Roman barrel padlock found at the Rath of the Synods, Tara"[119] and notes that it was likely an import from Roman Britain. Although peculiar and noteworthy, those findings add little to our global understanding of the site. Unfortunately, the same applies to the other items dated between the 7th and 11th centuries, i.e. – in a putative chronological order – a dress fastener, an iron buckle, a bell clapper from the 7th or 8th century, several pointed and grooved iron objects, two horseshoes and a spur (11th century), to which must be added the aforementioned silver penny (12th–13th centuries) and a show buckle from the 18th century.

On the other hand, the discovery of a "furnace-bottom" and two crucibles suggests that, at some point of history, the site was used for small-scale smelting of iron and copper.[120] Similarly, "disc querns, iron knives, whetstones, a spindle-whorl, an awl and a bone needle" as well as jet bracelets and a bone pin of unknown date were found in Rathnew: they evoke domestic activities and artisanal work, although it remains impossible to tell which one exactly.

No object directly associates the ringfort of Rathnew to either warriors or priests.[121] This did not stop Macalister and Praeger from classifying Rathnew as the probable royal "palace" of Tuathal Techtmar.[122] Schot, citing the work of Richard Warner, opted for a more nuanced approach: she established a distinction between a "royal site" and a "royal residence". A royal site does not imply that the king and/or his family lived *in situ* on a permanent basis; it was simply the place where the rituals of his tribe took place ("the inauguration, feasting, treaty-making and numerous other royal duties");[123] the king could occasionally stay there, notably during important events. From that perspective, it truly stood as a place of power.

The idea that Uisneach, or more precisely the Phases II and III of Rathnew, corresponded to a royal site is most plausible. Perhaps the term "place of power" is preferable because the objects excavated do not confirm the "royal" nature of the site. Schot backs up her theory by reminding of the "sheer scale of the earthworks, the presence of bivallation and, to some extent, the material assemblage indicate that the occupants were of high status".[124] But this does not confirm the royal nature of the ringfort: its high-ranked occupants could as well have been members of the sacerdotal class, an intriguing hypothesis which will be developed *infra*.

Macalister and Praeger were even more specific in their identification of this hypothetical royal "palace". They believed that the fort of Rathnew later became a residence of the southern Uí Néill.[125] However, their analysis relied on incorrect assumptions: the archeologists had difficulty differentiating history and myth. For instance, they accepted without any reserve the account of Tuathal Techtmar's story made by Keating.

Still, the idea that the southern Uí Néill may have used, at one point of history or another, the ringfort of Rathnew as a royal site or residence is, once again, most plausible. The mere facts that they were called "Kings of

Uisneach" and that some of their members were associated with the hill since the 7th century at least is, of course, a good indicator. But the fact that the Uí Néill were clearly associated with Uisneach is not enough to establish that they chose the ringfort as their "royal residence" or "royal site". Once again, it is preferable to look at the problem from a different angle: given what the medieval texts and the archeological evidence tell us of Uisneach, it seems evident that a royal dynasty, namely the southern Uí Néill, envisaged the hill as a "place of power". Whether the power they held over Uisneach expressed itself at the ringfort of Rathnew under the form of sheer royal power (Rathnew being a royal residence or a royal site) or by the inclusion of members of the sacerdotal class is yet open to further investigation.

The interest of the objects dug up is very relative: they suggest a re-sidential or domestic use of the site, but not necessarily a royal one. The very layout of the site leaves the door wide open for interpretation: large partitioned spaces, a "house" in both of the two main enclosures, a couple of hearths, post-holes, stones from which very little can be inferred, sou-terrains whose purpose remain unclear, entrances almost systematically opened to the east, a general east-west orientation which may (or may not) indicate a possible symbolic significance etc. This is all too little, too vague, too partial: no theory seems to prevail.

The presence of traces of feasts is also ambivalent: they either suggest royal assemblies or ritual gatherings – for instance, those connected with the celebration of *Bealtaine*. The numerous ash-beds also raise questions, although they date, for the most part, to the Phase I of Rathnew, i.e. *before* the creation of the ringfort *per se*. In this regard, the connections between Phase I and Phases II–III of the site must not be neglected. As Roseanne Schot notes:

> There is strong reason to suspect that the Phase I ditch still retained a physical presence, however slight, when the earthworks were erected. (...) Moreover, the spatial layout of the enclosures in general suggests that a deliberate effort was made to incorporate the older monument within the new.[126]

The idea was probably to preserve the sacred dimension of Phase I so as to incorporate it in the symbolism of Phases II and III.[127] In other words, preserving traces of Phase I when building the fort conferred it a symbolic significance, inscribed it in historical continuity and, given the very essence of the ancient enclosure, made it sacred: the Phase I enclosure was indeed a sanctuary. It is within this enclosure that large, intense fires were lit; simi-larly, within this enclosure, animal sacrifices most likely took place: there is little doubt that Phase I of Rathnew was intimately connected with rituals and the sacerdotal class.

The ringfort of Rathnew was built at the heart and around a sanctuary in a deliberate attempt to perpetuate and benefit from the ritual symbolism of

Phase I: the new constructions became sacred, in the sense that they were connected with the ancient sanctuary and, as a consequence, with the religious and spiritual world. The sacredness of the whole was most likely reinforced by the presence of two burial sites at the top of the two summits of Uisneach. It is therefore possible to suggest a timeline of events.

In the prehistoric period, Uisneach was chosen as a place of burial and/or commemoration, probably because of the commanding position of the hill and its central location but also because it was a fertile land where a lake seemed to spring from nowhere and where a mysterious monumental rock excited the imagination. Between the 3rd and 5th centuries, a ritual enclosure was built: huge fires were lit and sacrifices were probably made. Later, the first traces of settlement appeared: the ringfort of Rathnew – the *figure of eight* – was built at the same location as the ritual enclosure, perhaps in the 7th century. This construction was possibly made under the initiative of the Uí Néill; interestingly enough, the attempts at political manipulation that can be found in the medieval documents mentioned *supra* started in that period. The fort was maintained for several centuries. In the 16th century, it was already in ruins. The items found on-site are for the most part dated before the 11th – and to a lesser extent the 13th – century, which is a good indicator of the period of occupancy.

It is therefore more than conceivable that the ringfort was associated with the dynasty of the southern Uí Néill. The use of the site as a royal dwelling, in the strict sense of the term, is still debatable, at least for an extended period of time, first and foremost because of the scarcity and plainness of the items that were dug up – although this could be explained by a looting of the site. Other elements, such as the presence of a forge and objects connected with artisanal work, traces of feasts and ash-beds suggest a recurring use of the site, perhaps as a place of inauguration or crowning and possibly as a place of assemblies where the convention of Uisneach may have taken place. Still, no evidence is perfectly conclusive: as a consequence, it is still unclear whether the conjoined ringfort of Rathnew was a royal residence or a temporary royal or sacred site limited to periods of assemblies or ceremonies.[128]

The presence of tumuli and enclosures is compatible with what is known of inauguration and assembly places in Ireland; furthermore, the existence of funerary monuments most likely played a role in the legitimation of the power and territories claimed by the Irish medieval dynasties, as they established a form of symbolic continuity.[129] But the most intriguing hypothesis was articulated by Schot at the end of the main paper she dedicated to the site:

> Another intriguing possibility is raised by a practice referred to in early legal sources which stipulate that some of the land attached to the office of kingship may be assigned to members of the king's household, such as his chief poet, judge, physician, etc. (Kelly 1988, 101), who perhaps served as "stewards" or "keepers" of the royal site. Such a scenario would more readily allow for occupation at Rathnew on a permanent basis, and indeed

could potentially account for the presence of several other ringforts and related enclosures on the lower slopes of Uisneach.[130]

It is obviously impossible to prove that Rathnew was occupied by one or several "chief poets, judges, physicians" – in other words, members of the sacerdotal class – at one point of history or another, unless future archaeological digs unveil new persuasive evidence. However, contemplating the fact that one or several members of the sacerdotal class occupied the ringfort of Rathnew – built on the site of the sacred enclosure of Uisneach which was most likely connected with their rituals – is a most stimulating theory. This is to the very least compatible with our knowledge of the site, from an archaeological, mythical and historical perspective.

We could therefore envisage that the members of the medieval sacerdotal class – heirs to the druidic tradition – were the "keepers" of Uisneach, which was perhaps intermittently inhabited or visited by the Kings of Uisneach, possibly during periodic ritual assemblies – in May? Ancient feasts and sacrifices, evidenced by archaeological investigations in connection with the sanctuary of Rathnew, may have symbolically relied on the memory of the ancestors buried and the deities commemorated on the tops of Uisneach: after all, Lugh is said to have been killed on the hill during a "great meeting" and the authors of the *Dindshenchas* believed the eastern summit to be his grave. The spiritual significance of the prehistoric megalithic tomb of the western summit and the alleged burial mound of the eastern summit was perhaps exploited for purifying or prophylactic purposes at given times of the year. *Bealtaine* seems the obvious choice as its celebration marked the connection between the world of the living and that of the dead – an ideal moment for the veneration or commemoration of ancestors and gods, most distinguished members of the Otherworld.

Notes

1 The precise date is important since, according to Macalister and Praeger, it was raining heavily on that day, which could explain some of the rudimentary descriptions made by O'Donovan. "Report on the Excavation of Uisneach", *op. cit.*, 71.

2 The etymology proposed by O'Donovan has already been mentioned: he derived *Carraig an Chait* (the "stone of the cat") from *Carraig Coithrigi* (the "stone of Patrick"), noted *Ailnamireann* on his map.

3 http://map.geohive.ie/mapviewer.html. Uisneach "will be found indicated on the six-inch Ordnance Map of Westmeath, sheet 24, in the right-hand upper corner", "Report on the Excavation of Uisneach", *op. cit.*, 69.

4 Ferguson, Samuel. 1872. "On Ancient Cemeteries at Rathcrogan and Elsewhere in Ireland (as affecting the question of the site of the cemetery at Taltin)" in *Proceedings of the Royal Irish Academy*, XV, 114-24.

5 Borlase, William Copeland. 1897. *The Dolmens of Ireland*. London: Chapman & Hall, 372.

6 Woods, James. 1907. *Annals of Westmeath: Ancient and Modern*. Dublin: Sealy, Bryers & Walker, 239-49, esp. 247 for an attempt at describing the site.

7 "Report on the Excavation of Uisneach", *op. cit.*, 75.

8 See "Report on the Excavation of Uisneach", *op. cit.*, 69-70 and in "Uisneach Midi", *op. cit.*, 39-41 for all the necessary information on the carboniferous limestone terrain "which has mostly a thin covering of gravelly drift, under a foot or so of brown soil".

9 "Report on the Excavation of Uisneach", *op. cit.*, 69.

10 "Uisneach Midi", *op. cit.*, 41 for a list of neighboring hills.

11 Most studies mention "182 meters" but the difference is, of course, negligible to the present discussion.

12 *Mythic Ireland, op. cit.*, 206.

13 In more scientific terms: "The crest of the hill comprises a broad east-west ridge, about 1km long and 500m wide, with two gently rounded summits of similar height. The ridge slopes quite steeply to the west and north, while to the east and south the ground falls away more gently to form a complex micro-topography of swells and hollows". "Uisneach Midi", *op. cit.*, 42-3. The only "official" summit remains *Saint Patrick's Bed*.

14 See chap. V.5.

15 "From Cult Centre to Royal Centre", *op. cit.*, 107.

16 "L'Omphalos chez les Celtes", *op. cit.*, 194.

17 *The Bardic Poems of Tadhg Dall Ó Huiginni, op. cit.*, "Brian na Murratha", 72-9.

18 The only exception is a large field north of the hill. Schot, R., Stuijts, I., McGinley, S. & Potito, A. 2014. "Reflections on a Lake: a Multi-Proxy Study of Environmental Change and Human Impacts at *Lough Lugh*, Uisneach, Co. Westmeath" in *Late Iron Age and "Roman" Ireland, Discovery Programme Reports 8*, Dublin: Wordwell, 113–26: 113. However, excavations unveiled "several disc querns [...] attesting to the processing of cereal, rather than its cultivation, at Uisneach during the early medieval period". "Reflections on a lake", *op. cit.*, 117.

19 "Report on the Excavation of Uisneach", *op. cit.*, 69.

20 "Reflections on a lake", *op. cit.,* 117.

21 See Annex II.6.

22 "Report on the Excavation of Uisneach", *op. cit.*, 70.

23 *Ibid.*, 69-70.

24 Once again, see https://www.townlands.ie/westmeath/conry/ for detailed maps.

25 "Uisneach Midi", *op. cit.*, 43-4.

26 "Report on the Excavation of Uisneach", *op. cit.*, 77-84.

27 See Annex II.3. See also Annex II.5 for a simplified version.

28 For the chronology and traditional phases of Irish prehistory, see Annex IV.

29 "Uisneach Midi", *op. cit.*, 39.

30 "Report on the Excavation of Uisneach", *op. cit.*, 117-22 for a full list.

31 See *infra*. The *Triumphs of Torlough*, a document dating back to the 14th century calls the hill "Usnach of the golden goblets", an obscure mention which was unfortunately not clarified by archaeological excavations. O'Grady, Standish Hayes, (ed.). 1929. "*Caithréim Thoirdhealbhaigh*" in *Irish Texts Society*, XXVI, London, 29.

32 The absence of pottery also surprised the authors, all the more so than other elements (mentioned *infra*) suggest the holding of large feasts. Macalister and Praeger vaguely mention a possible "religious taboo", which is never explained in detail. Another – perhaps more convincing – explanation could simply be that utensils made of other materials such as wood or leather were used.

33 "Uisneach Midi", *op. cit.*, 42.
34 O'Donovan favored this idea. See *supra*.
35 *Mythic Ireland*, *op. cit.*, 197.
36 Kaulins, Andis. 2003. *Stars, Stones and Scholars*. Bloomington: Trafford Publishing, 219-22.
37 "Report on the Excavation of Uisneach", *op. cit.*, 78.
38 18 meters according to Roseanne Schot in one of her papers ("Uisneach Midi", *op. cit.*, 45), 21 in another ("From Cult Centre to Royal Centre", *op. cit.*, 101-2).
39 *Ibid.*, 102.
40 "L'Omphalos chez les Celtes", *op. cit.*, 199.
41 "Report on the Excavation of Uisneach", *op. cit.*, 78.
42 "From Cult Centre to Royal Centre", *op. cit.*, 102.
43 *Ibid.*
44 "L'Omphalos chez les Celtes", *op. cit.*, 199.
45 "From Cult Centre to Royal Centre", *op. cit.*, 102.
46 *Ibid.*
47 "L'Omphalos chez les Celtes", *op. cit.* 206.
48 "Report on the Excavation of Uisneach", *op. cit.*, 70.
49 "Reflections on a Lake", *op. cit.*, 123.
50 *Ibid.*, 117.
51 *Ibid.*, 117-8.
52 "Uisneach Midi", *op. cit.*, 42 and esp. "Reflections on a Lake", *op. cit.*, 113.
53 *Annals of the Four Masters*, *op. cit.*, M3510.2: "The eruption of Eithne, in Ui Neill", Ui Neill meaning "the province of [Mide]" here, which is rather telling.
54 Especially when considered that, according to myths, Eithne was confined to a tower on Tory Island – the "isle of Balor" and birthplace of Lugh – which is in turn connected to *Bealtaine* and/or early May by folkloric tales. See chapter IV.4.
55 The general configuration is reminiscent of another Irish site, i.e. the stone enclosure of *Cathair Crobh Dearg*, Co. Kerry. The site was also venerated in early May. From the stone enclosure, the two twin mountains called *Dá Chích Anann* (the *Paps of Anu*) can be seen in the distance. Between the two breast-shaped mountains, at a place very appropriately called *the Cleavage*, a small pond forms a rivulet which flows further down between the two mountains. The *Paps of Anu* and Uisneach are, to some extent, similar in the sense that they are both twin or double summits; in both cases, a water source lies halfway between the summits and one or several enclosures are connected with a veneration in May. The comparison is all the more intriguing that the "Anu" from the site of Co. Kerry refers to the goddess Dana, who gave her name to the famous tribe – the Tuatha Dé Danann – led by Lugh. On the other hand, although the *Paps of Anu* are twin mountains whose breast shape is unmistakable, the general aspect of Uisneach is far less remarkable. There are indeed two summits on the hill of Uisneach but they are barely noticeable from the central plateau: *Lough Lugh* reaches about 166 meters in altitude when Uisneach culminates at ~180m only. Still, the comparison between the two sites may require further investigation.
56 Schot only explains that "The spring issues near the base of a natural, rounded hillock on whose summit lies a large, prostrate pillar-stone". "Uisneach Midi", *op. cit.*, 45.
57 "Report on the Excavation at Uisneach", *op. cit.*, 78.
58 Quoted in *ibid.*, 73 and 75.
59 "Reflections on a Lake", *op. cit.*, 117.
60 "Uisneach Midi", *op. cit.*, 43.

61 "Reflections on a Lake", *op. cit.*, 117.

62 *Ibid.*, 123-4.

63 *Ibid.*, 124.

64 *Ibid.* A subsequent in-depth archaeological study later confirmed this hypothesis: McGinley, Seamus, Potito, Aaron P., Molloy, Karen, Schot, Roseanne, Stuijts, Ingelise & Beilman, David W. 2015. "*Lough Lugh*, Uisneach: from natural lake to archaeological monument?" in *Journal of Irish Archaeology*, XXIV, 115-30: 125.

65 "*Lough Lugh*, Uisneach: from natural lake to archaeological monument?", *op. cit.*, 125.

66 *Ibid.*, 126 where it is suggested that *Lough Lugh* was already turned into an "open water environment" in the 11th century.

67 *Ibid.*, 127.

68 This is, of course, the whole point of the article "*Lough Lugh*, Uisneach: from natural lake to archaeological monument?".

69 *Ibid*, 127.

70 "Reflections on a Lake", *op. cit.*, 117.

71 "From Cult Centre to Royal Centre", *op. cit.*, 104.

72 "Report on the Excavation of Uisneach", *op. cit.*, 83.

73 Schot uses the term "bowl-barrow".

74 "From Cult Centre to Royal Centre", *op. cit.*, 110.

75 *Dindshenchas*, *op. cit.*, IV, 279-81.

76 See *supra* "Pillar or navel: reality of Uisneach".

77 *Ordnance Survey Letters*, *op. cit.*, 42.

78 "Uisneach Midi", *op. cit.*, 44. See also "From Cult Centre to Royal Centre", *op. cit.*, 99.

79 *Ibid.*

80 "From Cult Centre to Royal Centre", *ibid.*

81 The author also suggests that it may have played a role in potential royal ceremonies in the medieval period "The prominence of Carn Lugdach (...) raises the distinct possibility that it served as the inauguration mound of the kings of Uisneach—the final destination, perhaps, in a royal procession that also took in other significant monuments such as the Cat Stone". "From Cult Centre to Royal Centre", *op. cit.*, 110. The idea is interesting but remains conjectural.

82 *Ibid.*, 105. See the paragraphs dedicated to the ringfort of Rathnew for the potentially royal nature of the site. The existence of possible graves on two summits which are equidistant from a watering place may remind, as already mentioned, of *Cathair Crobh Dearg*, Co. Kerry and its famous *Paps*. Hopefully, further analysis will back up this claim in the near future.

83 *Ibid.*, 99.

84 *The Bardic Poems of Tadhg Dall Ó Huiginn*, *op. cit.*, "Lios Gréine", 26.

85 *Ibid.*, 1.

86 See Annex II.4-5.

87 "Uisneach Midi", *op. cit.*, 47.

88 The Irish Iron Age corresponds to a thousand-year long era starting around 600 BCE. *The Prehistoric Archaeology of Ireland*, *op. cit.*, 4. See Annex IV.

89 *Ibid.*, 63.

90 See Annex II.4. There are also two auxiliary trenches in the north and southeast which are unfortunately barely visible and difficult to interpret. See *ibid.*, 50-1.

91 "Report on the Excavation of Uisneach", *op. cit.*, 89.

92 "Uisneach Midi", *op. cit.*, 52.

93 "Report on the Excavation of Uisneach", *op. cit.*, 90.
94 More precisely, a group of four post-holes (the two southernmost of which were filled with ashes), two others (conic-shaped) and a smaller one. *Ibid.*, 90.
95 *Ibid.*, 91.
96 *Ibid.*, 93.
97 Macalister and Praeger even mention "five large dogs" who "lived in Uisneach". *Ibid.*, 123.
98 *Ibid.*, 122.
99 *Ibid.*, 93.
100 *Ibid.*, 115.
101 "Uisneach Midi", *op. cit.*, 71.
102 *Ibid.*, 54.
103 See Annex II.4.
104 "Uisneach Midi", *op. cit.*, 65. See *infra* for further discussion.
105 The precise reasons for this theory are detailed *ibid.*, 58, the most convincing being the absence of pits near the two enclosures.
106 *Ibid.*, 55.
107 *Ibid.*
108 *Ibid.*, 59.
109 "Report on the Excavation of Uisneach", *op. cit.*, 101.
110 "Uisneach Midi", *op. cit.*, 59, quoting Lynn, C.J. 1978. "Early Christian Period Domestic Structures: a Change from Round to Rectangular Plans?" in *Irish Archaeological Research Forum*, V, 29-45.
111 "Report on the Excavation of Uisneach", *op. cit.*, 102.
112 *Ibid.*, 103 and "Uisneach Midi", *op. cit.*, 60.
113 "Report on the Excavation of Uisneach", *op. cit.*, 102.
114 See "Uisneach Midi", *op. cit.*, 61.
115 See *ibid.*, 60 etc. for detail.
116 "Report on the Excavation of Uisneach", *op. cit.*, 111.
117 *Ibid.*, 114.
118 "Uisneach Midi", *op. cit.*, 62.
119 *Ibid.*, 63.
120 *Ibid.*
121 The work of the forge could be an exception as it is always placed at the boundaries of the two classes.
122 "Report on the Excavation of Uisneach", *op. cit.*, 126-7. See also *Annals of Westmeath*, *op. cit.*, 247.
123 Warner, Richard B. 2000. "Clogher: an Archaeological of Early Medieval Tyrone and mid-Ulster" in Dillon C. & Jefferies H.A. (ed.) *Tyrone: History and Society*, Geography Publications: Dublin, 39-54.
124 "Uisneach Midi", *op. cit.*, 65.
125 "Report on the Excavations of Uisneach", *op. cit.*, 125.
126 "Uisneach Midi", *op. cit.*, 65.
127 Roseanne Schot mentions several interesting examples of such "incorporations" elsewhere in Ireland, *ibid.*
128 *Ibid.*, 65-6.
129 *Ibid.*, 66.
130 *Ibid.*

6 Modern and Contemporary Aspects of Uisneach

Archaeology confirms the symbolic importance of the hill in the Early Middle Ages and arguably as early as Irish prehistory. However, the site gradually fell into disuse. By the 16th century, it was already in ruins; in the 17th century, Keating wrote about it in the past tense; evidence from the 18th century is rare and usually holds little value.

Uisneach has to wait until the 19th century and the rather laconic topographical and archaeological comments of O'Donovan in 1837, then the excavations of the 1920s, to catch up with the train of history. Between the two investigations, little or no scholarly study was conducted on the hill, with the notable exception of a book entitled *Annals of Westmeath* by James Woods, published in 1907. The work is remarkable in the sense that it fosters reflection on the place Uisneach occupied in the Irish imagination at the time of the *Gaelic Revival*.

6.1 Uisneach and the Gaelic Revival

"*Gaelic Revival*" is a generic term which refers to a global resurgence of interest in the Gaelic/Irish culture that took place at the turn of the 19th and 20th centuries in Ireland. Its main purpose was to bring the Celtic or Gaelic culture – as opposed to the English and British cultures – to the fore: interest in ancient Irish history and literature as well as Celtic mythology was at the center of this new movement. Some authors focused on the importance of the Gaelic language and wrote exclusively in Gaelic Irish; other artists and intellectuals wrote in English and focused on other forms of engagement: for instance, the (Anglo-)*Irish Literary Revival* was a significant part of the wider *Gaelic Revival* movement and its members tried to revitalize the supposedly glorious Celtic past of Ireland through literature while still writing in English.

Since the 1880s and during the first quarter of the 20th century, intellectuals, artists, and politicians – professions that are obviously not mutually exclusive – produced a considerable number of works, frequently steeped in romanticism and nationalism, praising the all-too forgotten Irish culture.

DOI: 10.4324/9781003143161-7

As already mentioned above, a considerable number of authors made a strong case for Uisneach in the context of the story of *Deirdre* and the *Sons of Uisneach*; from Lady Gregory to Synge, from Yeats to Ferguson, most of the essential figures of the *Gaelic Revival* offered a version of the story. Interestingly enough, James Joyce is said to have visited Uisneach on at least on two occasions, in 1900 and 1901.[1] Some commentators even see an allusion to Uisneach in one passage of his major work, *Finnegans Wake*;[2] the hill is never directly mentioned but is supposedly described as the "mountainy molehill".[3] As this work of the novelist and poet is famously and especially cryptic, this correspondence is far from certain, to say the least.

Returning to the *Gaelic Revival*, and perhaps more significantly to the (Anglo-)*Irish Literary Revival*, the purpose of this urban, intellectual and to some extent *bourgeois* movement was to bring Ireland into the 20th century in a rather peculiar way: the "brilliant past" of the Celtic civilization was to be the tool by which the Irish identity was rebuilt from the ground up. The protagonists of the *Gaelic Revival* prompted their followers to show respect and cherish their centuries-old Irish traditions, which were considered as the cement of their nation-building effort and the cultural reinvention of Ireland.[4] The Celtic past was not only conceived as a matter of pride for the Irish: it stood as proof of the legitimacy of Ireland as a nation and possibly a country.

Several national myths stood at the core of the political and artistic approach offered by the movement: farmers were good and sensible holders of ancient wisdom and the Irish Celts of yore were considered or presented as intellectually and artistically superior:

> From Douglas Hyde to Yeats, from Charles Gavan Duffy to Lady Gregory and the playwrights of the Irish Literary Theatre (1899) then National Theatre of Ireland, these intellectuals gave birth to a literary nationalism which soon veered towards the political sphere.[5]

In particular, the opening of the *Irish Literary Theatre* by William Butler Yeats on 8–9 May 1899 came with the creation of its first theatrical pamphlet sold to the audience. This pamphlet was described as "The Organ of the Irish Literary Theatre" and included its seasonal programme. The poet chose to officially name the pamphlet "*Beltaine*" so as to "stress the Irishness of the venture as well as confound his English critics, who would be able neither to translate nor to pronounce it":[6] Yeats believed that the festival of *Bealtaine* was the epitome of Irishness, which is rather telling.

James Woods' *Annals of Westmeath* clearly falls within the scope of this revival and regeneration of the Irish identity: the Celtic past of Ireland is constantly referenced and glorified in the early 20th-century book. Its title is a rather misleading reference to the ancient history of Ireland: *Annals of Westmeath* has nothing to do with the traditional Irish "Annals" compiled in the Middle Ages. It is in fact a supposedly historical collection of the miscellaneous traditions attached to the different places of Co. Westmeath. A lyrical, emphatic tone dominates. In the case of *Annals of Westmeath*, the form is actually more informative than the substance: the book is interesting because it does shed light on the conception an Irish person may have of the county of Uisneach at the time of the *Gaelic Revival*, which is interesting and noteworthy in itself. The inscription of Uisneach in Irish history, even through the prism of "cultural exploitation" or the recycling of national identity, is part of the complex reality of the hill.

The nine pages dedicated to Uisneach unsurprisingly show the hill in a most favorable light. The tone is set from the start:

> Royal Uisneach, on whose summit St. Patrick preached, where St. Bridget made her religious profession, and received the white veil from Bishop Macaile; and where the pagan kings ruled in regal splendour long before Tara was known, an- sacred relics of the past.[7]

Later on, Uisneach is associated with the "former greatness" of Ireland, to its "ancient splendour" at the time were "great men" or even "a great race" lived.[8] Tuathal is presented as a "renowned king" and the obvious founder of Uisneach. For James Woods, "the history of this king reads like a powerful romance, and if his deeds were acted, they would form a drama of thrilling interest". Tuathal was a "prince, a great ruler whose wise laws and good government brought peace and plenty into the land".[9] The author also mentions a "coronation chair of Uisneach" without further explanation and explains that "the history of Ireland might be written from the hill-top and the ruined palaces of Royal Uisneach".[10] The history of Uisneach is presented as particularly rich and "would take long to relate". Woods also dwells on the comparison with other major sites and connects the hill with the rest of the Irish tradition and, more widely speaking, the history of the Western world:

> What Tara is to Royal [Mide], what Emon is to Ulster, what Cashel is to Munster, and what Cruachan is to Connaught, Uisneach is to Westmeath. This noble seat is sacred as the ancient meeting place of the renowned men of Ireland, the city of Laberos, mentioned by Ptolemy.[11]

Woods associates Uisneach with spirituality – as opposed to materialism – a comparison which is quite consistent with the *Gaelic Revival* and the *zeitgeist* of the early 20th century in Ireland as a whole:

> The spirit of the age is material, earthly, unspirited. There is nothing held sacred in our day, if money can be made by its desecration and spoliation [...] The fame of the old hill extends far back into the misty past, and for its early story one must seek in the twilight waste, where pale tradition sits by memory's grave.[12]

The author then makes a series of interpretations which are perfectly coherent with his vision; unfortunately, they reveal nothing about the "actual" history of Uisneach. Perhaps unknowingly, James Woods seemed in fact to follow the old tradition of the Irish mediators of myths. For instance, the author mentions *Bealtaine* fires and explains they were dedicated to the god "Beal" (Bel), allegedly a god of the sun;[13] his remarks on Lugh and the ancestors of Ireland are directly inspired by Keating. He believes that the decline of Uisneach can be attributed to the diverse incursions of Danish Viking tribes, the loss of power of the Uí Néill and, later, the arrival of the Normans, without further specification. There is no doubt external influences did harm to the symbolic importance of an essentially "Irish" hill; actually, the three reasons conjured up by Woods most likely played a role in the disuse and later relative oblivion of Uisneach. But, once again, it appears that, under the guise of a historical account, the main purpose of Woods is to oppose the Irish culture to other allegedly inferior traditions: *Annals of Westmeath* is about Irishness, not the history of Ireland.

Other statements are even more characteristic and even less credible: asserting that "Eiri" – that is, Ériu – is buried under *Ail na Mireann* is a very free interpretation or embellishment of the myths associating the goddess with Uisneach: although tradition holds that she had her abode on Uisneach, the idea that Ériu died on Uisneach or was buried under the *Catstone* appears nowhere in authenticated mythological documents or folklore – and it is obviously not documented by archaeological studies. Similarly, the following statement lacks credibility: according to Woods, in clear weather, "the O'Connell monument in Glasnevin Cemetery is distinctly visible"[14] from the top of the hill. The tower marking the grave of Daniel O'Connell, the Irish hero of Catholic emancipation, peaks at 55 meters and is situated on the northern side of Dublin, about 130 kilometers east of Dublin. The map proposed by Macalister and Praeger in 1928 shows that although one can see and be seen from far away from the top of Uisneach, the limits of the city of Dublin are *a priori* out of reach.[15] Arguably, Wood's fanciful statement stemmed from his ardent desire to stress on its Irishness.

One of the most intriguing allusions made by Woods in the few pages he dedicated to Uisneach is perhaps this laconic sentence: "The Dublin Branch of the Gaelic League visited Royal Uisneach on 12th August, 1906".[16] Founded by Douglas Hyde to promote the Irish culture and language, the *Gaelic League* was the spearhead of the *Gaelic Revival*. If one is to believe Woods, the fact that members of the organization visited Uisneach at the turn of the century – on Old *Lughnasa*– stand as direct evidence of the interest aroused by the hill in a pro-Gaelic political and cultural context. Unfortunately, the statement is difficult to corroborate, so much so that the precise names of the members of this Dublin Branch of the *Gaelic League* – which was still presided over by Douglas Hyde in 1906 – are not specified.

In his account, James Woods also alludes to the legend of Connla,[17] which does seem to be connected with Uisneach and certainly had a notable impact on Irish literature, especially in the early 20th century. A translation of the story was offered by Patrick Weston Joyce, a founding member of the *Gaelic Union*, historian, musicologist and linguist close to the *Gaelic League* and acting, on several occasions, as its musical and cultural advisor. Joyce's version of the legend is closer to a romantic adaptation than a translation *stricto sensu*. Incidentally, it was published in a collection called *Old Celtic Romances*, a title which is unequivocal in its signification:

> Connla of the Golden Hair was the son of Conn the Hundred-fighter. One day as he stood with his father on the royal Hill of Usna, he saw a lady a little way off, very beautiful, and dressed in strange attire. She approached the spot where he stood; and when she was near, he spoke to her, and asked who she was, and from what place she had come. The lady replied, "I have come from the Land of the Living – a land where there is neither death nor old age, nor any breach of law. The inhabitants of earth call us Aes-shee, for we have our dwellings within large, pleasant, green hills. We pass our time very pleasantly in feasting and harmless amusements, never growing old; and we have no quarrels or contentions".[18]

The style is much more poetic and refined than that of the original transcription and the references to sin and transgression[19] were omitted by Joyce, probably because they did not correspond with his idealized and romantic vision of the Celtic past of Ireland. In 1892, another – and even freer – adaptation was proposed by Joseph Jacobs in a book whose title was no less evocative, *Celtic Fairy Tales*: Jacobs even used English archaisms and outdated turns of phrases so as to consolidate – or rather, recreate – the supposedly antique and authentic quality of the legend.[20]

In the late 19th and early 20th centuries, the *Gaelic Revival* took over and exploited a part of the symbolism of Uisneach. Even if the movement generally favored other ancient sites – first and foremost the hill of Tara, which was already more famous, more impressive-looking and more frequently mentioned in the literature of the Middle Ages – a number of Irish artists and intellectuals did embrace the hill's symbolic value and brought it into the great historical Irish tradition. Uisneach became one of many means to consolidate the identity of the nation; its renewed conceptualization was modelled by a clearly romantic and idealized vision of "the Celt". However, this urban, intellectual, political interpretation of Uisneach was – quite unsurprisingly – far from the preoccupations of the Irish people living in the vicinity of the hill at the time, as evidenced by the work conducted by the *Irish Folklore Commission*.

6.2 Modern Folklore of Uisneach

The folkloric collections compiled in the 20th century are one of Ireland's many scholarly treasures. The manuscripts of the *Schools' Collection*

(1937–9) provide a most valuable insight of the beliefs and traditions that were customary at the time in each and every Irish county – and, better yet, each and every barony and parish. The pupils conducting this study under the supervision of their schoolteachers were supposed to interview their elders, which means that the data collected also pertained to the time of both their parents and grand-parents; as a consequence, the *Schools' Collection* provides a record of the 1930s as much as the beginning of the 20th century and a significant part of the second half of the 19th century. The manuscripts that correspond to the surroundings of Uisneach – the barony of Rathconrath – are denoted NFCS 742 to 744 and are now available on-line.[21]

In 1947, the *Irish Folklore Commission* focused on the celebration of *Bealtaine* in Ireland. The information collected for the study of *Bealtaine* in the barony of Rathconrath and Co. Westmeath as a whole complements the manuscripts of the *Schools' Collection*: both collections provide a thorough snapshot of the state of play of Uisneach's popularity at a particular moment, and may reveal potential traces of ancient traditions and myths left in the customary landscape of the barony.

Authenticity of Traditions

The most striking and perhaps most crucial characteristic of the manuscripts relative to Rathconrath is the language used. Most of the manuscripts of the *Schools' Collection* tend to switch between Irish and English, especially those collected from the western parts of Ireland. However, the pages dedicated to Uisneach and its surroundings are exclusively written in English. One informant from Lakenstown, Ballynacargy – about eight kilometers north of Uisneach – explains that "the oldest person in the district does not remember anyone who ever spoke Irish. The language is dead about 100 years here".[22] Some pupils from the barony even compiled the few Irish words that were still in use in the area "fifty year ago"[23] and specified that some of them were still known: the lists are rather short and include a few dozen words or phrases at most. It is clear that, in the vicinity of Uisneach by the 1930s, the Irish language had already become a part of *folklore*, in the common sense of the term.

This observation reminds us of the geographical position of Uisneach, at the center – and consequently at the crossroads – of Ireland: the centrality of the hill probably went against the preservation of traditions, as suggested by the local decline of the Irish tongue. Similarly, the relative proximity of Dublin probably played an important role in this process, as the city most likely influenced the whole area over the centuries, since its foundation by the Vikings – at a site that was already occupied by Christians – until its economic and political use and exploitation by the English Crown. The Scandinavian, Norman and English influences over Ireland are a demonstrated fact: Uisneach has been part of the sphere of influence of Dublin for a thousand years, which could not be without consequence.

The connection uniting the barony of Rathconrath and the capital city of Ireland is also evident in the manuscripts of the *Schools' Collection*. An informant explains that the local custom was to get married in Dublin when people could afford it. According to one's social status and fortune, the honeymoon was spent in Dublin, London, Paris or elsewhere in Ireland or Europe.[24] Surprisingly enough, the townland of Bracknahevla, four kilometers to the south-west of Uisneach, was connected with Dublin through a rather peculiar weather superstition: "A sure sign of rain in this locality is what is called 'the Dublin red' that is a red sky in the direction of Dublin. It surely rains that day".[25]

Uisneach is situated about a hundred kilometers west of the Irish capital and is certainly not a part of its suburbs. Still, it remains within its sphere of influence, so much so that the axis of communication connecting the hill to the capital was already very much in use at the time of – and even centuries before – the redaction of the *Schools' Collection*.

Finally, like everywhere in Ireland, one last element put the area at a disadvantage as to the "authenticity" or antiquity of the traditions collected by the pupils in the 1930s. A quotation from an informant of the village of Ballymore, a few kilometers west of Uisneach, is rather telling:

> There are a few old people over seventy in the townland. Very few if any know Irish but they can tell stories in English. Quite a number of people emigrated from this townland to foreign countries long ago as the fare to foreign land was very reasonable and there was good employment there.[26]

The barony of Rathconrath was not spared by the most difficult times Ireland experienced in the 19th century, first and foremost the Great Famine of 1845–9. The departure from Ireland caused another disaster: the erosion, or rather dilution of Irish and Gaelic cultures. A diaspora is obviously not limited to a physical dispersion of individuals neither does it simply amount to a potential enfeeblement of the national identity: an exodus implies a disaggregation – or at least a profound mutation – of traditions. Actually, some customs that were expected to be found in the modern folklore of Uisneach are never mentioned in the manuscripts: this absence may be explained, at least partially, by the mass exodus of the 19th century.

Importance of Uisneach

Still, the folkloric accounts of the 1930s and 1940s did include references to Uisneach. Several informants mention the hill, although usually without going into much detail. Some pupils and teachers did not really understand what the folkloric collection of 1937–9 was about and on several occasions, the "accounts" were reformulations or even reproductions of entire sections of James Woods' *Annals of Westmeath*:[27] the *Gaelic Revival* also influenced some of the manuscripts, which is worth noting. Occasionally, informants added rather peculiar details to the descriptions by Woods, such as the "coronation stone" of Tuathal – the "coronation chair" mentioned by Woods? – which was supposedly "afterwards taken to Tara, stolen from there to Scotland and from there sent on to Westminster".[28] There is probably nothing historical in this statement, but the fact that, once again, the legend of Uisneach was connected with the struggles for national identities – Ireland versus England – is informative in itself.

Generally speaking, the manuscripts give the impression that Uisneach was known, sometimes used as a landmark ("The hill of Rathskeagh, or rather the three hills are situated in the centre of Westmeath, one mile from the famous hill of Uisneach"),[29] but that most informants were not truly familiar with the hill in itself. We are told of an "obscure place at the centre of Ireland"[30] which could have played a role in the past of Ireland – the idea of a "royal residence" was, once again, inspired by Woods. Most informants settle for general and often inaccurate statements but also for rather exotic remarks, which are quite suggestive of their conception of the hill:

> Uisneagh or Kellybrook is only 300 perches asunder it is called Kellybrook locally, as it contains four or five spring wells. On the breast of the hill there is a rock about 130 tons weight. It is in five parts. If it was possible that it would be handled each piece would fit in its own place, so it was supposed that is was rent asunder at the death of our Saviour.[31]

Arguably, the most surprising characteristic of the accounts is the relative scarcity of mentions of Uisneach: other hills are cited again and again – such as Knocknasta, presented as the highest hill of Westmeath[32] and most of all Croughal/Croughill,[33] in the vicinity of Uisneach, on which towers a fort attributed to the Normans. Uisneach does not seem to be the first hill to come to the mind of informants, although their task was to collect *local* customs. More often than not, when the pupils make a list of the local ruins or "fairy-forts" – that is, supposedly inhabited by the fairies, a very common belief in Ireland at that time – they forget to mention Uisneach.[34] There also seems to have been fewer holy wells venerated on the hill than elsewhere. *Lough Lugh* and the ringfort of Rathnew are never mentioned, which is also quite surprising. Still, a few essential elements were known to some informants: for instance, *Saint Patrick's Bed* did earn its place in the *Schools' Collection*, although the mentions are scarce.

Saint Patrick's Bed

The references are as follows:

> On the top of the hill of Uisneagh, about two miles from Killare there is a rock, shaped like a bed, where St. Patrick is supposed to have slept.[35]

There is a stone shaped like a bed on the hill of Uisneagh where St. Patrick is supposed to have slept. There is a big flat stone in Killare. There is a track of Saint Patrick on the stone, because it was there he slept. It is called Saint Patricks Bed.[36]

On Uisneac[h] there is a field called *Saint Patrick's Bed* where the saint rested for two days and two nights.[37]

Some say St. Patrick and St. Brigid are our patron saints. There are a lot of stones near Uisneach and they are called "*Saint Patrick's Bed*". St. Patrick is supposed to have slept there.[38]

Saint Patrick's Bed on Hill of Usna. A bed of stones. He spent three nights there. Thirty on day – looked down at ground, a well appeared – quenched his thirst – stream still there.[39]

Those passages are quite typical of the confusion and possibly mis-interpretations of the informants. This *Saint Patrick's Bed* remained rather mysterious, even for those mentioning it. Sometimes placed on the top of Uisneach, sometimes in Killare (that is in the lower part of the hill, next to the holy well dedicated to St. Brigid), either described as a heap of stones, a stone shaped like a bed or even merely a field. It is as if the informants themselves have never visited the place in person. At no point is an allusion to a custom or a tradition contemporary to the redactors ever cited: in the 1930s, *Saint Patrick's Bed* was a somewhat fuzzy memory and was not linked to any custom hypothetically connected with an ancient Celtic tradition or with a Christian pilgrimage – which is even more surprising.

Conglomerate of Uisneach

The folkloric sources relative to *Ail na Mireann* are even more elusive. For instance, whether all of the following extracts actually deal with the boulder or not remains unclear:

There is a huge rock in Carrickan that Saint Patrick is said to have thrown from the hill of Uisneagh a distance of fifteen miles.[40]

There is another monument near our house known as the Cat and Mouse. It consists of an enormous rock over hanging the road side and a very small one opposite. The big one is the cat and the small one is the mouse.[41]

In our field are rocks known as the pipers rock, the cat and mouse and a big fort.[42]

According to James Woods, *Ail na Mireann* was already called "Cat Rock" by the locals at the turn of the century and O'Donovan referred to the conglomerate as the "Cat's Rock" as early as 1837.[43] This suggests that the stone here called "cat" is in fact the conglomerate of Uisneach, even though the terms "Cat Rock" or "Catstone" are not explicitly used[44] and even if, today, there is no smaller second stone in the immediate surrounding of *Ail na Mireann*. The coupling with a secondary rock called "the mouse" is nowhere to be found in more ancient traditions but is indirectly used today but the current owners of the hill ("[The Stone of Divisions] is more commonly known as the 'Catstone', named so because it resembles a cat watching a mouse"),[45] which is by no means proof of the antiquity of the tradition. Remarkably enough, those testimonies reveal nothing about possible traditions and customs attached to the stone in the 1930s: the stone of Uisneach had apparently no spiritual importance at the time for the locals – at least no visible one.

Three different theories could account for this apparent lack of popularity: either the traditions and spiritual significance of *Ail na Mireann* never actually existed outside of books and manuscripts or they faded over time – following the gradual disuse of the site in the previous centuries – or perhaps they had been eradicated or proscribed by an external force. In that regard, the local clergy may also not have welcomed the hypothetical worship of the boulder and was arguably unable and perhaps unwilling to integrate it into the Christian traditions. The first hypothesis can be quickly dismissed, especially thanks to the archaeological discoveries: the enclosure surrounding *Ail na Mireann* is a clear indication of the importance of the place. At this point, it is still hard to decide between a gradual neglect caused by a fading in popularity on the one hand and the possible determination of the local clergy to ban any Pagan custom attached to the stone on the other. Fortunately, a couple of elements detailed hereafter may throw light on this issue.

In the 1930s, the symbolic and ritual dimension of *Ail na Mireann* had completely disappeared – or had perhaps become a very well-kept secret. Only one example taken from the *Schools' Collection* catches our attention. It makes of the stone a standard-bearer, in the literal sense of the term: "Now there is a flag post out of this rock [Aill na míre] and the tricolour is hung on it on national festivals".[46] From spiritual, the importance of the boulder rock had become political. The hole had already been noticed by Macalister and Praeger. According to Michael Dames, it was carved in the context of the struggle for Irish independence.[47] As often, Dames does mention his sources but the idea seems congruent with Irish history: the mention of the tricolor flag of the Irish Free State – that had become Éire in 1937 – by an informant of the *Schools' Collection* leaves little doubt regarding its political use and its importance in terms of national identity: from the top of *Ail na Mireann*, on the sides of Uisneach, people claimed their attachment and affiliation to the Republic.

Once again, the terseness and brevity of the informant's account are most unfortunate: it could have been useful to know whether this raising of a flag was a part of a large gathering and was complemented by merriments and festivities or if, on the contrary, it was a solemn, grave and perhaps intimate event. Fortunately, the event may be connected with an article published in *The Irish Examiner,* which, without quoting its sources, tells about a comparable assembly that took place 20 years before the manuscripts of the *Schools' Collection* were redacted:

> In 1919, *Sinn Féin* held a huge rally at the spot, attaching the tricolour to the Catstone, while three years later the same stone was desecrated by Catholics who felt this pagan place held too much power over Irish people.[48]

This testimony makes of 1922 a turning point in the history of *Ail na Mireann* and Uisneach. The statement seems to answer the question of whether the disuse of the site was gradual or caused by an external force: there is a possibility that the *Catstone* was stripped of its symbolic importance and of the customs attached to it by the local clergy at that specific date; 15 years later, the informants of the *Schools' Collection* may have thought it inappropriate to go over this story and the past traditions attached to the stone for fear of the clergy's response.

From the perspective of the political significance attributed to the place, historian Ruth Illingworth goes a step further and claims:

> A week before the Mansion House meeting, the Westmeath *Sinn Féin* organization held a rally on the historic Hill of Uisneach near Mullingar. The meeting was attended by Alice Ginnell – the wife of Larry, who had made history at the 1918 General Election by being the first female election agent in Irish or British history. Others at the rally included Countess Plunkett and Mrs. Margaret Pearse (mother of Patrick and Willie). The main speaker was future Irish President, Sean T. O'Kelly.[49]

The official website of the Visitor Center of the hill of Uisneach states the following:

> In more recent years [Uisneach] became a site of political rallies, with Daniel O'Connell, de Valera and Padraig Pearse addressing the masses from Aill na Mireann.[50]

This idea was apparently inspired by an article of the *Irish Times* published in 1988, which does not quote its source.[51] The mention "Eamon de Valera held a rally on Uisneach" is rather laconic. A tour guide of the Visitor Center of Uisneach claims that he owns pictures featuring the pioneer of Irish independence on the hill of Uisneach;[52] there is no reason to question his good faith, although those pictures remain unpublished and no major biography of De Valera actually alludes to this episode.

Although they are usually lapidary and rarely backed up by credible sources, the mentions of great names of Irish Republicanism suggest a strong association of the site with the Irish national identity, as opposed to the English and British ones, in the wider context of the Irish War of Independence. There are no objective reasons to doubt the historicity of these political gatherings but the vagueness of the few accounts mentioning them is regrettable. Notably thanks to the *Gaelic Revival*, it is quite possible that Uisneach experienced an increased popularity in the 1900s–20s. Interestingly enough, this renewed popularity was particularly marked among political and intellectual elites of the country; the local rural tradition was far less impacted and the 1922 article from the *Irish Times* actually suggests quite the opposite: the local clergy may have successfully attempted to thwart any interest in this evidently Pagan site.

Local Tales and Legends: Stone(s) of Uisneach

The rituals connected with the boulder of Uisneach had disappeared – or were kept hidden – in the 1930s. Fortunately, two manuscripts from the *Schools' Collection* introduced legends that directly alluded to stones: *Ail na Mireann* is clearly mentioned in the first account and mysterious "stones on the top of Uisneach" are detailed in the second.

The first legend is here transcribed in its entirety:

> There were two men of the Fiana named Finn and Oisín. They often spent many months hunting around the hill of Uisneach. One day while resting there they saw a beautiful princess approaching them on a beautiful white horse. She stopped when she met them and said to Oisín "I have heard you are a great warrior, will you come with me to *Tír na nÓg*". Oisín said he would and he mounted the horse behind the lady. Immediately the horse mounted into the air and flew across land and sea to *Tír na nÓg*. There Oisín and the prince[ss] were married. They were always young and always happy and hundreds of years slipped by and they never noticed it.

> At last Oisín got a longing to return to see his own people. The princess gave him her own lovely horse to travel on. He found on his return that all his friends were dead and he was very sad. He was about to return home when he met some men trying to lift a huge rock. They asked Oisín to help and he leant sideways and gave the rock a shove and landed it miles and miles away from where it stood and it rested on the side of the hill of Uisneach and now it is known as "Aill na míre". Meanwhile while heaving the rock Oisín's feet tipped the ground. Immediately the horse went from under him and he sank to the ground with a weight of years age and sadness and then he died.[53]

The story is remarkable as it is in fact a version of *The Lay of Oisín in the land of youth (Laoi Oisín as tir na n-óg)*.[54] The original text was written by Micheál Coimín, a poet from the mid-18th century, and was edited and translated in 1896. The presence of a woman from the Otherworld associated with a white horse suggests that the substance of the poem is much more ancient: in the Welsh story of Pwyll and Rhiannon, Rhiannon has a white mare, which foaled every night of the calends of May. The connection of the female character with the pre-Christian goddess Epona – a goddess of agricultural fertility and fecundity, a Gallo-Roman *matres* connected to the Otherworld – has already been mentioned *supra*. In Coimín's version, the story is essentially the same as that of the *Schools' Collection* – including the mention of a rock almost impossible to lift – although neither Uisneach nor *Ail na Mireann* are explicitly mentioned by the 18th-century poet. As noted by Tomás o'Flannghaile, editor and translator of *The Lay of Oisín in the land of youth*, "there are but few places mentioned in the *Laoi* [...]. Doubtlessly some archaeologists would think the poem 'very poor in topography'",[55] The only hill alluded to is that of Allen, about halfway between Dublin and Uisneach, around 50 kilometers south-east of the latter.

The question of whether the version provided by the *Schools' Collection* is "more original" or simply more ancient that Coimín's poem is not easy to answer. It is of course quite possible that the redactor of the manuscript knew about Coimín's poem and decided to adapt – voluntarily or not – the story to the local topography. The mythological substance of *The Lay of Oisín* is indeed quite compatible with the topography of Uisneach, namely because of the presence of a boulder on its side. Another possibility is that the narrative provided by the *Schools' Collection* actually derived from local oral stories, which may stem from more ancient traditions. If that is the case, the similarities with other ancient stories of displacement of stones on Uisneach are particularly intriguing: as mentioned earlier, in the *Life of Áed* (7th–8th centuries), the saint of the Uí Néill is said to have discovered *Ail na Mireann* and moved it to its current location while blessing it with healing powers; in the *History of the Kings of Britain* (12th century), Merlin also used his magic to move the stone of Killaraus.[56]

As Coimín's *Lay of Oisín* also drew from oral tradition, there is a possibility that both stories are different versions of the same ancestral narrative that may date back to and be connected with those early stories of "displacing of stones".

The second legend, or rather "tale", that can be found in manuscript NFCS 742,[57] tells us: "Once upon a time a giant lived on Uisneach named 'Usher'. He carried all the stones from the top of the hill of Uisneach to Conra to build the old church there". Usher is baptized by Patrick, who accidentally sticks his staff in his foot: "On seeing what had happened St. Patrick apologized, but Usher said he thought it was part of the ceremony". The "Conra" here mentioned is in fact Croughill, a hill in the vicinity of Uisneach that is frequently cited in the manuscripts from the barony of Rathconrath. The tale symbolically connects Uisneach to Croughill: this matches with local tradition, which still tends to use both hills as landmarks today; additionally, it serves to justify the existence of what is called *Saint Patrick's Foot*, in Killare, a rock visibly marked with what looks like a footprint and which is occasionally mentioned by local informants.[58]

The redactor continues and tells us that "around [an] old church whose walls are still standing are the graves of seven bishops":

> These bishops were in hiding in the cave of Lockerstown in Cromwell's time but the soldiers found them and murdered them. Usher carried the large flags which are over their graves and put them in position. There is a chalice engraved on them. The English soldiers destroyed the church later on. Some of the walls are still standing and one of the windows is in good repair.[59]

Another informant, who had made a list of the local persecutions against Catholics, confirmed the story. His tone is much more neutral and prosaic and the giant Usher is not mentioned: "There were seven bishops hid in a cave in Uisneach and the English found out where they were and they killed them".[60] It is of course difficult to know where history starts and myths end. Assuming that seven bishops were actually killed by Cromwell's soldiers on Uisneach – which would not be surprising – it is still worth noting the inclusion of the episode in a tale and the appropriation of the hypothetical massacre by local tradition: just as *Ail na Mireann* literally became a standard-bearer of the Republicans, the English persecutions towards Catholics became a part of the mysticism of the hill.

Local Tales: Witchcraft

Of course, the local legends and tales of Uisneach are not limited to a few scattered allusions to *Ail na Mireann* in the manuscripts of the *Schools' Collection*. Several informants report stories connected with witchcraft or even milking-hares. Those mentions are remarkable because they confirm the link uniting Uisneach to the festival of *Bealtaine*: the Irish – and pan-European – witches were said to be particularly active in early November and May, the latter month being especially connected with their ability to turn into hares capable of sucking the udders of the cows and stealing the fortune of their owner.

> Once St. Patrick met a witch on the hill of Uisneach. She was practicing black magic. St. Patrick banished her away from the hill of Uisneach and sent her to the lake of Derravaragh[61] and she never returned.[62]

The association of the tale with the Patrician legend is not unconventional and it was quite common for the saint to be included in folkloric stories of that type. Occasionally, the connection is not established with a Christian character but with a more ancient mythological figure. This is notably the case for the following tale, which describes the usual story of a witch transformed into a red hare – the color of the Otherworld – while connecting it to the legend of the hero Finn/Fionn mac Cumhaill, the main protagonist of the Fenian Cycle:

> Once there was a hare on Uisneach and he was bigger and stronger and redder than any hare that ever was seen. Every hunter tried to catch her but none succeeded. At last one day Finn Mac Cumhail was out hunting and he saw the hare. He put the dogs on her and they chased her. She was nearly caught but she jumped in through the window of the house. As she jumped one of the dogs bit her leg. When the hunter came up he went into the house to see would he get the hare. When he went in he saw nothing only an old hag of a woman lying on the bed in the corner. He was surprised but then he saw the track of blood from the window to the bed and he knew then that the hare and hag were the same.[63]

Patrick in one case, Finn in the other: the character chosen actually matters little as, in both cases, the idea was to encode the story into the great Irish tradition – either Celtic or Christian Celtic – by associating it with one of its great champions. The connection of one of Ireland's "champions" with a specific place is not unheard of in the Irish folkloric corpus: this simply confirms that Uisneach was considered, probably in ancient times but also in modern folklore, as a mystical place attached to the Otherworld whose symbolic power was supposedly exploited by the character of the witch. The same idea can be found in another – far more cryptic – story:

> A man one time passed by Scallys. As he went he was turned into a black pig. He went towards Uisneach. He was shot by a man before he reached the Shannon. If he got to the river safely he would drown Ireland.[64]

Pigs are, together with the color red and the cauldron of abundance, one of the well-known attributes of the Otherworld. Conceivably, the fact that the animal tried to go to Uisneach confirms that the hill was a gate to the Otherworld; the black pig was supposedly able to unleash the symbolic power of the Otherworld on the whole island by "getting to the Shannon" in an attempt to use the mystical power of the hill: tradition indeed holds that Uisneach is the source of all rivers of Ireland. Incidentally, River Rath flows south and west of Uisneach and is a tributary of the Inny which is itself a tributary to the Shannon.

Local Tales: Fairies

Unsurprisingly, fairies – the other main figures of the *sídh* – were evidently not forgotten in the tales and legends associated with the hill.

In the 1930s, the belief in the fairy people was a most tangible reality in rural Ireland, in Co. Westmeath as elsewhere. This is confirmed by an informant of the barony of Rathconrath, who explained that "Belief in fairies is still quite strong in this locality".[65] The manuscripts of both the *Schools' Collection* and the 1947 *Irish Folklore Commission* are crammed with stories of fairies stealing milk or butter, abducting children or elders, going on a hunt or changing their abode, especially in early May and November.

Sometimes the interactions with humans bring joy and good fortune; more often, the fairies are seen as a peril to humans, hence the host of customs aimed at keeping them away or calming their anger. A handful of testimonies explicitly mention the hill of Uisneach:

> There were two old women living on Uisneach hill once. One morning one of them went to milk. While she was milking a fairy came up and asked her for a noggin of milk. She gave it to her and she drank it and asked for another, which was given to her. Then the fairy spat it all back into her face. The woman asked why she did this and the fairy said to her while she lived she would want for nothing as it was luck to her and they were wealthy ever after.[66]

The inscription of this fairy-tale in the broader context of milking and milk-customs is quite typical. The informant does not particularly focus on Uisneach, which is simply presented as the setting of the encounter. Once again, the main idea is to place the encounter with the Otherworld at an appropriate location, that is, a point of confluence uniting the world of human and that of fairies. The next account follows the same pattern:

> The midnight hunt is said to come across the hill of Uisneach at midnight. It crosses to the hill of Carne, and you can easily hear the cry of the hounds, and the master calling them, and the fox is never captured. He usually gets lost.[67]

Quite similarly, a story depicts a certain Paddy Ward who, on *Halloween* night, had decided to go visit a cemetery: he met a "pooka" – a common character of Irish folklore associated with the fairy people. The pooka knocked him unconscious, put him on his back and "soared into the air with him". The rest of the story is characteristic of fairy abduction tales but is noteworthy for its clear mention of Uisneach as well as "every hill in Ireland":

> Paddy on the Pooka's back was taken for a ride over the hill of Uisneagh, the hill of Skeigh, the hill of Knackasta and in Paddy's opinion over every

hill in Ireland. In very quick time he was landed at his own doorstep, much earlier than his comrades arrival. There they found him, blubbering like a child. He was very exhausted and didn't leave his bed for three weeks. Never after did Paddy venture abroad after ten o'clock.[68]

The leprechaun, another typical character of Irish folklore and fairy people, is mentioned by another informant in connection with Uisneach:

A family named Carberrys lived in Molloys house in Killare long ago. One day one of them went up the hill of Uisneagh to milk a cow. She caught a leipreachan when she was coming down the hill. She was going to bring the leipreachan home in her apron. There was a bull in the field and he said to her "O look the bull is after you". The very moment he spoke, she looked behind and the leipreachan slipped from her apron. She never saw him again.[69]

A milking story where a young girl is fooled by a leprechaun, master of deception and tricks, is in no way surprising. Although the local folklore of the 1930s did consider Uisneach as a passageway between the world of the living and that of the dead – a place where one could encounter fairies and witches – the hill was by no means exceptional from that perspective. To some extent, Uisneach was an "unremarkable magic place" – perhaps with the exception of the obscure extract, where Uisneach is presented as the cause of the "drowning" or submersion of Ireland. It is never presented as particularly noteworthy "fairy dwelling".

One last fairy-tale mentions an "ancient Killare Castle", in the vicinity of Uisneach:

[Joe Keegan and Patrick Magann] saw fairies while sheltering under a quick [set] near the ruins of the ancient Killare Castle, opposite Patrick Noonan's door in the vicini[ty] of Uisneach hill. It was on the nights of the Big Wind 27th and 28th February 190[?]. The tiniest little men and women came out on a stile and passed along an ancient passway. Shortly afterwards two little caps were found. Local tradition has it that the local doctor came and took them away and sent them to the National Museum.[70]

"Killare Castle" corresponds to the ruins of a motte castle probably dating back to the 12th century; the site comprises a "Ringfort, Castle and Earthworks, Church and Holy Well".[71] Killare is situated in the immediate surroundings of the south-western slope of Uisneach and is often mentioned by the informants, who usually discuss the ruins of the church,[72] which was supposedly founded by Saint Brigid herself and the "ancient" cemetery,[73] now abandoned.[74] But the most popular and most frequently cited location is by far St. Bride's/St. Bridget's Well,[75] the holy well of Saint Brigid (or sometimes "Brigit"), next to the cemetery and ruins of the church.[76]

Brigid's Well at Killare

The two main holy wells of Uisneach – *Tobernaslath* and Saint Patrick's Well – had completely fallen into desuetude in the 1930s;[77] conversely, St. Brigid's Well had remained extremely popular.

Today, the source is still well-maintained and well-advertised. It borders the road connecting Athlone to Mullingar, the two main towns in the vicinity – around 20,000 inhabitants each – which could explain its lasting notoriety.[78] A signpost and a small wrought-iron gate indicate "St. Brigid's" and is clearly visible from the road.

In the *Schools' Collection*, many informants mention the site and the annual visits, which were generally held on Good Friday,[79] on 2 February (for *Saint Brigid's Day* or the ancient festival of *Imbolc*)[80] and even the Assumption, on 15 August,[81] a day traditionally associated with the worship of the Virgin Mary.

The pilgrimage was apparently extremely popular as most informants mention "crowds" who gathered to pray or do the Stations of the Cross around the well, while heavily insisting on the reputation of the place.[82] According to popular belief, the water of St. Brigid's Well, which could either be sipped or brought back home,[83] could cure eyes,[84] warts[85] and toothaches for a whole year[86] or several other unspecified illnesses.[87] Saint Brigid herself was the Patron Saint of the locality;[88] she supposedly built the low stone walls surrounding the spring with her own hands[89] and took her vows at the spring or in the church now in ruins.[90] A statue of the saint, still standing, was erected above the well in 1929[91] by a certain Mrs Keane Bal [l]tacken,[92] probably as a token of gratitude for the healing of her son.[93]

An ash tree[94] used to hang over the well until the 1920s.[95] The beliefs attached to the tree are quite remarkable: "It was said, that it proved its sacredness, as refused to burn, though petrol and paraffin were thrown on it".[96] Obviously, this modern tree[97] cannot possibly be the famous "tree of Uisneach" from the *The Settling of the Manor of Tara* or from the *Dindshenchas* – though the latter was indeed an ash tree.[98] Still, the fact that this tree was associated with both water and fire in local folklore is intriguing. It was occasionally connected with rituals linked with the holy wells:

> There are nine stones at the well and when doing the stations people pray at each stone. They begin and end at the ash tree. People leave rags beads or pennies on the tree when they have finished. Then they wash or drink the water from the well, and so they get cured.[99]

> The people drink the water from the well when they go there. There is a paling round the well and there is a tall tree growing beside it. Relics such as pins, medals, rosary beads, washers and other small articles are left as tokens at the well.[100]

Today, people still come and visit St. Brigid's Well, do the Stations of the Cross or simply pray and leave small votive objects – coins, rosaries, sometimes St. Brigid's crosses etc.

In the 1930s, the well was surrounded by several other beliefs and legends, which confirm the mystical potency attributed to the well. The sacred water of St. Brigid's Well could not be used for washing clothes, bathing, cleaning or cooking. It was often said that it could not boil[101] or would turn to blood if one tried to heat it up.[102] An informant tells the story of an "ignorant woman" who broke those rules: the well dried out and the water only came back after many prayers and sprinklings of holy water.[103] Another tells us about a "Protestant" who had taken away "a load of stones" from the well and "got terrific pain in his big toe":

> He visited every doctor in all parts of Ireland but worse and worse the pain got. At last a neighbour advised him to go and interview the parish priest – Father Ferley. The priest told him to go home and draw back again to their original place the load of stones he had drawn from the well. He did so, and immediately on emptytying [sic] the load of stones at the well the pain left his toe. It never returned again.[104]

Other informants explain that trout occasionally appeared in the well.[105] Once, a man supposedly killed one of the fish and died soon after; the blood of the animal "can still be seen on a stone-slab".[106] This type of belief – fish miraculously appearing or water that would not boil – is very common when it comes to holy wells, in Ireland or elsewhere: those traditions are by no means exceptional and simply confirm the sacredness – or rather, the holiness – of the spring. A more detailed account unites both ideas:

> One night fresh water ran scarce in the local Uisneach Inn. Some person who was ignorant of the tradition filled a kettle in St. Bride's Well, brought it in and hung it on the kitchen fire to boil for punch-making. The kettle was on a considerable time but the water could not be brought to the boil. Someone lifted the lid of the kettle to see what was the matter. Lo! and behold, a great brown trout jumped out, shook his tail and out on the door of the inn. The local innkeeper was a man named Ben Carberry – a great grand-uncle to the present teacher in Moyvoughley School.[107]

The *Uisneach Inn*[108] existed until 2015, when it officially closed permanently.[109] It was situated at the crossroads of R390 (connecting Athlone to Mullingar) and L5241, the small road leading to the locality of Killare, and stood only a few dozen meters from the holy well.[110] Until recently, the inn displayed on its front an impressive sign, several meters wide, which read "The Uisneach Inn" written in a "Celtic-looking" font before a "Celtic-looking" sun in the background. The fact that the *Uisneach Inn* was situated in the immediate vicinity of St. Brigid's Well confirms that both Uisneach and Killare were considered, in modern times at least, to be connected and perhaps part of a wider symbolic entity. Of course, the holy well is situated in Killare, which is, technically speaking, not part of Uisneach *per se*. But the bond uniting St. Brigid's Well, and even the character of Brigid, to the hill of Uisneach is attested by many informants. Sometimes, people explain that the holy well is situated "not very far from the Hill of Uisneagh"[111] or "at the foot of Cnoc Uisnig [=Uisneach]",[112] which is a hard fact. An informant explains that the saint took the veil on "Usna", and not in Killare.[113] Two others explain that the well, which "could not be emptied",[114] provides all the mills in the locality with water power, which may or may not recall the belief according to which Uisneach was the source of all Irish waters:

> An old man told me that it is said locally that St. Brigid made a pond at the Church, which she got built at Killare and it is said that a small stream flows form the pond increasing in size and from that river all the mills in the locality are driven.[115]

The veneration of St. Brigid's Well is as intriguing as it is problematical. That its sacredness overshadowed all other local holy wells and springs, including those on the slopes of Uisneach, is remarkable. Moreover, the pilgrimage at St. Brigid's Well was in fact the most renowned modern tradition of the whole barony of Rathconrath, well ahead of all the beliefs and rituals connected to the center of Ireland. This reputation was arguably caused by one or several factors: first, the location of the source undoubtedly worked to its benefit. It lies in a plain which is accessible to all, contrary to Uisneach, slightly off the main roads and requiring a short but somewhat steep walk to its top. St. Brigid's Well is directly adjacent to a moderately busy lane of traffic, next to a crossroads. Most of all, the holy well is presented as a Christian spring by all folkloric informants of the modern era: the local clergy most certainly supported and sustained its veneration at the expense of potential Pagan rituals.

It is always difficult to trace back the sacredness of a spring, that is to know precisely whether it was celebrated since ancient Pagan times (and later Christianized) or was primarily bestowed its sanctity by the Christian religion. In the case of St. Brigid's Well, the source is situated next to a hill which was venerated before Christian times, next to an ancient road, and is mainly honored at a date corresponding to an ancient Irish celebration, *Imbolc*, later Christianized as *St. Brigid's Day*.[116] Incidentally, many scholars successfully argued that the Christian saint Brigid was connected to the Irish goddess Brigit. *Cormac's Glossary* presents Brigit as a triple goddess[117] who had two sisters – a blacksmith and a healer, two themes often connected to the powers of the Otherworld. Brigit is often presented as a fire goddess and most mythological sources explain that she was the daughter of the Dagda:[118] just like his daughter, the deity was a fertility figure but also a god of druids, the master of the Otherworld whose house was Uisneach.

Trying to reconstruct the original myths connected to the holy well of Brigid would prove useless and irrelevant: too little is known of its past and this approach, perhaps inherently flawed, would only generate a string of questionable hypotheses. Nevertheless, the connection between the veneration of Uisneach and that of St. Brigid's Well remains more than probable, precisely because of the geographical proximity of the two places and the compatibility of the characters of the Dagda and Brigit/Brigid. Furthermore, the recurrence of dates corresponding to ancient Celtic festivals is obviously striking: St. Brigid's Well was visited on *Imbolc*, Uisneach on *Bealtaine*.

Bealtaine/May Day *at Rathconrath*

At the time of the folkloric questionnaires, the celebration of *Bealtaine* was known in the barony of Rathconrath. Actually, since all of the informants were English speakers, the festival and the date were exclusively referred to as *May Day*. The local notoriety and importance of the festival was comparable to that of *Bealtaine/May Day* in Co. Westmeath or even in Ireland as a whole, with a few notable exceptions.

In the manuscripts of the *Schools' Collection* covering the barony, the first day of May was sometimes presented as the most important day of the year, especially by the elderly. It is quite clear that most informants felt somewhat uncomfortable or even embarrassed writing about the beliefs connected to the festival, which was already moribund at the time:

> There are many legends connected with the first day of May.[119]

> *May Day* superstitions did not quite die away yet. Many of the old people carry the old superstitions yet. *May Day* is one of the most important days throughout the whole year.[120]

> *May Day* superstitions are dying away now [...]. In olden times the Irish people were very superstitious and on *May Day* especially. They practiced many things that appear very foolish nowadays.[121]

In Rathconrath, the most common superstitions were without a doubt those linked with magic butter/milk-stealing. As in just about everywhere in Ireland – although the traditions were most popular in Ulster and Leinster – people feared that witches (or fairies) could steal from the farmers on *May Night* or *May Morning*. The counter-spells were similar or most often identical to the ones mentioned previously: people refused to give away milk, butter or fire in any form;[122] they used metal objects as means of symbolic protection;[123] would not throw away ashes and dust after grooming the house or stables;[124] tied a red ribbon to the tail of cows to scare fairies away or welcome them;[125] tried not to be the first house of the neighborhood to light their fire on *May Morning*;[126] or even "lighted a blessed candle and with it singed the hairs off the cows udder" to protect them.[127] Some informants explain that a special churning was made on *May Day*[128] in order to get "plenty of butter for the whole year".[129] Anyone paying a visit during churning was strongly encouraged to give a hand – while saying "Let me lay the weight of myself in butter"–[130] so that it was absolutely clear he/she could not steal the wealth or fortune from the farmer.[131]

One manuscript, which directly mentions Killare, explains the belief in detail. The description is quite typical of what was heard elsewhere in Ireland, with one notable exception: the milk cows were passed between branches of sallies so as to protect them.

> The pishrogue[132] of taking one's neighbour's butter by intoning a magic incantation has been tried out in the locality and district. It seems that the would-be thief of the butter must shout the incantation while planting sallies in the gaps through which the milch cows pass. A man by the name of Mooney (of Lough near Killare) once observed a woman sticking down the scollops[133] in the gaps and she was inchanting the cantation [sic]. He followed her in jest and copied her actions adding "That I may have half the butter". On the next churning his wife had such a huge churning that she was unable to turn the hand of the churn. She was very annoyed and she went to the priest. He instructed her to give a pound of butter to each of her neighbours. She did so and from that on her churnings were normal.[134]

"Planting sallies in the gaps through which the milch cows pass" to protect them from milk-stealing was not common in the Irish folklore of *Bealtaine* and the description of the custom is remarkable, perhaps unique. The tradition may derive from the ancient passing of cattle between two large fires for protection, with the assistance of the sacerdotal class.

In Uisneach and its vicinity, the symbolic significance of dew was known and its relation with witchcraft and putative magic powers confirmed. Sometimes the substance was associated with magic stealing: collecting the dew from a field amounted to stealing the wealth or fortune of the owner.[135] It was even more frequently used to wash one's face or feet in order to protect oneself from diseases for a whole year,[136] notably headaches and chilblains.[137]

Like almost everywhere in Ireland – more specifically in the areas where the influence of the Anglo-Normans was the strongest – dew was supposed to make people more beautiful and younger-looking, and give them a good complexion. It was also a way to prevent or get rid of freckles, which were deemed undesirable in those times and places.[138]

There were multiple ways to protect oneself from the ill influence of the fairies and the barony of Rathconrath was not significantly different from the rest of Co. Westmeath: a few informants confirm the importance of May flowers and branches when they were brought back to the house or stable on *May Morning* and used as ornamentation.[139] Compared with the rest of the county or even the country, the mentions of such customs are relatively rare and were sometimes transferred to other dates, namely Palm Sunday.[140] The custom had clearly fallen into disuse and was often adapted to the Christian tradition by the local clergy.

The May flowers were sometimes used to decorate *May branches*, also called *May Bushes*: those small familial or "individual" *May Bushes* should not be confused with "collective" *May Bushes*, which were larger, significantly more impressive and sophisticated and which were usually carried out in procession through villages, towns and cities. Concerning Rathconrath, the informants mention the decoration of "individual" *May Bushes* using ribbons, primroses or other spring flowers. On *May Morning*, the branch of May thus adorned was placed in front of the stable, usually on a manure heap. It was left there until it withered.[141] Most informants from Rathconrath write about the custom in the past tense, sometimes starting their account with "long ago" or similar phrases confirming the obsolescence of the custom.[142] More often than not, the tradition is connected with Christianity, either by explaining that the *May Bush* was planted "in the name of the Father, the Son and the Holy Ghost"[143] or by specifying that a statue or an altar dedicated to the Virgin Mary also had to be decorated in a similar fashion.[144]

At the time of the redaction of the *Schools' Collection*, informants therefore still assimilated the beginning of the month of May to the Otherworld and its main protagonists – witches and fairies – although most superstitions and customs were either falling into disuse or heavily Christianized. Some accounts from the vicinity of Uisneach are quite remarkable. An informant tells us that children born on *May Day* were able to see fairies.[145] Calves born on the same day brought good luck for the following year as well as eggs laid on the first of May, which were considered lucky.[146] Conversely, meeting a lone magpie on the road on *May Day* was believed to be an ill omen.[147] Interestingly enough, a very peculiar superstition associated the beginning of the month of May with a white horse: "If certain people in parish meet a white horse on the road on a *May Day* they will turn back as they say it is unlucky".[148] Unfortunately, the account is unique in the barony: the possibility that it was reported by someone passing through or by a family that had recently settled in the area cannot be ruled out. Still, it is evident that the substance of this belief is ancient and probably echoes Irish legends and myths connected with Rhiannon/Epona/Macha – and therefore the Otherworld *par excellence*.

Remarkable Absences

The *Bealtaine/May Day* rituals and beliefs of the environs of Uisneach seem at first glance relatively similar to the traditions linked with the celebration of the first of May elsewhere in Ireland. However, a number of superstitions and customs, although quite popular in other Irish regions in the first half of the 20th century were almost absent from the folkloric manuscripts of Rathconrath.

First, the dichotomy between *Old Bealtaine/New Bealtaine* or *Old May Day/New May Day* is never mentioned in the manuscripts from the *Schools' Collection* of Rathconrath. In the *Irish Folklore* manuscripts pertaining to *Bealtaine* in Co. Westmeath, it is alluded to only once by an informant from the south of the county.[149] Similarly, no mention is made of quarter-days or even the first of May corresponding to the beginning of summer in the barony.[150] In Rathconrath, no account specifies that the date marked the beginning of transhumance, although the tradition did exist in other parts of Co. Westmeath.[151] The customs connecting agriculture to the celebration were almost non-existent in the surroundings of Uisneach: only but one informant indicates that plantings were to be in the ground before *May Eve*.[152] Apart from a few proverbs – which were incidentally also very common in Ireland–[153] May weather and May diseases, so feared and anticipated elsewhere, are never mentioned.

Generally speaking, the date was not specifically a boundary or a turning point of the year, with an exception mentioned but once and seemingly unrelated to the agricultural world: "It is a local *May Day* Custom to start children schooling in *May Day*. Most children commence their school career on *May Day*".[154]

In Rathconrath, *May Day* was not a payday or a "gale day".[155] No May fair seems to have existed on Uisneach or its immediate vicinity, which is quite remarkable: the most famous fairs were often held on a monthly basis – for example, in Mullingar and Athlone.[156] A great horse fair in Mullingar (or Moate) in April and November is sometimes alluded to and a fair in Emper (or Empor), a few kilometers north of Uisneach, seems to have been held "in ancient times":

> At Empor a fair was held on the last day of May when the sales of cattle and sheep were over, the girls of every class used to gather in-to the village. A stage was erected on which were pipers and fiddlers. There would be much dancing and merry-making. After the fair several matches were made.[157]

An informant explains that there used to be a fair in Uisneach "long ago" but he clearly relies on his own readings rather than on the local oral tradition:

Long ago they used have a fair in Uisneach. All the provinces of Ireland met at "Aill na míre" and every one from each province came to the fair there. At the fair in Uisneach they spent the whole week in story telling dancing feasting and in feats of athletic prowess.[158]

There were no popular social manifestations connected with *Bealtaine* in the 1930s in Rathconrath: no "collective" *May Bush* or *May Pole* was erected or decorated in the vicinity of Uisneach. One informant from Rathconrath explains quite appropriately that "the Bush and Pole tradition came from across the Channel. There was no such customs in the Gaeltacht".[159] Although marriage divination practices in May were quite common in Ireland, they were almost absent from Co. Westmeath.[160] People knew that May marriages were either banned or frowned upon but the belief did not seem to be of particular importance.[161]

Surprisingly enough, even if the superstitions of magic stealing were common, the tales of "milking hares" seemed unknown in Rathconrath or are at least never mentioned, with the possible exception of the "red hare of Uisneach", although the animal is never said to have been seen milking a cow.[162]

Finally, the most remarkable feature of the modern folklore of Uisneach and its surroundings is undoubtedly the complete absence of "purifying fires" or even bonfires in May or for *Bealtaine*. In that regard, the following account from the *Irish Folklore Commission* manuscripts is rather telling:

It was either on *May Day* or *St. John's Day* that sparks of fire were thrown across the cows after being milked. Sparks were afterwards taken [?] out and put in the fields with crops.[163]

The connection with the great fires through which cattle were passed is not evident; furthermore, the informant himself is not certain of the date, which confirms that the tradition had already died out. The absence of purifying fire rituals in May is even more transparent in the manuscripts of the *Schools' Collection*, in which nothing is written about May fires or bonfires. An informant tried to compile all seasonal customs of the area and wrote: "*St. John's Day*. No Customs. *St. Peter & Paul's Day*. Bon-fires at cross-roads".[164] The allusion to potential bonfires at *St. Peter and Paul's Day* (29 June) is unique for the barony. Only one rather imprecise mention of bonfires of St. John can be found in relation with Rathconrath but it may well be a general statement and not a description of a local tradition:

St. John's Day falls on the twenty first of June. People gather furze bushes and sticks and light a bonfire. Then they dance and sing all around the fire.[165]

As already mentioned, bonfires of St. John are a celebration of summer and of the sun, at the zenith of its yearly path in the sky; the celebration substantially differs from the two purifying fires of *Bealtaine* as described in the medieval sources – the celebration of a "passage", that is a transition to summer, a lynchpin of the year combining fear and hope.

Thus, in the 19th century and most of the 20th century, there were apparently no large prophylactic or purifying May fires on Uisneach but also no large fair, no "convention" and, as a matter of fact, no real celebration at all, as well as few superstitions and collective rituals; in the 1930s and 1940s, the hill – and the sacredness of the center of Ireland as a whole – had indeed fallen into relative oblivion – or were a very well-kept secret.

Once again, the proximity to Dublin was probably one of the leading causes of this drop in reputation and status. In the early 20th century, the traditional system of fairs was for example already dying in Ireland, especially in well-served areas. The contacts with the urban population of nearby Dublin followed centuries of Anglo-Norman influence: in the Late Middle Ages, the *English Pale* – the fortified area under the direct control of the English crown – was only a handful of kilometers east of Uisneach. When time came for the *Pale* to disappear, its population – together with its traditions – gradually mingled with the Gaelic population. The language used by the speakers and transcribers of the folkloric manuscripts is but the tip of the iceberg. In the 1930s, the Irish language had literally disappeared from the surrounding of Uisneach and a large part of Ireland as a whole. There is no doubt that the language used is a reflection of the antiquity of traditions: the more the Irish language is used, the more probable the speakers were infused by the Gaelic culture and traditions. The barony of Rathconrath strikingly shows to what extent the opposite was also true.

The other significant reason for this apparent oblivion was undoubtedly the tragedy that afflicted Ireland in the 19th century: the Great Famine mainly affected the poorest and notably the rural population – incidentally Gaelic-speaking farmers first and foremost. Over one million people died; another million emigrated. One way or another, a quarter of the Irish population disappeared and with it, their traditions and customs.

Finally, the undermining influence of the Christian tradition cannot be disregarded. All over Ireland, priests usually chose to enfold ostensibly Pagan sites into Christianity, a decision which led to the preservation of a host of priceless information and the creation of the well-known Irish "Celtic Christianity". Unfortunately, no such process seems to have unfolded on Uisneach: only the sites that were identified, rightly or wrongly, as fundamentally Christian (for example, St. Brigid's Well) were accepted and promoted by the local clergy. How and when this undermining actually happened will probably remain a mystery, although this laconic – and hard to confirm – statement from the *Irish Examiner*, already mentioned *supra*, may be of some help:

> In 1919, *Sinn Féin* held a huge rally at the spot, attaching the tricolour to the Catstone, while three years later the same stone was desecrated by Catholics who felt this pagan place held too much power over Irish people.[166]

Similarly, it is hard to confirm the impact of such a "desecration" and spiritual pressure: local people may or may not have kept venerating the site in secret. The disapproval of the clergy most likely infused a sense of shame that led people to either renounce their ancient beliefs and traditions entirely or to continue worshipping Uisneach one way or another – but discreetly enough so as not to mention them when asked.

Decades later, the influence of the Catholic Church of Ireland waned significantly: from the late 1980s onwards, infamous scandals involving the Irish clergy were disclosed and prosecuted. This contributed largely to the gradual secularization of Ireland; eventually, a non-negligible proportion of Irish people turned to new spiritual horizons. As the current owner of the hill of Uisneach explains, the contemporary celebration now held on the top of the hill could not have emerged without the loss of power – either spiritual or factual – of the Catholic Church in the preceding decades. The contemporary rise in popularity of Uisneach is symptomatic of both the Irish *zeitgeist* and its evolution throughout centuries.

6.3 Uisneach and the Contemporary World

Uisneach Today: Site

Uisneach is now a private property. In 1998, the current owner, David Clarke, bought the domain which included the hill. Before that, Uisneach used to belong to a Scotsman, who had bought the property from a German owner. With David Clarke, the hill returned to the – very local – Irish bosom: Mr. Clarke is a native from Loughnavalley, in the immediate vicinity of Uisneach. Most of the elements mentioned hereafter are taken from personal interviews conducted with both the owner and the staff of the Visitor Center of Uisneach.

In his own words, David Clarke is a "farmer and a businessman" who grew up and worked all his life in the surrounding area. The hill was, and is still today a part of a vast domain, where a large number of livestock is bred for export: cattle-breeding has been intensive on the hill as early as 1850 at least according to archaeological investigations[167] and has therefore persisted.

From 1998 to 2009, Mr. Clarke exclusively conducted agricultural activities: the hill was not open to visitors and no celebration whatsoever was held on Uisneach. In 2009, a first step was taken: the owner decided to light up a fire on the top of the hill with a couple of friends and chose to invite some of the locals. The news spread rapidly and dissenting voices made themselves heard. Surprisingly enough, critics did not come from the local Catholic clergy but from what are referred to by Clarke as "Irish druids":[168]

> So, we had to meet with the local druids, Irish druids that frowned on this very much. People that said "you cannot do this, this is a sacred site". People did not want us changing anything here. But we invited

them along to that evening and after the evening everybody felt so good they said this is terrific and away we went, with the backing of everybody. 2009 we would have done the little fire. I'm sure it was 2010 we started with something bigger.[169]

Therefore, as soon as May 2010, a formal festival, open to the public, was held on Uisneach. The gathering was not so much a ritual celebration as it was a music festival with an admission fee, which gathered about 1,500 spectators. A large bonfire was lit for the occasion. Year after year, the small music festival held in early May continued and expanded, while incorporating new attractions and entertainments.[170] Eventually, it became a rather sizeable and popular event. In 2014, however, heavy rains led to the postponement and then cancellation of the festival. The financial loss was estimated at around 50,000 euros. David Clarke deems the experience as "terrifying for everybody both mentally and financially" and it caused him to scale down his ambitions and adjust his aspirations.

Opening to the Public

Soon after, he made the decision to organize paid guided visits of the hill. Today, it is still possible to visit Uisneach all year round, for a price ranging between a dozen and fifty euros, depending on whether the tour is collective or private. The visits are made from Wednesday to Sunday and are hosted by a tour guide. Unsupervised tours are prohibited and the official website of the hill, www.uisneach.ie, explains that "the sacred site is not open to the public at other times, as it is a private working farm"[171].

Special events are held throughout the year at moments deemed particularly important from a symbolic perspective: hence, *Sunrise* and *Sunset Tours* or *Winter Solstice* and *Midsummer Tours* as well as *Lughnasa Tours* are organized every year.[172] Although the four Celtic festivals are indeed taken into consideration by the owner, it was decided to add celebrations connected with solstices and equinoxes, even if they are quite secondary – to say the least – in Celtic myths and Irish history. With the permission of the Visitor Center, third parties also organize other types of visits which are centered on a more "spiritual approach" of the hill.[173] The very name of those "*Spiritual Tours*"[174] – during which one does not pay a visit but rather does "guided meditations"[175] – is rather telling and quite in line with the great social and spiritual themes of the late 20th and 21st centuries:[176] the influence of the *New Age* movement on the celebrations and contemporary manifestations of Uisneach must not be overlooked.

A new milestone was reached in 2015–6 with the construction of a Visitor Center and the addition of new infrastructures, including a large parking lot, which facilitated the care and guidance of visitors. The appearance and aesthetics of the building of the Visitor Center were carefully planned; it even competed for the 2017 *Irish Architecture Awards*.[177] The hill was also included as early as 2016 on the preliminary list of UNESCO world heritage sites,[178] alongside with Tara, Cashel, Cruachan, and Dún Ailinne, Co. Kildare.

Popularity

Generally speaking, visitors seem to enjoy their experience on Uisneach: as of May 2020, 103 out of the 113 web users who shared their opinion on TripAdvisor rated it as a "five-star" experience, which is perhaps not as anecdotal as it seems. Although people do receive a warm welcome when visiting Uisneach, the overwhelmingly positive feedback could also be explained by the fact that visitors do not come to Uisneach by accident. Incidentally, the only negative feedback expresses the frustration of an overly-enthusiastic visitor:

> Guided tours only.
>
> We were hoping to walk to the ancient monument, however we were advised when there you could only access it via a tour and this was estimated 2-3 hours, and was approximately 12 euros per person. Seemed a shame that with a historic site there isn't more flexible access.[179]

Admittedly, everything was planned to welcome visitors in the best possible conditions. The small Visitor Center is, by all accounts, agreeable and well-designed. The insistence on the "respect" owed to the site does not fail to impress the customers. A large sign explains that the hill is "one of the most sacred and historical sanctuaries of the world" – a subjective assessment indeed. The entrance to the site is marked by another large sign displaying the words "Uisneach Fire Festival" and which is itself positioned on a tall structure reminiscent of a pyre.[180] Finally, depending on the seasons, between one and four guides welcome the visitors; they specialize on either archaeological or mythical aspects of the site.

Of course, the success of the hill is quite modest in comparison with other great Irish sites. With the exception of the large events held in connection with ancient celebrations or astronomical events, between 4 and 5,000 people visit the hill every year. As a matter of comparison, Tara apparently attracted 26,000 people in 2016 and just under 190,000 (!) in 2017.[181] According to the numbers publicly provided by Facebook (May 2020), 4,000 members of the social network declared a visit "in person" since the official creation of the official Facebook page of Uisneach; the figure must be compared with the official Facebook page of Tara, which counts ten times more visits to the hill of Co. Meath.[182] On the other hand, about 20,000 people "followed" the Facebook page of Uisneach, which is twice as much as the official page for Tara, which could be explained by an intensive promotional and commercial work carried out by the owners of Uisneach and its Visitor Center.[183]

Fire Festival *of* Bealtaine: *History and Motives*

On 6 May 2017, over 2,000 people gathered on the top of Uisneach to attend the great gathering held on *Bealtaine*. In spite of its success, the May celebration almost disappeared a few years after its (re-)creation. Following the bad weather and cancelled festival of 2014, the moral and financial situation of the organization team was at its lowest: David Clarke had even decided to give up the idea of holding a May festival altogether. According to the current owner of Uisneach, he received a most providential e-mail precisely at that time:

> I have decided earlier that year that we would not light the fire because I just got enough. So with that decision came an email from a lady in Hawaii, which is very unusual, a lady called [Ellen][184]. So Ellen had said she was watching what was going on on social media so she had seen we had wet days, we had failed to do the festival and she understood it couldn't have been good and we lost a lot of money and she was really keeping an eye on everything and she was very disappointed and said "are you going to do it again" and I said "no, we're not going to do it again, because this is just such a crazy situation, so much pain with it all, we said we'd drop it". [...] She said, "okay, what if I make a financial contribution to help you with this festival" and I said "really I don't want to do it". So she wrote back again, "how much do you need?" And I said "even to do a small festival costs about 8-10,000". So she said, "right, I would give you 5,000 for the fire". And I said, "if you want it that badly, we'll do the fire!" So we've done the fire last year and I think if it weren't for Ellen it might have stopped. So, on we go again.

When asked about the motivations of the generous benefactor, the owner became evasive, citing the attachment to the site and the "energies" emerging from it – energies he said he himself could feel, which does shed light on his global approach to the hill. Actually, the current owner of Uisneach does not seem motivated by self-interest and profit alone, as could have been expected from a self-proclaimed businessman owning one of the major sites of Irish history: Mr Clarke appears to be sensible to a more mystical approach and holds a more intimate connection with Uisneach, which may explain the distinctiveness of the celebrations held on the hill today.

Commerce and Traditions

A native from the area, David Clarke has "always known Uisneach"; he claims that every morning, on his way to school, he crossed the land adjoining the hill. Like most locals, he had heard that Uisneach had sup-posedly been a "royal site" and "the Fifth Province". In his childhood, that is the 1960s and 1970s, "very few people came up here. It was a rough terrain. It was a farm, a wild farm in my younger days": the difficult access to the hill worked against the popularity of its tradition, probably to the benefit of St. Brigid's Well.

The first fire he lit up on Uisneach, in May 2009, was apparently dictated by the desire to "rekindle what was already there, so it was just the re-kindling of the *Bealtaine* fires". This achievement was made possible by the decreasing influence of the Church. According to the businessman, his schoolteachers never told him about Uisneach because of the influence of the local clergy. Furthermore, "20–25 years ago we would not have been allowed [to do it] because the Church would have put a stop on this".

David Clarke believes the contemporary celebration of Uisneach and the annual kindling of the fire on the hill to be a "re-enactment" and not a ceremony:

> It's a re-enactment of the ancient festival. I have to be very true to tell that participants that this is not a ceremony, this is a re-enactment. [...] It has to be universal, it has to be open, it has to be for everyone. So we do not want to say we are this, that or the other so it is whatever you want it to be yourself.

As will be demonstrated *infra*, the contemporary celebration of Uisneach can hardly be described as a "re-enactment": its unfolding and general atmosphere have very little to do with what is known of the ancient festival. On the other hand, the decision to aim for ecumenism and in-clusiveness is quite noteworthy: David Clarke did not want Uisneach to become the flagship of any creed, religion or spiritual movement, let alone revive old religious antagonisms which are still very much a reality in Ireland.

When asked about his source of inspiration and what guided him in those "re-enactments", the current owner of Uisneach offers an interesting an-swer. The friction between Mr. Clarke's multiple functions and identities – his occupation, his personal history, his anchoring in the territory, both local and national – is quite apparent:

> I'm a businessperson, I'm a commercial person. If I wasn't a commer-cial person I wouldn't be here today in this situation talking about Uisneach because I wouldn't be the landowner here. We're just passing through so I suppose you're trying to recreate something. There was a major void, and even in this area there still is a major void as people leave the area so you're trying to rekindle and bring Uisneach back. I feel that's something we have to do and put it back right where it rightfully belongs: at the center. The people respect it.

This "commercial" side is echoed in the date chosen to hold the event. The contemporary celebration is preferably organized in the week-end following *May Day*, so as to secure a predictable minimum attendance: in Ireland, the first Monday of the month of May is still a bank holiday which bears the name of *May Day/Lá Bealtaine*. During our face-to-face interview, the businessman explained:

> It would have to be ideally on the bank holiday weekend but we have changed that completely now. We would still like to have [the festival] close to a weekend for convenience to people. So we would always choose a festival now that is after *Bealtaine*, not before. If we can be on it, good, but there's no experts out there to tell us exactly what time it should be done so we are more inclined to go after the occasion now, we'd think if we go before we are forcing it.

For the same commercial reasons, the contemporary celebration of Uisneach could have geared towards exponential growth as the years passed. But this escalation never happened: David Clarke claimed he had other ambitions for the hill and invoked his desire to preserve the spirit of the event. Perhaps the failure of 2014 also played an important part in this decision.

The first contemporary celebrations gathered a few hundred participants. The maximum so far came "a couple of years later", with around 6,000 or 7,000 people attending the kindling of the *Bealtaine* fire on Uisneach: "back then, it was more of a commercial event. So we pulled back from there and now we're running in around 2,000 people, 2,000-2,500 today". The celebration is therefore supposed to remain "manageable and to be very true to itself". Mr. Clarke also seems anxious to preserve a local, family-friendly atmosphere; in the owner's words, the local community will always be given the priority for the purchase of tickets. Arguably, the choice of a "family-friendly event" was also a strategic bet: David Clarke is quite conscious that he cannot compete with his rivals – first and foremost, Tara – either in terms of cultural significance or economic firepower. The owner decided to "respect the site", that is not to make of *Bealtaine* a nakedly commercial event, and therefore focused on "authenticity" – either real or reinvented – which may prove beneficial and perhaps more profitable in the long term as more and more visitors will potentially be attracted by this approach: "There's no thinking about it, in three or four years we will be, let's say, stopping people coming. That will all come".

During the last celebrations of Uisneach, the focus of the celebration was the fire, which was supposed to be the star of the show. Although, in the years preceding, several musical bands shared the stage of Uisneach, music now only plays a secondary role:

> It's funny, we took away all the really good music, you know we had very good bands here and at the end of the day the best art we have ever

had is the fire and that draws the crowd and the fire now that is the art you want to see. If you come in for the music, don't bother, the fire is the star attraction, if you don't like fire, don't come!

The choice was perhaps equally dictated by historical aspirations, the desire to create a quality event as well as a business necessity: the hypothetical return on investment provided by expensive bands was potentially too unreliable. Additionally, the cancelled event of 2014 was an experience Mr. Clarke did not want to go through again.

Accessing the celebration of *Bealtaine* on Uisneach has a cost: in 2017, there was no fixed admission fee and participants were encouraged to give at least ten euros per person. In 2019, the price was fixed to 20 euros per adult and admission was free under 16 years of age.[185] On 21 December 2019, an e-mail was sent to the "Friends of Uisneach" – that is the people who had already attended the event – to inform them that they would have an exclusive opportunity for the purchase of tickets until the first of February for the 2020 event: the price had gone up to 30 euros per person. Incidentally, due to the COVID-19 crisis, the 2020 event was cancelled. Another e-mail was sent on the first of May and explained that another form of gathering would take place:

> Bealtaine is a very special time for all of us, so there will be a fire. It will be with only the Keeper of the Hill,[186] David Clarke present and his immediate family. We request that no attempts are made to visit the Hill whatsoever.

> We would love if you could join us on our Facebook platform where the Bealtaine fire will be lit and streamed live. The fire will take place at 21:21 GMT on 5th May, where together we can unite in this ancient tradition, albeit in a virtual space, in welcoming-in the Summer.[187]

As far as the price increases are concerned, David Clarke explained that it was more about balancing the books than actually turning a profit. Certainly, money has to come from somewhere. Uisneach receives only small national subsidies: 2,000 euros in 2016, then 3,500 in 2017, which is quite insufficient to cover the expenses of such an event. The owner of the hill insisted that the entrance fee ought to be compared with the 15 euros people pay locally to attend "a bad football match" and explained that no commercial endorsement is accepted. The celebration of *Bealtaine* on Uisneach has never had a private sponsor. Patronage is possible but subject to anonymity – or at least discretion. Plastering the hill with billboards, for example, advertising alcoholic beverages, could have been an easy way of turning out profit but this option was apparently never contemplated. The temporary bar set up for the occasion in the first years was closed in 2015 and alcohol forbidden on the site. Mr. Clarke gives a very specific reason for this choice:

We don't believe in drinks companies or anybody like that taking over. I myself is Keeper of the Hill. I have the responsibility of not … Alright I'll put it in a different way. We cannot be bought. It has to be true and respectful and yeah, all of that.

Of course, such a decision was also highly compatible with the aspirations of the audience targeted: prohibiting alcohol, opting for a spiritual approach rather than a commercial one, placing the "large fire" rather than Pop music at the heart of the celebration was also a way to meet the expectations of a certain fringe of the public. This public, craving authenticity and "ancient" spirituality, could have turned away from Uisneach. At the end of the day, aiming for authenticity was also perhaps a way to ensure the continuity of the site and the popularity of the event over the long term, while at the same time avoiding large annual investments such as the remuneration of popular bands.

Today, the economic pattern of the celebrations of *Bealtaine* on Uisneach is essentially based on volunteer work. Between 30 and 40 people took part in the organization of the 2017 event; all were unpaid volunteers with the exception of temporary technical jobs, such as electricians, pyrotechnicians and a film crew hired for the occasion. The artists who exhibit their work are not paid; some musicians only have their expenses reimbursed, such as percussionists coming from Galway in 2017. Once again, the fire is supposed to be at the center of all attentions but a certain degree of ambiguity remains, perhaps hiding greater ambition: "the fire is the [star] so we don't want any big stars. We will see in time to come the big stars will come themselves and they will ask can I please play? That will come".

In spite of those few nuances, there is little reason to doubt the good faith of Mr. Clarke when he presents himself as the "Keeper of the Hill", the guardian of the authenticity of Uisneach. This last extract from the interview he gave brings up the sensitivity of the owner – or rather "Keeper" – of the place. His attachment to the hill of Uisneach is *a priori* genuine: he apparently wants to do what he considers good for his community and the land he feels in charge of. To the question: "How would you describe the contemporary Fire Festival of Uisneach to someone who has never heard of it?" David Clarke offered the following answer:

It's very basic, very simple, it's very beautiful, it's very emotional, it's very calm. It's very special you know. It's a rekindling of a 5,000 year-old festival[188]. It depends on where you're coming from yourself, on what your beliefs are, or what you want to believe but within us all we all want to believe in something, some little thing that keeps us motivated, keep going. I suppose this today will bring that out in people. It's a little bit of a pilgrimage, to come here. Yeah, no, I have yet to see somebody that said he didn't like it. It goes down very well. Yes, it can be wet, it can be cold, it can be a whole lot of things but at the end of the day … You know it's not Disneyland. You have to use your imagination and I think it'll all come together.

A Fire Festival?

As could have been expected, the event organized on Uisneach at the time of *Bealtaine* since 2010 is not presented as a "great assembly", let alone a "convention". Actually, the contemporary gathering has nothing in common with what is known of *Mórdháil Uisnigh*. The name chosen can easily be explained in terms of marketing strategy: the term *Fire Festival* has a certain ring to it. The Neo-Pagan community and the Celtic enthusiasts probably see in it a reference to supposedly ancient traditions; arguably, families in search of cultural and visual thrills may be intrigued by this promising title.

Furthermore, a large proportion of Irish people have heard of those famous "*Fire Festivals*" which punctuated the year in ancient times. The four seasonal festivals – *Samhain, Imbolc, Bealtaine* and *Lughnasa* – are usually popularized and alluded to in Ireland as "*Fire Festivals*", although the use of fire is not formally proven for each and every one of the ancient celebrations. Most popular books, and most children's stories, choose this enticing denomination over the more neutral – but probably more accurate – "four seasonal festivals". Incidentally, this is also how a fringe of the Neo-Pagan community refers to *Samhain, Imbolc, Bealtaine* and *Lughnasa*. Today, a quick search for "four fire festivals" on Google, which is currently the most popular web search engine available, gives four times more answers than the terms "four Irish festivals", almost five times more that "four Celtic festivals", ten times more that "four Gaelic festivals", although the latter terms are much more appropriate. With 201 results only in May 2020, the combined words "four quarter day festivals" are even less common on the Internet – although, of course, those numbers are not absolute, as the results provided by search engines are usually adjusted to the prior search history of the user.

The term "*Fire Festival*" strikes the imagination of many: it is all the more appealing and attention-grabbing today that it echoes prominent social gatherings such as the famous *Burning Man* in the Black Rock Desert of Nevada, which attracts dozens of thousands of visitors every year. The comparison with the *Beltane Fire Festival* held in Edinburgh is even more apposite. Every year, on the evening of 30 April, crowds gather around artistic performances usually connected with the theme of fire. A procession takes place and generally includes a *May Queen* and a *Green Man*, who is often associated with a Celtic horned god (usually referred to as Cernunnos) by the participants. As indicated on the official website of the Scottish event:

> Our festival is a living, dynamic reinterpretation and modernisation of an ancient Iron Age Celtic ritual and is the largest of its kind. Having been resurrected as a practice in 1988 it has become a central focus for our community, bringing many many people together to acknowledge

and revel in the birth of the Summer and the fertility of the land. It is important to note that the purpose of our festival is not to recreate ancient practices but to continue in the spirit of our ancient forebears and create our own connection to the cycles of nature.[189]

The gathering is held on Calton Hill, a small hill in central Edinburgh, right next to the Parliament of Holyrood and about 1.5 kilometers north-west of Arthur's Seat. As a matter of fact, Arthur's Seat is identified by the organizers as the original ancient place of *Beltane* celebrations in Scotland – a statement which is quite in tune with the brief study of the Scottish hill featured *supra*.

The *Fire Festival* of Uisneach seems to have drawn its inspiration from the *Beltane Fire Festival* of Edinburgh, at least as far as its name is concerned. Furthermore, terms such as "convention", "congregation" or "assembly" are virtually devoid of connotation, either positive or negative, for the general public. Conversely, a *Fire Festival* is likely to more readily attract a large number of visitors, which is probably what happened in the case of Uisneach. Without even mentioning the 6000–7,000 spectators when the gathering was a large music festival, the *Fire Festival* of 2017 attracted more than 2,000 people, including visitors coming from "the United Kingdom, France, Germany, the USA, Canada, Australia, New Zealand, Argentina, India, Egypt and South Africa", according to the organizers. The contemporary gathering of Uisneach is now, in the literal sense of the term, an international event. However, in 2017, David Clarke insisted on the fact that "locals" had the priority: "We are very much trying to encourage more of the locals to come here. There's a lot of locals that has never been to Uisneach". The owner of the hill detailed his marketing strategy as follows:

> What we have been doing over the last two years with the help of Justin[190] here: when somebody wants to attend the festival, they will send him an email, he will reply to them then he'll be asked to leave a donation so we're trying at this stage only to get the people who really want to come. You know if it's a Saturday evening and the sun is shining and [they] have nothing better to do, we don't really want that sort of person, we want people who want to be here.

The re-introduction of a fixed fee and a more traditional Internet registration in 2018–9 suggests that Clarke's position has evolved since. This minor adjustment did not change the substance of the event, which remains a compromise that is perfectly congruent with the Irish *zeitgeist* of the 21st century, as confirmed by the investigation carried out on Uisneach during the *Bealtaine Fire Festivals* 2017 and 2019 for the making of this book.

In both 2017 and 2019, the bonfire kindled on the top of the hill was the culmination of the event. The gathering was, to some extent, informally divided into two parts: the celebration started with secular events and re-joicing, followed by the re-enactment of sacred customs, which ended late in the evening.

Contemporary Fire Festival: *Secular Aspects*

The gates of Uisneach open at around five in the afternoon. After a quick search and the presentation of the entry ticket, the visitors climb up the hill, walking a path – decorated with greenery for the occasion – which leads to the top of the hill. The ascent usually takes five to ten minutes. The first point of gathering, which is ostensibly "profane", is situated right next to *Lough Lugh*: people meet up and have a good time. Many tables and chairs are set up and several large tents and wagons accommodate drink and food stalls.[191] Only soft drinks are offered since, as mentioned before, alcohol was prohibited in 2015; today, the temporary bar called *Tír na nÓg* – the Land of Youth, that is the Otherworld – is but an empty platform. *Rogan's Smokehouse* from Rathowen Co. Westmeath stands next to *GG's Philly Cheese*, *Sally's Hand Rolled Ice Cream*, *Lough Owel Organic Farm* and other pancake and beverage vendors, gluten-free, vegetarian or vegan stalls and other eco-friendly food shops. Next to *Lough Lugh*, musicians, dancers, marching bands and majorettes take turns on a small platform; most of them are amateurs, usually from the area, with a couple of exceptions, including a marching band coming all the way from Galway in 2017. Visitors eat, drink, listen and watch while having fun and talking among guest jugglers and street artists. Vendors sell articles which they feel are connected to the spirit of the place, that is supposedly ancient traditions – but not necessarily Celtic or Irish ones – and a revised form of "authenticity": decorated mugs, design-your-own leather bracelets, dream-catchers, costume jewelry, wrought iron craftsmanship etc.

Here and there, a few peculiar stalls and stands are set up. For instance, in 2017, an archery booth and children's play areas met some success. In 2019, a large canvas was stretched over a round horizontal framework, creating a large *bodhrán* – an Irish frame drum – which produced a very deep and rather impressive sound, especially when it was hit by dozens of hands in unison. The most studious visitors could attend a cycle of conferences more or less directly dealing with Uisneach; those conferences were sponsored by *Ireland's Ancient East*, an agency attached to the *Department of Transport, Tourism and Sport* whose purpose is to promote tourism in the East[192] of Ireland, which is indeed often neglected by the major tour operators.

More surprising and perhaps even more illustrative, in 2019, a part of the site was turned into a "Yoga & Holistic" area. Collective yoga classes for both adults and children were organized in large tents. The *Institute of Pranic Healing UK & Ireland* offered "Healing Sessions" and "Courses & Events to Enhance All Areas of Your Life",[193] which were supposed to offer

"Physical & Emotional Healing through 11 Major Chakras" so as to "flush out stress & Increase Energy Levels". The success of the stall proves that it met real customer demands: a part of the visitors of Uisneach were queuing for several minutes in order to have their "aura purified" by the members of the Institute. Without making value judgments on the inclusion of those practices in a supposedly "re-enacted" Celtic festival, it is already clear that the term of "historical re-enactment" is quite ill-suited to qualify the contemporary gathering of Uisneach.

The decoration of the site receives careful attention. Artificially aged panels and signs guide the visitors. Huge colored flags float everywhere on the upper part of the hill and garlands and multicolored festoons adorn the site. Many – unpaid – artists set up the artworks around the upper plateau of Uisneach: once again, the gathering is placed under the sign of a "return to the origins" as most of the works of art are supposed to represent mythical characters or allegedly ancient symbols. Depending on the year, one can find monumental horse statues, winged female characters, faces reminding of male or female deities – including Lugh – a large wheel symbolizing the sun or the course of time, large adorned Celtic harps etc.[194] As evening falls, imposing metal structures in the shape of triskeles, spirals or other geometrical figures – and even dragons and other mythical beasts – are wrapped in flammable materials and set ablaze.

As mentioned earlier, the visitors of Uisneach come from a large number of different countries. However, in both 2017 and 2019, most of them were Irish. Although the exact figures are not known, the general, anecdotal impression was that the visitors were quite young: most were teenagers or young adults coming in small groups, parents with their toddlers or young children or couples between the age of 20 and 50. People over 60 seemed largely underrepresented but only a more systematic approach could confirm this suspicion. There was no obvious imbalance between genders, although the presence of many female dancers and "ritual practitioners"[195] may tip the scale in their favor. The visitors attending the 2017 and 2019 celebrations appeared quite representative of the different ethnic groups of Ireland and their proportions.

Some women chose to wear meticulously adorned dresses and had placed flowers, leaves and ribbons in their hair;[196] people could get their face painted or their make-up done by volunteers for a small fee, or rather tip. Other protagonists – both male and female – wore clothes that were visibly inspired by the Hippie/New Age movements.[197] Quite often, visitors had come in a costume and spent their afternoon and evening wearing their attire. Fairies, "Celtic" warriors – usually inspired by the blue make-up popularized by the film *Braveheart* – either wearing kilts or not, elves, princesses, bards but also – and this is perhaps more peculiar – pirates, demons and gothic-looking witches:[198] the profusion of symbols traditionally condemned or disapproved of by the Catholic Church is striking. Undoubtedly, Uisneach had to get rid of the influence of the local clergy before even considering the re-creation of this festival.

In both 2017 and 2019, a man wore a *Green Man* costume. This popular Neo-Pagan figure is supposed to echo the cycle of seasons and remind of certain ancient deities, such as the horned god usually referred to as Cernunnos, a continental Celtic god whose attributes and exact function are still debated in scientific literature. In 2019, the *Green Man* of Uisneach wore a boa around his neck and offered people to pet it – an attraction amongst others which takes us further away from the concept of "historical re-enactment" *per se.*

Contemporary Fire Festival*: Sacred Re-enactments*

The secular side of the celebration mainly takes place on the large meadow next to *Lough Lugh*. Three distinct places are or were dedicated to its "sacred side" – or rather, to putative re-enactments of sacred customs. Remarkably, the ringfort of Rathnew was not one of those places, as it is slightly off the beaten track and also may legitimately be considered too fragile and precious to be included in contemporary celebrations.

In 2017, the re-enactment of these supposedly ancient and sacred traditions first took place near *Ail na Mireann*. As soon as the gates of the site open, it is possible to go pay a visit to the boulder rock: some choose to stay there for a while and rest or meditate, others sing or play music with the instruments they brought with them; occasionally, children climb it to its top and go through the narrow passage crossing the stone.[199] But in 2017, a quite intriguing event was held at the *Catstone* by Patsy Preston,[200] with the help of Treasa Kerrigan, the owner of www.sacredsites.ie, which, as mentioned earlier, offers spiritual tours of Uisneach.

Just like David Clarke, the two organizers of this parallel event were kind enough to answer to a couple of questions, this time not in person but via e-mail: the complete answers of Patsy Preston are featured in Annex III.[201] For the sake of brevity, only the elements essential to the comprehension of the celebration are mentioned hereafter.

Patsy Preston presents herself as the "Artistic Director of the Uisneach *Bealtaine* Fire Festival since its inception". From the very beginning, she sets the scene and explains that she has been visiting Uisneach for 30 years "on [her] own personal Spiritual journey" and "built a strong connection there on an energetic level". Mrs. Preston admits that she was quite skeptical when David Clarke told her he wanted to kindle a fire on Uisneach: the owner had indeed mentioned that the "local druids" originally viewed his project unfavorably. Mrs. Preston does consider herself as a fully-fledged druidess, since she was "initiated as a Druid around 25 years ago, and have followed this path, as a way of life since". She details her spiritual function as follows:

> This involves celebrating and marking the Celtic Wheel of the Year and honouring the Divinity within the Land and all of Nature. [...] Last

year I was asked to co-ordinate the celebration and ritual to raise the Devine [sic] Feminine energy at the Catstone, and bring this to meet the main procession. Our main procession has always walked from the Palace [of Rathnew] to the top of the Hill and, although containing many women, always seems to feel more Masculine in nature. The symbolism we were working with was bringing the Spear of Lugh, to meet the Divine Cauldron of the Goddess Ériu and join in the central fire, impregnating the land and awakening Ériu's Fire Eye, so the Goddess may survey the land in a physical context through her people.

The neo-druidess places the notion of authenticity at the heart of her speech. She explains that she finally accepted the kindling of a fire on Uisneach because she believed that it was "what would have happened in times past". Just like David Clarke, she draws a parallel or even a corre-lation between the growing popularity of the contemporary celebration of Uisneach and the decline of Christianity in Ireland. She then adds an es-sential – and very contemporary – parameter to her argumentation: the importance of ecological issues.

This search for an authentic connection with Earth or Nature-based Spirituality, stems in many ways, I feel, from general dis-satisfaction with, not just the larger, established religions, but also an awareness of the damage mankind are doing to our home planet, an ecologically minded, Spiritual path, attempting to re-create balance, by looking at our indigenous heritage, here on the Western Seaboard of Europe.

Interestingly enough, Mrs. Preston also develops the ideas of inclusiveness already mentioned by David Clarke ("It has always been one of my main objectives that the gathering at Uisneach should be inclusive and not just a Pagan celebration") and uses, just like the current owner of Uisneach, the notion of "guardians/keepers of the hill". Both Mr. Clarke and Patsy Preston also explained in detail their desire for the celebration not to be a commercial event but rather a spiritual one. It is quite clear that the current owner of the hill and his artistic director speak with one voice:

From small beginnings, the festival quickly grew and was in danger of becoming just one more Music and Arts Festival, so we have pulled it right back, to the core element, of Lighting the *Bealtaine* Fire and joining with the community to celebrate the arrival of summer. [...] While the procession is in effect a spectacular performance, it does have a genuine Spiritual aspect.

Prior to the celebration, Patsy Preston put out a general call to any women that wanted to be included to wear white[202] for *Bealtaine* 2017, "mainly to give visual cohesion to the ceremony and performance. In the dark and by the fire-light this looked incredible and helped differentiate those involved in the ceremony from the public". In the late afternoon, those women gathered around the *Catstone* and readied themselves for the ceremony: Mrs. Preston had prepared ornaments and headdresses for most of the participants, who painted their faces in white and blue colors[203]. Shortly before sundown, a secret ceremony – or perhaps more appropriately an "exclusive" event – took place at the boulder of Uisneach. Men and "unbelievers" were politely – though quite firmly – asked to leave. Fortunately, Mrs. Preston was kind enough to briefly summarize the rituals as follows, although the "ceremony" in itself is not detailed:

> The ceremony itself followed a fairly standard form for gathering in circle and each of the celebrants was open to add their piece without censure. We had a healing voice session and everyone was blessed with water by some women who have been working with the waters for healing for some years.

Although the importance of water is attested in the ancient Irish traditions and myths related to *Bealtaine*, the connection between those contemporary rituals and what may have taken place on Uisneach is quite questionable, to say the least. Interestingly enough, Mrs. Preston is quite aware of that fact:

> Of course, unlike other indigenous cultures, we here do not have an unbroken tradition, and so a certain amount of guesswork is involved in forging this authentic connection.

The statement in itself is rather contradictory: there is an obvious paradox in trying to "create" or "forge" authenticity. Still, the spiritual and intellectual approach hiding behind this desire is rather clear and undoubtedly sincere: perhaps what should be remembered is that the "mysterious past" of Ireland remains a stimulating vector of artistic creation and identity affirmation today.

The holding of such specific events raises the question of the spiritual affiliation of its participants. Although the inscription of Neo-Paganism in general on to the event is beyond reasonable doubt, Patsy Preston and Treasa Kerrigan insisted on the plurality and ecumenism of their approach. Mrs. Kerrigan explains that she has been a member of *Keepers of the Well* since 2014, a "progressive witchcraft group" with only about a dozen affiliated members.[204] A "High Priestess" is at the head of this group; according to Mrs. Kerrigan, she was trained by Janet Farrar and Gavin Bone, two distinguished members of the Wicca religion in Ireland who had apparently been initiated by the pillars, if not the founders of this spiritual movement, Alex and Maxine Sanders.

Treasa Kerrigan also explained that she has been involved in what she calls the "Irish spiritual community" since 2003 thanks to the study of

Reiki. The association of this alternative pseudo-medical practice based on spirituality with a Neo-Pagan celebration is not surprising: the successful stall of the *Institute of Pranic*[205] *Healing UK & Ireland* on Uisneach proves that the aspirations of some visitors of the hill are compatible with such beliefs. Mrs. Kerrigan started with Reiki but soon "expanded to channelling, angel therapy, crystal healing etc." It will be interesting to see if, in the years to come, those pseudo-medical practices will take the lion's share at Uisneach and if the celebration of *Bealtaine* will turn into a forum of "alternative medicines". Should that occur, it would be easy to regret it and lament over the misappropriation of an ancient sacred site. Conversely, one could point out a certain form of continuity in history: trying to purify the cattle of a farmer by having them passed between two fires or attempting to "cleanse the aura" of people by brushing their forehead and waving at them is perhaps not so fundamentally different. This is, of course, provided that the "cures" are offered in perfectly good faith, without trying to take advantage of the credulity of impressionable participants.

Treasa Kerrigan continues:

> I became definitely pagan around 2009, but was a solitary practitioner for many years until joining the witchcraft group. We are quite loosely structured here as Ireland is small most people get to know each other, whether they identify as shaman, druid or witch, or just pagan.

She makes it clear that her involvement in the celebrations of Uisneach came as an individual and regardless of her affiliation with *Keepers of the Well*. Patsy Preston confirms:

> it was not one group, but a coming together of like-minded souls, to raise the Devine Feminine Energy on Uisneach. So although there would have been a range of "Spiritual affiliations" there was a joint Spiritual connection, focused on healing and empowering.

However, the Artistic Director seems clearly affiliated with www.paganfederationireland.co, which she mentions openly: the creed of the federation of Neo-Pagan groups (ecumenism, ecological approach, affiliation with Wicca and neo-druidic movements as well as "traditional witchcraft" and "heathenry") seems indeed rather in tune with the discourse of Mrs. Preston and the rituals that took place at the *Catstone*, or at least what is known of them.

During the *Bealtaine* gatherings, those rituals are not limited to the vicinity of the *Catstone*. The second notable place of interest was, in 2017, *Saint Patrick's Bed* on the western summit. In the late afternoon, a dozen or so men – not wearing any type of costume or specific attire – gathered and formed a circle around the concrete pillar marking the top of the hill, which had been crowned with a gilded pyramidal structure, evidently of contemporary manufacture, adorned with shapes and drawings of Celtic inspiration. They remained assembled for several minutes, talking or reciting what sounded like litanies or prayers. Once again, the laypeople were asked not to stand too close and interfere, which confirms the sacred intent of the gathering. The site was most likely chosen because it marked the actual top of the hill as well as a probable ancient megalithic tomb – and obviously not because of its late association with Patrick. The vaguely phallic shape of the monument thus adorned may or may not explain why only men gathered there on that day.

Finally, the third place of interest in terms of "re-enactment" stands only a few meters from *Saint Patrick's Bed*. During the days preceding the event, a large hut,[206] about five meters in height, is built at the place called the "*Bealtaine* fire ceremony site" by the Visitor Center. The hut is made of branches and various greeneries and is decorated with little statues. Four entrances are opened to the four cardinal points.

As night falls, all visitors are invited to gather around the hut to attend the kindling of the fire. Depending on the year, various protagonists liven up the ceremony: riders dressed as Celtic warriors, dancers – usually, but not exclusively female – giant puppets, street artists, plow races or stunts, choirs, musicians – including many people playing the Irish traditional drum, the *bodhrán* – entertain the audience while the fire, discreetly kindled next to the ringfort of Rathnew, is carried in procession up to the *Bealtaine* fire ceremony site. The four little gaps opened to the four cardinal points are celebrated by several protagonists: for example, some people are supposed to represent the four Classical elements of fire, water, earth and air; they come from different points of the site and meet up at the hut. In 2016, Mrs. Kerrigan "was invited as an individual, by Patsy, to represent the element of Fire by being the Priestess of the south".[207] The High Priestess of *Keepers of the Well* was the Priestess of the east and represented Air.

From the ringfort of Rathnew, a procession composed of selected members – local or national personalities but also men and women dressed in costumes for the occasion – slowly goes up to the large hut, carrying the fire. When the procession reaches the *Bealtaine* fire ceremony site, the fire is kindled. For safety reasons, the public is kept at a reasonable distance and a team of professionals oversees the whole process, which seems very well-managed. Depending on the year, the kindling is preceded by speeches from the tour guides of the Visitor Center, who go over the main lines of the history of the hill.[208]

The lighting of the fire in itself is well-documented: the current owner of the hill usually hires a professional film crew to capture the *Fire Festival*. Several cameras, some of which are set up on drones, record the event and the result is generally published on line. Although technically speaking a promotional video, the YouTube clip "*Bealtaine @ UISNEACH 2017*"[209] is particularly convincing and well done, in the sense that it conveys the general atmosphere of the celebration quite faithfully.

Celebration of Irishness

The fire kindled today on Uisneach is a huge bonfire whose purpose is probably better expressed in the French translation of the term, a *"feu de joie"* – literally a "fire of joy". The contemporary *Fire Festival* of Uisneach, though at times quite solemn and intense, is before anything a joyful event, which makes the notion of a potential "historical re-enactment" all the more questionable.

In fact, the contemporary celebration is neither an attempt to faithfully recreate the ancient celebration as it may have unfolded nor a re-enactment of a mythological episode – Midhe's fire.

The documents relating to *Bealtaine*, both from a folkloric and a mythological perspective, do suggest that not *one* but *two* large fires were kindled in ancient times; "joy" as a whole was most likely not a part of the essence of the festival: a historical re-enactment would have been performed under the sign of solemnity exclusively. The two fires of *Bealtaine* through which cattle and people were passed to be protected for the coming year were prophylactic fires implying a fear inherent to the passing of time that was only countered by customs performed to bring a counterbalancing good luck. Nothing indicates that, in ancient times, the crowd enjoyed itself and people danced around those fires and welcomed the summer joyfully as it was the case for *Midsummer* fires.

Similarly, if the idea behind the *Fire Festival* was to re-enact the mythological episode of Midhe and his "first fire" lit in Ireland, the contemporary celebration would probably not have been the popular success it is today: no matter how symbolically important they are, political claims – either real of fictional – usually lack the glamorous and entertaining quality of a contemporary *Fire Festival*.

Consequently, the new *Fire Festival* of Uisneach cannot be considered as a re-enactment. It is a reinvention, a contemporary reinterpretation, an update of an ancient event, which probably existed but remains poorly known and understood – and is destined to remain so. This statement is of course not a value judgment. Quite the contrary, it is fascinating to see that, as years and centuries passed, Irish history took over again the sacredness of Uisneach, adapted it to its time, seized it to better adore it. To that extent, the contemporary event held at *Bealtaine* on Uisneach is better described as a creative commemoration of Ireland, perhaps a true celebration of Irishness.

This appropriation of the Irish past is manifold – or rather threefold and arguably "trifunctional". The *Fire Festival* of Uisneach attracts thousands of onlookers; it is a *"popular"* event in the first sense of the term, that is relative to the people themselves. It is also a *sacred* celebration connected to the sacerdotal world through the prism of neo-druids, who attach the greatest importance to the coordination and supervision of the festival. Finally, it is a *political* statement, the expression of the power of the ruling elite: in 2017, the most striking characteristic of the festival was un-doubtedly the participation of Michael D. Higgins, the president of Ireland, who kindled the great fire on the hill of Uisneach.

Michael D. Higgins and Uisneach

According to the current owner of the hill, who had met Michael D. Higgins at the time he was still minister for arts, culture and the *Gaeltacht*, the Irish president has always taken a great interest in Uisneach and wished to attend the celebration for several years. A first formal contact had been made some years before the 2017 event: it took David Clarke genuine determination and several years to get an official answer from the entourage of the president.[210]

Michael D. Higgins was supposed to attend the celebration in 2016 but had to cancel only a few hours before his scheduled arrival: after two months of intense negotiation, the two major Irish political parties, *Fine Gael* and *Fianna Fáil*, had decided to approve the formation of a new government headed by Enda Kenny on 6 May 2016 precisely. The cere-monial duty of the president of Ireland, who must symbolically appoint the head of government, obliged him to stay in Dublin. As a consequence, his visit to Uisneach was postponed to the following year.

In 2017, there was no such setback and Michael D. Higgins therefore accompanied the flame from the ringfort of Rathnew to the western summit of Uisneach. He kindled the fire himself by throwing a burning branch on the hut of the "*Bealtaine* fire ceremony site".[211]

David Clarke explains the motivation of Michael D. Higgins as follows:

> I believe, he's very excited today to be coming here, with his family I might add, to light the fire on the hill of Uisneach. So, this is hugely significant to see the president of Ireland light the fire on that pre-Christian hill. Go back again let's say twenty years ago, it definitely wouldn't have happened or even ten. He's a great man [who] under-stands where we're all coming from. It's a great honour for us but a great honour for him to lighten the fire.

Michael D. Higgins is a proficient Irish speaker and spent a significant part of his career promoting the Gaelic Irish culture, language, history and art. The poems he published as early as 1990 are deeply rooted in the Gaelic past of Ireland and their somewhat mystical nature is well-established.

His kindling of the fire of Uisneach, which was only very moderately covered by the press,[212] was as symbolic as it was political. On Uisneach, the president of Ireland, the supreme representative of the Irish state and its constitution, became a part of a millennial tradition – either real or my-thical – that of holders of power and knowledge literally bringing the "light" of fire over the island. In fact, his gesture is a probable attempt to re-enact or honor the mythical episode of druid Midhe, who lit the first fire of

Ireland. This probable commemoration of the mythical episode was not insignificant: this powerful symbolic move undoubtedly highlighted the unity of Ireland – the Republic but also perhaps the island as a whole – which appeared federated around its center.

Interestingly enough, the Ireland of 2017 accepted without batting an eye the involvement of her president in such a formerly iconoclastic event: the national scandal that would have undoubtedly ensued a few decades prior did not happen.

In an interview he gave to the press, Ruairí McKiernan, a then member of the Irish Council of State, confirmed the federating, ecumenical and fundamentally political nature of such a gesture:

> The gathering on the hill is a celebration of community, a coming together at a time of so much suffering, isolation, fear and division. The reawakening of Uisneach is about reawakening a deeper consciousness in our country. It's about lighting the fires of the imagination which are so badly needed in our world today.[213]

In order to complete this study, the entourage of Michael D. Higgins was contacted in 2018, then in 2019: the idea was to get a clearer picture of the motivations of the president and, more generally, to appreciate the connection that seemed to unite him with the hill. On 11 February 2020, the Irish president finally answered this call; the text he wrote was directly sent via e-mail by his head of communications and information: it now serves as preface to this book.

Michael D. Higgins reminds us that he will go down in history of the first president of Ireland to kindle the fire of Uisneach. Significantly enough, he is quite conscious of being a part of this historical as well as mythical continuity of Ireland ("a celebration not only of Ireland's history and rituals, but also its mythical past").

More than a mere "tribute to our rich cultural heritage", the gesture was inherently symbolic: the use of what he calls the "power of fire" is of course not trivial. Michael D. Higgins used this "power" to political ends. The fire, which symbolizes renewal and a form of "new light", was once again associated with an ecumenical and inclusive approach. The idea was to unite Ireland around ancient – Gaelic and Celtic – themes and its supposedly federative past.

There are several ways to interpret the bringing-together of "communities" mentioned by the president. As Michael D. Higgins is clearly not affiliated with the Irish ultra-nationalist creed, his statement was by no means a territorial or nationalist claim nor was it meant to imply that Ireland was one and indivisible, north and south of the border. Still, the most obvious interpretation is that this allusion to communities echoes the tragic and tumultuous history of Catholicism and Protestantism in Ireland. Kindling the fire on Uisneach was arguably a way to emphasize the Irishness of *all* Irish citizens regardless of their religion – a statement which is all the more relevant given that the archaeological, historical and mythical past of the island started centuries, if not millennia before the introduction of Christianity. However, the rhetoric of Michael D. Higgins suggests that the scope of his speech is even wider. The lighting of the *Bealtaine* fire on Uisneach is about "re-awaken[ing] our sense of belonging as people on a shared planet". The ecumenism promoted by Higgins transcends communities as much as it transcends borders. In his own words, the president's gesture was not only about uniting different religious, national and political identities of Irish people; it was a way to unite individuals and peoples on a global scale by reminding them of their common destiny. The president of Ireland thus made himself the spokesman of reconciliations, or perhaps more appropriately the humanist *mediator* of peoples.

Uisneach, the Fifth Province and the Spiritual Center

The ecumenical, inclusive vision of Michael D. Higgins, who thus placed Uisneach at the heart of Ireland, is not a creation *ex nihilo* of the current President. Although arguably inspired by Irish myths and folklore as well as the *Gaelic Revival* of the early 20th century, the notion according to which Uisneach was a center of Ireland – and most of all the *spiritual* center of Ireland – had been revived a second time in the 1970s. This specific revival most likely strongly influenced Michael D. Higgins' perception of the hill.

The periodical called *The Crane Bag* was published by Richard Kearney and Mark Patrick Hederman twice annually between 1977 and 1985 in two annual editions. Its mission was to "disseminate modern Irish thinking and culture, while also engaging the critical participation of artists and thinkers from other countries".[214] Interestingly enough – and as noted by historian Michael Böss – the two editors believed their role to be that of "mediators" of knowledge and held that truth "could not be derived from any doctrine once and for all. It was neither an *a priori* nor a product, but a process, a 'becoming'".[215] Their strong emphasis on the Fifth Province of Ireland was to play a pivotal role in the general perception and historiography of Uisneach: Kearny and Hederman believed that the symbol of Ireland's Fifth Province "invoked a vision of an Ireland which would be open, tolerant and culturally inclusive".[216]

The two editors explained that the "spiritual middle" of Ireland counterbalanced the political center of Tara. This correspondence was supposedly a well-kept secret, originally known to druids and poets only:

> It seems clear to us that in the present unhappy state of our country it is essential to restore this second centre of gravity in some way. [...] This province, this place, this centre, is not a political position. In fact, if it is a position at all, it would be marked by the [absence] of any particular political and geographical delineation, something more

like a dis-position ... Uisnech, or the secret centre, was the place where all oppositions were resolved, the primeval unity. The discovery of points where unrelated things coincide was always one of the great arts of seers, poets and magicians. Thus, the constitution of such a place would mean that each person must discover it for himself within himself. Each person would have become a seer, a poet, an artist. The purpose of The Crane Bag is to promote the excavation of the unactualized spaces within the reader, which is the work of constituting a fifth province. From such a place a new understanding and unity might emerge.[217]

While Tara is here presented as the ancient political center of Ireland, Uisneach is considered by Kearney as its spiritual center with an influence even more crucial, and more potent, to Ireland: he conceives its power as a unitive, federative one – the secret heart and soul of Ireland "where all oppositions were resolved, the primeval unity" or a "transcendent location" as coined later by dramatist Brian Friel.[218] In the 1980s, Kearney went a step further and suggested "a new notion of a non-territorial, cultural, Irish nation in which the local community and Irish diaspora merged into an entity beyond the nation-state".[219] According to this conception, Uisneach was, or could become, symbolically the spiritual center of Ireland but also the spiritual center of Irish people throughout the world – the embodiment of Irishness.

Of course, the dichotomies according to which Ireland had two centers – Tara, the political one and Uisneach, the spiritual one – must not be understood in sheer historical terms; nothing, either in ancient Irish historical records or myths, substantiates the claim in such a clear and unambiguous fashion, although the two hills were indeed like "the two kidneys in a beast" according to one medieval commentator. Rather, it suggests that to this day, a fraction at least of the Irish population still chooses to think "their history in mythical terms"[220] and use – or rewrite – the past of Ireland in order to re-imagine its present and possibly shape its future.

When Mary Robinson campaigned for the presidency in 1990, she also relied on this notion of a "Fifth Province", which may have been appealing for a number of reasons. Ireland in the 1970s and 1980s was intimately connected to the concept of "Europeanisation":[221] most Irish people envisioned their future within Europe and there is no doubt that this new political architecture played a pivotal role in the evolution of Irish identity. In her campaign, Robinson tried to conciliate the natural anchoring of Irish people in local tradition with a more universal approach, while at the same time "combining her strong commitment to the protection of universal human rights with an equally strong belief in the values and resources of the local community":[222]

With her background in academia, Mary Robinson was familiar with the cultural and intellectual debate in Ireland in the 1980s. She was personally acquainted with many of its leading figures, and she later acknowledged her debt to both *The Crane Bag* and Field Day[223]. Ideas and sentiments expressed there filtered into her presidential speeches, and, on a few occasions, they even provided drafts. Importantly, this was the case when Robinson, exhausted by months of campaigning, made a phone call to Kearney to ask him for ideas for her inaugural speech.[224]

This phone call inspired Robinson to include mentions of a "Fifth Province" in her inaugural speech. The president used the ideas of Kearney to underline the inclusiveness of the new Ireland that was emerging. Her speech began as follows:

> The Ireland I will be representing is a new Ireland, open, tolerant, inclusive. [...] The recent revival of an old concept of the Fifth Province expresses this emerging Ireland of tolerance and empathy. The old Irish term for province is *coicead*, meaning a "fifth"; and yet, as everyone knows, there are only four geographical provinces on this island. So where is the fifth? The Fifth Province is not anywhere here or there, north or south, east or west. It is a place within each one of us – that place that is open to the other, that swinging door which allows us to venture out and others to venture in. Ancient legends divided Ireland into four quarters and a "middle", although they differed about the location of this middle or Fifth Province. While Tara was the political centre of Ireland, tradition has it that this Fifth Province acted as a second centre, a necessary balance. If I am a symbol of anything I would like to be a symbol of this reconciling and healing Fifth Province.[225]

The new nation thus defined was not inclusive merely because the Fifth Province was supposed to be the center of an open-minded, tolerant Ireland: it was inclusive because the Fifth Province was also "a place within each one of us". Therefore, the Province was implicitly defined as the center of Irishness as a whole – arguably the spiritual center of humankind. Most of all, the President of Ireland, as imagined by Robinson, was supposed to be a representative of this "reconciling and healing" Fifth Province: whereas Tara was the political center, the Fifth Province was the "second centre, a necessary balance" – a spiritual *just middle-ground*, one might add. This second center, located by Kearney at the hill of Uisneach, was symbolized by the representative power of the president of Ireland, who therefore became a "symbol of a symbol", as noted by Böss.[226] In other words, this vision suggests that the president symbolizes Uisneach, which itself symbolizes spirituality and the very higher ideal of humankind as a whole.

Incidentally, the concept of a Fifth Province was scarcely used afterwards and virtually disappeared from public debate in the following years: the symbol had apparently lost its appeal. Robinson herself subsequently preferred references to "the tolerant society" or the notion of "plurality", which was adopted and promoted by the Fianna Fáil in the 1990s. Perhaps the original claims were too excessive to be sustained; they were also possibly too mystical to find their place on the political stage or even for the average person to relate to.

In 2002, historian Michael Böss very elegantly explained this development by theorizing that, although Robinson did popularize "a cultural pluralist vision of Ireland which had hitherto only been the imaginative possession of a small intellectual elite",[227] the problem lay in an original misconception:

> Kearney had assumed only two centres – the centres of political and spiritual powers – ignoring the fact that, in the contemporary world, there is a third centre which is even more powerful than these, namely the virtual centre of the transnational, global economy.[228]

Michael D. Higgins's gesture may or may not prove this statement wrong in the years to come. On 6 May 2017, the president chose to inscribe himself in tradition – both ancient and reinvented: he decided to play his part as a "symbol of a symbol". The fire he kindled was indeed a spiritual, political fire as well as a federative, humanist flame. It illuminated the top of a hill rife with symbols and powers, of spirituality and mediation – a hill at the center of Ireland, of Irishness, perhaps of humankind's spiritual world as a whole. Only time will tell whether this flame was destined to burn for centuries or be shrouded in the darkness of spiritual paucity.

Notes

1 The statement is featured prominently on the official website of Visitor Center of Uisneach (http://uisneach.ie/fire-festival/) and was inspired by Daly, Leo. 1975. *James Joyce and the Mullingar connection*. Dublin: Dolmen Press. A visit paid by Joyce to Mullingar in 1902 is mentioned in Barfoot, C.C. & D'Haen, Theo. 1995. *Troubled Histories, Troubled Fictions: Twentieth-century Anglo-Irish Prose*. Leiden: Brill Rodopi, 83. See also Garvin, John. 1976. *James Joyce's Disunited Kingdom*. Dublin: Gill & Macmillan, 29.

2 "In *Finnegans Wake* Joyce calls the stone 'Mearing Stone' – an archaic English term meaning 'boundary stone', and chiming, if not rhyming, with Aill na Mireann". *Mythic Ireland, op. cit.*, 197.

3 Joyce, James. 1939 (1966). *Finnegans Wake*. New York: Viking Press, 473.

4 *Histoire et Civilisation de l'Irlande, op. cit.*, 75.

5 *Ibid.*

6 Kelly, John, Schachard, Ronald (ed.). 1997. *The Collected Letters of W.B. Yeats: Volume Three, 1901–1924*. Oxford: Oxford University Press, 250. /beltein/ is a common mispronunciation of Irish *Be[a]ltaine* (usually pronounced /belt(ʃ)ənə/) by English speakers.

7 *Annals of Westmeath, op. cit.*, iii.

8 *Ibid.*, 239–41.

9 *Ibid.*, 239.

10 *Ibid.*
11 *Ibid.*, 240. The idea can be found in Lewis, Samuel. 1837. *A Topographical Dictionary of Ireland*. S. Lewis & Co., London, II, 695. "[The provincial assemblies of Westmeath] were held at the hill of Usneagh, supposed by some to be the Laberus noticed by Ptolemy as one of the inland cities of Ireland". But the most ancient association Laberus/Uisneach dates back to 1607, in the words of English historian William Camden. Camden, William. 1607. *Britannia*. London: Georgii Bishop and Joannis Norton. Recent studies tend to associate Laberos to Tara rather than Uisneach. See Darcy R. & Flynn, William. 2008. "Ptolemy's map of Ireland: a modern decoding" in *Irish Geography*, XLI:1, 49–69.
12 *Annals of Westmeath, op. cit.*, 240.
13 *Ibid.*, 242.
14 *Ibid.*, 240–1. The idea was inspired by an article published in the *Dublin Daily Independent* on 10 August 1906 by James Tuite.
15 "Report on the Excavation of Uisneach", *op. cit.*, 70. See also Annex II.6.
16 *Annals of Westmeath, op. cit.*, 247.
17 *Ibid.*, 245.
18 Joyce, Patrick Weston. 1879. "Connla of the Golden Hair and the Fairy Maiden" in *Old Celtic Romances*. Dublin: the Educational Co. of Ireland, 106–11: 106.
19 *The Gaelic Journal, op. cit.*, 307 and "Mythological Legends of Ancient Ireland. I, the Adventures of Condla Ruad", *op. cit.*, 120, already mentioned in chap. III.6.
20 "Connla of the Fiery Hair was son of Conn of the Hundred Fights. One day as he stood by the side of his father on the height of Usna, he saw a maiden clad in strange attire coming towards him. 'Whence comest thou, maiden?' said Connla. 'I come from the Plains of the Ever Living,' she said, 'there where there is neither death not sin. There we keep holiday always, nor need we help from any in our joy. And in all our pleasure we have no strife. And because we have our homes in the round green hills, men call us the Hill Folk". Jacobs, Joseph. 1892. "Connla and the Fairy Maiden" in *Celtic Fairy Tales*. London: David Nutt, 1–4.
21 https://www.duchas.ie/en/cbes.
22 *NFCS 742*, page 190.
23 *NFCS 743*, 1–4, 189–8, *NFCS 744*, 144–7.
24 *NFCS 742*, 417–8.
25 *NFCS 744*, 73.
26 *NFCS 743*, 307.
27 *NFCS 742*, 5–9, *NFCS 744*, 82.
28 *NFCS 742*, 5.
29 *NFCS 743*, 231. The local population continued using the hill as a reference point throughout centuries. Dermot Ó Cobhthaigh, a local poet from the barony of Rathconrath even started one of his poems by "two clouds of woe over the land of Uisneach", as a reference to the murder of his wife in 1556. *Oxford Dictionary of National Biography*, ref. *Ó Cobhthaigh family*, XLI, 435–6.
30 *NFCS 744*, 24. To some extent, the idea according to which Uisneach was the center of Ireland survived among the local population. In a report from 1971, already mentioned in chapter I.2, a journalist interviewed the inhabitants of three localities (Uisneach, Tubberclair Co. Westmeath and Birr, Co. Offaly) claiming to be the center of Ireland. There was clearly no consensus over Uisneach as the center of the island: from national, its fame had become local. https://www.rte.ie/archives/exhibitions/681-history-of-rte/705-rte-1970s/139386-dead-centre-of-ireland/.
31 *NFCS 744*, 24–5.

32 *NFCS 744*, 23.
33 *NFCS 742*, 229–30, 232, 238, 276–7, 375 etc. The two hills were connected by a local saying which lived on until the 20th century in the locality of Croughal: "between the two hills" meant between Croughill and Uisneach. See also *infra* the tale of the giant Usher.
34 *NFCS 742*, 435–6, 506, etc.
35 *NFCS 742*, 476.
36 *NFCS 742*, 498.
37 *NFCS 742*, 245.
38 *NFCS 742*, 323.
39 *NFCS 744*, 66.
40 *NFCS 743*, 50. See also *NFCS 743*, 51 for the mention of a large rock in a field of Moyvoughly.
41 *NFCS 742*, 345.
42 *NFCS 742*, 245.
43 *Annals of Westmeath*, op. cit., 246.
44 MSS. *NFCS 742*, 5–9 and 338 are not taken into account here, as they plagiarize the work of Woods and do not provide further information.
45 http://uisneach.ie/history/.
46 *NFCS 742*, 329.
47 *Mythic Ireland*, op. cit., 197.
48 https://www.irishexaminer.com/lifestyle/artsfilmtv/a-fire-burning-in-irelands-heart-192774. html.
49 https://www.facebook.com/mullingarnewsandviews1/posts/2372681252761689.
50 http://uisneach.ie/history/.
51 O'Farrell, Padraic. "An Irishman's Diary", 30 Nov., 1998, https://www.irishtimes.com/ opinion/an-irishman-s-diary-1.220209.
52 "De V[a]llera was definitely on the hill – I have the photos – There were several political rallies on the hill – Some even laid on special trains out of Dublin". Personal e-mail to F.A. from one of the Visitor Center's tour guides, 22 Jan. 2020.
53 *NFCS 742*, 338–9.
54 O'Flannghaile, Tomás (ed.) 1896. *The Lay of Oisín in the Land of Youth by Micheál Coimín*. Dublin: M.H. Gill & Son.
55 *Ibid.*, 94.
56 See chap. I.3 and I.6
57 *NFCS 742*, 339–40.
58 *NFCS 742*, 323, *NFCS 742*, 476 for example.
59 *NFCS 742*, 340.
60 *NFCS 742*, 248.
61 A lake about 15 kilometers north-east of Uisneach.
62 *NFCS 742*, 337.
63 *NFCS 742*, 359–60.
64 *NFCS 742*, 310.
65 *NFCS 743*, 11.
66 *NFCS 742*, 311.
67 *NFCS 742*, 337.
68 *NFCS 744*, 11–2.
69 *NFCS 744*, 49–50.
70 *NFCS 743*, 12.
71 See *Preservation Orders*, June 2019, National Monuments Service, Seirbhís na Séadcomharthaí Náisiúnta https://www.archaeology.ie/sites/default/files/media/publications/po19v1-all-counties.pdf, 41.

72 See for instance *NFCS 743*, 365.

73 An informant explains that it is the oldest local cemetery. *NFCS 744*, 80.

74 *NFCS 742*, 278, 323, 379, 448, 476, *NFCS 743*, 310, *NFCS 744*, 66 etc.

75 Bride, Brigit, Bridget etc. are common alternatives to Brigid.

76 *NFCS 742*, 476, *NFCS 743*, 310.

77 Other local holy wells (such as Sunday's Well, mentioned in *NFCS 743*, 241) are almost completely overshadowed by St. Brigid's Well.

78 A very thorough description of the site can be found in *NFCS 744*, 85.

79 *NFCS 743*, 9 "The Stations of the Cross are performed around the well on Good Friday", *NFCS 742*, 178, *NFCS 743*, 310, 311, *NFCS 444*, 66; *NFCS 742*, 305 mentions the evening of Good Friday and *NFCS 744*, 90 people visited the well before six o'clock.

80 Traditionally, *St. Brigid's Day/Imbolc* was celebrated on 1 February but the dates were of course flexible. *NFCS 742*, 456. *NFCS 742*, 476 mention both possibilities.

81 *NFCS 742*, 448 (Good Friday and 15 August).

82 *NFCS 742*, 278, 448, 456, *NFCS 743*, 310, 312.

83 *NFCS 742*, 448, 456, 476.

84 *NFCS 743*, 330.

85 *NFCS 742*, 278.

86 *NFCS 742*, 305.

87 *NFCS 742*, 448, 456, *NFCS 743*, 312. An informant even explains that "in St. Brigid's time, there were a great many camps around the well. Some terrible diseases were prevalent among the inhabitants of the camps. Each patient went over to the well and ate some of the water-cress growing on it. As soon as they did so they were cured of the disease". *NFCS 744*, 94.

88 *NFCS 742*, 476. *NFCS 742*, 476 which explains that many women were named Brigit in the locality. The similarity between the words "Killare" and "Kildare" – Brigid of Ireland is usually referred to as St. Brigid of Kildare – may partially account for the extensive association of the holy well with the saint.

89 *NFCS 743*, 310.

90 *NFCS 742*, 323, 448, 476, 507, *NFCS 744*, 85–6.

91 *NFCS 742*, 278. The date is engraved under the altar.

92 *NFCS 742*, 278, 323, 448.

93 *NFCS 744*, 85–6.

94 *NFCS 742*, 278, *NFCS 744*, 85–6.

95 *NFCS 744*, 85–6. Apparently, the tree was cut for safety reasons.

96 *NFCS 744*, 86–7.

97 Ash trees are not expected to live more than two centuries. In any case, this specific tree was not on Uisneach *per se*, but rather at the foot of the hill.

98 See *supra*.

99 *NFCS 742*, 278.

100 *NFCS 742*, 448.

101 *NFCS 743*, 311.

102 *NFCS 743*, 312.

103 *NFCS 744*, 93.

104 *NFCS 744*, 92–3.

105 *NFCS 743*, 311, *NFCS 744*, 85–6.

106 *NFCS 743*, 311.

107 *NFCS 743*, 10.

108 Annex I.27.

109 According to the Visitor Center of Uisneach.

110 Another rather peculiar story from the *Schools' Collection* mentions the inn. At the time of the Irish Rebellion of 1798, a group of thieves led by Boyle the Robber supposedly looted the locality and finally "reached the slopes of Royal Uisneagh where they rested & partook of deep draughts of Killahugh 'dew', whilst a raging storm swept across the wide historic hill. The party reached Killare and when right in front of where the 'Uisneagh Inn' now stands, the robbers heard the noise of the approaching coach. They shout to the driver 'Pull up or you are a dead man'. [It] was unexpectedly answered by a sudden discharge of firearms from the inside of the vehicle". Three thieves were injured, three others killed NFCS 742, 21–2.

111 *NFCS 742*, 448–9.

112 *NFCS 744*, 85.

113 *NFCS 744*, 66.

114 *NFCS 742*, 448.

115 *Ibid.* and 477.

116 The visits on 15 August and Good Friday are without a doubt late Christian adaptations.

117 "Brigit i.e. a poetess, daughter of the Dagda. This is Brigit the female sage, or woman of wisdom, i.e. Brigit the goddess whom poets adored, because very great and very famous was her protecting care. It is therefore they call her goddess of poets by this name. Whose sisters were Brigit the female physician [woman of leechcraft,] Brigit the female smith [woman of smithwork]; from whose names with all Irishmen a goddess was called Brigit. Brigit, then, breo-aigit, breo-shaigit a fiery arrow'". *Three Irish Glossaries, op. cit.*, entry: Brigit.

118 See for example *Lebor Gabála Érenn, op. cit.*, IV, 133, 159, 197.

119 *NFCS 743*, 334.

120 *Ibid.*, 333.

121 *Ibid.*, 331–2.

122 See *NFC 1097* (Westmeath), 75–82, *NFCS 742*, 456, *NFCS 743*, 20, 263, 265, 331, 334.

123 *NFC 1097* (Westmeath), 75–82, *NFCS 743*, 263.

124 *NFCS 742*, 456 for instance.

125 *NFCS 743*, 263, 332.

126 *Ibid.*, 20.

127 *Ibid.*, 332.

128 *NFCS 742*, 314, *NFCS 743*, 20, 331, 333–4.

129 *NFCS 743*, 333.

130 *NFCS 742*, 296–7.

131 *NFCS 743*, 263, 331, 333–4.

132 The informant meant "pishogue", Irish for incantations and superstitions connected to magic.

133 Rods used to pin down thatch.

134 *NFCS 743*, 20–1. See also *NFCS 742*, 296–7 for another detailed account.

135 *NFC 1097* (Westmeath), 75–82.

136 *NFCS 743*, 260, 292.

137 *NFCS 742*, 456, *NFCS 743*, 331–4.

138 *NFCS 743*, 332–4 for example.

139 *NFC 1097* (Westmeath), 75–82, *NFCS 742*, 296, 515.

140 *NFCS 742*, 309, 515.

141 *NFC 1097* (Westmeath), 75–82. *NFCS 742*, 296, 515, *NFCS 743*, 333 (which mentions a turnip rather than a branch), 334, 385.

142 *NFCS 743*, 334.

143 *NFCS 742*, 296.

144 For example *NFCS 742*, 456.
145 *NFCS 743*, 333.
146 *NFCS 743*, 333–4.
147 *Ibid.*, 263.
148 *Ibid.*
149 *NFC 1097* (Westmeath), 59–66.
150 However, the idea is mentioned by three informants of the *IFC* for Co. Westmeath but never in the vicinity of Uisneach. *NFC 1097*, 59–66, 91–98, 99–106. In Rathconrath, the following proverb is arguably a – very remote – resurgence of a quarterly division: "The cuckoo comes in April/He sings his song in May/In leafy June he whistles a tune/And in July he flies away". *NFCS 742*, 290.
151 *NFC 1097*, 59–66, 87–90, 91–98, 99–106.
152 *NFCS 742*, 296.
153 "A wet and windy May fills the haggards with corn and hay" (*NFC 1097*, *op. cit.*, 75-82, *NFCS 742*, 289, 293, 454), "Ne'er cast a clout till May is out" (*NFCS 742*, 289), "A swarm in May is worth a guinea a day", (*NFCS 742*, 288), "April and May keep out of the sea, June and July swim till you die" (*NFCS 742*, 292). In Irish tradition, the ocean is often identified as a possible incarnation of the *sídh*.
154 *NFCS 743*, 21.
155 For the remainder of Co. Westmeath, the idea is mentioned by four informants in *IFC 1947*: *NFC 1097*, 59–66, 87–90, 91–98, 99–106.
156 *NFCS 742*, 235, 478.
157 *Ibid.*, 419. See also 478.
158 *Ibid.*, 329–30.
159 *NFC 1097*, 75–82. Collective *May Bushes* or *May Poles* traditions existed in the *Gaeltachtaí* but were rare and most likely imported in recent times from Great-Britain.
160 There are actually mentioned but once for the whole county. *NFC 1097*, 59–66.
161 *NFCS 743*, 22. The proverb "Marry in the month of May/You will surely rue the day" can be found in *NFCS 742*, 289. For the remainder of Co. Westmeath, it is only mentioned twice, *NFC 1097*, 91–8, 99–106.
162 Only two informants mention milking-hares in the rest of the county. *NFC 1097* (Westmeath) 67–74 and 91–8.
163 *NFC 1097*, 75–82.
164 *NFCS 744*, 79.
165 *NFCS 742*, 306.
166 https://www.irishexaminer.com/lifestyle/artsfilmtv/a-fire-burning-in-irelands-heart-192774.html.
167 "Reflections on a Lake", *op. cit.*, 125.
168 Later identified as Patsy Preston. See *infra*.
169 Interview with David Clarke, 6 May 2017.
170 Details will be given for years 2017 and 2019 *infra*.
171 A more recent version of the website features the following announcement: "Unauthorised access to the Hill is not permitted for insurance and safety reasons. A suitable level of physical fitness and appropriate footwear and clothing are necessary. Please be advised that the Hill is private property and a working farm with livestock, machinery and other dangers". http://uisneach.ie/guided-tours/.
172 Especially during the "National Heritage Week": https://www.heritageweek.ie.
173 http://www.sacredsites.ie/.
174 https://www.eventbrite.ie/e/winter-solstice-spiritual-tour-of-uisneach-tickets-80714534345?aff=ebdssbdestsearch.

175 http://www.sacredsites.ie/.
176 See for instance http://www.sacredsites.ie/sacred-sites/uisneach/. A meditation CD and an MP3 file are available for purchase. An extract can be listened to here: https://www.youtube.com/watch?reload=9&v=z3Fqn0fZ75U. The website is quite well documented, in spite of a couple of "adjustments" regarding the mythology of the hill and its interpretation. The poems inspired by Uisneach (https://www.sacredsites.ie/bards-corner-2/bards-corner/) use the most common themes connected with the alleged sacredness of the hill and adapt them to the spirituality and beliefs of the authors.
177 See Annex I.4. http://www.irisharchitectureawards.ie.
178 https://www.chg.gov.ie/app/uploads/2016/07/heritage-ireland-issue-4.pdf.
179 https://www.tripadvisor.com/ShowUserReviews-g7146944-d7142589-r291734623-Hill_of_Uisneach-Killare_County_Westmeath.html#REVIEWS.
180 Annex I.3.
181 http://www.westmeathexaminer.ie/2017/12/29/hill-of-tara-unable-to-cope-with-visitor-numbers/.
182 All figures from 30 January 2020. https://www.facebook.com/pg/HillofTara and https://www.facebook.com/hillofuisneach.
183 Uisneach has also been present on Twitter since March 2015: https://twitter.com/uisneachfire?lang=en. As of August 2020, they had 845 followers, which seems consistent with the reputation of the hill.
184 Due to privacy concerns, the last name has been omitted.
185 See Annex III.1-2a.
186 See *infra*.
187 See Annex III.2b for full e-mail.
188 This claim is of course controversial. See chapters II and V and *infra*.
189 https://beltane.org/about/about-beltane/.
190 Justin Moffatt is one of the tour guides working for the Visitor Center of Uisneach.
191 Annex I.2, 9, 10.
192 Technically speaking Uisneach is now part of Leinster. Uisneach joined the *"Ireland's Ancient East heritage trail"*.
193 Annex I.11.
194 Annex I.12–14.
195 See *infra*.
196 Annex I.18.
197 Annex I.19–20.
198 Annex I.15–17.
199 Annex I.6.
200 See http://www.patsypreston.com.
201 Annex III.3.
202 "It was important that everyone would be actively involved in the ceremony and many would have been involved in healing, or working with energy in some way". See Annex III.3 for more details on the selection process.
203 Annex I.7-8.
204 "It's based in Kells and run by High Priestess Gemma McGowan, who studied witchcraft with Janet Farrar and Gavin Bone". 1 Feb. 2018, personal e-mail.
205 From "prana", a reference to "vital energy".
206 Annex I.21.
207 Personal e-mail from Treasa Kerrigan, 1 Feb. 2018.
208 Annex I.23-6.

209 *Bealtaine @ UISNEACH 2017* (https://www.youtube.com/watch?v=WX2SCp_ Dj5I is a short trailer presented the 2017 celebration. See also *2017 Uisneach Bealtaine Fire Live* (https://www.youtube.com/watch?v=z_0OGuPmJds), an unedited 100-minute-long film – or rather, a recording of a live stream – showing the last part of the celebration.

210 Ruairí McKiernan, at the time a member of the Irish Council of State, played a pivotal role behind the scene; this study is also greatly indebted to Mr. McKiernan.

211 Annex I.22.

212 See for example "Watch: President Higgins 1st Leader in almost 1,000 years to light fire on the hill of Uisneach", Irish Examiner, 12 May 2017: https://www.irishexaminer.com/breakingnews/ireland/watch-president-higgins-1st-leader-in-almost-1000-years-to-light-fire-on-the-hill-of-uisneach-789399.html.

213 *Ibid.*

214 As stated in each issue of *The Crane Bag.*

215 Böss, Michael. 2002. "The Postmodern Nation: a Critical History of the 'Fifth Province' Discourse" in *Etudes Irlandaises*, XXVII-1, 139–59: 143.

216 *Ibid.*

217 1979. "Ireland's Identities", in *The Crane Bag*, III-1, 23, cited *ibid.*

218 Howe, Stephen. 2000. *Ireland and Empire*. Oxford: Oxford University Press, 111, also quoted by Böss, to whom we are much indebted.

219 "The Postmodern Nation", *op. cit.*, 150.

220 *Dieux et Héros des Celtes*, *op. cit.*, 3.

221 This was confirmed later by a White Paper published by the Department of Foreign Affairs: "Irish people increasingly see the European Union not as an organization to which Ireland belongs, but as an integral part of the future". Department of Foreign Affairs, 1996, 58–9, as quoted in "The Postmodern Nation", *op. cit.*, 151.

222 "The Postmodern Nation", *op. cit.*, 151–2.

223 The Field Day Company was a cultural and artistic project of the 1980s which also attempted to include the notion of a "Fifth Province".

224 "The Postmodern Nation", *op. cit.*, 152.

225 Robinson, Mary. 3 Dec. 1990. "Inaugural Speech", Dublin Castle.

226 "The Postmodern Nation", *op. cit.*, 153.

227 *Ibid*, 155.

228 *Ibid*, 156.

Conclusion

The hill of Uisneach was and remains sacred for a fraction of the Irish population, even though the nature of this sacredness has necessarily evolved through time. Uisneach is at the center of Ireland, it was a probable *omphalos* and an *Axis mundi* – a "navel" and a "cosmic axis" – and is considered by many medieval documents to be a mystical place, a place of transcendence, "above" and "outside" of the tangible world. This symbolic potency derives from a number of factors, prominently including its geographical situation, approximately at the center, slightly hanging over a vast plain that enables an occupant to see and be seen kilometers around: Uisneach is the "full-center", the *Mediolanon* of Ireland. Coupled with the large number of water sources and the fertility of the surrounding area, Uisneach earned its reputation as a primordial source of Irish waters.

The impressive *Ail na Mireann* undoubtedly played a great role in the hill's establishment as a place of transcendence and then power. The existence of the stone possibly may have led to the creation of the first – most likely funerary – site at an undetermined period of time. The first traces of settlement or consecration of the hill are usually said to date back to "at least 5,000 years". The megalithic tomb and the barrow sited on the two summits, *Saint Patrick's Bed* and the so-called burial mound of Lugh, could indeed date back to the Neolithic period and, as a consequence, predate the Celtic era. It must be noted, however, that the most recent archeological investigations focused mainly on *Lough Lugh* and Rathnew: further archeological studies of both the megalithic tomb and the barrow will hopefully back up this claim one day.

The study of *Lough Lugh*, a lake at the approximate geographical and perhaps symbolic center of the site, reveals an occupation of its surroundings at least since the late Irish Bronze Age.[1] The idea according to which the lake could have played the role of a ritual point of water is not confirmed. For Rathnew, the settlement is even more recent. The creation of the site could date back to the 3rd–5th centuries CE and the traces of feasting noted by archeological investigations vouch for the ritual significance of the place. Better still, the presence of ash beds confirms the likelihood of the lighting of large ritual fires. The idea that the "first phase" of Rathnew most likely corresponded to a sanctuary prevails. The sacredness of the place is only reinforced by the megalithic tomb and the tumulus at the two summits – the ancient *necropolis* of Uisneach. At that time, the value of the site appears to have been spiritual before anything, most likely sacerdotal in nature, and inspired by mythology: the necropolis of Uisneach arguably inspired the creation of its sanctuary.

This sacredness was exploited so as to establish power, be it political or religious: Uisneach was indeed a place, if not *the* place of "ritual procla-mation of sovereignty" in Ireland, which complemented Tara. As argued by Richard Kearney, it is indeed quite fitting to consider Uisneach as the *spiritual middle* of Ireland, which counterbalanced the *political center* of Tara. The purported will of Patrick to inscribe his power – along with that of the Christian religion and his monastery, Armagh – specifically on Uisneach was a 7th-century invention that is quite symptomatic of this exploitation. More generally speaking, it is with the lineage of the Kings of Uisneach and a fraction of the Uí Néill dynasty that this symbolic im-portance was the most prevailing and triumphant. Arguably, the pre-dominance of Tara to the detriment of Uisneach in Irish history and imagination followed the downfall of the Uí Néill and their "Kings of Uisneach" or was at least reinforced by the gradual collapse of the dynasty.

On Uisneach, a ringfort was built in lieu and place of the sanctuary of Rathnew, thereby appropriating its sacredness and inscribing itself in the symbolic and historical continuity. Most of the objects found there date to the 7th–11th centuries CE. That period corresponds to the pinnacle of the influence of the southern Uí Néill and it is conceivable to attribute the construction, then use of the fort to the dynasty. The southern Uí Néill considered the hill as a "place of power" at the center of Ireland: Uisneach may have been a royal residence or, to be more cautious, a royal site; the sacred dimension of the place was probably still prevalent at that time and members of the sacerdotal class may have maintained close connections with Rathnew, either by living there in the long term or using it as part of social or ritual manifestations. If this hypothesis is confirmed, the medieval sacerdotal class, heirs to the druidic traditions, arguably played the role of "keepers of the place".

In the 12th century, the reputation of Uisneach had extended beyond Ireland, as demonstrated for example by the links connecting Stonehenge to Uisneach. The fact that the Irish hill was indirectly presented as the ancestor of Stonehenge stands as vivid evidence of its rising – although still limited – renown abroad. Simultaneously, it seems that this period saw a relative neglect for the site in Ireland: the objects found in the ringfort of Rathnew that are dated to the 11th to 13th centuries are scarce. This correlates broadly with the decline in influence of the Uí Néill as early as the 10th century and the end of the lineage of the Kings of Uisneach from the 12th century onward: it must be remembered that Brian Boru was said to have "harried Mide and went to Uisneach" in 988, at a time where the Uí Néill were the rulers of the place. The attack of Boru on Uisneach weakened and even probably ended the dynastic hegemony of the Uí Néill. The hill was no longer a "place of power", at least temporarily. We know that "Ushnagh's castle", which must be interpreted as the fort of Rathnew, was in ruins in the 16th century, which gives a rather precise idea of the period of occupancy.

Between the 12th and 16th centuries, history turned into myth: it is at this time that the largest amount of documents, mainly inspired by older mythological texts, mention the hill. The place of Uisneach in ancient Irish mythology is, in any event, clearly established: according to tradition, the hill stood at the very center of Mide, the mythological province of the center; the mythical druid Midhe supposedly lit the first fire of Ireland on its summit; the Fir Bold divided the island from Uisneach; the Dagda, master of time, seasons and druids had its "house" on the hill; Lugh, the greatest god of the insular Celtic pantheon, drowned in the lake near its summit; the god was killed by three brothers who were husbands to a triple goddess representing Ireland; the eastern summit of Uisneach, a few dozen meters from the mythological killing ground, was believed to be his resting place; Balor, the grand-father of Lugh, had given his name to the "hill of Balar"; Dian Cécht, the god of healing, was said to have created three lakes from its top; the fire of Delbáeth had generated five streams and Uisneach was presented as the primordial source of Irish waters; according to several authors from the Middle Ages, its stone(s) was/were supposed to possess prophylactic and medical virtues when heated by fire, dipped in water and associated with herbs; the hill was considered as one of the gates to the *sídh*, a place where deities and characters from the Otherworld would meet, including Connla the Red and Ériu; precisely, Ériu, the personification of Ireland, supposedly gave her name to Éire because she lived on the central hill and granted power over Ireland to Men from Uisneach.

Year after year, century after century, the myths nurtured the sacredness of the place. Some of them were even probably consubstantial to its sacred nature. While most of the texts were transcribed in the Middle Ages, it must be remembered that they reflect much older traditions. The Christian monasteries diffused beliefs connected to Uisneach from "time immemorial". Some of those myths – although it is impossible to tell which ones – were likely contemporary to the establishment of the first sanctuary of Rathnew and existed originally to justify the sacredness of the hill. The best candidates are perhaps the myths uniting the themes of fire, water, prophylaxis, fecundity and sovereignty, all placed in a specific calendar context, that of *Bealtaine*.

Along these same lines and consonant with the idea of "diffusion", it is in the 17th century that the concept of an assembly of *Bealtaine* on Uisneach, *Mórdháil Uisnigh*, was popularized by Keating. The historical reality of *Mórdháil Uisnigh* remains unresolved. Although unprovable, the idea of an Assembly on Uisneach at the time of *Bealtaine* is compatible with what is known of this time and this place. However, Keating could as easily have been inspired by traditions still fashionable at his time and a number of medieval texts mentioning other ritual assemblies: he therefore could have fabricated a "convention of Uisneach" using those elements so as to adjust the symbolism of the hill with the traditions in effect at the time of his *History of Ireland* to make the place an integral part of his epoch.

The mentions of the hypothetical god "Bel" notoriously do not hold water. However, the archaeological findings suggest that one or several large fires were actually lit on Uisneach, maybe as early as the time of the sanctuary of Rathnew. It is tempting, though not provable, to believe that they were lit in connection with the festival of *Bealtaine* and its trail of traditions, all stemming back to ancient myths and beliefs. Nothing clearly confirms the existence of past human sacrifices. Animal sacrifices, on the other hand, seem to have been a reality at one moment of the history of Uisneach or another – perhaps at least at the time of the sanctuary, possibly that of the ringfort of Rathnew. Once again, it is conceivable that those sacrifices were made – and those large fires were lit – for *Bealtaine*. Conversely, the fact that this all happened in the context of a hypothetical "great assembly" cannot be confirmed.

The comparison with other allegedly Celtic traditions, other central points, other assembly or judgment places proved partially fruitful. Uisneach, along with *Ail na Mireann*, the stone of division – or perhaps the "rock of judgment" – may have found its counterpart in other Celtic, or perhaps more broadly speaking Indo-Europeans traditions. Arguably, the Indo-European concept of being crowned at "the center of the four cardinal points" is a "total" coronation that unites the three Dumezilian functions. In the case of Uisneach, it has been shown that this archetype of symbolic centralization is as much political and religious as it is connected to the "productive" class. More importantly, a coronation at the center of the four cardinal points – at the center of the mythical provinces of Ireland – amounts to a spiritual, transcendent declaration of sovereignty: it takes place at the heart of both the tangible and otherworldly realms. Symbolically speaking, Uisneach was supposed to be both "above" and "out of this world": it was the epitome of the *juste milieu*, the "just midpoint".

It was conjectured that Uisneach could have been, at one time in its history, mainly dedicated to the sacerdotal function. The members of the sacerdotal class that had inherited the druidic tradition may have lived or performed their tasks in Rathnew as keepers of the place. They were perhaps visited on a more or less regular basis by rulers for periodic ritual assemblies, possibly in connection with the festival of *Bealtaine*. Whereas Tara could have been the main seat of royal power, Uisneach possibly was, at some point of history, its sacerdotal, religious and symbolic counterpart. The two hills were the two faces of the same coin or, in the wording of the 14th–15th-century *Settling of the Manor of Tara*, "the two kidneys in a beast". The idea is partially confirmed by archaeological investigations. The

symbolic potency of Uisneach could rely on the memory of putative ancestors or deities that were buried or commemorated on the hill – for instance Lugh on the eastern summit and possibly Ériu. Since *Bealtaine*
marked the moment of the year when the gates between the world of the
living and the *sídh* were said to open, the connection uniting the hill to the
month of May appears to be transparent.

For ancient populations, the veneration of the hill was an echo of the
"cosmic cycle", the temporal sequence of divine origin. Uisneach was *out of*
this world and was to be celebrated at a moment that was *out of time*. A
fraction of early Irish literature indicates that Uisneach played the role of a
spatial mediator between two worlds and was venerated in connection with
a *temporal* connector between those two worlds, i.e. *Bealtaine*. It therefore
stood as a form of mediation between the living and the dead – a spatio-
temporal hyphen.

The significance of Uisneach probably went beyond that of a potential
"cult of the center". The hill may have functioned as an imagined median
point, a balancing boundary, a *juste milieu* – the acknowledgment "of a
necessary equilibrium between two poles, two realities that oppose and
complete each other" as explained by Laurent and Tréguer.[2] In other
words, it is possible that Uisneach played the symbolic role of a vertical
mediator between the world of the living and that of the dead. This inherent
symbolism is probably best described as a liminal zone (and time) of
mediation, an allegorical passageway between real and imaginary, between
the realm of humans and that of the *sídh*: the sacred hill *was* the Irish
Medionemeton. The guarantors and representatives of this "in-between"
might have been the druids and the ensuing sacerdotal class, mediators *on*
the hill of the just midpoint *at* the just midpoint of the year, *Bealtaine*.

This symbolic richness was exploited repeatedly by some redactors and
transcribers from the Middle Ages and began to peter out and almost
completely disappear after the fall of the dynasty of the Kings of Uisneach.
The ruin of the ringfort of Uisneach was concomitant with the symbolic
ruin of Uisneach. The local folklore of the 18th, 19th and 20th centuries
only remembered the hill as a place of passage between two worlds: the
purifying fires were missing, so were the assemblies, the social gatherings
and the collective rituals, with the notable exception of the veneration of
St. Brigid's Well at the foot of the hill. This disaffection was due to a range
of factors: the relative proximity with Dublin and, as a result, the overwhelming English and British influence, the Great Famine, the power of
both local and national clergies throughout the centuries. To the moribund
"power" of the Uí Néill succeeded an aggregation of forces that were for
the most part external to the Gaelic world. Those forces relegated the hill of
Uisneach to the footnotes of history for reasons both of ideological burn-
ishing and simple palimpsestual overlay.

It took no less than the *Gaelic Revival* to have Uisneach – partially and
very gradually – regain its position. The intellectual and artistic movement

breathed new life into the place, although the original traditions were often intertwined with a romanticized conception of the past and were heavily influenced by the political agendas of its proponents. This revival, however, did not succeed in completely rescuing Uisneach from oblivion: the references to the hill remained peripheral at best, perhaps with the noteworthy exception of James Woods' *Annals of Westmeath*. The protagonists of the *Gaelic Revival* most often laid the emphasis on other places, first and foremost Tara, a hill which is more remarkable in the sense that it is perhaps more impressive-looking or easier to trace down in Irish history.

The real turning-point took place well after the *Gaelic Revival* – and actually well after Irish independence. The roles of Richard Kearney and Mark Patrick Hederman as editors of *The Crane Bag* and the renewed emphasis on the concept of a Fifth Province in the 1970s and 1980s undoubtedly played a pivotal role – not least because their work as "mediators of knowledge" later inspired Mary Robinson in the writing of her 1990 inaugural speech in Dublin Castle.

The decline of the Irish Catholic Church in the late 20th and early 21st centuries was also one of the catalysts of the real revival of Uisneach. Secularization has been a fairly widespread tendency in large portions of the Western world, especially Western and Northern Europe. It proved all the more true in 21st-century Ireland, notably because of the various scandals engulfing the Catholic Church since the 1980s and 1990s. This loss of power had two major consequences: a defiance toward Christianity and its representatives led a number of Irish people to actively seek a new form of spirituality, one that would be in keeping with their expectations and values. In parallel, the loss of power of the Church enabled some trends and sympathies to show themselves in broad daylight and grow unhampered, with no fear of potential censure. Whereas Irish Neo-Pagans were ostracized and had to keep a low profile for decades, their new faith – steeped in "Celticism" and romantic influences – could now emerge.

The contemporary gathering of Uisneach is far from being either the continuation or a historical re-enactment of an ancient Irish celebration: it is perhaps precisely for that very reason that it is also worth studying. To the putative Celtic-Irish prophylactic fires succeeded a joyful bonfire – a "contemporary" bonfire in many respects. Obviously, the new festival is not about fearing the agro-pastoral, divine cycle of the year and climatic variations. Just as evidently, the Irish people of the 2010s and early 2020s no longer feel compelled to drive their cattle between two fires to protect them from witches and fairies; they also do not pay their taxes on a hill and they would rather settle their disputes in courts than around a large boulder. Times have changed and, along with them, mindsets, customs, traditions, the structure of society and spiritual aspirations as a whole.

At the dawn of the 21st century, a new Irish society is on the rise. It is arguably more ecumenical and inclusive as it freed itself from a number of political and religious constraints that had left profound detrimental marks in its history: the *Fire Festival* of Uisneach stands as striking evidence of this evolution. At the beginning of the month of May, people dress as fairies, witches, demons or warriors; they dance around a joyful bonfire; they chant reconstructed Pagan prayers and litanies etc. It is a strictly speaking a *popular* event: the people, as opposed to elites, occupies the central place. By celebrating the festival of *Bealtaine* on the hill, the people proclaim their own sovereignty: to that extent, Uisneach still is today an outstanding political, spiritual and religious driving force.

* * *

The history of Uisneach does not lack consistency. Successively necropolis, sanctuary, fort then ruins, forgotten during the centuries of the English and British hegemony then flagship of the 20th-century Celtic/Gaelic revivals and concretization of a form of Pagan rebirth, the hill never ceased to be a significant piece of the history of Ireland and, to some extent, the evolution of Western societies. Today, the contemporary *Fire Festival* of Uisneach is the product of its time.

It can therefore be argued that "sacred Uisneach" was and is a place of remembrance and commemoration as much as a place of power. The memory of the mythologized ancestors granted the ancient sanctuary of Rathnew its spiritual, then political power. Today, the memory of the Celtic and Gaelic past of Ireland nurtures its symbolic and political significance as well as fosters its (still modest) commercial impact. While it was fundamentally connected to the sacerdotal and royal worlds in ancient then medieval Ireland, Uisneach is renewing itself in the expression of power by people, who play at attempting to re-enact the past. Some could argue that the hill had implications over the three Indo-European "classes" (i.e. the clergy, warriors and farmers). To that extent, Uisneach could be defined as trifunctional and *total* in its sacredness: the fact that the myths attached to Uisneach seemed inherently connected with threefold characters and triplism in general is but another proof of this total and trifunctional essence.

In May 2017, this Irish people were accompanied in their allegorical proclamation of sovereignty by their symbolic leader, Michael D. Higgins, whose participation must be interpreted through this reading grid. Although it was meant to perpetuate the ancestral tradition of the Irish elite declaring their power, his gesture is not as anachronistic as may seem at first glance. On that night, Michael D. Higgins followed the path laid out by Mary Robinson and her inaugural speech. More importantly, he played a role himself, that of a representational leader of the people, a president of Ireland: by lighting the fire of Uisneach, he aligned with the historical continuity of the island. This noteworthy symbolic – and political – move asserted the coherence of the country, possibly the island as a whole: Ireland appeared federated around its factual and spiritual center. Perhaps even more significantly, the unity of mankind in its entirety was celebrated precisely at a point of mediation, Uisneach.

By attempting to revive its past, Ireland is reinventing itself in the present tense: the gesture of Michael D. Higgins verges on a "historical re-enactment" more than any other, precisely because it must be interpreted as an archetype of mediation, a theme which is so fundamentally connected to the hill of the *just midpoint*.

For lack of *forging authenticity*, Uisneach is actually a means of creativity – artistic, symbolic, spiritual but also philosophical and inherently connected to Irishness. On 6 May 2017, the president ignited the heart of the island. That very night, on Uisneach, at *Bealtaine*, the mythical past of Ireland fleetingly united with its present. It was meant to make history – or recreate it altogether.

Notes

1 See Annex IV.
2 Laurent, Donatien & Tréguer, Michel. 1997. *La Nuit Celtique*. Rennes: Terre de Brume Editions, Presses Universitaires de Rennes, 126.

Annexes

Annex I Photographs

All photographs by F. Armao unless mentioned otherwise.

Figure 1 Overview of Uisneach (May 2017).

Figure 2 Aerial view of *Lough Lugh* and preparations for the *Fire Festival* (May 2017).

Figure 3 Entrance to the site (May 2017).

Figure 4 Visitor Center of Uisneach (April 2019).
Taken by and published on the official Twitter account of Uisneach, @uisneachfire.
Credit: www.uisneach.ie.

Figure 5 Ail na Mireann (May 2017).

Figure 6 Ail na Mireann (May 2019).

Figure 7 Gathering at *Ail na Mireann* (May 2017).

Figure 8 Priestess at *Ail na Mireann* (May 2017).

Figure 9 Gathering near *Lough Lugh* (May 2019).

Figure 10 Gathering near *Lough Lugh* (May 2019).

Figure 11 "Healing sessions" (May 2019).

Figure 12 Artwork: winged woman (Mórrigan?) (May 2019).

Figure 13 Artwork: deity and cosmic wheel (May 2017).

Figure 14 The Green Man of Uisneach (May 2017).

Figure 15 Costume: horned demon/witch (May 2017).

Figure 16 Costume: *Green Man and snake* (May 2019).

Figure 17 Costume: warrior (May 2019).

Figure 18 Costume: women wearing flower crowns (May 2019).

Figure 19 Visitors (May 2019).

Figure 20 Visitors on their way to the Catstone (May 2019).

Figure 21 Bealtaine fire ceremony site: hut (May 2017).

Figure 22 Bealtaine fire ceremony site: Michael D. Higgins kindling the fire.
Credit: www.uisneach.ie and Verona McQuaid (6 May 2017).

Figure 23 Bealtaine fire ceremony site: crowd (May 2019).

Figure 24 Bealtaine fire ceremony site: fire (May 2019).

Figure 25 Bealtaine fire ceremony site: fire (May 2017).

Figure 26 Bealtaine fire ceremony site: fire (May 2019).

Figure 27 Uisneach Inn (May 2017).

Annex II Maps and illustrations

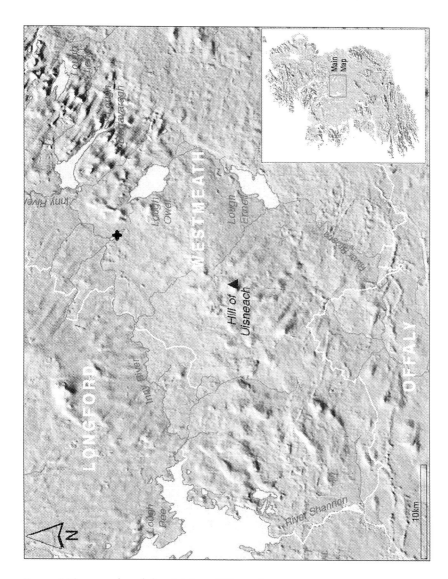

Figure 1 Topography of the vicinity of Uisneach.

Credit: © Copyright The Discovery Programme.
"Reflections on a Lake", *op. cit.*, 114. *Lough Iron* is here noted by a +.

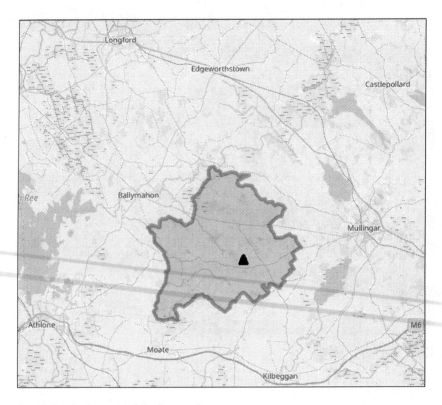

Figure 2 The barony of Rathconrath.

Credit: http://townlands.ie. © OpenStreetMap contributors.
See https://www.openstreetmap.org/copyright

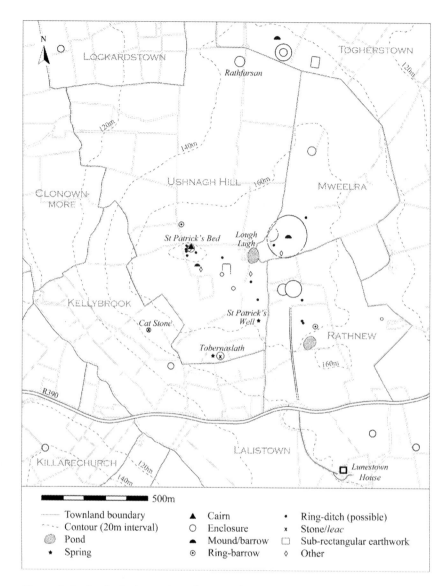

Figure 3 Archeological complex of Uisneach.

Credit: Roseanne Schot.
"From Cult Centre to Royal Centre: Monuments", *op. cit.*, fig. 5.2 and "Reflections on a Lake", *op. cit.*, 115.

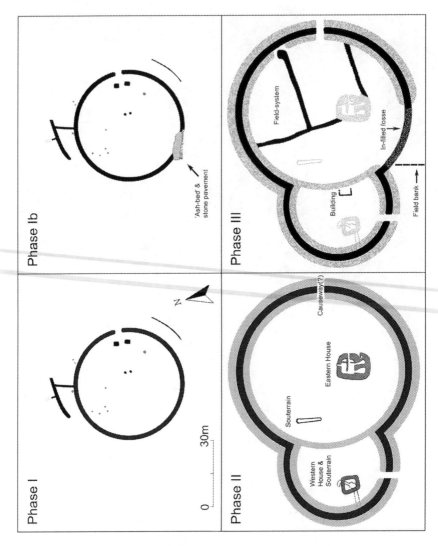

Figure 4 Schematic diagram of the principal structural phrases at Rathnew.

Credit: Roseanne Schot.
"Uisneach Midi", *op. cit.*, 50. Phases I and Ib correspond to what is referred to in this volume as the "sanctuary of Uisneach", Phases II and III to the ringfort of Rathnew.

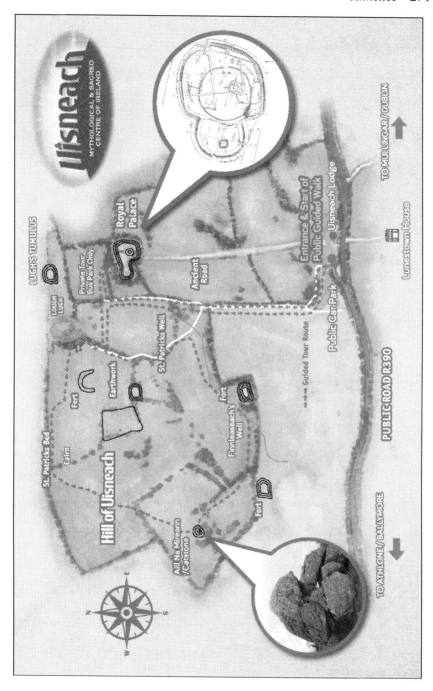

Figure 5 Map of the site made by the Visitor Center of Uisneach.

On the right, a sketch of Rathnew according to Macalister and Praeger.
Credit: Credit: www.uisneach.ie.

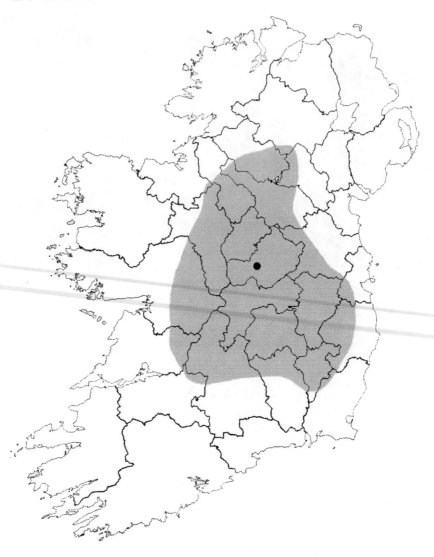

Figure 6 Range of country commanded from the hill of Uisneach.

Source: "Report on the Excavation of Uisneach", *op. cit.*, 70.

Annex III E-mails

General e-mail sent by the organizers of the celebration of Uisneach as a preamble to the festival of 2017. Credit: Credit: www.uisneach.ie.

* * *

Information for Bealtaine Fire Ceremony - May 6th 2017

We look forward to welcoming you to the Bealtaine Fire ceremony on May 6th at the hill of Uisneach. This years event, like last year is focused on the lighting of the Bealtine fire.

Here are some pointers to make the event as safe & enjoyable as possible for everyone.....

- The event starts at 7pm - You may arrive from 5pm to park.
- The event finishes at 10.30pm - There is NO CAMPING on site.
- There is no charge but adults are asked to leave a donation -To help defray costs of this not for profit community event...we suggest a minimum of €10 per person...
- You must bring a good quality flash-lamp/torch.(not cell phone torch)
- There will be a selection of food & drinks available to purchase on site
- You are advised to "dress for the weather" with appropriate rainwear/ footwear - Please note that it does get cold after sunset
- We ask that you follow the instructions of our volunteer stewards/ Parking stewards.
- Mullingar is our nearest town if you wish to book a Hotel/B&B - Trip Advisor has an excellent list of available accommodation.
- There is no public transport to/from Mullingar so we suggest a taxi.
- There are guided tours on the Fri 5th & Sunday 7th at 1pm from the main entrance.
- Children are welcome but **must** be accompanied by an adult.
- Dogs are not permitted on/off a leash (We are on a working farm)
- The event will be filmed, photographed & may be publicly broadcast -. If this is a problem for you please let us know.
- Commercial photographers **must contact us in advance** -

You may contact us at **info@uisneach.ie** or call +353 87 7189550
For regular updates please be sure to sign up to our mailing list on **www.uisneach.ie**

Figure 1 E-mail, Uisneach 2017.

2a. E-mail, Uisneach 2019

General e-mail sent by the organizers of the celebration of Uisneach as a preamble to the festival of 2019. Credit: www.uisneach.ie.

***

A Message from Uisneach:

> Below, Please find, at the bottom of this email, our programme for Sunday 5th May @ Uisneach. We are also including a site-map on our Facebook page/Twitter feed for your information.

You will also read some important safety information -

Information for Bealtaine Fire Ceremony - Sunday May 5th 2019.

We look forward to welcoming you to the Bealtaine Fire Celebration on **Sunday**May 5th at the Hill of Uisneach. Postcode - N91WNW2 (works great in SatNav/Google Maps)

Here are some tips to make the event as safe & enjoyable as possible for everyone ... ..

Temperatures are expected to be very low on the night - Please dress well for the weather & make sure that children have adequate layers!

- The event starts at 5pm - You may arrive from 4pm to park.
- You must arrive before 9.00pm –
- The event finishes at 11.30pm - There is NO CAMPING on site.
- Please print out your tickets or save the QR code to your smartphone
- wallet & have them ready as you approach the entrance. Screenshots are not recommended - The Eventbrite App works best.
- There will be NO TICKETS for sale on the day at the gate.
- We will have transport up & down the hill for people with lesser mobility.
- You must bring a good quality flash-lamp/torch.(not cell phone torch)
- There will be a selection of food & drinks available to purchase on
- site.
- There will be no bar on site- You may BYO but please bring empties
- home with you. There is NO GLASS allowed on-site. This is a community, family friendly event - We ask everyone to act responsibly.
- We ask everyone to bring their recycling/rubbish home with them.
- You are advised to "dress for the weather" with appropriate rainwear/
- footwear - Please note that it does get cold after sunset. Temps are due to be low on the evening of the 5th - Wrap up warm!!

- We ask that you follow the instructions of our volunteer Stewards/Fire stewards/ Parking stewards.
- There is no public transport to/from Mullingar/Athlone so we suggest a taxi.
- There is a guided tour on Monday 6th @ 1pm sharp –
- If you have mobility issues please get in touch with us by email in advance - tours@uisneach.ie.
- Children are welcome(ticketed) but must be accompanied & supervised at all times by a ticket-holding adult.
- Dogs are not permitted on/off a leash (We are within a working farm)
- Please excercise patience in relation to parking in advance and leaving in an orderly manner, following security/steward instruction.

*Please do not walk to the site or walk home afterwards. Taxi drop off/ collection will be in operation. Please avail of this service and do not walk home.

*Please do not park on public road verges, private driveways around the external perimeter of the event site. Vehicles will be towed. Parking only in designated event car parks.

Our event team, most of whom are voluntary have worked tirelessly to create and deliver this event. We ask for your support and understanding in keeping this special and unique event family friendly. The event is produced in good faith and we ask for good faith in return.The event will be filmed, photographed & may be publicly broadcast -

- If this is a problem for you please let us know in advance.
- Commercial photographers must contact us in advance -
- You are invited to bring a small piece of wood from your locality -
- There will be a collection point near the main fire - These will be added to the Bealtaine Fire -
- You may contact us at info@uisneach.ie or call +353 87 7189550 (No Texts please)
- Below please find some important safety information -
- These terms and conditions apply between you, the patron of Uisneach & The Bealtaine Celebrations (the "festival")
- Please read these terms and conditions very carefully, as they affect your legal rights. Your agreement to comply with and be bound by these terms and conditions is deemed to occur upon purchase of tickets. If you do not agree to be bound by these terms and conditions, you should not purchase tickets. In these terms and conditions "staff" means any individuals attending the festival who is either (a) employed acting in the course of their employment or (b) engaged as a consultant or otherwise providing services to Uisneach Bealtaine Celebrations and accessing the site in connection with the provision of such services.

- "You", "attendee", "the public" or "patron" means any individuals at-tending the festival and who are not staff, except staff who are off-duty.
· "Kids" means any individuals attending the festival who are aged 12 or under. "Teens" means any individuals attending the festival who are aged 13 to 17. "Children" means Kids and Teens collectively.
- "Site" means the grounds upon which the festival occupies.

Security

- You may be body and/or bag searched at the entrances. Persons suspected of carrying items that may be used in an offensive or dangerous manner, or carrying out illegal activities onsite may be searched. Any person who refuses to be searched by a steward or other person acting on the behalf of the Promoter will be refused admission or ejected from site.
- Entry to the premises will be refused to any person who appears to be intoxicated, acting in a threatening or violent manner. Anyone caught burning toxic materials, creating fires, throwing gas canisters or aerosols onto fires, throwing missiles or taking part in anti social behaviour that en- dangers other attendees will be evicted from site.
- Security staff will be patrolling throughout the event. They are there to help and are also watching for suspicious behaviour. There is also CCTV that is monitored

  - Please contact event staff or security if you need any assistance.

Children

- Uisneach Bealtaine Celebrations is a festival for the whole family so patrons are reminded that children will be present in all public areas at all times.

  - Children who are attending the festival must be accompanied by a parent or guardian aged 18 or over at all times It is therefore paramount that all children are supervised at all times and any children found to be unsupervised, or misbehaving could be asked to leave the festival along with their parents or guardians. Please note that we will not tolerate the consumption of alcohol by persons under 18 years of age.
  - If a child is found, please notify the nearest steward immediately who will radio the Control Centre. A steward will then go to the location of the lost child. A parent who has lost a child should follow the same procedure, making contact with nearest steward
  - We advise that all parents write their mobile numbers on a child's wristband which is located at the main gate.

- Always hold hands or carry your children through busy areas
- Educate your children on what to do if they get separated from you. Advise them to stay where they are and not to move or go with anyone until a Garda or Steward approaches them. They should indicate their phone number to the Garda or Steward.

Fire and Safety

- Anyone involved with starting a fire or throwing anything onto a fire will be evicted from site.
- The event is outdoors. You are strongly advised to bring appropriate clothing and footwear to protect against inclement weather.
  - Sleeping or camping in vehicles in the car parks is not permitted.
  - Please do not climb on any trees onsite. It is dangerous and may damage the tree.
  - No entry to any of the lakes or ponds
  - Uisneach Bealtaine Celebrations takes place on uneven land with stone track ways.. Whilst we take every effort to ensure that suitable walkways are available there will be some areas where care should be taken due to uneven ground conditions. Take care, especially at night and during periods of adverse weather. Strong shoes for walking are a good idea – as is a torch after dark.

Prohibited Items:

- Aerosols over 250 ml, air horns & megaphones, gas canisters of any size (including nitrous oxide), any items which may reasonably be considered for use as a weapon
- Clothing with discriminating and/or provocative texts
- It is prohibited to distribute flyers or hang posters during the festival
- Illegal substances
- Large or framed backpacks
- Glass containers of ANY kind
- Skateboards, scooters, or personal motorized vehicles
- Bicycles inside Festival grounds
- Fireworks and explosives
- Instruments and laser pointers
- Selfie sticks
- Spray paint
- Tents
- Pets (Except animals that assist people with disabilities).

- No illegal vending is permitted (no unauthorised or unlicensed vendors allowed)
- Drones - Strictly NO DRONES to be flown onsite.

Leave No Trace

When the festival is over it's important to take home everything you brought with you, or dispose of items you do not want in the correct way.

Damage/Losses

- The promoter is unable to accept any liability for personal or property damages, loss- es (including confiscations) or injuries sustained at this event -. Any personal property brought to the event is at your own risk.
- We may prosecute you if you cause damage to the site, or infrastructure, or cause harm to any other person onsite.

Programme

MUSIC

> 5pm–6pm Ragairí Drummers
> 5.30pm Mullingar Town Band
> 6pm: Touch the earth (Lake Stage)
> 6.30pm Harpist & Singer (Lake Stage)
> 7pm: The Fox Family (Lake Stage)
> 7pm–8pm Midlands Uilleann Pipers (Tearoom)
> 8pm: Westmeath Ceomhltas Fleadh music group
> 9pm: KuKu Drummers (Fire Arena)
> 9.10pm: Fire Dance Group (Fire Arena)
> 9.15pm: Procession Horses (Fire Road)
> 9.20pm: Procession (Fire Road)
> 9.30pm–9.45pm: Lighting of Bealtaine Fire (Fire Arena)
> 10pm: Fire Dancers (Fire Arena)
> 10pm: Fire Dancers (Fire Arena)
> 10.30pm: Alp Luchra (Lake Stage)
> 11.30pm: Close.

HOLISTIC AREA

Yoga Tent 1
> 5.30–6.15 Kundalini Yoga with Gerard O'Connor
> 6.30–7.15 Shamanic Journeying & Drumming with Anna Coote
> 7.30 to 8.15 Kundalini Mantra Meditation with Olive McDonagh
> 8.30 to 9 Sound Bath Healing with Melanie Walsh

Yoga 2
   5.30 to 6 Rainbow Yoga for Kids with Caro Bridie
   6.15 to 6.45 Radiant Child Yoga with Lily Ennis
   7 to 7.30 Parent & Child Meditation with Amanda Connell
   7.45 to 8.15 Vinyasa Flow for Adults with Kim Darby

HERITAGE TENT

   6.15pm Simon Tuite (Monumental Ireland) Talk on Dún Aillne & royal
      sites
   7pm - Talk by Dan Curley, Rathcroughan
   7.30 - Talk by Damien Houlahan, Emain Macha, Armagh
   8.00pm - Talk by Jack Roberts
   8.30pm - Talk by Anthony Murphy

ARTS & CRAFTS

We have various pieces of art dotted around the site & also some amazing local craft displays & stalls

We encourage you to speak with the artists/crafts people & artisans who are showcasing their skills!

2b. E-mail, Uisneach 2020

General e-mail sent by the organizers of the celebration of Uisneach following the Covid-19 crisis of 2020. Credit: www.uisneach.ie.

***

Dear Friends of Uisneach,
   We hope this mail finds you and yours well. We are navigating very strange times but together-apart, our spirits will not be broken.
   At the moment given the circumstances, we remain completely closed until we get the go ahead to reopen to the public. We are endeavouring to bring you as much from the Hill as we possibly can. We understand just how important Uisneach is to many of us and we miss not being able to engage with this sacred space.
   Bealtaine is a very special time for all of us, so there will be a fire. It will be with only the Keeper of the Hill, David Clarke present and his immediate family. We request that no attempts are made to visit the Hill whatsoever.
   We would love if you could join us on our Facebook platform where the Bealtaine fire will be lit and streamed live. The fire will take place at 21:21 GMT on 5th May, where together we can unite in this ancient tradition, albeit in a virtual space, in welcoming-in the Summer.

Let us take a moment on 5th May to reflect on recent months and think of those that may have lost loved ones, those affected by or those that are suffering with Covid-19. A moment too for those who have given their lives to save others in this strange and sometimes sad time of uncertainty. This will be a moment for many of us to reflect and to heal, together in support of one another.

If you intend to have your own token Bealtaine fire lit, we would love to see you share it onto our page after the Uisneach fire is lit. We will also make an animation available to share on all social media platforms in case it's not feasible for you to light a token fire.

You will all be in our thoughts, blessings and well wishes when the Bealtaine Fire is lit and the flames dance in the skies.

We wish each and everyone of you a warming and heartfelt 'Lá fheile Bealtaine' and look forward to welcoming you all back onto the Hill of Uisneach soon.

Blessings,

Uisneach

3. E-mail: Patsy Preston

E-mail sent to F.A., extract (12 Feb. 2018).

* * *

"There is such a growing awareness of, and interest in diverse Spiritual practice these past few years, with a particular focus on Pagan practice. This search for an authentic connection with Earth or Nature based Spirituality, stems in many ways, I feel, from general dis-satisfaction with, not just the larger, established religions, but also an awareness of the damage mankind are doing to our home planet, An ecologically minded, Spiritual path, attempting to re-create balance, by looking at our indigenous heritage, here on the Western Seaboard of Europe. Of course, unlike other indigenous cultures, we here do not have an unbroken tradition, and so a certain amount of guesswork is involved in forging this authentic connection. There is much diversity within the Pagan community, many different groups who perhaps work in different ways, but with broadly similar ethos. www.paganfederationireland.com is a good place to start.

I have been going to Uisneach on my own personal Spiritual journey for over 30 years now and have built a strong connection there on an energetic level. Personally, I was initiated as a Druid around 25 years ago, and have followed this path, as a way of life since. This involves celebrating and marking the Celtic Wheel of the Year and honouring the Divinity within the Land and all of Nature. Often I will do this alone but also within a circle or Grove. The Owl Grove is a group I often join in circle with, were featured in this production, looking at ancient Irish Spiritual practice, you may find it of interest. http://tilefilms.ie/productions/sacred-sites-ireland/ So, back to Uisneach. I have been Artistic Director of the Uisneach Bealtaine Fire Festival since its inception around 10 years ago. Although I was wary initially, of such a large gathering at such a sacred site, I realised that a gathering such as this is just what would have happened in times past. From small beginnings, the festival quickly grew and was in danger of becoming just one more Music and Arts Festival, so we have pulled it right back, to the core element, of Lighting the Bealtaine Fire and joining with the community to celebrate the arrival of summer.

We have had Karen and John from http://www.slianchroi.ie involved in the procession fro[m] the beginning. While the procession is in effect a spectacular performance, it does have a genuine Spiritual aspect.

I have personal tended to shy away from becoming involved in being in the public focus and work more behind the scenes, working on sculptural art and creating the visual language of the event ... all within a very limited budget. However, last year I was asked to co-ordinate the celebration and ritual to raise the Devine Feminine energy at the Catstone, and bring this to meet the main procession. Our main procession has always walked from the Palace to the top of the Hill and, although containing many women, always seems to feel more Masculine in nature. The symbolism we were working with was bringing the Spear of Lugh, to meet the Divine Cauldron of the Goddess Ériu and join in the central fire, impregnating the land and awakening Ériu's Fire Eye, so the Goddess may survey the land in a physical context through her people. These elements were decided on by a working group, co-ordinating the performance with our procession people LUXe, Sli na Croi, myself and several others connected with the hill. It was such an honour to have Uachtarán na hÉireann, Michael D. Higgins actually light the fire. Amazing!

It has always been one of my main objectives that the gathering at Uisneach should be inclusive and not just a Pagan celebration. It is about bringing people together, and this was how I approached the women's circle. A group of people ... perhaps you could consider them guardians of the Hill spent time in meditation at the Catstone to ask for ways we could honour the Goddess in our ceremony.

The Priestess' chosen for each of the Directions were women who are practicing Pagan Priestess,' but not from one particular group. The Element carriers brought elements from around the country to meet at the ceremony. We had decided for practical reasons to have around 100 women, I asked the groups associated with the hill to offer suggestions of who to invite and made sure to invite women from many paths. However it was important that everyone would be actively involved in the ceremony and many would have been involved in healing, or working with energy in some way. I decided not to have the public present at the ceremony, as I wanted everyone to participate fully and not feel they were on 'show' for this important part of the day. The women I invited, I asked each to invite 3 or 4 more, to spread the net wide, so to speak. The ceremony itself followed a fairly standard form for gathering in circle and each of the celebrants was open to add their piece without censure. We had a healing voice session and everyone was blessed with water by some women who have been working with the waters for healing for some years.

So as you can see, it was not one group, but a coming together of like minded souls, to raise the Devine Feminine Energy on Uisneach. So although there would have been a range of 'Spiritual affiliations' there was a joint Spiritual connection, focused on healing and empowering.

We asked everyone to wear white mainly to give visual cohesion to the ceremony and performance. In the dark and by the fire-light this looked incredible and helped differentiate those involved in the ceremony from the public.

We have not decided yet exactly what will happen this year, but I am certainly looking forward to gathering on Uisneach again. Will you be joining us this year.? The Uisneach Fire Festival will be on May 5th, which it the astronomically aligned date for Bealtaine."

Annex IV Chronology

Traditional Periodization of Irish Prehistory

Early Mesolithic	7000–5500 BCE
Later Mesolithic	5500–4000 BCE
Neolithic	4000–2400 BCE
Copper Age	2400–2200 BCE
Early Bronze Age	2200–1500 BCE
Middle Bronze Age	1500–1000 BCE
Late Bronze Age	1000–600 BCE
Iron Age	600 BCE–400 CE

From John Waddell, *The Prehistoric Archeology of Ireland*, *op. cit.*, 4.

Tentative Chronology of Uisneach

The asterisks indicate that the date or the historical reality of the elements mentioned are not clearly established.

Late Glacial Period: *Lough Lugh* formed.

*Neolithic-early Bronze Age: constructions on both summits of Uisneach (later referred to as *Saint Patrick's Bed* and burial mound respectively)

3rd–5th centuries CE: creation of the sanctuary of Uisneach (or Rathnew I).

*End of 4th century CE: Niall/Néill Nóigiallach (Niall "the holder of the Nine Hostages"), ancestor of the Uí Néill dynasty.

*480: Conall, son of Néill, first King of Uisneach.

*514: Fiachu, King of Uisneach.

*565: Diarmait, leader of the southern Uí Néill becomes King of Uisneach.

*7th century: ringfort of Uisneach (or Rathnew II) built around the sanctuary. First possible mention of an assembly at Uisneach (*The Cause of Mongán's Frenzy*, 7th-9th c., only transcribed in the 12th c.).

7th–11th centuries: numerous objects from that period, suggesting an intensive occupation of the site. Transformation of the ringfort (or Rathnew III). Probable use by the southern Uí Néill as a place of power.

*988: Brian Boru gathers a fleet on *Lough Ree* and attacks Uisneach. Probable end of the dynastic and symbolic hegemony of the southern Uí Néill on Uisneach.

*11th century: *Lough Lugh* possibly dug out.

11th–13th centuries: progressive desertion of the site.

*1111: "Great Synod of Uisneach".

*1135: Peace conference at Avall Keherny.

*1141: Peace on Uisneach between King of Connacht and King of Tara.

12th century: most Irish oral narratives transcribed; numerous mentions of Uisneach in the insular manuscripts; probable tipping point from a historical to a mythical relevance of the hill. Writings of Jocelyn of Furness and Geoffrey of Monmouth. Transcription of *The Cause of Mongán's Frenzy*.

15th century: late transcriptions of the story of Deirdre/Sons of Uisneach.

16th century: Ringfort of Uisneach in ruins, as suggested by Tadhg Dall Ó Huiginn.

1634: *History of Ireland* by Geoffrey Keating.

*1820s–30s: possible date of construction of a cottage next to *Lough Lugh*.

1837: description of the site by O'Donovan.

*1900–2: James Joyce visits Uisneach and Mullingar.

*1919: *Sinn Féin* rally on Uisneach.

*1922: *Ail na Mireann* "desecrated by Catholics". Birth of the Irish Free State.

1925–31: main archeological excavations by Macalister and Praeger.

1937–9: manuscripts of the *Schools' Collection*.

1947: manuscripts of the *Irish Folklore Collection* (*Bealtaine*).

1988: first official *Beltane Festival* in Edinburgh; possible source of inspiration for contemporary Uisneach gatherings.

1998: Uisneach domain bought by David Clarke.

2009: first contemporary kindling of the fire of Uisneach.

2010: first contemporary *Fire Festival* of Uisneach.

2014: first guided tours.

2016: the Visitor Center of Uisneach opens.

6 May 2017: Michael D. Higgins kindles the fire of Uisneach during the *Fire Festival*.

Bibliography

PRIMARY SOURCES

Ireland (up to the 17th century)

Bambury, Pádraig (ed.). 2008 (2001). *Annals of Connacht*. Cork: Corpus of Electronic Texts, University College Cork.

Bambury, Pádraig & Beechinor, Stephen (ed.). 2020 (2000). *Annals of Ulster*. Cork: Corpus of Electronic Texts, University College Cork.

Best, Richard Irvine (ed.). 1910. "The Settling of the Manor of Tara" in *Ériu*, IV, 121–72.

Best, Richard Irvine & Bergin, Osborn (ed.). 1938. "Tochmarc Étaíne" in *Ériu*, XII, 137–96.

Best, Richard Irvine, Bergin, Osborn & O'Brien, Michael A. (ed.). 1954. *Book of Leinster formerly Lebar na Núachongbála*. Dublin: Dublin Institute for Advanced Studies, I.

Bieler, Ludwig (ed.). 2000 (1979). *The Patrician Texts in the Book of Armagh*. Dublin: Dublin Institute for Advanced Studies.

Binchy, Daniel Anthony (ed.). 1962. "Patrick and his Biographers—Ancient and Modern" in *Studia Hibernica*, II, 7–173.

Binchy, Daniel Anthony (ed.). 1955–8. "The Fair of Tailtiu and the Feast of Tara" in *Ériu*, XVII–XVIII, 113–38.

Bourke, Angela (ed.). 2005. *The Field Day Anthology of Irish Writing Volumes IV and V: Irish Women's Writing and Tradition*. Cork: Cork University Press.

Comyn, David & Dineen, Patrick (ed.). 2016 (1898–1908). *Geoffrey Keating. History of Ireland*. Cork: Corpus of Electronic Texts, University College Cork.

Cross, Tom Peete & Slover, Clark Harris (ed.). 1936. *Ancient Irish Tales*, New York: Henry Holt & Co, 488–90.

Dillon, Myles (ed.). 1962. *Lebor Na Cert. The Book of Rights*. Dublin: Irish Text Society.

Dillon, Myles (ed.). 1953. "The Wasting Sickness of Cú Chulainn" in *Scottish Gaelic Studies*, VII, 47–88.

Dillon, Myles (ed.). 1951–2. "Taboos of the Kings of Ireland" in Proceedings of the Royal Irish Academy: Archaeology, *Culture, History, Literature*, LIV, 1–36.

Donahue, Annie (ed.). 2004-5. "The Acallam na Senórach: A Medieval Instruction Manual" in Proceedings of the Harvard Celtic Colloquium, *XXIV–XXV*, 206–15.

Dooley, Ann, Roe, Harry (ed.). 2008. *Tales of the Elders of Ireland*. Oxford: Oxford University Press.

Dunn, Joseph (ed.). 1914. *The Ancient Irish Epic Tale: Táin Bó Cúailnge*. London: David Nutt.

Forester, Thomas (ed.). 2000. *Giraldus Cambrensis. The Topography of Ireland (Topographia Hibernica)*. Cambridge, Ontario: In Parentheses Publications.

Fraser, J. (ed.). 1916. "The First Battle of Moytura" in *Ériu*, VIII, 1–63.

Guyonvarc'h, Christian-Joseph (ed.). 1980. *Textes Mythologiques irlandais I*. Rennes: Ogam-Celticum.

Guyonvarc'h, Christian-Joseph (ed.). 1965. "La Conception de Cuchulain" in *Ogam*, XVII, 367.

Guyonvarc'h, Christian-Joseph (ed.). 1960. "L'Ivresse des Ulates (*Mesca Ulad*)" in *Ogam*, XII, 487-506.

Guyonvarc'h, Christian-Joseph (ed.). 1959. "La Courtise d'Emer" in *Ogam*, XI, 413-23.

Gwynn, Edward. (ed.). 1941 (1903). *The Metrical Dindshenchas*. Dublin: Hodges, Figgis & Co.

Gwynn, Edward. (ed.). 1913. *Liber Ardmachanus: the Book of Armagh*. Dublin.

Heist, W. W. 1965. *Vitae Sanctorum Hiberniae: ex codice olim Salmanticensi nunc Bruxellensi in Subsidia Hagiographica*. Brussels: Société des Bollandistes. Translated as *Life of Áed Mac Bricc from Codex Salmanticensis* by Kate Peck in 2006.

Henderson, George (ed.). 1899. *The Feast of Bricriu, Fled Bricrend*. London: Irish Text Society.

Hennessy, William M. (ed.). 1871. *The Annals of Loch Cé*. Oxford: Longman & Co.

Hennessy, William M. (ed.). 1866. *Chronicum* Scotorum: A *Chronicle of Irish Affairs*. London: Longmans & Co.

Hull, Vernam (ed.). 1971 (1949). *Longes Mac n-Uislenn: The Exile of the Sons of Uisliu*. New York: Kraus Reprint.

Hull, Vernam (ed.). 1930. "The Cause of Exile of Fergus mac Roig" in *Zeitschrift für celtische Philologie*, XVIII, 293–8.

Hull, Vernam (ed.). 1930. "An Incomplete Version of the Imram Brain and four Stories concerning Mongan" in *Zeitschrift für celtische Philologie*, XVIII, 409–19.

Hyde, Douglas (ed.). 1899. "Deirdre" in *Zeitschrift für Celtische Philologie*, II, 138–155.

Knott, Eleanor (ed.). 1922. *The Bardic Poems of Tadhg Dall Ó Huiginn (1550–1591)*. London: Irish Texts Society, XXIII.

Mac Airt, Seán (ed.). 1988 (1944). *The Annals of Inisfallen* (MS. Rawlinson B. 503). Dublin: Dublin Institute for Advanced Studies.

MacAirt, Seán (ed.). 1944. *Leabhar Branach. The Book of the Ó Byrnes*. Dublin: Dublin Institute for Advanced Studies.

Macalister, Robert Alexander Stewart (ed.) 1938 (1932), 1939 (1933), 1940 (1937), 1941 (1939), 1956 (1942). *Lebor Gabála Érenn (Book of the Taking of Ireland).*). Dublin: Irish Text Society.

Mac Giolla Léith, Caoimhin (ed.). 1994. Oidheadh Chloinne Uisnigh in *Ériu*, XLV, 99–112.

Mackinnon, Donald (ed.). 1904–8. "The Glenmasan Manuscript" in *The Celtic Review*. Edinburgh: Norman Macleod, I–IV.

Meyer, Kuno (ed.). 1901. "Brinna Ferchertne" in *Zeitschrift für Celtische Philologie*, III, 41–6.

Meyer, Kuno (ed.). 1888. "*The Wooing of Emer*" in *Archaeological Review*, I, 68–75; 150–5; 231–5; 298–307.

Meyer, Kuno. 1890. "The oldest version of Tochmarc Emire" in *Revue Celtique*, XI, 434–57.

Meyer, Kuno & Nutt, Alfred (ed.) 1895. *The Voyage of Bran, Son of Febal to the Land of the Living. 2 vols, I: The Happy Otherworld*. London: David Nutt.

Murphy, Denis (ed.). 1896. *The Annals of Clonmacnoise, Being Annals of Ireland from the Earliest Period to A.D. 1408*. Dublin: Royal Society of Antiquaries of Ireland.

Murphy, Gerard (ed.). 1955. "Finn's Poem on May-Day" in *Ériu*, XVII, 86–99.

O'Beirne Crowe, J. (ed.). 1874. "Mythological Legends of Ancient Ireland. I, the Adventures of Condla Ruad" in *Journal of the Royal Historical and Archaeological Association of Ireland*, Fourth Series, III, No. 18, 118–33.

O'Cuív, Brian (ed.). 1945. *Cath Muighe Tuireadh: The Second Battle of Magh Tuireadh*. Dublin: Dublin Institute for Advanced Studies.

O'Curry, Eugene (ed.). 1863. "The Fate of the Children of Tuireann (Oidhedh Chloinne Tuireann)" in *Atlantis*, IV, 157–240.

1863. "The Fate of the Children of Lir'", in *Atlantis*, IV, 113–57.

O'Donovan, John (ed.). 1869. *Senchus Mór, Ancient Laws of Ireland*. II. Dublin: Longman, Green, Reader, and Dyer.

O'Donovan, John (ed.). 1868. *Cormac's Glossary*. Calcutta: the Irish Archaeological and Celtic Society.

O'Donovan, John (ed.). 1865. *Senchus Mór, Ancient Laws of Ireland*. I. Dublin: Longman, Roberts and Green.

O'Donovan, John (ed.). 1847. *The Book of Rights*. Dublin: Celtic Society.

O'Duffy, Richard (ed.). 1901. *Oide Cloinne Tuireann, The Fate of the Children of Tuireann*. Dublin: M.H. Gill and Son.

O'Grady, Standish Hayes, (ed.). 1929. "Caithréim Thoirdhealbhaigh" in *Irish Texts Society*, 26, London.

O'Grady, Standish Hayes, (ed.). 1892. *Silva Gadelica*. London & Edinburgh: Williams and Norgate. 2 vol.

Peck, Kate (ed.). 2006. *Life of Áed Mac Bricc from Codex Salmanticensis*. Brussels: Société des Bollandistes.

Ryan, Emma (ed.). 2002 (1997). *Annals of the Four Masters*. Cork: Corpus of Electronic Texts, University College Cork.

Stokes, Whitley (ed.). 1993 (1895-6). *The Annals of Tigernach, Trans. Reprinted from Revue Celtique*. Felinfach: Llanaerch Publishers.

Stokes, Whitley (ed.). 1908. "The Training of Cúchulainn" in *Revue Celtique*, 29, 109–52.

Stokes, Whitley (ed.). 1891. "The Irish ordeals, Cormac's Adventure in the Land of Promise, and the Decision as to Cormac's Sword", in *Irische Texte mit Wörterbuch*, 4 vols, III: 1, Leipzig, 183–221.

Stokes, Whitley (ed.). 1891. "The Second Battle of Moytura" in *Revue Celtique*, XII, 52–130, 306–8.

Stokes, Whitley (ed.). 1887. *The Tripartite Life of Patrick*. London: Eyre and Spottiswoode.

Stokes, Whitley (ed.). 1887. "The Death of the Sons of Uisnech" in *Irische Texte mit Wörterbuch*. Leipzig, II, 109–84.

Stokes, Whitley (ed.). 1862. *Three Irish Glossaries, Cormac's Glossary, Ó Davren's Glossary, a Glossary to the Calendar of Oingus the Culdee*. London: Williams and Norgate.

Swift, Edmund (ed.). 1809. *The Life and Acts of Saint Patrick: the Archbishop, Primate and Apostle of Ireland*. Dublin: Hibernia Press Company.

Todd, James Henthorn (ed.). 1848. *Leabhar Breathnach annso sis: The Irish version of the Historia Britonum of Nennius*. Dublin: Irish Archaeological Society.

Ireland (17th-21st centuries)

National Folklore Collection (Main Collection) noted NFC

NFC 1095: Munster.
NFC 1096: Connacht & Ulster.
NFC 1097: Leinster.

National Folklore Collection (Schools' Collection) noted NFCS

NFCS 742: 1–12. Newbristy south, Co. Westmeath. Teacher: Bríd Murphy.
NFCS 742: 13–48. Milltown, Co. Westmeath. Teacher: Sean O'Casey.
NFCS 742: 49–216. Milltown, Co. Westmeath. Teacher: Margt. McNally.
NFCS 742: 217–228. Irishtown, Co. Westmeath. Teacher: Margt. McNally.
NFCS 742:229–396. Loughanavally, Co. Westmeath. Teacher: Mrs. O'Connor.
NFCS 742: 397–519. Moyvore, Co. Westmeath. Teacher: Mrs. Kelly.
NFCS 743: 1–138. Moyvoughly, Co. Westmeath. Teacher: C. Ní Fhlannagáin.
NFCS 743: 139–305. Ballymore, Co. Westmeath. Teacher: P.G. Cooney.
NFCS 743: 306–425. Ballymore, Co. Westmeath. Teacher: K. Kavanagh & Mrs. Kearney.
NFCS 744: 1–147. Bracknahevla, Co. Westmeath. Teacher: T. Kavanagh.
NFCS 744: 148–169. Ballymore, Co. Westmeath. Teacher: S. Murphy.
NFCS 744: 170–187. Ballymore, Co. Westmeath. Teacher: T. Hanley.

Other Irish primary sources

Cameron, Alexander, Macbain, Alexander & Kennedy, J. (ed.). 1894. "The Book of Clanranald" in *Reliquiae Celticae*, Inverness: The Northern Counties Newspaper and Printing and Publishing Company, Limited, II, 149–288.

Coulter, John. 1944. *Deirdre of the Sorrows*. Macmillan Company of Canada.

Feltham, John. 1798. *A Tour through the Island of Mann in 1797 and 1798*. Unknown: R. Cruttwell.

Ferguson, Samuel. 1887. *The Death of the Children of Usnach*. Dublin: Sealy, Bryers & Walker.

1880. *Deirdre: A one-act Drama of old Irish Story*. Unknown.

Hedderman, B.N. 1917. *Glimpses of my Life in Aran, part I*. Bristol: John Wright and Sons Ltd.

Hull, Eleanor. 1906. "The Story of Deirdre and the Lay of the Children of Uisne" in *Celtic Review*, 11, 288.

Jacobs, Joseph (ed.). 1892. "Connla and the Fairy Maiden" in *Celtic Fairy Tales*. London: David Nutt, 1–4.

Joyce, James. 1966 (1939). *Finnegans Wake*. New York: Viking Press.

Joyce, Patrick Weston. 1879. "Connla of the Golden Hair and the Fairy Maiden" in *Old Celtic Romances*. Dublin: the Educational Co. of Ireland, 106–11.

Moore, Thomas. 1850. *Irish Melodies*. Philadelphia: Lea & Blanchard.

O'Flannghaile, Tomás (ed.). 1896. *The Lay of Oisín in the Land of Youth by Micheál Coimín*. Dublin: M.H. Gill & Son.

Stephens, James. 1970 (1923). *Deirdre*. New York: The Macmillan Company.

Steven, Kenneth. 2017. *Deirdre of the Sorrows*. Edinburgh: Birlinn.

Stoker, Bram. 1994 (1897). *Dracula*. London: Penguin Books.

Synge, John Millington. 1910. *Deirdre of the Sorrows*. Dublin: Cuala Press.

Trench, Herbert. 1901. *Deirdre Wedded: Song for the Funeral of a Boy, Shakespeare, A Charge, & Other Poems*. London: Methuen.

Russell, George William. 1907. *Deirdre*. Dublin: Maunsel.

Yeats, William Butler. 1907. *Deirdre*. Dublin: Maunsel.

Websites: primary sources

1/ Mythology and medieval sources

CELT, Corpus of Electronic Texts The Free Digital Humanities Resource for Irish history, literature and politics. https://celt.ucc.ie

2/ Media

BBC: http://bbc.co.uk
Irish Examiner: http://irishexaminer.com
Irish Times: http://irishtimes.com
Meath Chronicle: http://meathchronicle.ie
RTE: http://rte.ie
Westmeath Examiner: http://westmeathexaminer.ie

3/ Modern and contemporary

Department of Culture, Heritage and the Gaeltacht: http://chg.gov.ie
National Folklore Collection: http://duchas.ie/
National Heritage Week: http://heritageweek.ie
RIAI: http://irisharchitectureawards.ie
Sacred Sites: http://www.sacredsites.ie
Uisneach (Visitor Center): http://uisneach.ie

4/ Social networks and sharing platforms

http://eventbrite.ie
http://instagram.com
http://facebook.com
http://tripadvisor.com

http://twitter.com
http://youtube.com

Non-Irish primary sources

Camden, William. 1607. *Britannia*. London: Georgii Bishop and Joannis Norton.

Davies, Sioned (ed.). 2007. *The Mabinogion*. Oxford: Oxford University Press.

Hamilton, H.C. & Falconer W. (ed.). 1854. *The Geography of Strabo in Three Volumes*. London.

Jones, Alexander. (ed.). 2000 (1966). *The Jerusalem Bible*. New York: Doubleday.

McDevitte, W. A. & Bohn, W. S. (ed.). 2012 (1869). *The Gallic Wars. Julius Caesar*. Merchants Books.

Munch, Peter Andreas (ed.). 1874. *Chronica Regvm Manniae et Insvlarvm. The Chronicles of Man and the Sudreys from the Manuscript Codex in the British Museum*, I. Douglas: The Manx Society.

Rackham H., Jones, W.H.S. & Eichholz, D.E. (ed.). 1949–54. *Pliny's Natural History*. London: William Heinemann.

Reeve, William (ed.) 1907 [?]. *The Apology of Tertullian*. London: Griffith, Farran, Okeden & Welsh.

Thompson, Aaron (ed.). 1999. *Geoffrey of Monmouth. History of the Kings of Britain*. Cambridge, Ontario: In Parentheses Publications.

Website used as a primary source

Beltane Fire Festival on Calton Hill: https://beltane.org/

SECONDARY SOURCES

Irish and Celtic worlds

Arbois de Jubainville, Henri D'. 1884. *Cours de Littérature celtique*. Paris: Ernest Thorin Editeur.

Arbois de Jubainville, Henri D'. 1880. *Les Assemblées publiques de l'Irlande*. From *Séances et Travaux de l'Académie des sciences morales et politiques*. Paris: A. Picard.

Armao, Frédéric. 2018. "Dá Chích Anann: mythes et rituels associés aux 'Seins de Dana'" in *Ollodagos*, Institut des Hautes Etudes de Belgique, Brussels, XXXIII, 157–217.

Armao, Frédéric. 2013. "La Charnière de mai: Beltaine, fête celtique ou fête irlandaise?" in *Ollodagos*, Institut des Hautes Etudes de Belgique, Brussels, XXVIII, 61-128.

Armao, Frédéric. 2002. "De Beltaine à Pâques" in *Etudes irlandaises*, XXVII-2, 29-43.

Barfoot, C.C. & D'Haen, Theo. 1995. *Troubled Histories, Troubled Fictions: Twentieth-century Anglo-Irish Prose*. Leiden: Brill Rodopi.

Bhreathnach, Edel. 1995. *Tara: A Select Bibliography*. Dublin: Royal Irish Academy.

Birkett, Helen. 2013. "Plausible Fictions: John Stow, Jocelin of Furness and the Book of British Bishops" in Downham, Clare (ed.), *Jocelin of Furness. Essays from the 2011 Conference*. Donington: Shaun Tyas, 91–120.

Böss, Michael. 2002. "The Postmodern Nation: a Critical History of the 'Fifth Province' Discourse" in *Etudes Irlandaises*, XXVII–1, 139–59.

Breatnach, Caoimhín. 1994. "Oidheadh Chloinne Uisnigh" in *Ériu*, XLV, 99–102.

Broderick, George. 2003. "Tynwald: a Manx cult-site and institution of pre-Scandinavian origin?" in *Cambrian Medieval Celtic Studies*, XLVI, 55–94.

Brunaux, Jean-Louis. 2014. *Les Celtes. Histoire d'un Mythe.* Paris: Belin.

Brunaux, Jean-Louis. 2005. *Les Gaulois.* Paris: les Belles Lettres.

Bury, John Bagnell. 1902. "Tírechán's memoir of St Patrick" in *English Historical Review*, XVII, 235–67.

Byrne, Francis John. 1973. *Irish Kings and High-Kings.* London: Four Courts Press.

Carey, John. 1995. "On the Interrelationships of some *Cín Dromma Snechtai* texts" in *Ériu*, XLVI, 71–92.

Charles-Edwards, Thomas. 2008 (2000). *Early Christian Ireland.* Cambridge: Cambridge University Press.

Daly, Leo. 1975. *James Joyce and the Mullingar connection.* Dublin: Dolmen Press.

Dames, Michael. 1996. *Mythic Ireland.* London: Thames & Hudson.

Doherty, Charles. 2005. "Kingship in early Ireland", in Edel, Bhreathnach (ed.), *The Kingship and Landscape of Tara.* Dublin: Four Courts Press, 3–31.

Duval, Paul-Marie. 1993 (1957). *Les Dieux de la Gaule.* Paris: Payot.

Duval, Paul-Marie & Pinault, Georges. 1986. *Recueil des Inscriptions gauloises. Vol. III: les calendriers (Coligny, Villards d'Héria).* Paris: CNRS Editions.

Edmonds, Fiona. 2013. "The Furness Peninsula and the Irish Sea Region: Cultural Interaction from the Seventh Century to the Twelfth" in Downham, Clare (ed.), *Jocelin of Furness. Essays from the 2011 Conference.* Donington: Shaun Tyas, 17–44.

Etchingham, Colmán. 1993. "The Implications of Paruchia" in *Ériu*, XLIV, 139–63.

Fackler, Herbert V. 1978. *That Tragic Queen: The Deirdre Legend in Anglo-Irish Literature.* Salzburg: Institut für Englische Sprache und Literatur.

Fellows-Jensen, Gillian. 1993. "Tingwall, Dingwall and Thingwall" in *North-Western European Language Evolution*, XXI–XXII, 53–67.

Flanagan, Marie Therese. 2013. "Jocelin of Furness" in Downham, Clare (ed.), *Jocelin of Furness. Essays from the 2011 Conference.* Donington: Shaun Tyas, 45–66.

Garvin, John. 1976. *James Joyce's Disunited Kingdom.* Dublin: Gill & Macmillan.

Gourvest, Jacques. 1954. "Le Culte de Belenos en Provence occidentale et en Gaule" in *Ogam*, VI, 257–62.

Green, Miranda Jane. 1992. *Dictionary of Celtic Myth and Legend.* London: Thames and Hudson.

Green, Miranda Jane. 1989. *Symbols and Image in Celtic Religious Arts.* London and New York: Routledge.

Gricourt, Jean. 1954. "Epona – Rhiannon – Macha" in *Ogam*, VI 25–40, 75–86, 137–8, 155–68, 165–89, 269–72.

Griffin-Kremer, Merrie-Cozette. 1999. *May Day in Insular Celtic Traditions.* PhD thesis. Brest: Université de Bretagne Occidentale.

Guyonvarc'h, Christian-Joseph & Le Roux, Françoise. 2016 (1991). *La Société Celtique.* Fouesnant: Yoran.

Guyonvarc'h, Christian-Joseph & Le Roux, Françoise. 2016 (1990). *La Civilisation celtique.* Fouesnant: Yoran.

Guyonvarc'h, Christian-Joseph & Le Roux, Françoise. 2016 (1987). *Morrigan-Bodb-Macha. La Souveraineté Guerrière de l'Irlande*. Fouesnant: Yoran.

Guyonvarc'h, Christian-Joseph & Le Roux, Françoise. 2015 (1995). *Les Fêtes celtiques*. Fouesnant: Yoran.

Guyonvarc'h, Christian-Joseph & Le Roux, Françoise. 1986. *Les Druides*. Rennes: Ouest-France.

Hamp, Eric. 1974. "Varia" in *Ériu*, XXV, 253–84.

Hutchinson, John. 1987. *The Dynamics of Cultural Nationalism: The Gaelic Revival and the Creation of the Irish Nation State*. London: Routledge.

Irwin, Philip. 2004. "Fiachu mac Néill (fl. 510–516)" in *Oxford Dictionary of National Biography*. Oxford University Press.

Kaulins, Andis. 2003. *Stars, Stones and Scholars*. Bloomington: Trafford Publishing.

Kelly, John, Schachard, Ronald (ed.). 1997. *The Collected Letters of W.B. Yeats: Volume Three, 1901–1924*. Oxford: Oxford University Press.

Kenney, James Francis. 1929. *The Sources for the Early History of Ireland: An Introduction and Guide. 1: Ecclesiastical*. New York: Columbia University Press.

Kohl, Johann Georg. 1844. *England, Wales and Scotland*. London: Chapman and Hall.

Kohl, Johann Georg. 1843. *Reisen in Irland*. 2 vol. Dresden & Leipzig: Arnold.

Kruta, Venceslas. 1985. *Les Celtes en Occident*. Paris: Atlas.

Lonigan, Paul R. 1996. *The Druids, Priests of the Ancient Celts*. Westport: Greenwood Press, Westport.

Loth, Joseph. 1915. "L'Omphalos chez les Celtes" in *Revue des Études Anciennes*, XVII-3, 193–206.

Loth, Joseph. 1914. "La croyance à l'omphalos chez les Celtes" in *Comptes rendus des séances de l'Académie des Inscriptions et Belles-Lettres*, LVIII-5, 481–2.

Lucas, Anthony T. 1965. "Washing and Bathing in Ancient Ireland" in *Journal of the Royal Society of Antiquaries of Ireland*, XCV-1/2, 65–114.

Lucas, Anthony T. 1963. "The Sacred trees of Ireland" in *Journal of the Cork Historical and Archaeological Society*, LXVIII, 16–54.

Macalister, Robert, Alexander, Stewart. 1931. *Tara, a Pagan Sanctuary of Ancient Ireland*. New York: Charles Scribner's Sons.

Markale, Jean. 1993 (1971). *L'Epopée celtique d'Irlande*. Paris: Payot.

Markale, Jean. 1983. *Le Christianisme celtique et ses survivances populaires*. Paris: Imago.

Markale, Jean. 1969. *Les Celtes et la civilisation celtique*. Paris: Payot.

Mathews, P.J. 2009. *The Cambridge Companion to J. M. Synge*. Cambridge: Cambridge University Press.

Mathews, P.J. 2003. *Revival: The Abbey Theatre, Sinn Fein, the Gaelic League and the Co-operative Movement*. Cork: Cork University Press.

McDonald, Russell Andrew. 2007. *Manx Kingship in its Irish Sea Setting, 1187–1229: king Rǫgnvaldr and the Crovan dynasty*, Dublin: Four Courts Press.

MacKillop, James. 1998. *Dictionary of Celtic Mythology*. Oxford: Oxford University Press.

McMahon, Timothy G. 2008. *Grand Opportunity: The Gaelic Revival and Irish Society, 1893-1910*. Syracuse: Syracuse University Press.

MacNeill, Eoin. 1929. "The Origin of the Tripartite Life of Saint Patrick" in *Journal of the Royal Society of Antiquaries of Ireland*, Sixth Series, XIX-1, 1–15.

MacNeill, Eoin. 1928. "The Earliest Lives of St Patrick" in *Journal of the Royal Society of Antiquaries of Ireland*, LVIII, 85–101.

Maignant, Catherine. 1996. *Histoire et Civilisation de l'Irlande*. Paris: Nathan.

McCone, Kim. 1990. *Pagan Past and Christian Present*. Maynooth: Department of Old Irish, National.

O'Curry, Eugene. 1873. *On the Manners and Customs of the Ancient Irish*, Dublin: Williams and Norgate.

O'Leary, Philip. 1994. *The Prose Literature of the Gaelic Revival, 1881–1921: Ideology and Innovation*. Pennsylvania State University Press.

O'Rahilly, Thomas Francis. 1946. *Early Irish History and Mythology*. Dublin: Dublin Institute for Advanced Studies.

O'Rahilly, Thomas Francis. 1942. *The Two Patricks, a Lecture on the History of Christianity in Fifth Century Ireland*. Dublin.

O'Reilly, David. 2001. *The Hill of Uisneach Co. Westmeath*. Thesis, University College Dublin.

Rees, Alwyn & Brinley. 1988 (1961). *Celtic Heritage, Ancient Tradition in Ireland and Wales*. London: Thames and Hudson.

Savignac, Jean-Paul. 2014 (2004). *Dictionnaire Français-Gaulois*. Paris: La Différence.

Sergent, Bernard. 2013. "Préface" in Armao Frédéric (ed.), *Les Nations Celtiques et le monde contemporain. Babel-Civilisations & Sociétés*. Toulon: Université de Toulon, VIII, 17–20.

Sergent, Bernard. 2004. *Celtes et* Grecs. II, *Le livre des dieux*. Paris: Payot.

Sergent, Bernard. 1999. *Celtes et* Grecs. I, *Le livre des héros*. Paris: Payot.

Sharpe, Richard. 1982. "Palaeographical Considerations in the Study of the Patrician Documents in the Book of Armagh" in *Scriptorium*, XXXVI, 3–28.

Sharpe, Richard. 1972. "Churches and Communities in Early Medieval Ireland: Towards a Pastoral Model" in Blair, J. & Sharpe, R. (ed.), *Pastoral Care Before the Parish*. Leicester.

Sheehan, Jeremiah (ed.). 1996. *Beneath the shadow of Uisneach: Ballymore & Boher, Co. Westmeath*. Ballymore: Ballymore-Boher History Project.

Sjoestedt, Marie-Louise. 1940. *Dieux et Héros des Celtes*. Paris: Presses Universitaires de France.

Sterckx, Claude. 1996. *Dieux d'eau: Apollons celtes et gaulois*. Brussels: Ollodagos.

1986. *Eléments de Cosmogonie Celtique*. Brussels: Editions de l'Université de Bruxelles.

Swift, Catherine. 1994. "Tírechán's Motives in Compiling the 'Collectanea': An Alternative Interpretation" in *Ériu*, XLV, 53–82.

Vendryes, Joseph, Bachallery, Édouard, & Lambert, Pierre-Yves. 1978. *Lexique étymologique de l'irlandais ancien*, IV, 21–2.

Vendryes, Joseph. 1935. "L'Unité en trois personnes chez les Celtes" in *Comptes rendus des séances de l'Académie des Inscriptions et Belles-Lettres*, 79th year, III, 324–41.

Watson, Alden. 1981. "The king, the poet and the sacred tree" in *Etudes celtiques*, XVIII, 165–80.

Williams, Mark. 2016. *Ireland's Immortals. A History of the Gods of Irish Myths*. Princeton: Princeton University Press.

Wyatt, David R. 2009. *Slaves and Warriors in Medieval Britain and Ireland: 800–1200*. Leiden: Brill.

Archeology, geography, toponymy

Borlase, William Copeland. 1897. *The Dolmens of Ireland*. London: Chapman & Hall.

Burl, Aubrey. 2000. *The Stone Circles of Britain, Ireland and Brittany*. New Haven: Yale University Press.

Clément, Michel. 1979. "Le Tesson aux Svastikas de Trogouzel et la Pierre de Kermaria (Finistère)" in *Etudes Celtiques*, XVI, 53–61.

Daire, Marie-Yvonne & Villard, Anne. 1996. "Les Stèles à décors géométriques et curvilignes. Etat de la question dans l'Ouest armoricain", in *Revue Archéologique de l'Ouest*, XIII, 123–56.

Darcy, R. & Flynn, William. 2008. "Ptolemy's map of Ireland: a modern decoding" in *Irish Geography*, XLI-1, 49–69.

Day, Angelique & McWilliams, Patrick (ed.). 1990-7 (1834–6). *Ordnance Survey Memoirs of Ireland*. Dublin: Institute of Irish Studies.

Donaghy, Caroline & Grogan, Eoin. 1997. "Navel-Gazing at Uisneach, Co. Westmeath" in *Archaeology Ireland*, XI-4, 24–6.

Ferguson, Samuel. 1872. "On Ancient Cemeteries at Rathcrogan and Elsewhere in Ireland (as affecting the question of the site of the cemetery at Taltin)" in *Proceedings of the Royal Irish Academy*, XV, 114–24.

Lewis, Samuel. 1837. *A Topographical Dictionary of Ireland*. London: S. Lewis & Co., 2 vol.

Lynn, Christopher J. 1978. "Early Christian Period Domestic Structures: a Change from Round to Rectangular Plans?" in *Irish Archaeological Research Forum*, V, 29–45.

Macalister, Robert Alexander Stewart & Lloyd, Praeger Robert. 1928–1929. "Report on the Excavation of Uisneach" in *Proceedings of the Royal Irish Academy: Archaeology, Culture, History*, XXXVIII, 69–127.

McGinley, Seamus, Potito, Aaron P., Molloy, Karen, Schot, Roseanne, Stuijts, Ingelise & Beilman, David W. 2015. "*Lough Lugh*, Uisneach: from natural lake to archaeological monument?" in *Journal of Irish Archaeology*, XXIV, 115–30.

O'Donovan, John. 1927 (1841). *Ordnance Survey Letters*. Dublin: Ordnance Survey Ireland.

O'Donovan, John. 1837. Letters Containing Information Relative to the Antiquities of the County of Westmeath collected during the Progress of the Ordnance Survey in *1837 (2 vols.)*. O'Flanagan Michael (ed.). Bray: National Library of Ireland.

O'Murchadha, Diarmaid. 2005. "A Review of Some Placename Material from Foras Feasa Ar Éirinn" in *Éigse, A Journal of Irish Studies*, XXXV, 81–98.

O'Reilly, David. 2010. "Some Forgotten prehistoric Rock Art from the Hill of Uisneach, Co. Westmeath" in *Journal of the Royal Society of Antiquaries of Ireland*, CXL, 73–82.

Rivet, Albert Lionel Frederick & Smith, Colin. 1979. *The Place-Names of Roman Britain*. London: Batsford Ltd.

Schot, Roseanne. 2011. "From Cult Centre to Royal Centre: Monuments, Myths and Other Revelations at Uisneach" in *Landscapes of Cult and Kingship*. Dublin: Four Courts Press, 87–113.

Schot, Roseanne. 2006. "Uisneach Midi a medón Érenn: A Prehistoric 'Cult' Centre and 'Royal Site' in Co. Westmeath" in *Journal of Irish Archaeology*, XV, 39–71.

Schot, Roseanne, Stuijts, Ingelise, McGinley, Seamus & Potito, Aaron. 2014. "Reflections on a Lake: a Multi-Proxy Study of Environmental Change and Human Impacts at *Lough Lugh*, Uisneach, Co. Westmeath" in *Late Iron Age and 'Roman' Ireland, Discovery Programme Reports 8*, Dublin: Wordwell, 113–26.

Suess, Barbara A. 2003. "Progress & Identity in the Plays of W.B. Yeats, 1892–1907". New York: Routledge.

Villard-le Tiec, Anne, Cherel, Anne-Françoise & Le Goff, Elven. 2003. "Aspects de l'art celtique en Bretagne au Ve siècle avant J.-C." in *Supplément à la Revue archéologique du centre de la France*, XXIV, 221–36.

Waddel, John. 2000 (1998). *The Prehistoric Archaeology of Ireland*. Dublin: Wordwell.

Waddel, John. 1982. "From Kermaria to Turoe?" in Scott B.G. (ed.), *Studies on Early Ireland. Essays in honour of M. V. Duignan*. Belfast, 21–8.

Warner, Richard B. 2000. "Clogher: an Archaeological of Early Medieval Tyrone and mid-Ulster" in Dillon C. & Jefferies H.A. (ed.) *Tyrone: History and Society*. Dublin: Geography Publications, 39–54.

Wollaston, William Hyde. 1814. "On Fairy-Rings" in *Abstracts of the Papers Printed in the Philosophical Transactions of the Royal Society of London*, I.

Websites

http://archaeology.ie/
http://map.geohive.ie/
http://megaliths.co.uk/
http://www.osi.ie/
https://www.townlands.ie/
https://www.ucd.ie/archaeology/

Mythology and Indo-European studies

Allen, Nicholas J. 1999. "Hinduism, Structuralism and Dumézil" in *Miscellanea Indo-Europea*. Washington: Institute for the Study of Man, 241–60.

Camps-Gaset, Montserrat. 1994. *L'Année des Grecs, la fête et le mythe*. Paris: Annales Littéraires de l'Université de Besançon.

Dubuisson, Daniel. 2005. *Impostures et pseudo-science: l'œuvre de Mircea Eliade*. Lille: Presses Universitaires du Septentrion.

Dubuisson, Daniel. 1978. "Le Roi indo-européen et la synthèse des trois fonctions" in *Annales. Économies, Sociétés, Civilisations*, 33rd year, I, 21–34.

Dumézil, Georges. 1963. "Le Puits de Nechtan" in *Celtica*, VI, 50–61.

Dumézil, Georges. 1955. "Triades de calamités et triades de délits à valeur tri-fonctionnelle chez divers peuples indo-européens" in *Latomus*, XIV, 173–85.

Dumézil, Georges. 1946. "'Tripertita' fonctionnels chez divers peuples indo-européens" in *Revue de l'Histoire des Religions*, CXXXI-1-3, 53–72.

Dumézil, Georges. 1940. "La Tradition druidique et l'écriture: le vivant et le mort" in *Revue de l'Histoire des Religions*, CXXII, 125–33.

Eliade, Mircea. 1965 (1957). *Le Sacré et le profane*. Paris: Gallimard.

Lajoye, Patrice. 2006. "Borgne, manchot, boiteux: des démons primordiaux aux dieux tonnants" in *Ollodagos*, XX-2, 211–45.

Le Quellec, Jean-Loïc, Sergent, Bernard. 2017. *Dictionnaire critique de mythologie.* Paris: CNRS Editions.

Sergent, Bernard. 2005 (1995). *Les Indo-Européens.* Paris: Payot.

Sergent, Bernard. 2004. "Le Sacrifice des femmes samnites" in *La Fête, la rencontre des dieux et des hommes.* Actes du 2e Colloque international de Paris "La fête, la rencontre du sacré et du profane". Paris: L'Harmattan.

Smith, Williams. 1973. *Dictionary of Greek and Roman Antiquities.* London: Milford House.

Zair, Nicholas. 2012. *The Reflexes of the Proto-Indo-European Laryngeals in Celtic.* Leiden: Brill.

Folklore studies

Armao, Frédéric. 2017. "Cathair Crobh Dearg: From Ancient Beliefs to the Rounds 2017" in *Estudios Irlandeses, Electronic Journal of the Spanish Association for Irish Studies,* XII-2, 8–31.

Armao, Frédéric. 2016. "Les Superstitions du lièvre-trayeur en Irlande" in *Babel-Civilisations & Sociétés,* Univ. Toulon, XI, 23–40.

Buhociu, Octavian. 1957. *Le Folklore Roumain de Printemps.* PhD Thesis. Paris: Université de Paris.

Briody, Mícheál. 2016. *The Irish Folklore Commission 1935–1970, History, Ideology, Methodology.* Helsinki: Studia Fennica Folkloristica.

Cronin, Dan. 2001. *In the Shadow of the Paps.* Killarney: Crede, Sliabh Luachra Heritage Group.

Cronin, Denis A., Gillian, Jim & Holton, Karina (ed.). 2001. *Irish Fairs and Markets, Studies in Local History.* Bodmin: Four Courts Press.

Danaher, Kevin. 1972. *The Year in Ireland.* Dublin: Mercier Press.

Danaher, Kevin. 1964. *In Ireland Long Ago.* Dublin: Mercier Press.

Frazer, James. 1996 (1922). *The Golden Bough.* London: Penguin Books.

Gaignebet, Claude. 1987. "A la Pêche aux Enfants" in *Civilisations,* XXXVII-2 "Ethnologies d'Europe et d'ailleurs", 35–41.

Giraudon, Daniel. 1997. "*Belteine,* les Traditions du premier mai en Irlande" in *ArMen,* LXXXIV, 26–35.

Guibert de la Vaissière, Véronique. 1978. *Les Quatre fêtes d'ouverture de saison de l'Irlande ancienne.* PhD thesis. Montpellier: Université Paul Valéry.

Holton, Karina. 2001. "From Charters to Carters: Aspects of Fairs and Markets in Medieval Leinster" in *Irish Fairs and Markets, Studies in Local History.* Bodmin: Four Courts Press, 18–44.

Hutton, Ronald. 2001. *The Rise and Fall Of Merry England: The Ritual Year 1400–1700.* Oxford: Oxford Paperbacks.

Judge, Roy. 2000 (1979). *The Jack-in-the-Green: A May Day Custom.* London: The Folklore Society Books.

Laurent, Donatien & Tréguer, Michel. 1997. *La Nuit Celtique.* Rennes: Terre de Brume Editions, Presses Universitaires de Rennes.

Laurent, Donatien. 1990. "Le Juste milieu. Réflexion sur un rituel de circumambulation millénaire: la troménie de Locronan" in Tenèze, Marie Louise (ed.). *Tradition et Histoire dans la culture populaire. Rencontres autour de l'œuvre de Jean-Michel Guilcher.* Grenoble: Centre Alpin et Rhodanien d'Ethnologie, 255–92.

Logan, Patrick. 1986. *Fair Day, the Story of Irish Fairs and Markets*. Belfast: Appletree Press, 121.

Lysaght, Patricia. 1998. "Seán Ó Súilleabháin (1903–1996) and the Irish Folklore Commission" in *Western Folklore*, LVII-2/3, 137–51.

Lysaght, Patricia. 1994. "Women Milk and Magic at the Boundary Festival of May" in *Milk and Milk Products from Medieval to Modern Times*. Edinburgh: Canongate Academic, 208–29.

Lysaght, Patricia. 1993. "*Bealtaine*: Irish Maytime Customs and the Reaffirmation of Boundaries" in *Boundaries and Thresholds: Papers From a Colloquium of the Katharine Briggs Club*. Stroud: Thimble for the Katharine Briggs Club, 28–43.

Lysaght, Patricia. 1991. "Maytime Verdure Customs and their Distribution in Ireland" in *International Folklore Review*, VIII, 75–82.

MacDermott, Mercia. 1998. *Bulgarian Folk Customs*. London: Jessica Kingsley Publishers.

MacLeod, Sharon Paice. 2003. "*Oenach Aimsire na mBan*: Early Irish Seasonal Celebrations, Gender Roles and Mythological Cycles" in *The Proceedings of the Harvard Colloquium*, XXIII. Harvard: Harvard University Press, 257–83.

MacNeill, Máire. 1982 (1962). *The Festival of Lughnasa*. Dublin: Comhairle Bhéaloideas Éireann.

Meehan, Cary. 2002. *The Traveller's Guide to Sacred Ireland*. London: Gothic Image Publications.

Mehler, Natascha. 2015. "Þingvellir: A Place of Assembly and a Market?" in *Journal of the North Atlantic*, spec. VIII, 69–81.

Moore, Arthur William. 1994 (1891). *The Folklore of the Isle of Man*. Felinfach: Llanerch Publishers.

Ó Súilleabháin (Sullivan), Seán. 1977 (1967). *Irish Folk Custom and Belief*. Cork: Mercier Press.

Ó Súilleabháin (Sullivan), Seán. 1974. *Folklore of Ireland*. London. B.T. Batsford, London.

Ó Súilleabháin (Sullivan), Seán. 1973. *Storytelling in Irish Tradition*. Cork: Mercier Press.

Ó Súilleabháin (Sullivan), Seán. 1968 (1966). *Folktales of Ireland* Chicago: University of Chicago Press.

Ó Súilleabháin (Sullivan), Seán. 1963. *A Handbook of Irish Folklore*. London: Herbert Jenkins.

Rodgers, Michael & Losack, Marcus. 1996. *Glendalough, a Celtic Pilgrimage*. Harriburg: Morehouse Publishing.

Rhys, John. 1901. *Celtic Folklore, Welsh and Manx*. Oxford: Clarendon Press.

Stany-Gauthier, Joseph. 1953. "Les Saints Bretons protecteurs des récoltes et des jardins" in *Arts et traditions populaires*, 1st year, IV, 307–21.

Trevelyan, Marie. 1909. *Folk-Lore and Folk Songs of Wales*. London: Elliot Stock.

Van Gennep, Arnold. 1999 (1937–58). *Le Folklore français. II. Cycles de mai, de la Saint-Jean, de l'été et de l'automne*. Paris: Robert Laffont.

Van Gennep, Arnold. 1998 (1937–58). *Le Folklore français. I. Du berceau à la tombe, cycles de carnaval - Carême et de Pâques*. Paris: Robert Laffont.

Westropp, Thomas J. 2000 [?]. *Folklore of Clare*. Ennis: Clasp Press.

Westropp, Thomas J. 1902. "Bewitching" in *Journal of the Royal Society of Antiquaries of Ireland*, XXXII (XII of the 5th Series), 1902, 265.

Wilde, William R. 1995 (1852). *Irish Popular Superstitions*. New York: Sterling Publishing.

Woods, James. 1907. *Annals of Westmeath: Ancient and Modern*. Dublin: Sealy, Bryers & Walker.

Uisneach or the Center of Ireland

The hill of Uisneach lies almost exactly at the geographical center of Ireland. Remarkably, a fraction at least of the ancient Irish population was aware of that fact. There is no doubt that the place of Uisneach in Irish mythology, and more broadly speaking the Celtic world, was of utmost importance: Uisneach was – and probably still is – best defined as a sacred hill at the center of Ireland, possibly *the* sacred hill *of* the center of Ireland.

This book explores the medieval documents connected with the hill and compares them with both archaeological data and modern Irish folklore. In the early 21st century, a *Fire Festival* started being held on Uisneach in connection with the festival of *Bealtaine*, in early May, arguably in an attempt to echo more ancient traditions: the celebration was attended by Michael D. Higgins, the current president of Ireland, who lit the fire of Uisneach on 6 May 2017.

It will be argued that the symbolic significance of the hill has echoed the evolution of Irish society through time, be it in political, spiritual and religious terms or, perhaps more accurately, in terms of identity and *Irishness*.

Frédéric Armao is currently an Associate Professor at the University of Toulon (France). His primary research focuses on the link between Irish folklore (both modern and contemporary) and Celtic mythology. His work has examined the evolution of Irish calendar festivals from their pre-Christian beginnings through their syncretic contemporary celebration.

Index

Printed in the United States
by Baker & Taylor Publisher Services